D1622092

ON THE ROAD

ON THE ROAD

An Inside View of Life with an NHL Team

HOWARD BERGER

Warwick Publishing Inc.
Toronto   Los Angeles

Published by Warwick Publishing Inc.
• 24 Mercer Street, Toronto, ON. M5V 1H3
• 1424 Highland Ave., Los Angeles, CA 90027

ISBN: 1-895629-51-9

Cover design: Kimberley Davison
Text design: Kimberley Davison
Front cover photo: Doug MacLellan, HHOF
Back cover photo: Paul Hunter, Toronto Star

Distributed in the United States and Canada by:

Firefly Books Ltd.
250 Sparks Ave.
Willowdale, ON
M2H 2S4

Printed and bound in Canada by Webcom.
Fourth printing August 1996.

To my cousin, Marty Brown,
whose courage
and self-deprecating sense of humour
in the face of cancer
has been a true inspiration

ACKNOWLEDGEMENTS

While travelling with the Maple Leafs to write this book, my efforts were enhanced by a number of people.

I'd like to thank Mary Speck of the Maple Leaf administration office for taking care of my hotel bookings out of town.

Terrie Ashton of *Sportscorp Travel Ltd.* has been arranging flights for the Maple Leafs during the past 11 years and her professionalism and friendly smile were of great assistance.

Bob Stellick and Pat Park of the Maple Leaf publicity office have tolerated me for a number of seasons. My thanks, once again, to them.

A special debt of gratitude goes to Eugene McEleney of *Global* TV, who offered me countless rides to and from airports in all varieties of weather conditions. He was a great friend all season long.

Like always, my mentor Scott Metcalfe — news and sports director at The *Fan-590* — lent his support and patience.

Publishers Nick Pitt and Jim Williamson at *Warwick* poured a few dollars into this venture and I'd like to thank them for believing in yet another project.

But most of all, I want to salute head coach Pat Burns and the players of the 1995 Toronto Maple Leafs for their acceptance and cooperation throughout a trying season.

CONTENTS

*(Photos and a brief bio for each of the
team members I traveled with.)*

PREFACE
Living A Dream

The idea came together quickly.

Follow a famous hockey team on the road during a season marred and short-ened by labour strife, and write a book about it.

That famous team: the Toronto Maple Leafs.

Ever since I was old enough to read a newspaper, I have dreamed about cov-ering the Maple Leafs throughout an entire season. The hockey scrapbooks from my youth bear the names of the men who have previously done so... Red Burnett, George Gross, Paul Dulmage, John Iaboni, Frank Orr, Dan Proudfoot. Writing from places that no longer exist, or won't be around much longer... the Detroit Olympia, Chicago Stadium, Boston Garden, St. Louis Arena, Montreal Forum.

There was something mystical about the Leafs playing on the road; wearing their predominantly white uniforms in the 1960s.

I'm too young to remember the days when Maple Leaf road games were shown in Toronto-area movie theatres. An advertisement from a Gardens hock-ey program in January, 1963, lists the entire Leaf road schedule of 1962-63 alongside an action photo of defenceman Carl Brewer. It reads:

> *NOW! SEE ALL THE AWAY GAMES ON THE BIG SCREEN AT THE COLLEGE THEATRE!*
> *Live! Direct from: Montreal, New York, Boston, Chicago and Detroit.*
> *You can be one of the few hockey fans to see the away games in the Maple Leaf schedule. For the first time, a closed-circuit hook-up will bring you every game, as it's played. New Eidopher projection gives a brighter, sharper picture on the giant 30-foot screen.*
> *TICKETS: $1.25, $2.00, $2.50*

In those days — and later in the '60s — my only linkage to Maple Leaf road hockey was the radio, where Foster Hewitt called games on his privately owned station CKFH-1430. *Hockey Night In Canada*, which used to telecast nationally on Saturday and Wednesday nights, showed Maple Leaf mid-week games when they were played in Montreal, but no place else. On the rare Saturday nights when the Leafs were out of town, the coast-to-coast telecast would originate from Montreal. And vise versa. Only in the playoffs would Maple Leaf road games be available on local TV and, quite often, the Canadiens provided the opposition.

My earliest memory of watching a Leaf regular-season game on TV from somewhere other than Montreal was during the 1969-70 season. In fact, I wrote about the game in my book last year, *MAPLE LEAF MOMENTS*. It was a Sunday afternoon telecast on CBS from the Met Center in Bloomington, Minnesota. The Leafs played the North Stars (Mar. 1, 1970) and lost the game, 8-0. The final score, believe it or not, was overshadowed by one of the great tantrums in NHL annals — thrown by Maple Leaf defenceman Jim Dorey. The rambunctious Dorey clobbered Minnesota's Claude Larose in a pair of altercations, and also planted a right hook squarely on the chin of linesman Pat Shetler. He then tossed a chair onto the ice from the bench area as he left in a huff for the dressing room.

The '69-70 season was the last year NHL teams wore their primarily coloured uniforms on home ice, and their white sets on the road. The CBS games on Sundays provided the first chance to see the other clubs play at home. Colour TV was still in its infancy, and my parents had purchased a large *Admiral* console sometime in 1968. It was downstairs in the family/recreation room and made hockey watching a terrific, new experience. Particularly with expansion having occurred just more than a year earlier, bringing six new teams and a bunch of new colours into the NHL. I vividly remember marvelling at the green, yellow and white uniforms the North Stars wore in that March, 1970 telecast from the Met Center. The Maple Leafs wore predominantly white, with blue pants and blue piping on their shoulders.

At the start of the 1970-71 season, NHL teams switched to wearing their coloured uniforms on the road (as they do today). The reasons were two-fold: a) it would give fans around the league a chance to see the more attractive sets that each team wore, and b) cleaning the primarily white uniforms had become a chore while away from home — especially on three or four-game road trips. I had no idea of this rule change when I attended the Maple Leafs' first home exhibition game of that '70-71 season, against Minnesota. And I remember my eyes almost bulging out when Gump Worsley led the North Stars onto the ice wearing their primarily green uniforms. I went to the next pre-season game as well and the Chicago Blackhawks were decked out in their red sweaters.

A pleasant surprise occurred on a Saturday night late in the 1971-72 season. There was a messy technicians' strike at the CBC, and it was wreaking havoc on the weekend telecasts from Maple Leaf Gardens and the Montreal Forum. I remember watching in dismay as a Maple Leaf home game in early March against Los Angeles abruptly went off the air during the first period — right in the midst of the play. It was followed seconds later by an apologetic announcement from somebody at CBLT in Toronto, who explained the strike would preempt the remainder of the telecast. Instead, the network switched to the Boston at Detroit game from the Olympia. Emotional trauma overcame me when my Saturday night Maple Leaf fix disappeared from the screen.

Three weeks later, it happened again. On Saturday night, Mar. 25, 1972, the CBC strike actually turned into a blessing in disguise for Maple Leaf fans. The Leafs were in Los Angeles and the *Hockey Night In Canada* national telecast had New York at Montreal. Just prior to the 8 p.m. faceoff, however, the screen again went blank and the announcement came forth, this time, that *no* telecast would be available. Being a Montreal game, it wasn't so gut-wrenching and I remember staying up late that night to watch a TV special on Canadian boxer George Chuvalo, who was preparing for his second career fight against Muhammad Ali.

The special ended at 11 o'clock and I decided to flip through the channels once more before going to bed. Suddenly, I noticed two hockey teams skating around in a wide-angle shot. The team on the right of the screen was wearing yellow and my eyes instantly focused on the center-ice circle, where a pair of crown logos flanked the red line. It donned on me that this was a TV picture from the Los Angeles Forum, where the Kings and Maple Leafs were about to face off. But, how could this be? I was all set to go upstairs and turn the game on radio. And now, for the first time ever, I was seeing a live shot from a hockey game at the L.A. Forum. I remember there was no sound initially — just a wide-angle view of the Leafs and Kings skating around before the anthem.

A few minutes later came an announcement that in appreciation of the patience hockey fans across the country had shown, the CBC network was piping in the L.A.-produced telecast of the Leafs-Kings game. Then came the voices of Ken (Jiggs) MacDonald and Dan Avey, who called the action on TV station KTLA in Los Angeles. What a bonanza! And to top it off, the Maple Leafs skated to an impressive 4-0 blanking of the Kings.

The first Maple Leaf road game I ever *attended* was in Pittsburgh during the 1976 Christmas holidays. A friend and I were visiting my cousins, Steven and Judy Tobe, in the suburb of Monroeville and upon arriving in Pittsburgh late Friday afternoon, we bought three tickets for the Leafs-Penguins game Sunday night (Dec. 26). Our luck, there was a dreadful snowstorm in Pittsburgh Sunday afternoon. We were watching the Steelers at Oakland AFC championship game on TV and Steven wasn't overly enthusiastic about having to drive downtown for the hockey game. The radio and TV stations were flashing warnings, imploring motorists to stay off the roads unless it was absolutely necessary. However, my near-tantrum at possibly having to miss the game prompted Steve to give it a try. And what an adventure it was.

We inched westward along Interstate 376 (the Penn-Lincoln Parkway) and Steven kept abreast of the traffic and road conditions over his C-B radio. It took more than an hour to get to Pittsburgh and the parking lot we entered at Civic Arena had a downward slope. As long as I live, I'll never forget Steven's car sliding *sideways* towards the bottom of the lot before he was able to re-gain control of the wheel.

The announced crowd that night was 6,603 but no more than 3,000 fans had actually braved the conditions to be on hand. Pittsburgh beat the Maple Leafs 4-2 on goals by Jean Pronovost, Dennis Owchar, Pierre Larouche and Rick Kehoe. Toronto scorers were Pat Boutette and the late Don Ashby. I remember the Penguins were still wearing powder-blue trim on their home white uniforms (they switched to black and gold in 1979), and neither club had player names sewn on the backs of its jerseys (that would happen the following season).

With the arena so empty, we were able to move down beside the Leaf bench in the second period. And when Boutette scored the first Toronto goal (at 4:13 of the third), I was the only fan in the arena cheering. A big, burly man sitting six or seven rows behind me yelled out, "Hey, you, there's a bus leaving for Toronto after the game... be underneath it." Everybody around him laughed, but I didn't care.

I eventually saw games in all of the old arenas. And even today, when I go to Pittsburgh, or Philadelphia, or Los Angeles, it reminds me of a small pamphlet-book I had in the 1969-70 season — two years after expansion. It was called *Where They Play* and it had exterior photos and data on all 12 NHL arenas. As I mentioned earlier, only Leaf road games from Montreal were shown on TV back then and we could merely imagine what the other buildings looked like, particularly the newer ones. When Bill or Foster Hewitt came on the radio from one of the expansion arenas, we were left with only their verbal descriptions: a Romanesque-columned facility in Los Angeles; a sardine-can shaped arena in Philadelphia; a flat-topped, white-stone building in Minnesota, and an all-glass mecca in Oakland, known euphemistically as the "Jewel Box."

In the summer of 1978, I went to California for the first time and remember seeing the Los Angeles Forum out the right-hand side of the aircraft as we flew over Inglewood on final approach. Just to view the inside of the arena, we bought tickets a few days later to see Lionel Ritchie and The Commodores in concert. Later during that west coast trip, my buddy and I were in San Francisco and we decided to take the BART train to Oakland. There was a *Coliseum* exit and we knew that the Oakland Coliseum-Arena (where the Seals used to play) was next to the baseball/football stadium where the A's and Raiders played.

I'll always remember seeing that round, glass-walled structure as we approached on the train — looking exactly like it had in *Where They Play* a decade earlier. There was a circus at the arena and someone gave us a pair of tickets outside. We went in and looked about the place — remembering how we used to stay up late and listen on radio to Maple Leafs/Seals games that began at 11 p.m. Toronto time. It was all rather haunting.

The first road trip I made with the Leafs during my work career was to research a magazine article early in the 1983-84 season. It was a three-gamer — to Minnesota, Winnipeg and Calgary. I saw my only game at the old Met Center, but I recall a moment earlier that day even more vividly. Metropolitan Stadium, former home of the Vikings and Twins, was still standing across the parking lot from the hockey arena, even though both teams had moved into the Metrodome in downtown Minneapolis a year-and-a-half earlier. Having watched so many NFL playoff games on TV from Met Stadium, when the legendary purple gang of Fran Tarkenton, Allan Page, Carl Eller and Co. were so powerful in the 1970s, I wanted to have a look at the place.

Late in the afternoon, I walked over there from the Bloomington Marriott and could see into the stadium through a gate down the left-field line. The seats were still in place but many of the sockets from the giant light-towers were broken, and the grass — which hadn't been cut in more than two years — seemed terribly long. I discovered just *how* long when I walked around to the opposite end of the stadium and stood beneath the massive former scoreboard (in back of the south end zone). Had the grass been a normal length, I would have strolled out onto the field and looked around more closely. However, this would have been like walking into a forest, as the grass and weeds were actually taller than me — probably more than seven feet high. I looked back towards the home-plate area and could only view the upper-deck seats and press box over the swaying foliage. It was eerie to see a formerly well-manicured baseball and football pitch looking like a swamp in the Everglades. A security guard came over on a motorbike and warned me not to proceed any further, saying that nobody knew exactly what creatures lurked in that jungle-like mass of shrubbery.

The Met — as it was known — fell to the wrecking ball just more than a year later, and the territory on which it stood is now occupied by the giant Mall Of The Americas.

Later that night, a sell-out audience of more than 15,000 jammed the Met Center to see the North Stars humble the Maple Leafs. Minnesota had a good team back then and the low ceiling in the building enhanced crowd noise. Built for the arrival of big-league hockey in 1967, the Met Center has also since been demolished — the franchise now located, of course, in Dallas.

So these are some of my earliest memories of watching on TV, and later attending Maple Leaf road games. Getting around nowadays is sure a lot different than it was a generation ago.

Travel during the six-team era could hardly be termed glamorous. NHL teams moved from city to city by train almost exclusively until the league doubled in size for the 1967-68 season. Going from New York to Los Angeles on the ground was no longer an option, and jet travel came into vogue. The rail era was altogether different.

"It was usually a rush situation," remembers George Gross, who covered the Maple Leafs in the '60s for the old Toronto *Telegram.* "We would play in Toronto on Saturday night, and go by train to an out-of-town game Sunday. After filing our stories from the Gardens, we would rush down to Union Station. The train would pull away sometime after midnight and very few of us could sleep right away. So, we'd sit and talk to Punch Imlach before going to bed in our sleeper cars.

"The trip would take all night and sometimes part of the next day. Occasionally, we'd go right to the arena then get back on the train and return home after the game. Imlach would tell us in the dressing room, `You guys have 20 minutes to write your stories.' It was nothing at all glamorous, yet we loved every minute of it."

Throughout the years, weather conditions have occasionally played havoc with Maple Leaf travel plans. None more-so than on a weekend in November, 1969. The Leafs played a rare Saturday night game in Montreal and were scheduled for a charter flight to Chicago afterwards. The Habs prevailed 6-3 and when the Leafs had finished showering, they were informed that fog had closed O'Hare airport in Chicago.

Howard Starkman, who is currently public relations director of the Toronto Blue Jays, held the same post with the Maple Leafs back then and it was his responsibility to arrange the club's travel itinerary. Having to make a quick decision, Starkman phoned the train station and discovered there was a midnight departure to Windsor, Ont. that would connect with another train to Chicago. The Leaf players were hustled to Montreal's Windsor Station (where the new Forum now sits) and they were placed in sleeper cars for the overnight trip.

"What a mess that was," Starkman recalls. "The trip took something like 18 1/2 hours and we got to the Chicago train station around 6 p.m. on Sunday (for a

7:35 start). I called ahead for a police escort to the Stadium and I don't remember whether or not they delayed the game a few minutes. All I *do* remember is that we got killed."

He's not kidding. The game *was* delayed a half-hour, but Chicago drubbed the Maple Leafs 9-0 for their worst defeat of the season.

Travelling with a sports team provides an exciting paradox. While certain routines become second-nature — going to the airport... flying to a city... bussing to the hotel... bussing to and from the arena for practices and games... heading back to the airport to fly someplace else — there's a refreshing variety to almost everything that happens.

With the Maple Leafs, the routine part is plainly indicated in the travel itineraries prepared by administrative assistant Mary Speck. For example, here is the dispatch players, coaches and media received this season prior to the Leafs' four-game west-coast trip, March 14-22:

Trip 7

TORONTO to SAN JOSE to ANAHEIM to LOS ANGELES to VANCOUVER to TORONTO

TUESDAY, MARCH 14, 1995

9:10 a.m.	AIR CANADA #757 to SAN FRANCISCO
11:36 a.m.	AIR CANADA #757 arrives in SAN FRANCISCO
	Bus to FAIRMONT HOTEL, San Jose
	(Royal Coach Bus Lines)
1:30 p.m.	PRACTICE at SAN JOSE ARENA

WEDNESDAY, MARCH 15, 1995

10:30 a.m.	Bus to SAN JOSE ARENA
11:30 a.m. - 12:30 p.m.	Skate
12:45 p.m.	Pre-game meal
4:30 p.m.	Pre-game snack
5:00 p.m.	Bus to SAN JOSE ARENA
7:35 p.m.	GAME vs. San Jose
After Game	Bus to hotel

THURSDAY, MARCH 16, 1995

12:00 noon	Bus to SAN JOSE AIRPORT
12:50 p.m.	SOUTHWEST AIRLINES #851 to ORANGE COUNTY
2:05 p.m.	SOUTHWEST AIRLINES #851 arrives in ORANGE COUNTY
	Bus to WESTIN SOUTH COAST PLAZA HOTEL
	(Pacific Coast Busline)

FRIDAY, MARCH 17, 1995

10:30 a.m	Bus to ARROWHEAD POND
11:30 a.m. - 12:30 p.m.	Skate
12:50 p.m.	Bus to hotel
1:15 p.m.	Pre-game meal
4:30 p.m.	Pre-game snack
5:00 p.m.	Bus to ARROWHEAD POND
7:35 p.m.	Game vs. Anaheim
After Game	Bus to LOEWS SANTA MONICA HOTEL
	(Pacific Coast Busline)

SATURDAY, MARCH 18, 1995

10:30 a.m.	Bus to GREAT WESTERN FORUM
11:30 a.m. - 12:30 p.m.	Skate
12:50 p.m.	Bus to hotel
1:30 p.m.	Pre-game meal
4:30 p.m.	Pre-game snack
5:00 p.m.	Bus to GREAT WESTERN FORUM
7:35 p.m.	Game vs. Los Angeles
After Game	Bus to hotel

SUNDAY, MARCH 19, 1995

11:15 a.m.	Bus to LOS ANGELES AIRPORT

12:20 p.m.	**DELTA AIRLINES #989 to VANCOUVER**
3:07 p.m.	**DELTA AIRLINES #989 arrives in VANCOUVER**
	Bus to WESTIN BAYSHORE HOTEL
	(Vancouver Tour Bus)

MONDAY, MARCH 20, 1995

T.B.A.	**PRACTICE at PACIFIC COLISEUM**

TUESDAY, MARCH 21, 1995

10:30 a.m.	**Bus to PACIFIC COLISEUM**
11:30 a.m. - 12:30 p.m.	**Skate**
12:50 p.m.	**Bus to hotel**
1:15 p.m.	**Pre-game meal**
4:30 p.m.	**Pre-game snack**
5:00 p.m.	**Bus to PACIFIC COLISEUM**
7:35 p.m.	**Game vs. Vancouver**
After Game	**Bus to hotel**

WEDNESDAY, MARCH 22, 1995

7:40 a.m.	**Bus to VANCOUVER AIRPORT**
9:00 a.m.	**AIR CANADA #142 to TORONTO**
4:18 p.m.	**AIR CANADA #142 arrives in TORONTO**

If this seems like a complicated timetable, let me assure you there is precious little deviation to the schedule.

Like on all sports teams, most of the players are paired up for hotel room assignments. Some athletes prefer being alone and stipulate the request in their contracts. Here were the pairings from the hotel list at the Hyatt Regency Dallas on April 21st of this season:

BILL BERG and DAMIAN RHODES, MIKE RIDLEY and MIKE CRAIG, PAUL DIPIETRO and RICH SUTTER, TIE DOMI and WARREN RYCHEL, DAVE ELLETT and BENOIT HOGUE, MIKE GARTNER and KENT MAN-

*DERVILLE, TODD GILL and RANDY WOOD, MATT MAR-
TIN and DARBY HENDRICKSON, JAMIE MACOUN and
GRANT JENNINGS, MATS SUNDIN and KENNY JONSSON,
DAVE ANDREYCHUK and FELIX POTVIN*

To ensure his privacy, Maple Leaf captain Doug Gilmour checks into each
hotel under an assumed name and normally reserves his own room.

*   *   *   *   *   *

Over the years, several books have been written by media personnel about
their experiences travelling with a professional sports team. My friend Roy
MacGregor of the Ottawa *Citizen* penned a superb chronicle of the Senators' first
year back in the NHL (*Road Games*). At home, I have diary books by various former NHLers. Ex-Boston goalie Gerry Cheevers wrote *Goaltender* with columnist Trent Frayne after the 1970-71 season. Former Bruin coach (and current general manager) Harry Sinden penned *Hockey Showdown* — a daily chronicle of
the famed 1972 Canada-Soviet series (he coached Team Canada). And former
Ranger Vic Hadfield wrote *Vic Hadfield's Diary*: the story of his acrimonious
departure from Team Canada and the Rangers' successful 1972-73 season. All
were interesting reads and were written in a manner that respected the private
lives of people around them. In other words, they were not exposés.

I've applied the same philosophy to this book. While my foremost aim was
to take the reader behind the scenes with the Maple Leafs, I've done so in at least
moderate deference to the athletes. There is plenty to be seen and heard when you
spend an entire season travelling with a group of young, handsomely-paid men.
But it's my belief that you cannot execute a project like this in a proper manner
without first gaining the trust and confidence of the people involved. If you go
on to betray that trust, your credibility becomes worthless.

Yes, there have been books — in fact, best-sellers — exposing the dark,
seedy aspects of public figures. Written, in all likelihood, by people who are generally squalid themselves. You will read passages in this chronicle that may surprise you, but all of the stories are either directly or indirectly related to the game.
I think you'll agree they are plentiful. You will not read about family crises or
sexual preferences of the subjects. That's their business — just like it would be
our's — and that business must be respected.

Instead, you will read about the assortment of Western Conference cities we
visited in 1995. And about the arenas in each city... most of them new and
exceedingly modern. I take you onto the Maple Leaf team bus, and aboard commercial and charter flights (from the perspective of a slightly nervous flyer). Into

the dressing room for both good times and bad. As well, you'll be introduced in varying depth to the people who comprised the 1995 version of Toronto's NHL team.

So I invite you now to come along with me as I live a dream, and travel through an historic season with the Toronto Maple Leafs.

Enjoy the ride,

Howard Berger,
Toronto,
September, 1995

INTRODUCTION
THE LONGEST DAY
January 9-10, 1995
New York

Occasionally, we test the endurance of the human body beyond reason, and discover that its aptitude for withstanding punishment is quite extraordinary.

Such was the case during the climactic hours of the longest and most damaging labour dispute in National Hockey League history. With the ill-fated 1994-95 season hanging precariously in the balance, the principals involved with the league and the Players' Association — as well as the attending media — were forced to go without sleep for more than a day and a half. Complicating matters for us, was the painstaking lack of any rousing venture other than hanging around a faceless hotel ballroom in the event of a news break.

And it went on... and on... and on.

Dispatched to New York to cover the make-or-break negotiations for Toronto radio station The *Fan-590*, I awoke Monday morning, January 9th, at 7:30 and did not close my eyes until Tuesday night at 9:20. A quick calculation reveals that I stayed awake for 37 hours and 50 minutes —most definitely a record in my lifetime. This endurance mark did not impress those — including my wife, Susan — who had pulled frequent "all-nighters" while studying for final exams in college. However, my attention span for such matters was roughly six minutes... or until the start of the next hockey game on TV.

For more than four months, NHL players and management had been posturing and squabbling over a number of issues — most prominently, the various euphemisms for a salary cap. Phrases such as "luxury tax", "giveaway", "take-back", "small-market", "hawks" and "doves" had become more agonizingly common than "hello" and "goodbye".

The primary actors in this dull, drawn-out production were NHL commissioner Gary Bettman and his 26 board of governors (with Harry Sinden and John McMullen in leading and support roles). And the NHL Players' Association, led by executive-director Bob Goodenow and his negotiating elite of Mike Gartner, Marty McSorley and Ken Baumgartner. More "final" deadlines were tendered than during a war summit.

It ultimately came down to a marathon gab-fest in the second week of January, from which both sides agreed they could not depart without first cancelling the entire schedule. And they ventured within a razor-blade's width of such a conclusion. In the end, the man who came across as the story's villain wound up playing the hero's role.

To detail the union/management mayhem from beginning to end would induce slumber among any of you reading this book. I remained conscious only because it was my work's obligation to do so. In summary, the mess officially began in August, 1994, when Bettman unveiled a list of 19 economic sanctions against the players for their refusal — he claimed — to engage in the collective bargaining process. Player salaries began to escalate immeasurably during the 1993-94 season, when the two sides were in labour limbo; playing under the guidelines of an expired previous agreement. It was Bettman's contention that repeated offers to commence negotiations on a new pact had fallen on deaf ears. His public revelation of monetary and beneficiary rollbacks would be the ultimate catalyst, he hoped, in getting the two sides to the table.

The gamble proved successful.

Not unlike most labour scuffles, this one grew unavoidably nasty before common sense intervened. With tangible support from high-profile players like Maple Leaf captain Doug Gilmour, the NHLPA executive waged an all-out war against the implementation of a salary "drag" — without question, the primary objective of league governors. The PA understood it would be a take-back negotiation from the league's standpoint, but did not want to yield to a cap on wages — citing the ever-increasing disparagement among players and governors in the National Basketball Association. Once the two sides dug in their heels, the stalemate grew.

The negotiating process, or lack thereof, was so pitiful that the NHL announced at a mega news conference in New York, Sept. 30, that it was "postponing" the start of the 1994-95 regular season — scheduled for eight days hence. Bettman used the term "postponement" with vigour, while the players countered with the correct term: "lockout." A new league schedule, to begin a fortnight after the original version, was drawn up and presented as an alternative.

Not surprisingly, the quarrel extended far beyond the second date and it soon became a clash of one-upsmanship among the two figureheads — Bettman and Goodenow — each of whom attained impressive heights of obstinacy. When first Christmas, and then the New Year came and went without any sign of accord, the NHL owners convened for an "emergency" session in New York and presented yet another "final" overture to the players. The meeting took place throughout the afternoon and early-evening hours of Saturday, January 7th, and it resulted in withdrawal of the salary cap requisition.

The subsequent press conference convened by NHL governors was not exactly a show of solitude. Several high-profile executives chose not to show up, as a pre-curser to the inner strife that would almost kill the season three days later. Columnist Al Strachan of the Toronto *Sun* took the most decided anti-league stance on the lockout and wrote after Saturday's board session:

> *The counterproposal (yesterday), despite Bettman's bleatings to the contrary, was not a compromise. It was a calculated affront, completely in line with the tactics the hard-line owners have been pursuing all along. Every move they have made during the past year has been meticulously planned. This one was no different and it was no accident that some of the moderate performers in this drama — including Cliff Fletcher of the Toronto Maple Leafs, Mike Ilitch of the Detroit Red Wings and Mike Shanahan of the St. Louis Blues — were absent from the press conference.*

Both sides clearly understood that playing a shortened season would not be plausible upon any further breakdown in talks, and while the new NHL proposal compensated with restraints in areas independent of the salary dispute, Goodenow realized it was now or never. He accepted Bettman's invitation to meet one last time in New York and the final countdown began.

Arising in the Marriott Marquis on Monday morning at 7:30, I had no idea that I wouldn't be using my hotel room again that night. The league established a media work center in the nearby Holiday Inn Crowne Plaza and that would be my home for the next day and a half. Several of us in the media camped out early Monday morning in the lobby of the NHL executive offices at the Rockefeller Center. When it was reasonably determined that Bettman and Goodenow were not convened there, we took a taxi to the Four Seasons Hotel in east Manhattan — Goodenow's usual hangout — and discovered the two leaders were inside. A clandestine telephone call to Goodenow's room confirmed as much, and the NHLPA boss immediately placed a "do-not-disturb" on his line.

Heading back to the Crowne Plaza around the noon hour, the vigil officially began. We sat in that ballroom throughout the afternoon, the early evening, and into the wee hours of Tuesday morning without a peep from either the players or owners. Rumours of a forthcoming settlement continued to swirl about — mainly because of confirmation that the two sides were still banging away at it. Leaving the ballroom for even the time it took to empty one's bladder was a risky proposition, though a group of us submitted to hunger around 7 p.m. and hustled to a take-out Chinese Food restaurant in Times Square.

Meanwhile, back in Toronto, union president Mike Gartner of the Maple Leafs was similarly anxious, holding a vigil with fellow players at the NHLPA offices on Dundas St.

"I had the option of going to New York with Bob (Goodenow) but I realized it would ultimately come down to a one-on-one meeting between Bob and Gary Bettman, so I stayed back with the negotiating committee," Gartner recalls. "We waited by a phone in the PA office — me, Marty McSorley, Ken Baumgartner, Andy Moog, Kelly Miller and Doug Wilson. When the meetings went into the wee hours of the morning, we tried to lay on some conference-room chairs and sleep, but it was futile. Some of us were able to conk out for 15 or 20 minutes at a time. Otherwise, we were awake through the night."

It was the same story in the press holding at the Crowne Plaza, where many of us sat through the ordeal trying to keep our heads in an upright position. Several reporters carved out a corner in the ballroom and passed out on the carpeted floor. Quadraphonic snoring intensified as the evening progressed. There was so little information to pass on that your's truly took to playing *Flintstones* trivia on the air around 3:30 a.m. with a trio of dedicated hosts back at the radio station.

The sun came up Tuesday morning without a hint of a settlement. I staggered outside and bought a muffin at the Roxy Deli then went up to my room, knowing that if I dared lay down on the terribly inviting bed, a crane would be required to erect me. Instead, I checked out of the hotel and dragged my suitcase up the road to the Crowne Plaza ballroom.

Extreme viewpoints continued to fly off the computer screens of columnists in attendance. Mike Lupica of *Newsday* in New York attacked Goodenow with the same fervour that Strachan had been assailing Bettman. Regarding the union boss's strategy in the four-month long dispute, and under a heading GOODE-NOW GOT HIS TAIL KICKED, Lupica wrote:

> *Goodenow never really wanted to negotiate. He was out of his weight class and never seemed to have much of a plan, except to wait. (But), in the end, Bettman has turned everything around on Goodenow. The salary cap is gone and the luxury tax on salaries is gone. Now it is Goodenow who has paid, with a list of concessions that is rather amazing. (The owners) will still come away with a system in which no hockey player can become a free agent until he is 30, or 31, or 32. All because Goodenow got Bettman to drop a salary cap. Only, no one is cheering Goodenow now.*

... Goodenow looks like a general left standing when his whole platoon is gone.

Ultimately, as Lupica pointed out, an agreement hedged on the free agency issue. A "final" deadline of Tuesday at noon had been declared by the league after Saturday's board meeting, and at 11:55 a.m., Arthur Pincus — the NHL's New York-based vice-president of public relations — made a long-awaited appearance in the media room to announce that the deadline had been extended. Big surprise. Tuesday afternoon dragged on and became early evening. Pincus then returned to the media center at 8:30 p.m. and made a rather bizarre announcement:

> *On a conference call with the National Hockey League Board of Governors this evening, Commissioner Gary Bettman was directed to present a revised proposal to the NHL Players' Association, and to effectuate the cancellation of the 1994-95 season if a new Collective Bargaining Agreement is not reached promptly.*

The ridiculously worded statement put Pincus in an uncomfortable spot. A barrage of questions was fired his way from the restless media mob, but Pincus had neither the authority nor the information to answer any of them.

"What does `promptly' mean... very soon?" he was asked.

"I don't know what promptly or very soon means," came his nervous reply. "That's all I have to say."

Meanwhile, Boston's Harry Sinden — whose "We will not capitulate" pledge became the most notorious of all labour-related quotes — held a news conference in Beantown to declare, on behalf of the owners, that "This is the final, final, final, final, final offer."

Where had we heard that before?

Information did leak out, however, that a frenzied conference call among league governors came within a hair of nixing the season. Bettman chose to present the owners a proposition that resulted from almost 27 consecutive hours of hammering away with Goodenow. The most militant, or "hawkish" owners — Abe Pollin (Washington), Jeremy Jacobs (Boston), and John McMullen (New Jersey) — promptly went for Bettman's jugular. As Toronto *Star* columnist Bob McKenzie wrote:

*They had the sense that Bettman was spending too much
time playing ball with NHLPA executive director Bob
Goodenow and not enough time wielding the big stick.*

Bettman's decision to throw open the proposal for a majority vote backfired
and created massive internal chaos during the conference call. As one management source told columnist Larry Brooks of the New York *Post,* "It was extremely heated. Teams were hammering away at each other and they were hammering
away at Bettman. A lot of owners were ticked off because they didn't think Gary
had the mandate from the board to restructure the (Saturday) deal the way he did."

The board voted 14-12 in defeat of the proposal and the militants pressed for
immediate cancellation of the season. But, Bettman would not buckle under. It
was his resolve and persuasiveness in the critical ensuing moments that got the
board to re-think its position, ultimately saving the schedule. In so doing,
Bettman laid to rest the notion that he, more than anyone, wanted to torpedo the
season.

He convinced the governors to slightly modify their stance and re-present
the players with one last-ditch proposal. At issue was the age which players could
file for unrestricted free agency. A six-year deal was drawn up by the league
whereby players could file for unfettered free agency at 32 for the first three
years of the agreement, and 31 for the remaining three years. The players were
bargaining for a 31-30 split and Bettman's offer to put the lower age grouping to
a vote had caused the uproar on Tuesday afternoon's conference call.

The NHL commissioner persuaded both the New Jersey and Vancouver
"hawks" to think along his lines, therefore ensuring a majority vote in his favour.
It was now, beyond any doubt, up to the players to decide.

More importantly, from the standpoint of the haggard media, was Arthur
Pincus's allusion after his 8:30 p.m. press briefing that, "In all likelihood, nothing will be announced until tomorrow (Wednesday) morning at the earliest."
Clearly, Bettman and Co. were looking for a decent night's sleep, along with
everybody else in New York.

Earlier in the day, I had dragged my weary self to the front desk of the
Crowne Plaza and checked into a room on the 32nd floor. Now, it was time to get
some rest. I crawled into bed at 9 absolutely paralysed from fatigue. After watching TV for about six minutes, I passed out and was aware of nothing else until
8:15 a.m. Wednesday, when Susan called from Toronto. An explosion during the
night wouldn't have aroused me.

A long, hot shower and shave was invigorating and I soon proceeded back
to the ballroom for the final decision on the labour crisis. For awhile in the late-

morning hours — as the talks seemed to drag on —there were grave misgivings among many of us in the media. Another day of deadline extensions and myopic press briefings seemed in the offing, and the vast majority of us in that ballroom had reached the end of the line. Our patience was exhausted.

Thankfully — and like a blessing — word came down just after the noon hour that the NHLPA executive, after meeting in Toronto, had voted to accept the owners' 11th-hour proposal. The 103-day lockout was over — pending ratification by the Players' Association membership (considered to be a formality). The joyous news spread quickly through the Crowne Plaza and within 90 minutes, Bettman and Goodenow were on a podium at the front of the ballroom... shaking hands.

"I'm thrilled, happy, relieved — every emotion in the spectrum," said the NHL commissioner. The (collective bargaining agreement) isn't the end, it's the beginning. We can take the game to new heights."

Added union boss Goodenow: "I'm very confident the membership will accept the bargaining committee's recommendation as it has throughout these negotiations. We've come to a conclusion that both sides can live with and now we can grow together. It's time to put the focus on hockey where it belongs... on the ice with the players."

In Toronto, Mike Gartner announced the NHLPA decision to a horde of media gathered outside the union offices.

Asked if he was pleased with the end result, Gartner rhetorically replied, "Are we happy about the scars that have been created for the game of hockey? Are we happy about losing millions of dollars? Are we happy the relations between owners and players have been severely hindered? No, we're not happy about that.

"But we are happy hockey is going to be played very soon."

In a later discussion with me over the phone, Gartner confessed, "I had a feeling it was going to get done. If you look at the whole dispute, all of the meaningful negotiating took place in the final four or five days, and that's usually the way it happens with these things. Yes, there were conversations through the course of four months, but the sides were so far apart philosophically.

"Why did it take so long? That's a simple question that deserves a simple answer. Unfortunately, there isn't one. When two sides become confident in a working relationship, and both feel they are benefitting in some way equally from that relationship, a deal can be done quickly. It's not usually a process that gets resolved overnight."

The six-year agreement was favourable in many ways to both sides. The owners got the inevitably larger slice of the pie they were looking for, and the players were able to save face. Wrote sports editor Scott Morrison of the Toronto *Sun*:

> *The decision (by the players) was no doubt easier to make armed with the knowledge that without a salary cap, and without a luxury tax (the two concessions the players could never make), not only does the NHL have the distinction of being the only professional league without either, but there remains the potential for the rich owners to still spend, and for the others to self-destruct. When it all plays itself out, it may not seem nearly as bad as it does today."*

A 48-game schedule was announced several days later — stretching into the first week of May — and there existed the possibility of a Stanley Cup presentation as late as July 1st. But, no one seemed to care. The 26 teams went through vigorous six-day mini camps to prepare for the shortened season.

After more than four months of agonizing inactivity, it was finally... GAME ON!

THE REGULAR SEASON
THURSDAY, JANUARY 19th
Pearson International Airport,
Toronto

The limousine pulled up to the U.S. Departures area of Terminal 2 after a somewhat harrowing drive through the morning rush-hour. For almost a week, the city of Toronto has been blanketed by a pea-soup-like fog — the result of unseasonably warm temperatures. January is normally the coldest month of the year in these parts, but the mercury has hovered well above the freezing point for the past ten days.

It was still dark outside as I ventured into the quiet terminal, looking for a familiar face. The daily flock of early morning business commuters formed a line at the Air Canada check-in counter but nobody from the Toronto Maple Leaf organization was visible. Suddenly, I heard a voice say, "Howie, we check in down there." Turning around, I noticed Doug Gilmour, a folded suit-bag strapped over his shoulder, pointing towards the far west end of Terminal 2.

"Thanks, Doug," I sarcastically replied, as a devilish grin came upon the Leaf captain. Of course, I had flown long enough to know that flights to the U.S. do not leave from the Domestic departures area, but Gilmour — noticing my heavy equipment bag — was hoping to con me into an arduous trek through the building. Nice guy.

Realizing his first prank of the season had bombed, Dougie pointed me in the proper direction of Terrie Ashton, the trusty agent who has booked Maple Leaf travel for more than a decade. I had spoken to Terrie for the very first time just yesterday, begging and cajoling her to try and reduce the cost of my full-fare economy ticket.

Having booked at the eleventh hour an outbound trip from Toronto to Los Angeles, and a return from San Francisco, my publisher was on the hook for almost $1,400 — a hefty bite out of our projected budget for traveling with the hockey club. After a few moments of serious dickering, however, Terrie butchered roughly $800 off the round-trip and became an instant friend for life.

I got my ticket and proceeded through the customs/immigration routine. Once in the boarding lounge, Gilmour arrived and I began to realize how anxious he was to get this labour-reduced season underway. Though Doug postured freely with his fellow NHLPA brethren, he is at the apex of his brilliant hockey career and has thoroughly considered the perils of a lengthy disruption.

29

About six weeks into the NHL-imposed lockout, I met with Gilmour at a restaurant near Maple Leaf Gardens and during the course of our discussion, he mentioned the word retirement. "If this lockout cancels the whole season, I could see myself not coming back," he said with an irksome tone. At 32 years of age, and with hockey's biological clock ticking away, Gilmour feared the carnal results of prolonged idleness. Plus, he wasn't making any money.

Therefore, not more than ten days later, the Leaf captain was skating for Raperswil-Jona of the Swiss Elite League — his body doing what comes naturally; his heart and soul less able to adapt. After two weeks of trekking through the Alps with players nowhere near his rank, Doug realized it was the NHL or nothing. He played in one game of the Wayne Gretzky European tour then packed his bags and came home.

Now, he was the only member of the Maple Leaf entourage at Pearson Airport — a full hour and 15 minutes before the flight to California. Though the Air Canada boarding lounge was quieter than usual, a number of travelers recognized Gilmour and he willingly posed for photos and signed autographs. "I'm excited," he confessed, his words mirroring the boyish smile on his face.

It was 20 minutes before anyone else from the Maple Leaf party arrived in the lounge, but they soon came in droves. Dressed in jacket and tie, the players mingled about, seemingly anxious to board the aircraft. Tough winger Bill Berg glanced up from his newspaper and noticed Randy Wood, the club's newest acquisition. Teammates on the New York Islanders from 1988 to 1991, Berg and Wood greeted one another and appeared happy to be reunited.

The youngest member of the entourage stood alone in the middle of the lounge, wearing a body-length raincoat where others wore blazers. Kenny Jonsson glanced about inquisitively as he readied to embark on his first Maple Leaf road-trip. Born just more than 20 years ago in Angelholm, Sweden, the lanky, blonde-haired defenceman was the Maple Leafs' first selection (12th overall) in the 1993 amateur draft at Quebec City. Glamorized by the hockey establishment, it was natural for a long-time Maple Leaf observer to wonder if another Borje Salming stood in that terminal. Of course, only time will tell.

The call to board the Air Canada Lockheed 10-11 soon came. Having arrived seemingly unnoticed, coach Pat Burns stood in line: his interminable game-face in full bloom. As Gilmour rose to join the line-up, a patch of hair sprang loose and covered his forehead. "Window open in the cab?" asked a wise-cracking Rick Wamsley, bringing another smile to the Toronto captain.

Once aboard the aircraft, the Maple Leaf hierarchy proceeded to the roomy *Executive Class* cabin... among them, coach Burns, assistant general manager

Bill Watters, and Business Operations Director Bob Stellick. The players, trainers and equipment staff sat among the peasants in the *Economy* cabin. With all 238 seats on the L10-11 pre-sold, the loading of baggage and equipment seemed incessant. The captain finally confessed as much in a statement from the cockpit and it was soon learned that not all had been well at Maple Leaf Gardens.

Within the previous hour, the equipment truck, manned by trainers Jim Carey and Brian Papineau, had been blocked from leaving the arena by striking security staff at the Wood St. loading ramp. Cooler heads prevailed when Gardens' president Cliff Fletcher arrived on the scene and the truck was allowed to leave for the airport. As part of the deal, Fletcher stayed behind and hammered out a new contract with the three full-time and six part-time employees, who'd been on strike since December, seeking a pay increase. The Maple Leaf general manager would have to catch the next flight to Los Angeles.

Better late than never, the giant aircraft full of hockey players was soon hurtling northward on Runway 33. Within seconds of lifting off the pavement, we were enveloped by the relentless fog. But roughly 90 seconds after that, the quivering jetliner poked through the density and into brilliant sunshine, reminding us that we were indeed part of a solar system. Our mother star had been obscured by cloud and fog for ten consecutive days — most certainly, a record in my lifetime — and the concept of sunlight had become foreign to many of us on that plane.

Flying from Toronto to Los Angeles is an exercise in patience and creativity. Depending on head-winds, the trip takes roughly five hours and like most trips across the continent, time soon begins to drag. Traveling on a morning flight, many of the players had been awake since 6 a.m. and a goodly number of them passed out soon after boarding the aircraft — only to be roused by the meal service almost two hours later.

The flight-pattern approach to Los Angeles International Airport (known universally as L-A-X) can be spectacular, weather permitting. In-bound traffic almost always lands to the west, gently buffeted by winds blowing in-land off the Pacific Ocean. As the aircraft enters the Los Angeles basin, a passenger at a starboard (right-side) window will notice the splendour of the San Gabriel Mountains, which frame the city and surrounding areas to the east. The famed "HOLLYWOOD" sign, perched on the hills north of the city, is visible to those with keen eyesight.

The buildings of downtown L.A. soon come into view and roughly one mile northeast of the city — on a site known as Chavez Ravine — sits an empty Dodger Stadium, surrounded by acres of parking. Below us, are the countless homes of south-central L.A., whose neighbourhoods were ravaged in the riots of April, 1993.

Off the wing-tip, just southwest of the city, is the University of Southern California campus, and the nearby complex of the Los Angeles Coliseum and Sports Arena. Seconds later, the aircraft passes over the southern tip of Hollywood Park racetrack with the Maple Leafs' ultimate destination, the Great Western Forum, mounted on a parking lot across the street — its white Roman columns unmistakable. Flying over the 405 Freeway, which winds south towards San Diego, the jetliner softly descends to Runway 25-L, speeding past the phalanx of airport hotels that line Century Blvd. to the north.

As we touched down, the sun was peeking through a clump of thick clouds — forewarning us of yet another rainstorm expected in the L.A. area. Southern California has been deluged with Monsoon-like conditions for the entire month of January: causing wide-spread flooding in-land, and treacherous mud-slides in the coastal hills between Santa Monica and Malibu. The Pacific Coast Highway, a scenic and busily traveled motor route that skirts the ocean shoreline, was shut down completely in some areas and reduced to a single lane of traffic in others.

Grassy areas in the city are saturated beyond capacity, with five more consecutive days of rain expected. Quite a contrast to the drought conditions that had plagued the region for almost three years.

In the past 22 months, Los Angeles residents have experienced a week of race rioting, more than a month of destructive brush fires in canyons surrounding the city, a devastating 6.8-magnitude earthquake centered in the heavily populated San Fernando Valley, and now the excessive rainfall. Quite a litany of woe.

Upon leaving the plane, the players and coaches headed towards a bus that awaited them outside the Arrivals area; they had carried their personal belongings on-board and thus did not have to visit the luggage carousel. Meanwhile, team trainers Carey and Papineau were met on the tarmac by the Los Angeles Kings' equipment staff: part of a reciprocal arrangement that is honoured by all NHL teams (the home club sends a truck to the airport for the arriving visitors — quite often in the middle of the night). The Leaf equipment was loaded and transported directly to the Forum, where a team practice was slated to begin within 90 minutes.

For many years, when visiting Los Angeles, the Leafs had stayed at the Airport Marriott hotel — right in the middle of L-A-X. The airport itself is rather unique in that it actually flanks Century Blvd., with separate terminals and runways on each side of the busy street. Hotels at L-A-X are obviously convenient for business travelers and are also handy for visiting hockey and basketball teams, as the Forum (in the city of Inglewood) is only ten minutes away by car.

In the 1993 Campbell Conference final against the Kings, the Maple Leafs had set up camp at the Lowes resort: a luxurious hotel on Santa Monica beach, about a half-hour from the airport. They had planned to stay there during their 1994-95 stops in L.A. and Anaheim but their plans on this opening trip have been scuttled by the lockout-shortened schedule. It makes little sense to stay in Santa Monica for merely one night, so the club and traveling media are housed at the Doubletree Hotel at L-A-X. Nothing fancy, but if you enjoy watching planes take off (as I do), there's no better place in the world.

Media members who cover the Maple Leafs on the road are indebted to administrative assistant Mary Speck. Mary is the first person you encounter upon entering the Leaf executive offices at the Gardens and she's in charge, among other things, of formulating the club's travel plans. She books hotels, commercial and charter flights, as well as bus transportation to and from airports, hotels and arenas. No easy chore. Mary also books hotel rooms for traveling media at a special "team" rate. As a result, media organizations who staff road games rarely pay more than $90 per night at even the fanciest hotels. Broadcasters and writers are usually accorded the privilege of traveling on the team bus and (for a cost) on team charter flights.

On this first trip of the new season, I checked into the L-A-X Doubletree and immediately phoned Rick Minch, the Los Angeles Kings' director of media relations, who informed me the Kings were at the tail-end of a practice session. The aforementioned proximity to the arena came in handy, as I hopped in a cab and was standing in the Great Western Forum not more than 15 minutes later. The Kings, to my abundant relief, were still on the ice.

Wayne Gretzky, however, was not, so I ventured down to the Kings' dressing room and after the mandatory 15-minute wait, went inside. The Great One was standing in the middle of the room, talking with teammate Tony Granato. He was decked out in bluejeans and an old, beat-up hockey jersey — probably from his youth. Our eyes met and he reached out to shake hands. Gretzky and I aren't acquainted beyond facial recognition but he did receive the very first copy of my book, MAPLE LEAF MOMENTS. On that October day in 1994, Gretzky and Vancouver columnist Jim Taylor were launching Wayne's pictorial biography at Gretzky's restaurant in downtown Toronto. *My* book came back from the printer that same day and the publisher's office was just across the street. So I ran over there, signed a copy to Gretzky, and took it to him. Having both grown up in southern Ontario and being roughly the same age (he's 23 months younger), I figured Gretzky would be able to identify with the subject matter and I'm told he spent the entire flight back to Los Angeles later that day reading the book.

Standing in the Kings' dressing room today, Gretzky talked very much out of character. For years, hockey's greatest star had spoken out against excessive violence in the sport and had been particularly adverse to fighting. But after experiencing one of the most frustrating seasons of his career (and perhaps hardened by the lockout mess), he was quite willing to sing a different tune.

"We're not going to take the punishment anymore," he said in reference to the passive and horribly disappointing Los Angeles team of 1993-94. After making it to the Stanley Cup Finals the previous year, the Kings were pushed around like rag-dolls and plummeted 22 points in the standings, missing the playoffs.

"A lot of guys have taken liberties with players on this team and that's going to stop," he continued. "I've never been one to condone fighting but we'll do whatever it takes to make up for last year. What happened to us is the guys in the league who weren't so tough suddenly got brave. That was very annoying."

Exactly how the new muscle approach will translate to an improved season is unclear. The Kings have beefed up considerably with additions like Rick Tocchet (in a trade with Pittsburgh for 50-goal shooter Luc Robitaille), cement-handed Troy Crowder (former Red Wing and Devil who has been out of hockey since 1991), veteran defenceman Michel Petit and rookie behemoth Matt Johnson. As well, union sparkplug Marty McSorley is back from playing half a season with Pittsburgh. But, have the Kings up-graded their skill level? If so, it isn't apparent on paper.

As the Los Angeles players left the dressing room, the Maple Leafs walked by to suit up for their practice. Goaltender Kelly Hrudey, who had just signed a contract extension, paused while chatting with a reporter to shake hands with former L.A. teammate and new Maple Leaf Dixon Ward. Otherwise, the stoic Leafs filed nonchalantly past the departing Los Angeles players without even a glance. So much for union brotherhood.

During the practice session that followed, coach Burns skated two new line combinations: Mike Eastwood between Mike Craig and newcomer Randy Wood, and Kent Manderville between Bill Berg and Ken Baumgartner. Afterwards, in the Leaf dressing room, I asked the Bomber if he'll find it difficult to foster a hate-on for McSorley, with whom he worked so diligently on the NHLPA executive committee during the lockout?

"I don't think so," he replied. "At least, that hasn't been a problem in the past."

McSorley wasn't so willing to respond.

"I did enough talking during the lockout to last me a lifetime," he smiled. "Let's play hockey."

Having acquired enough tape for my scheduled braodcast, I walked up into the Forum seats and glanced wistfully around the building. It has been just more than a year-and-a-half since the Leafs and Kings battled through a memorable playoff semifinal and my thoughts drifted back to covering that series. On the ice in front of me stood the goal into which Gretzky scored the overtime winner of Game 6 — seconds after carving Doug Gilmour's chin with an accidental high stick. Wendel Clark had scored into that same net in the dying moments of regulation to tie the game.

Now empty, the Forum seems tattered and worn, even though it is less than 30 years old. Built in 1967 by the Kings' first owner, Jack Kent Cooke, it was hockey's most plush and modern arena when it opened in December of that year — its Romanesque facade creating a stately appearance. More than a quarter-century later, it sits near a notorious Los Angeles ghetto, devoid of the private luxury suites that drive the sporting economy. Still, it has a pleasant-enough feel to it and is one of the few "expansion era" facilities with some character.

Mounted on the north wall are enlargements of the five gold-and-purple uniforms retired by the NBA's Los Angeles Lakers: Ervin (Magic) Johnson, Kareem Abdul-Jabbar, Wilt Chamberlain, Jerry West and Elgin Baylor. To the right is a banner depicting the Kings' 1992-93 Campbell Conference championship and next to it, the two uniforms retired by the hockey club: Rogie Vachon and Marcel Dionne. Emblazoned on the south wall — illuminated by rays of light from the Forum ceiling — are the six Laker championship banners.

The 16,005 seats surrounding the rink are divided in a peculiar colour scheme... the stands on the east side are gold; on the west side they're orange. The two levels are separated by a walkway and the press box is located in the upper-level orange seats, directly at center ice.

The skies remained mostly sunny as I waited outside the Forum for a cab back to the hotel. Jetliners shrilled overhead on final approach to L-A-X. A security officer at the Forum Club entrance talked about his cushy job becoming not-so-cushy with the return of hockey.

Early tonight, my mother-in-law, Maxine, and brother-in-law, Andrew, picked me up and we went for dinner at the *Cheesecake Factory* in Marina Del Rey. As we were being seated on the outside patio, Andrew mentioned something about Toronto and the waitress asked, "Oh, are you going to the hockey game tomorrow?" I nodded yes and she explained that the entire Maple Leaf team was inside the restaurant having dinner.

"One of the players is real cute," she gushed. "He has long blonde hair and kind of a bashed-in nose."

Ah yes... another of the Bomber's secret admirers.

FRIDAY, JANUARY 20th
Los Angeles

Speaking of Ken Baumgartner, he was up with the seagulls today. Sitting in the hotel lobby at 7:30, working on the Los Angeles *Times* crossword puzzle, the Bomber had fallen victim to the three-hour time change. "I'm usually up early with the kids anyway," he shrugged. "No big deal." As we were chatting, Pat Burns stomped by in his sweat-suit, heading outside for his morning exercise. I had breakfast and then went upstairs to get my tape machine.

Every Maple Leaf road-trip is staffed by either Business and Communications Director Bob Stellick or Public Relations Coordinator Pat Park, who split the season-long duties. They more or less oversee the semantics of the trip, serving as a liaison between the club and the media. Their chores include ensuring that hotel-room keys are properly assigned; arranging boarding passes for commercial flights, and tickets for out-of-town friends and/or relatives. They also make sure that pre-arranged ground transportation arrives on time, such as the bus that would take us to this morning's skate at the Forum.

All NHL teams have a light skate the morning of a game to keep the muscles loose for the evening's combat. The workouts are often shorter and less-strenuous than normal practices and are occasionally optional (as on consecutive game days). The home team skates at 10 a.m. with the visitors following around 11:30. As the team bus prepared to leave for Inglewood this morning, the players were having some fun at the expense of Stellick, who made the season-opening trip.

Burns had not yet emerged from the hotel, but his sweatsuit jacket was on the front seat of the bus, where he always sits. From the back, several players implored the driver to leave for the Forum, saying that Burns had gone ahead in a taxi. Caught between a rock and a hard place, Stellick wanted to believe the players but with Burns' coat on the bus, he feared the coach was still inside. He walked back into the hotel to double check and as soon as he left the bus, one of the players cracked "Okay, now we can leave", bringing a chuckle from the others. Stellick returned without Burns a few moments later, and we were on our way.

The bus drivers who transport hockey teams from place to place are usually treated with dignity and respect by everyone on board, with one mild exception: the driver is always referred to as "bussie". He could be Harry, Pete, Norman, Irv, Roy... whatever, and his name is sometimes identified by a slide-in tag at the front of the vehicle. Still, it's, "Hey bussie, let's get a move-on", or, "Thanks for the ride, bussie." The coaching staff is usually more polite, calling the man "driver".

During the Maple Leaf skate this morning, Jerry West emerged from a concourse ramp at the Forum. The basketball hall of famer and current general manager of the Lakers was surprisingly in town, with his club across the country in Boston for an historic road game. The Lakers and Celtics — long-time NBA playoff rivals — will meet for their final regular-season encounter at the Boston Garden later tonight and I found it strange that West had not travelled east.

Introducing myself, we chatted for a few moments and he seemed quite knowledgeable about hockey — wondering aloud how the Maple Leafs were going to replace Wendel Clark. When I inquired about his absence from the Lakers' trip to Boston, he made a point that I've never heard from the general manager of a pro sports team.

"I hardly ever travel with the club because I don't feel there's any constructive purpose to it," West explained. "When I was a player and the G.M. was on a trip, I could almost feel his presence during the game. It's like the big eye in the sky was looking down on me and it made for additional pressure. I don't like doing that to my players and I find I get more work done at my office here in the Forum."

Interesting, when you consider that practically all G.M.s travel with their teams for varying reasons. Many believe that it's necessary to maintain contact with the players and coaching staff; others travel to initiate or field trade discussions, while a few undoubtedly do so as an escape from domestic chores. Whatever the case, travel budgets always encompass the presence of a general manager, and rarely does the G.M. chose not to go along.

On the team bus back from the skate this afternoon, I noticed an oddity: jetliners were taking off eastward from L-A-X over the city, rather than out over the ocean. Therefore, while doing my work, the Doubletree Hotel shook with noise every 30 seconds or so, as planes roared off the runway. It reminded me of covering a Maple Leaf game in Minnesota several years ago. We stayed at the Bloomington Marriott —directly across the street from the Met Center, and roughly a mile from the Minneapolis/St. Paul airport. There was no need for a wake-up call in that place, as ascending jetliners blasted you out of bed seconds after the 6 a.m. noise curfew had been lifted.

I mentioned earlier that, like many people, I've always been quite fascinated by the spectacle of giant airplanes lifting off the runway and our Los Angeles vantage point was perhaps the best I can remember. After sending voice clips and my Gretzky interview to the radio station, I went down to the lobby and outside to the fourth level of the hotel parking structure. From there, I could see the entire runway in the south tier of L-A-X. And I spent a glorious hour watching planes take off until the forecasted rainshowers began around 4:30

Prior to leaving for tonight's game, the players, coaching staff and media checked out of the hotel and placed their suitcases in the luggage compartment of the team bus. With a game tomorrow night in San Jose, the club has a charter flight booked out of L-A-X and will head to the airport immediately following the game. The luggage will remain locked on the bus in the Forum during tonight's opener with the Kings.

On my way down to check out, the elevator door opened and standing inside were Dave Andreychuk and Garth Butcher. Working in radio all of these years, I've been one to dress for comfort — usually in bluejeans and a shirt. My clothes have always been clean, but rarely flashy. Such was the case when I stepped on the elevator and Andreychuk said, "Gee, Howie, I see you're dressed for the occasion." In his not-so subtle way, Andreychuk sent me an important message... I was now travelling with the team (at times) and should therefore conform more closely to accepted practices while on the road. I quickly went back up to my room and put on a pair of slacks and a sweater. And I thanked Andreychuk while we were boarding the team bus.

There wasn't so much as a peep of noise during the 10-minute ride to the Forum. In contrast to a more jovial atmosphere on the ride back from the morning skate, the players and coaches grew quiet and introspective with the season opener two hours away. The bus wound east along Century Blvd. and made a left turn at Prairie Ave. To our right was the Hollywood Park Racetrack, whose entire length we had to traverse before the Forum came into view on the same side of the road. The white columns of the arena and its royal blue roof were bathed in floodlights, as the mid-winter darkness had enveloped Los Angeles. The letters "G-W" were prominent on the side of the roof, as Great Western Bank has been the Forum's primary sponsor for half a decade (beginning a trend that would catch on with other arenas).

Our bus turned left down a large ramp and disappeared into the bowels of the Forum. When it came to a stop, Burns rose from his front-row seat and hollered "Let's go boys!"; the players responded with unorganized chants, and we all filed off.

Walking up to the Forum press area, I turned and noticed that the players' benches and penalty boxes had been switched to opposite sides of the rink. The players' benches had previously been on the same side as the pressbox and TV cameras. I checked into it and was told that the television people had requested the move so cameras could more easily pick up facial expressions of players and coaches across the ice. They say that TV rules the world and here was another small example.

The pre-game festivities were comprehensive as the Kings and their fans observed the belated start to the season. P.A. announcer David Courtney brought a chuckle to the Toronto media while introducing the starting line-ups when he referred to the Leafs' rookie defenceman as Kenny "Jo-Honsson". Photos of the Leaf starters were flashed on the Forum sportstimer and both Gilmour and Burns were loudly booed. After the Leaf intros, the Forum lights were dimmed and the L.A. players were introduced to thunderous cheering. Meanwhile, an entire orchestra, it seemed, was wheeled out to the center-ice area for elaborate renditions of *O Canada* and the *Star Spangled Banner.*

My seat in the pressbox was one row behind the *Hockey Night In Canada* broadcast team of Bob Cole and Harry Neale. As a result, I was briefly removed in favour of a TV monitor and camera-light so that Cole and Neale could turn around and do their pre-game chat. When it ended, I got my seat back.

Doug Gilmour went to center-ice for the Maple Leafs, flanked by Dave Andreychuk and Nikolai Borschevsky. Dave Ellett and the rookie Jonsson started on defence with Felix Potvin in goal. After nearly four months of labour unrest, the abbreviated 1994-95 season was underway and when referee Don Koharski dropped the puck, the capacity audience at the Forum let out a sardonic cheer, as if to say... *"FINALLY!!!"*

As advertised, the bigger and supposedly braver Kings came out of the gate all full of piss and vinegar, launching their bodies at Maple Leaf players who had the audacity to get in their way. And as expected, the Kings went immediately overboard — union-leader McSorley rubbing his gloved hand into Mike Craig's face with 1:20 elapsed on the clock, drawing a roughing infraction, and officially ending NHLPA brotherhood.

Four seconds later, defenseman Dmitri Mironov scored the Maple Leafs' first goal of the season.

Mats Sundin won a draw to the right of Kelly Hrudey. Dave Ellett took the puck and passed across ice to Mironov, who one-timed a point shot into the L.A. net. The Leafs stormed Hrudey and recorded the first five shots of the game. Then ex-Leaf Michel Petit took a swipe at Gilmour, who did not retaliate, and the Kings were two men short. Mike Ridley made them pay, wristing a two-on-one pass from Mike Gartner into the net for his first goal as a Maple Leaf and it was 2-0 Toronto.

But the Leafs then ran into their own penalty trouble and the poisonous duo of Jari Kurri and Wayne Gretzky struck on consecutive powerplays to tie the score in the next five minutes. Koharski gave Gilmour a ridiculous goaltender interference penalty late in the period. Replays showed that Hrudey came out and bumped into the Leaf captain, who did not even skate through the goalcrease. It's a penalty referees are constantly tricked into calling by crafty netminders who know how to act. And being so close to Hollywood, Hrudey has obviously brushed up on his dramatics.

As the clock wound to a close in the opening frame, a large group of fans in our vicinity yelled out in unison, "How much time is left?!"

"One minute to play in the period," announced David Courtney.

"Thank you!" they replied.

Leaf defenceman Jamie Macoun scored the only goal of the middle period and he did so before many of the fans were back in their seats. His low shot from inside the point escaped Hrudey in the first minute. Midway through the period, the Kings flashed a "Hollywood Minute" on the scoreboard and the fans lustily booed the appearance of actress Heather Locklear, presumably for her bitchy demeanour on *Melrose Place*.

Meanwhile, Gretzky developed a nasty disposition towards referee Koharski as the period unfolded. While killing a penalty, Gretzky was hauled down by Mironov on a 2-on-1 break with Kurri. The Maple Leaf defenceman drew an interference call, but Gretzky argued vehemently for a penalty shot. On his next shift, Gretzky appeared to be breaking into the clear in the neutral zone when Mike Eastwood reached out and hooked him to the ice. Sliding on his belly, Gretzky looked up at Koharski but the referee shook his head, figuring the Great One had embellished his tumble. The crowd went ballistic and when the play ended, Gretzky broke his stick over the glass at the L.A. bench in an uncharacteristic fit of anger. The period ended 2-1 for the Maple Leafs.

The most excitement in the third period resulted from a brawl in the nosebleed seats up behind us. A couple of guys were just hammering on one another and when a third party became involved, all hell broke loose. A half-dozen cops rushed to the scene and broke it up. On the ice, meanwhile, Kenny Jonsson was having a rough time in his first NHL game. Caught out of position behind his own net, Jonsson reached out and tackled Kurri to the ice, drawing a blatant holding call. Gilmour joined him in the box for roughing six seconds later and Kurri tied the score with the two-man advantage. Poor Jonsson got duped again on his next shift and drew a tripping penalty. In the press box, Leaf general manager Cliff Fletcher threw his hands up in exasperation.

The game went into overtime and the Leafs had the best chance when big Sundin cut in towards the net off his wrong wing. But Hrudey came out to meet him and made a sprawling save. The match ended 3-3.

The Leafs were sloppy and appeared confused in the latter half of the hockey game and Jamie Macoun had a few gripes in the dressing room afterwards.

"The ice is always lousy and soft in this place and the style of game played tonight was ridiculous," he said. "The Kings were hacking and whacking out there and considering they're supposed to be the big skilled team, it was a bush game. There were a lot of bad hits and cheap shots on the ice and it really wasn't the type of game that I expected. But, I suppose that's the style they're going to try and play for the rest of the year."

While the Leafs ran out of stamina late in the game, there were a few bright spots — most notably, the play of Felix Potvin in goal, and the line of Ridley, Gartner and Sundin. "This was the Kings' opener and we came in here and walked away with a tie," said Leaf captain Gilmour. "I thought we jelled together pretty well for such a new team."

The Maple Leaf players dressed quickly after the game and boarded one of two buses waiting outside on the Forum's main ramp. The second bus had been arranged for the overflow media throng covering this first Leaf road trip. The group included Joe Bowen, Gord Stellick and myself from the *Telemedia* radio network; about a dozen announcers, producers and technicians from *Hockey Night In Canada*; three reporters from the Toronto *Sun* and two from the *Star*, plus a reporter and cameraman from CFTO-TV, Channel 9 in Toronto.

It was pouring rain when we boarded the second bus around 11 p.m. and began following the Maple Leaf vehicle to L-A-X. We had to go to the aviation/charter area, which was not a part of the main terminal, and it was obvious our driver had never been there before. Still, none of us realized the saga we'd encounter along the way.

Post-game traffic was still heavy on Prairie Ave. and our driver maintained radio contact with the Leaf bus, about a block ahead. We passed a store called "BAIL AND BONDS", and someone behind me made a rude crack about Bruce McNall. The gallows humour only intensified when we somehow lost sight of the Maple Leaf bus. Our driver was suddenly on his own and the poor guy had not a clue as to where he was heading.

Several long moments later, he pulled off the main road and we found ourselves in a remote parking area beneath an overpass of the Century Freeway. About a half-dozen cars formed a mini "RatLand" below us, with sexually active teens groping at one another, believing they had found uncharted territory. Come to think of it, a radar device might indeed have failed to locate us at that moment and our driver sheepishly attempted to radio his whereabouts to the now-distant Maple Leaf bus. He was told to look for the "guard gate" and we knew we were in big trouble when the driver began making a right turn into the Korean Airlines cargo terminal.

Talk about a long road trip: Los Angeles on Friday; Seoul on Saturday.

By then, it was painfully evident that our trusty chauffeur had lost not only his directions, but his confidence as well. Sitting in the front seat of the bus, Bob Cole did his level best to keep the guy from breaking down, saying things like, "C'mon now, we should be able to find the guard gate; you know this city." Backing out of the Korean Airlines lot, the driver pulled up to another gate and made a desperate radio plea to the Maple Leaf bus. No answer. He tried again. Still no answer. While sitting there, we had a great view of the south runway and main airport terminal at L-A-X. Suddenly, an *Airbus* took off in front of us, prompting Harry Neale to crack, "Whup, there she goes", in mock reference to the Maple Leaf charter.

The driver turned around and began heading for yet another gate. This time we passed through and his waffling became more obvious than ever. He inched the bus forward and stopped... inched forward and stopped... inched forward and stopped. "Another hundred or so lurches and we should be there," cracked *Hockey Night In Canada* producer Mark Askin. Suddenly, the long-lost Maple Leaf driver re-established radio contact, saying he had already dropped off the team and that we should look for "the last building on your right." Somebody at the back of the bus blared, "He'll probably drop us at the first building on our left!" Finally, we came upon one more gate that led to a DC-9 aircraft with a bus parked beside it. "That's the one," radioed the Leaf driver and our little odyssey was over.

We pulled up beside the DC-9 and walked off the bus, then up the airplane's portable stairwell. It was still teeming rain outside. The Leaf players and coaches were comfortably strapped into their seats and they glanced at us with bemused expressions, as if to say, "Where the hell have *you* guys been?" I wish we knew. Thankfully, our bewildered bus driver had not delayed the flight, as trainers Papineau, Carey and Chris Broadhurst were loading the team equipment. They had the truck pulled up right next to the cargo hold but as I looked out my right-hand window, I could tell they were getting drenched. And when they finally came on board, you would have thought they had just emerged from a swimming pool. A glamorous life, indeed.

The charter flight would take us to Oakland because of curfew restrictions at the San Jose airport, which is close to the center of town. Jet airliners cannot take off or land in San Jose after 11 p.m. and Oakland is only 30 miles north. The captain welcomed us on board, saying the flight would be 50 minutes in duration and that we'd likely be flying through an area of thunderstorms northeast of Los Angeles. As we lifted off the runway, I looked down and recognized the area of our impromptu bus tour. "There's the driver: he's going back the same way," I gibed, as my media colleagues chuckled and offered a little wave.

We then disappeared into the clouds.

*   *   *   *   *   *

It was 1:45 a.m. on the west coast when the captain radioed that we were taking the scenic route into Oakland. And he wasn't kidding. We flew to the north of San Francisco and then turned back south directly over the Golden Gate Bridge. In a spectacular approach to the airport, we followed the Bay waters over Alcatraz and the San Francisco-Oakland Bay Bridge. The city may have turned in for the night, but the lights of San Francisco shone brilliantly through broken clouds out my right-side window. Two minutes later, we were on the ramp in Oakland.

Stepping out of the plane, there were again two buses waiting to take us to San Jose. We glanced through dim lighting to ensure that our Los Angeles driver did not have a twin brother in northern California. It was also raining in Oakland and the cooler air had a bite to it. The luxuries of commercial flying were non-existent, as we had to walk on the tarmac to the opposite side of the DC-9 and fetch our luggage from the cargo hold. The Maple Leafs departed quickly and we followed on the media bus several minutes later. The trip down the Nimitz Freeway took three-quarters of an hour and we pulled up to the Fairmont Hotel in San Jose at 2:20 a.m. Thankfully, our room keys were waiting at the front desk (another advantage of traveling with the club) and after filing my reports from the L.A. game, I hit the sack at 3 o'clock.

SATURDAY, JANUARY 21st
San Jose

At breakfast this morning, I read the San Jose *Mercury News* about the Sharks' dismal performance in their season opener last night. They were out-classed 5-2 at home by St. Louis and Arturs Irbe, according to all reports, had a lousy game in net. It was a major disappointment for the 17,190 spectators, who had last seen the Sharks during their near-upset of the Maple Leafs in the Conference semifinal eight months ago.

St. Louis, however, did not impress Ray Ratto, the droll columnist at the San Francisco *Examiner*. He wrote:

> *The Blues? Well, they have Mike Keenan, a pretty new building and new ghastly uniforms this season to get in front*

of, rather than behind, the fashion curve. Of course, none of these ideas are new — especially the uniforms. The design is stolen outright from the Mighty Ducks of Anaheim, and the colour scheme is a ripoff of those 1880s Old West whorehouse curtains you see in all the right places.

The San Francisco Museum of Modern Art, for example, uses them for dropcloths. Or to wipe up the sneeze guards at the snack bar.

Still, it's hockey, even if the Blues chose to dress like they've all been stabbed in the left kidney, and everyone seemed just happy to be back at it. Brett Hull actually backchecked, which was almost never seen before the lockout.

Hull also scored a couple of gift goals against the Sharks and it was obvious, this morning, that San Jose coach Kevin Constantine would not tolerate a repeat performance from his hockey club.

Constantine looks like a Vietnam platoon officer and he's got the personality of a turnip. At least that's the way he presents himself to a visiting member of the media. His daily briefings occur in an office next to the Sharks' dressing room. Constantine reluctantly saunters in and sits painstakingly at a table, leaning on his elbow and rubbing his forehead from side to side — as if he's suffering from a kidney stone. His answers are curt, and frequently unenlightening. In that regard, he closely resembles Pat Burns but, like Burns, his persona changes when he's removed from the spotlight.

I found that out at a media briefing during the NHL Awards dinner last June. A deserving finalist for the Jack Adams Trophy as coach of the year, Constantine was in Toronto to attend the ceremony. My program director at The *Fan* asked me to gather information for a series we aired called *Jock 'n Roll*. Essentially, I went around to the Award nominees inquiring about their favourite rock musicians. Constantine was off in a corner by himself and I cautiously approached him, figuring all the while it would be an exercise in futility. You can thus imagine my surprise when the demure San Jose coach waxed poetically for almost 90 seconds about his affinity for the rock group America. It was probably the best piece of tape I acquired all night long.

But now at the San Jose Arena — seven long months later — Constantine was in no mood to be humming *Ventura Highway*. His club had bombed on opening night and I became privy, quite by accident, to his volatile response. Having gathered with a local radio reporter in the hallway outside the Sharks' dressing quarters, we were led into the briefing room by media relations assistant Roger Ross. Seconds later, a highly agitated Constantine could be heard reaming his charges about their brutal performance against St. Louis. This was the Riot Act in all its frightful glory, with "fucks" and "dammits" reverberating off the walls. Ross shuffled about uncomfortably and then thought it might be prudent to have us wait outside a little longer.

Gazing about the empty Arena moments later, it was eerie to realize that the 1994-95 NHL All-Star Game would have been played here in San Jose this afternoon. January 21st was supposed to be a big day for the Sharks and their loyal fans, but the lockout got in the way. And it's too bad, because this organization would have put on one heck of a show for the hockey world.

The San Jose Arena is a beautiful new facility with all the modern amenities. It is situated at the end of a busy street on the fringes of the main downtown area, a block west of the Guadalupe Parkway overpass. The rink is a comfortable 15-minute walk along palmtree-lined streets from the Fairmont Hotel. A small, quiet and clean city, San Jose has a distinctly Spanish flavour and the downtown core has been resurrected primarily by the Fairmont and the Arena. The hotel is a magnificent, white-stone edifice less than three years old, located on a main street round-about, adjacent to a small park. Its rooms are luxurious, with separate bath and shower stalls, and soft terri-cloth robes hanging in your closet. Behind the hotel is an L-R-T transit line and a promenade of boutiques and restaurants, including a great sports bar. The whole area is perfect for a two or three-day hockey visit.

Prior to leaving for the Arena tonight, Pat Burns sat at the front of the bus, stoic and expressionless. On the short ride over, Burns and assistant coach Mike Kitchen were discussing the initial segment of Don Cherry's *Coach's Corner* — a between-periods feature broadcast nationally in Canada — last night. Apparently, Grapes had once again railed on Maple Leaf management for trading feisty captain Wendel Clark in the off-season, and suggested the Leafs would not be as gritty a team because they had players with "too many visors". Burns grew slightly agitated and said, "Cherry is paid for his opinions, not his decisions." The conversation then became lighter, as Kitchen recounted playing for Cherry with the Colorado Rockies in 1979-80, and how Cherry came within an eyelash of slapping out maverick defenceman Mike McEwen. Burns had a good chuckle over that story as the bus pulled up to the Arena.

The main dinner course in the media room was enough to wipe the smile off anyone's face. It was a ground-beef concoction that must have been 30 percent meat and 70 percent *Tabasco*. Handkerchiefs were everywhere as teary eyed din-ers honked out the ingredients. Bob Stellick issued a desperate warning to coach Burns as he stood in line. And if the meal didn't bring a frown to Burns' face, you can be sure tonight's game certainly did.

Although they led 1-0 after the first period, the Leafs appeared tired and tentative. Mats Sundin bagged his first goal as a Maple Leaf on a powerplay in the game's opening minutes but the visitors were not able to sustain any form of attack. Midway through the period, Burns juggled his top forward lines, removing Sundin from his natural center position and placing him on right-wing with Gilmour and Andreychuk. He switched Mike Ridley to center on the second unit between Mike Gartner and Nikolai Borschevsky. He also double-shifted Gilmour, using him on a line with Bill Berg and Kent Manderville. But nothing seemed to work, and San Jose took control of the game with a 24-second outburst early in the middle frame.

Defenceman Mike Rathje slammed in Ulf Dahlen's feed from behind the net and less than half-a-minute later, Ray Whitney walked between Dave Ellett and Kenny Jonsson on a major defensive gaffe to give the Sharks a 2-1 lead. Felix Potvin was helpless on both plays. The fans at the Arena began taunting the Leaf goalie with cries of "*POT...VIN!*" but the Leafs were able to tie the game a few minutes later on Mike Craig's first goal in a Toronto uniform. Craig beat Arturs Irbe on a nifty two-on-one set-up from Mike Eastwood. The hockey game, however, swung in San Jose's favour moments after referee Paul Devorski penalized Sandis Ozolinsh for mugging Ellett late in the period.

Burns put Jonsson out on the powerplay, showing confidence in the fledgling rookie. While circling in the neutral zone, Jonsson stumbled — later saying that he lost an edge on his skate. He lunged clumsily at Sharks' rookie Jeff Friesen, who took a pass from Igor Larionov and marched in on a clear, 100-foot breakaway. Friesen whipped a wrist-shot past Potvin with just more than a minute remaining in the period and the shorthanded goal sent a wave of electricity through the Arena.

Jonsson was embarrassed on the play, and he played a large role (along with Ellett) in the mistake that enabled Whitney to pot the Sharks' second goal. This was only his second NHL game and the young Swede was zigging when he should zag. Both games on this trip were televised back home, and heaven only knows how Maple Leaf fans are reacting to Jonsson's glaring miscues. Patience is not a long suit among hockey observers in Toronto and despite his size and skating ability, the kid doesn't seem up to the NHL challenge just yet.

The San Jose hockey crowd is lively and excitable, even without its club scoring timely shorthanded goals. The Sharks have cornered the market on creating an event-like atmosphere. It starts when a large shark-head is lowered from the rafters prior to the game. The lights in the rink are extinguished, except for a spotlight that illuminates the shark. Dry ice mist begins to swirl about as the San Jose players skate onto the ice through the mammal's protracted jaw, while *The Final Countdown* blares out over the Arena sound system. It's quite a scene.

In the second intermission, I walked back into the press box and noticed an inflatable shark actually flying through the Arena. This helium-filled creature is known as *AirShark*. It is 23 feet long, 12 feet high and 10-feet wide, and is remote-controlled by an operator standing in the Zamboni entrance at the east end of the Arena. Soaring just beneath the rafters, *AirShark* swoops gracefully among the fans in the upper-seats, dropping souvenir items like caps and T-shirts. It's a concept that surprisingly hasn't caught on in other arenas, thought I suppose an inflatable penguin or panther might look ridiculous.

The Maple Leafs played by far their best hockey of the road trip in the final ten minutes of tonight's game but were unable to score the tying goal. Sundin failed to corral a loose puck to the left of Irbe at the midway point of the period. Andreychuk then directed a centring pass from Gilmour inches wide a few moments later. But the Leafs' best chance occurred with 3:50 left in regulation time when Kent Manderville deflected Todd Gill's point-drive off the inside of the left goalpost. Andreychuk and Mike Craig failed to score from the slot in the final 2 1/2 minutes and with Potvin on the bench in the dying seconds for an extra attacker, San Jose held on by a shoestring to win the game.

In the Leaf dressing room afterwards, the players took solace in the fact they did not wilt, as expected, in the late stages of the game and they quite accurately believed they were unlucky not to emerge with at least a point. "We could have beaten them tonight, but it's going to take time for this team to start playing well," explained Dave Ellett. "There's still some confusion out there, as guys are looking around and hesitating. We have to make quicker decisions and that will come."

Indeed, the Toronto defence appeared slow and tentative with just about every player guilty of coughing up the puck. The veteran blueline brigade under Pat Burns the past two years had been the strength of the hockey club. With Sylvain Lefebvre now in Quebec (part of the Mats Sundin-Wendel Clark trade), and Rob Rouse in Detroit via free agency, the Leafs have lost some savvy in that key area. Only Potvin, who may have played the finest 20 minutes of his career in the first period, was able to keep the Maple Leafs in this game. Otherwise, it was mass confusion in the Leaf zone.

Manderville spent 35 minutes in the trainer's room and then spoke about his near miss late in the third. "I thought it was in," he said. "(Mike) Ridley made a great play to Giller and Todd put a good shot towards the net. The puck hit the shaft of my stick and went off the inside of the post. Ridley then tried to make a play on the rebound and Irbe jumped on it. That's the way our luck seemed to go tonight."

Meanwhile, the focus of the post-game media blitz centred on the rookie Jonsson, and how terribly he was beaten by Friesen on San Jose's winning goal. It looked brutal from up in the press box. But Jonsson's teammates were trying to shield him from criticism. "You know it's tough... defence is the hardest position to come into the NHL and play and there are going to be a few bumps in the road for Kenny," said Ellett. "He just has to learn from his mistakes and bounce back." Added Jamie Macoun: "What happened to him happens to veterans as well. But when you don't have that much experience to draw on, you feel like the world's crashing down on you. But, tomorrow's another day and Kenny will get better. He has a load of talent."

The ride back to the Fairmont was understandably quiet. "Bus at 6:30 in the morning fellas," announced Mike Kitchen as we arrived. Walking into the hotel lobby, Cliff Fletcher asked me, "Whad'ya think, Howie?" We talked briefly and he seemed quite pleased with the way his team energized itself in the third period. "We'll be alright," he said.

SUNDAY, JANUARY 22nd
Aboard Air Canada Flight
From San Francisco

It was still pitch-dark outside as the Maple Leaf bus pulled away from the Fairmont Hotel this morning. With traffic not a factor, the ride up to San Francisco International Airport took only 35 minutes and the first hint of morning light glowed on the horizon as we entered the terminal. An all-purpose restaurant flourished with travellers inside the Departures lounge and the Maple Leaf players purchased traditional breakfast items like muffins and danish. All except Mats Sundin, who saw fit to order a salami and cheese sandwich at 7:20 a.m. Someone pointed out, however, that it was 4:20 p.m. in Sweden and, therefore, time for a late-afternoon snack.

Our Air Canada *AirBus* took off over Oakland at 8:30 with Pat Burns sitting in the flight-deck — a guest of the captain and first officer. The trip went by quickly as the majority of passengers settled back to watch *Forrest Gump*: undeniably one of the best movies ever made. The ending of that great film is enough to bring even the brawniest of people to tears, as witnessed by the number of Maple Leaf players who busted out the kleenex.

With just more than an hour remaining in the trip, I visited the flight-deck and shook my head in amazement after introducing myself to the first officer. Bruce Bornstein and I both attended high school at William Lyon MacKenzie in North York (he graduated four years ahead of me) and we grew up at opposite ends of the same street (Kennard Ave.). Talk about a small world! Here I was, 37,000 feet over Lake Michigan, reminiscing with the Air Canada co-pilot about my English and Biology teachers. Bruce and captain Michael Ennis invited me sit with them for the rest of the flight and it was quite an experience. On an *AirBus*, the pilots are essentially baby sitters — programming computers to fly the plane from practically the moment it starts its take-off roll, to the second its wheels touch down.

Being Sunday — a busy traffic day in the skies around Pearson Airport — the Maple Leafs had no idea how close they came to spending a few hours in our nation's capital. We went into a holding pattern over Kitchener-Waterloo, Ontario, and had we been forced to make more than one circuit, fuel guidelines dictated that we continue on to our alternate landing site: Ottawa. Thankfully, Air Traffic Control cancelled the hold and we landed in Toronto only 20 minutes late.

Customs procedures at Pearson can be endless at the best of times and today was one of the worst. A dozen international flights must have landed ahead of us and Customs looked like Macy's on Boxing Day. You had to see the dour faces on the tired Leaf players as the lengthy lines inched tediously forward. At one point, Doug Gilmour thought that a new position was opening and he darted out of line in anticipation —drawing 15 or 20 people with him. Turned out it was a false alarm and his followers sheepishly re-took their original spots. Seconds later, though, a Customs agent recognized the Leaf captain and did open up the new position. Finally, we were home.

MONDAY, JANUARY 23rd
Toronto

Nerves were frayed around the Gardens today as Burns and the Leaf players reacted to media criticism of Kenny Jonsson. The headline on Damien Cox's Toronto *Star* game story from San Jose said: SHARKS DEVOUR LEAF ROOK-

IE, with a sub-heading: JONSSON STRUGGLES TO FIND NHL LEGS IN LOSS TO SAN JOSE. After practice, Burns tried to remove the heat from Jonsson and played the age-old "us against the media" game in an attempt to get his men snarly for Wednesday's home opener.

Unfortunately, I got caught in the cross-fire.

In a brief meeting with Bob Stellick this morning, he mentioned that several Leaf players had expressed concern over me traveling with the club to write this book. Just last Tuesday, I sought and received Stellick's blessing to be accorded the same media privileges as others covering the team, but now he was changing his tune. A few players, he said, had told Burns they were uncomfortable with me "hanging around" and gathering information, perhaps believing I was in the process of researching a "kiss-and-tell" biography of their season.

Of course, they had it all wrong, and I immediately went down and knocked on Burns' office door. He invited me in and I assured him I had no interest in anyone's penis size or sexual mysteries. With the large number of new faces on the team, I could understand why there might be some suspicion, but I never figured it would be this much of a factor. Burns said he'd discuss it further and we'd speak again tomorrow.

When I got home from work tonight, I called Doug Gilmour to find out just where the team captain stood on this issue. He phoned back a few moments later and basically explained that any anger or resentment towards me had been a by-product of reaction to the Jonsson criticism. The players were upset at not winning either of their games out west; they were further annoyed when the media had the audacity to point out Jonsson's plight, and their frustrations were directed in large part towards "the guy writing the book". Gilmour told me not to fret and said he'd support me if the subject came up again.

All of this caught me by surprise because the Maple Leaf practice had ended on a humorous note. To lighten up the atmosphere, Burns organized a little game whereby the players fired towards an empty net from the far blueline. If they scored, they could leave the ice but if they missed, they'd have to do a wind-sprint to the other end and back. The big loser, quite incredibly, was Mats Sundin — normally a sharp-shooter, but a guy who today couldn't have hit a cow in the ass with a shovel. Poor Sundin skated himself silly to the roaring delight of his teammates and coach Burns, who cracked at one point, "What's the matter Matty, don't you *like* our little game?" After his eighth or ninth miss, Sundin looked around and spotted the NHL's fifth all-time leading goal-scorer leaning on the boards, smiling. He skated over to Mike Gartner, borrowed his stick, and buried his next attempt.

WEDNESDAY, JANUARY 25th
Toronto

This was a good news/bad news day for the Maple Leafs, who easily won their home opener, beating Vancouver 6-2. But afterwards, the mood was sombre when the club's only legitimate enforcer, Ken Baumgartner, revealed he would miss the bulk of the regular season while recovering from shoulder surgery. First to the game.

In this day of entertainment one-upsmanship, it was nice to see the Maple Leafs stick to tradition with the annual ceremony of the 48th Highlanders. The bagpipe unit has marched up and down the Gardens ice at home openers dating back to the Conn Smythe era, while other arenas have fallen into the laser-show and dry-ice trap of the '90s. There's a time and place for everything, including some formality, and that has always been a strong point of the Maple Leaf organization.

The evening's biggest surprise had to be the normally stoic Paul Morris at the public-address microphone. He rocketed through his pre-game player introductions with a rush of excitement normally produced by amphetamines. Or as one press box wag more crudely noted: "It sounds like he's getting a blow-job." Whatever, one of the higher-ups in the organization evidently instructed Morris to enliven his performance a notch and he sounded like an old 33-r.p.m. record spinning at 78.

After experiencing the audience fervour in San Jose Saturday night, the contrast at the Gardens tonight was monumental. For many years, we have heard about the dormancy of the Maple Leaf hockey crowd — how its collective intelligence apparently precludes the flow of emotion. Well, you can argue the rationale all you want, but there is no disputing the myth. Having been to every arena in the NHL, I'm certain that the Maple Leafs play before the undisputed champion of dead-ass crowds. The only exception occurs in April and May, during the playoffs, when the people suddenly come alive. But otherwise, there's no comparison elsewhere.

Like good Canadians, we stood silently on guard tonight during the national anthem and then politely applauded when it was over. A slight rumble of noise ensued when referee Dan Marouelli brought the players to center-ice but seconds later, you could have heard people *breathing* four sections away. When the Gardens crowd becomes that quiet, there is not only a lack of cheering, but an absence of conversation. Fans watch the game so intently, they abstain from chatting with their companions. People in San Jose make more noise in the main lobby of the Arena.

It took Randy Wood's first goal in a Maple Leaf uniform to induce a rise out of the Gardens audience. Jiri Slegr of the Canucks was off for tripping when Wood jammed a loose puck past Kay Whitmore early in the first period. Todd Gill set up the play with an impressive rush. A few moments later, Dmitri Mironov artfully tackled Pavel Bure in the neutral zone and had this been a football game, would've received high-fives all around. Instead, he was sent off for holding and Vancouver's Sergio Momesso converted Trevor Linden's pass from the corner to tie the score 1-1. The first period ended deadlocked.

Mats Sundin and Martin Gelinas traded goals early in the second before the Maple Leafs took control of the game. Having won the Western Conference championship last year, the Canucks are off to a horrendous start. Management hiked ticket prices by more than forty percent during the off-season and there were numerous empty seats for the Canucks' two opening home games, against Dallas and St. Louis. The Blues won the latter match 7-1 and the Canuck players were booed off the ice. It all came on the heels of the lockout (which fans in western Canada may not soon forget), and Pavel Bure's threat to quit the team if he was not paid his full season's salary. With a new coach behind the bench (Rick Ley), the Vancouver club seems very much in disarray.

Bill Berg scored his first goal of the season midway through the second period on a nice passing play with Sundin and Gilmour. It would be the eventual game-winner as the Canucks were blown away in the final frame. Mike Eastwood scored in the opening minute and the Leafs led by two. Mike Gartner then got untracked and blew a pair of slapshots past Whitmore late in the period to give Toronto a four-goal victory. His second marker came via both goalposts behind Felix Potvin. Bure fired the unfortunate double-clang, and the puck rebounded out to Gartner, who took it down the right-wing boards and beat Whitmore.

After Gartner's first tally, the line of Eastwood, Craig and Wood — the Maple Leafs' best unit so far — buzzed the Vancouver zone for a full minute and received a standing ovation. Sundin then got a big rise out of the crowd when he ploughed Vancouver defenceman Jyrki Lumme into the end boards with a monstrous body check. For the second game in a row, the Maple Leafs asserted themselves strongly in the third period and this time, they emerged with a victory.

The trading of Wendel Clark, one of the most popular Leafs of all time, left Mats Sundin in a quandary and the big Swede was not received that warmly during exhibition games before the lockout. But he was most certainly the star of the home opener and attracted a large media scrum in the dressing room afterwards. "It's been a bit difficult for me," he admitted. "Wendel was among the most accomplished players in the history of this team and a lot of people didn't like the trade. The fans obviously expect a lot and it was nice to hear them get behind me during the game tonight."

Bob Stellick asked for everyone's attention and announced that Ken Baumgartner would be out momentarily to make a statement. The Bomber emerged from the coat room a few seconds later and said that his left shoulder would have to be surgically reconstructed, sidelining him for at least three months. Ironically, the man who had spent so much time negotiating a collective bargaining agreement as vice-president of the Players' Association, would now miss the lockout-shortened campaign.

"Real glorious season, huh? — two games," he lamented.

Baumgartner originally injured the shoulder in that fateful game last Feb. 28 at Ottawa. He suffered a broken wrist when he fell to the ice in a fight with the Senators' Dennis Vial, and he also damaged his shoulder. He aggravated the injury in the playoffs last spring and in the ill-fated pre-season back in September. After fighting with Jeff Odgers in San Jose Saturday night, Baumgartner realized the shoulder wasn't responding.

"I'm told my career is not in danger but there's a possibility I won't play again this year," he said. When asked if he erred by not having the shoulder fixed in the off-season, he replied, "No, the only true test was the rigors of playing hockey. We couldn't have predicted anything during the summer."

Baumgartner's injury deprives the Leafs of their only legitimate enforcer and Cliff Fletcher was immediately surrounded after the game by media wondering if he will now have swing a trade for a player of similar ilk. "If Bomber's out for an extended period, I doubt the rest of the league will rush to help us," said the G.M. "For now, we'll stay the way we are. The future will depend on how we play."

FRIDAY, JANUARY 27th
Chicago

There was another up-lifting moment — literally and figuratively — on the Air Canada flight to Chicago this morning. Today began the fourth consecutive week of cloud cover in Toronto; the city hasn't seen a ray of sunshine since January 6th, and it's become damned depressing. But brighter days may be just ahead, as the DC-9 poked through a rather thin ceiling and into brilliant daylight only seconds after taking off from Pearson Airport at 9:40 a.m. And five minutes into the flight, or roughly 40 to 50 miles northwest of the city, the cloud-cover below us dissipated and we could actually see terra-firma.

Flying from Toronto to Chicago (by jet) normally takes about an hour and 15 minutes and the approach to the Windy City is dazzling on a clear day. If you're sitting on the left side of the aircraft (as I was), the giant skyscrapers of downtown Chicago come into view while you're still halfway out over Lake Michigan. From 40 miles away, and at 20,000 feet, the Sears Tower and Hancock Tower ascend through a veil of mist and smog, as the shores of the Great Lake meet the city.

Hockey writer Lance Hornby of the *Sun* was also on the flight today and he was entirely perplexed by the sudden disappearance of his return ticket. Poor Lance remained on the aircraft for almost 20 minutes after our arrival, searching desperately on the floor, between seat cushions, and in the overhead bin. Stunned by this inexplicable turn of events, he finally surrendered and joined me in a cab to the brand new United Center.

The up-coming Super Bowl between San Francisco and San Diego was a hot topic with our taxi driver, who was still bitter at the 49ers for annihilating his beloved Bears in the opening round of the playoffs. He spent the early part of the ride cursing Deion Sanders.

Driving through the slums of west Chicago about 20 minutes later, we noticed that the area of Madison St. near the arena has undergone something of a renovation. The old Chicago Stadium is still standing across the road from the United Center, in one of the most violent and neglected areas of the city. But a tiny stretch of Madison, about seven blocks from the arena, has been modernized with shops and restaurants, including *Cheli's Chili Bar* — owned by Blackhawks' defenceman Chris Chelios — and is fast becoming a popular hang-out for the hockey crowd.

The Chicago Stadium doesn't look a lot different then it did when we left it for the last time nine months ago. The marquee-sign over the south entrance has crumbled and there appears to be some destruction of the hallway inside the bolted doors. From the outside, however, the venerated old barn looks the same as when the Leafs eliminated the Blackhawks in the first round of the playoffs last April 28.

Walking into the United Center, a guard explained that asbestos insulation was being removed from inside the Stadium in preparation for the wrecking ball. Looking across the street, it's difficult to believe that all the history and memories will soon come tumbling down. It's obvious the land will be more viable as a parking lot, but one of these days, a city somewhere is going to preserve a bygone arena and convert it into an eternal museum. The ancient Romans didn't have it all wrong.

Lance and I knew for sure things had changed in Chicago when we entered the United Center and came upon an elevator. That's one luxury the Stadium never had... if you couldn't climb stairs, you stayed home. We went down to the lower level, where the dressing rooms are located, and when we got off the elevator, Lance said, "Howard, look at this." I turned around and he shook the right sleeve of his overcoat, spilling out the lost plane ticket. "Unbelievable," he sighed.

After checking out the two dressing rooms, we went up to the main level and into the arena. And it was an awesome first sight. Here, we could admire the full scope of the United Center's enormity, and more easily comprehend the notion that the entire Chicago Stadium would fit comfortably inside. There are three levels of seats in the new arena —all in the same licorice-red colour as across the street, but far-more handsomely upholstered. Above each level is a complete circumference of private luxury suites: 216 in all, and all of which are sold out for the minimum three-year duration.

A pair of small Blackhawk insignias used to flank the center red line in Chicago Stadium, but here, a giant Indian-head logo envelopes the entire center-ice circle, dominating the paid advertisements that surround it. Even the logo of United Airlines — the arena's primary sponsor — is lost in the colourful display.

There seems to be a major drawback involving the upper-level seats at each end. They're calling this place: "The House That Michael Jordan Built But Never Played In" and the fans sitting in those end zone pews likely wouldn't have seen him, anyway. In such an expansive auditorium, basketball must be a rumour from way up there.

While I gazed around the building, the Blackhawks completed their morning skate and I went back downstairs to get some tape. Waiting for coach Darryl Sutter to conclude a team meeting, a group of reporters gathered outside the Chicago dressing room and we reviewed the details of an incident during yesterday's practice involving Sutter and goalie Ed Belfour. The combative netminder had skated onto the ice ten minutes late, inciting a loud reprimand from his coach. He responded by leaning defiantly on his crossbar during a shooting drill, before storming off the ice in an apparent huff.

"I have a pulled groin muscle which has been bothering me and I was getting my leg taped," Belfour subsequently explained, justifying his late arrival. "It was bothering me on the ice, so I didn't want to make it worse."

Countered Sutter: "I have no idea why he left, I didn't tell him to go. He was late for practice and he left early. This is a team game and I'm not going to play the bad guy for telling him off."

The altercation was still topical a day later and Sutter finally emerged from the dressing room with the look of someone who had just sniffed a rotten egg. The pointed jaw matched his pointed nose and he seemed not at all in the mood for a lengthy conflab. Wanting to head upstairs for the Leaf skate, I began the impromptu media conference.

"Any backlash from the Belfour incident, coach?"

"I'm not getting into that."

"What about the larger ice dimensions here at the United Center? Will your club play a different style than it used to?"

"I talked about that already."

"Yeah, when?"

"Last April."

Thanks, Darryl, have a good life.

After a few more minutes of insightful commentary, Mr. Personality turned and walked away. I went in to speak with some Blackhawk players and immediately noticed that the new Chicago dressing room is the size of a small airport. An equipment guy told me it's a long-distance call from the shower to the trainer's room. The carpeting in the main area is embroidered with a gorgeous Indianhead logo and each player has a separate stall and name-plate in the spacious coat room. Chris Chelios walked in to get dressed and we began chatting about his restaurant.

"Chili isn't exactly traditional Greek food," I chided, prompting a smile from the veteran defenceman.

"Yeah, that's what my relatives have been telling me," he laughed.

I then asked Chelios about his much-ballyhooed harangue against Gary Bettman just prior to the lockout, and his subsequent hearing with the NHL Commissioner. It was back on Sept. 28, two days before Bettman and the NHL Board of Governers postponed the start of the season, that Chelios said: "If I was Gary Bettman, I'd be worried about my family. I'd be worried about my well-being now. Some crazed fans, or even a player — who knows? — they might take matters into their own hands and figure if they get him out of the way, things might get settled."

It was the most inflammatory comment made by anybody involved with the lockout and while it reflected the increasing tensions between the two sides, it was an absurd and irresponsible remark.

"I never considered the statement to be a threat," Chelios told me. "It was a stupid thing to say and I realized it almost immediately. Of course, the media then showed it over and over again and made me out to be another Charles Manson. That interview must have been on the air for a week. It was just a dumb remark made out of frustration. I want to be a role-model for kids and I made a bad decision, so I've got a little cleaning up to do on my image."

Despite incessant prodding, Bettman would not publicly address the Chelios diatribe, but once the lockout ended, he requested an audience with the two-time Norris Trophy winner. Chelios flew to New York with Blackhawks general manager Bob Pulford and just about everyone expected some form of disciplinary action. Bettman, though, limited his response to an adamant lecture, and warning of dire consequences in the event of a similar outburst.

"I think it's all straightened out now," Chelios said. "Everybody makes mistakes and, fortunately, no one got harmed from it. I can't say I wasn't surprised that Bettman didn't suspend me, but I was definitely relieved. I'm just glad we're back playing hockey."

In another corner of the coat room, Blackhawk star Jeremy Roenick was dressing and putting a rather desperate spin on tonight's game with the Leafs. "We've got to have this one tonight... it's a must-win for us," he said. "That may sound strange in only the second week of the season but we have a killer road trip coming up and we can't afford to waste any points in our building."

Indeed, the Hawks are facing an unusual grind of eight consecutive road games in 16 days. And what a circuitous trip it'll be, going from Los Angeles to San Jose to Edmonton to Calgary to Vancouver, back down to Anaheim, then across the country to St. Louis and Toronto.

The Maple Leafs completed their morning skate and then retreated to the visitor's dressing room at the United Center, which is far more modern and spacious than their own room at the Gardens. Tonight's game is being televised back home by *Global,* and after getting some pre-game tape from the Leafs, I walked into the Molstar studios across the hall. They were set up in the visitor's basketball dressing room and it's obvious that the arena builders made a point of catering to the larger NBA players. The urinals in the bathroom are practically at eye level, and the shower-heads are so high up on the wall, water would likely evaporate before reaching a normal-sized person. What a sight.

The unfamiliar nooks and crannies of the United Center had Maple Leaf players scurrying in all directions while searching for the team bus after practice. Bill Berg and Mike Eastwood passed each other two or three times. Poor Mike Craig looked like Ray Boldger in that scene from the *Wizard Of Oz* when

Dorothy first comes upon the Scarecrow. This time, however, nobody could find the damned yellow-brick road. Finally, an arena worker pointed out a door that led to the outside ramp.

I hitched a ride back on the Leaf bus and checked into the Drake Hotel: one of Chicago's eldest and most stately landmarks. The 12-story limestone structure is located on the corner of Michigan Ave. and East Walton Place: two blocks north of the 95-story Hancock Building. It was formally opened on New Year's Eve, 1920, with a dinner party attended by 3,000 of the city's most prominent citizens (Al Capone presumably notwithstanding). Over the years, the Drake has hosted visiting luminaries like former Egyptian President Anwar Sadat, Israeli Prime Minister Yizhak Rabin, and Britain's Queen Elizabeth. It was now graced by the likes of Bill Watters, Mike Kitchen and Damien Cox.

While relaxing in my hotel room and reading the newspapers this afternoon, a Chicago sporting paradox came to mind. When you watched a Blackhawk game on TV from the old Chicago Stadium, it was easy to think that the entire city was hockey mad. No crowd in the NHL cheered on its team as loudly or emotionally. Yet, people in the know often theorized that the Stadium contingent represented Chicago's entire hockey fandom; that the sport ranked far from the top in terms of overall popularity. Well, that theory seemed quite plausible when reading the sports pages. A quick review of the Sports Friday section in the Chicago *Sun-Times* —the daily tabloid paper — revealed the following:

Football and basketball dominated the front preview page, with a small note in the bottom right-hand corner that read: "Belfour, Sutter Clash at Practice". The inside-front contained a column by Dan Pompei at the Super Bowl in Miami. Page 3 had a game-story and photo from last night's Chicago Bulls NBA loss in Orlando. Page 4 had the NBA standings and box scores. Page 5 was also all basketball, featuring a story on the one-game suspension levied against Scottie Pippen of the Bulls for throwing a tantrum Tuesday night against San Antonio. Page 6 had a feature story by staff writer Lacy J. Banks on all the whining lunatics in the NBA. More basketball on Page 7, as writer John Jackson penned a mid-season report card on the struggling Bulls (who are 20-21). Pages 8, 9 and 10 were filled with preview stories on Sunday's Super Bowl. Page 11 was devoted solely to college basketball, while a giant SONY advertisement filled Page 12, and a headline reading "Clinton Says To Play Ball" dominated the baseball stories on Page 13.

Finally, on Pages 14 and 15 — just before the enthralling local tennis news — did I discover some material on the NHL.

It was much the same in the broadsheet paper, the Chicago *Tribune*: football, basketball and baseball on the front... baseball, basketball and skiing(!) on Page

2... basketball and college football on Page 3... and hockey on Page 4. Definitely, the No. 4 sport in this town. Further supporting that claim was my pal, George Ofman, who works at The *Score*: one of Chicago's two all-sports radio stations. George happens to be crazy about hockey and it was with heavy heart that he told me about a recent *Score* listenership survey, which revealed that only 20 percent of his audience gives a flying fidoo about the Blackhawks. Oh well.

A forecasted shower of wet snow was falling as the Maple Leaf bus pulled away from the Drake late this afternoon. The ride to the United Center was quiet and peaceful, with Led Zeppelin's classic *Stairway To Heaven* playing softly on a terrific stereo system. This time, the bus pulled right into the bowels of the arena and it was only a short walk up a ramp-like hallway to the dressing room. No one got lost.

The media diningroom at the United Center is located in the same corridor and is roughly the size of a banquet hall. Boy, are my Chicago media pals spoiled! The meal consisted of either orange-roughy or beef tacos, with rice, potatoes and vegetables. For desert, there were two kinds of chiffon layer cakes: chocolate and lemon. What a scoff. Only the press toilet, with an ear-splitting version of the United Airlines theme-song blasting in overhead speakers, detracted from the exquisite atmosphere. Fine dining, indeed.

After finishing my meal, Mark Hebscher of *Global* TV came into the room with a copy of The *Blue Line* — an underground publication sold on game nights. Calling itself "an unofficial guide to Blackhawks hockey" and "a real program", The *Blue Line* is relentless in its disrespectful treatment of Hawks' owner Bill Wirtz and is thus furiously unwelcomed in the United Center (as it was in the Stadium). But fans eagerly shell out three dollars to purchase it on city owned sidewalks outside the rink. I went out the concourse level to buy a copy myself and, heavens, did I draw some filthy looks on my way back in. Apart from slandering Wirtz, the maverick newsletter surely cuts into sales of the official Blackhawks program — *Face Off* — and arena staffers are poised to give you a "*fuck* off" look if you walk in with it.

The cover of Wednesday night's inaugural issue featured a hockey glove with its middle finger extended, and the sardonic message: "NHL still No. 1 with fans!" Inside, beneath the headline "DNA TESTS PROVE BETTMAN KILLED UNION!", were several poignant examples of Wirtz bashing. The accompanying article contained a Chicago *Sun-Times* quote from Wirtz on his supposedly reluctant participation in the labour dispute. "The lockout probably cost us more than any other team but we did it for the league," he said. The *Blue Line* evidently disagreed, and with some bite.

"We regard this as only a lapse in credibility on Mr. Wirtz's part likely due to short-term memory loss caused by excessive drinking," the publication said. "Bill just momentarily forgot that he was one of only seven hard-liners — Boston, Chicago, Edmonton, Detroit, New Jersey, Washington and Winnipeg — who voted to scrap the season rather than settle with the players. Drunks do forget things."

Another page featured the transposed faces of Bettman and Chelios on the bodies of two people enjoying champagne in bed, with Bettman saying, "I love when you talk dirty to me, Chris."

Tonight's edition was more humorous and not quite so outlandish. The front-page headline said "LEAFS DID HAWKS A LEVEBVRE" — extolling the virtues of the veteran defenceman Toronto traded to Quebec in the Wendel Clark deal. An inside page poked some fun at sightlines from the upper-reaches of the United Center. A cheeky list of "the top 10 things overheard in the 300 level on opening night" contained the following:

* "Those aren't ants, idiot! Those are Oilers."
* "Pass the binoculars... I think that's Al Cowlings driving the Zamboni."
* "Thank God there aren't too many Stanley Cup banners hanging up here to ruin my view."
* "With the bigger ice surface, it's taking the Blackhawks longer to dump and chase."

And, *my* personal favourite...

* "Hubbel telescopes! Get your Hubbel telescopes!"

A more profound controversy had developed within the Blackhawks organization in recent days, and it also received plenty of ink in The *Blue Line*. For many years, Wayne Messmer had been the Chicago Stadium tenor: whipping the crowd into a frenzy with his rousing rendition of The *Star Spangled Banner*. But Messmer had assumed the executive vice-presidency of Chicago's International Hockey League team, the Wolves, and was now persona non gratta with the Blackhawks. Fired by Bill Wirtz, he was allowed to sing one final anthem at the Hawks-Edmonton opener the other night but would be replaced for good at tonight's game. The *Blue Line* did yet another number on Wirtz.

"Bill Wirtz didn't have the decency to fire Messmer; he sent Bob Pulford to do the dirty work. The Blackhawks never treated Wayne with respect. It took them seven years to give him courtesy parking. On his last night of singing, the Hawks reluctantly gave Wayne two 300-level nose-bleeders for his wife and family."

Blue Line columnist Dan McNeil, talk-show host at The *Score*, also delivered a jab to the Hawk owner: "No surprise about Wayne Messmer's unceremonious release. I heard on good authority that Wirtz was so upset at Messmer's involvement with the Wolves last spring, the bastard didn't even send flowers or pick up the telephone after Wayne was shot at Hawkeye's." Messmer had recovered from a gunshot wound to the throat while leaving a Chicago nightclub last April.

His successor tonight will be Chicago baritone Stephen Powell — the subject of an elaborate news release by the hockey club earlier today. A local opera soloist and "longtime Blackhawk fan", Powell has sang the national anthem at sporting events in the past, including Game 6 of the 1993 American League Championship Series at Comiskey Park. If that rings a bell with Toronto sports fans, it's no surprise. The Blue Jays eliminated the White Sox that evening to advance to their second consecutive World Series (against Philadelphia).

Roaming the United Center press box before tonight's game, I could easily commiserate with the guy on Wednesday who confused the hockey players with ants. What *is* it with these new arenas? It's like they finish building them... hold ribbon-cutting ceremonies, and then say, "Oh shit, we forgot to put a press box in." This particular media domain is chiselled out of the upper reaches of the 300 level — sort of where Wirtz put Messmer after Wednesday's anthem. At least the box here is between the goal-lines and not behind the net, as it was across the street for all those years.

The Blackhawks skated onto the United Center ice during a high-tech laser show: one of the better pre-game spiels in the NHL. With the arena lighting dimmed, four Hawk logos were flashing and dancing on the ice — one in each faceoff circle — while a larger Blackhawk emblem, comprised of white laser light, circled the upper-deck seats.

As the Blackhawks expected (and slightly feared), Stephen Powell induced a round of hearty boos when first presented to the crowd before tonight's game. Of course, the audience was venting its spleen at Wirtz for canning the popular Messmer, and boos quickly turned to cheers when Powell unleashed immaculate versions of O Canada and the Star Spangled Banner. With that voice, he'll soon become a legend.

The Maple Leafs lost to the Blackhawks 4-1 tonight but rarely has a final score been so flattering to the loser. This game may well have been the worst all-around Maple Leaf effort in the Pat Burns era as the placid, nonchalant Toronto players were tossed around the rink like a pack of blow-up dolls. The forwards were unable to slow their fired-up Chicago counterparts in the neutral zone and the Maple Leaf defencemen were being plastered up against the end boards as soon as they touched the puck. On the few occasions they did have time to turn around, they either coughed up the puck, or forwards were out of position to receive a pass. In a word, the Leafs looked scared. Confused, too.

"There was no grit from anyone tonight," agreed Pat Burns after the game. "You look at their line-up and there's nothing to be afraid of. We shouldn't be so physically dominated by that team."

The Blackhawks did all the scoring damage they would need in a 27-second span midway through the first period. Joe Murphy whipped a high wrister past Felix Potvin from the left-wing circle to open the scoring (it was Chicago's first goal against Potvin in three games, dating back to last spring's playoff round). Brent Sutter then took advantage of a typical Maple Leaf defensive lapse to sweep in on Potvin and make it 2-0. Jamie Macoun was victimized on both plays.

Gilmour tapped in a goalmouth feed from Sundin on the powerplay five minutes later and the period ended 2-1 for Chicago. But the Hawks set the physical tone before the game was five minutes old, with their best player — Jeremy Roenick — leading the way. Roenick bowled over the tentative Maple Leaf defence on several occasions, and Tony Amonte decisioned Dixon Ward in the period's only scrap. All Chicago, except on the scoreboard.

Incredibly, the second period was even worse for the Maple Leafs, as Steve Smith and Murphy scored to give the Blackhawks a 4-1 edge. The defence pairing of Macoun and Garth Butcher had a dreadful 20 minutes with Butcher's neutral-zone giveaway sending Murphy in alone to score Chicago's fourth goal. Adding injury to insult, Dave Ellett took Rich Sutter's high pass off his cheekbone late in the frame and dropped like a rock. He was helped off the ice and did not return.

The Maple Leafs could manage only six feeble shots at Ed Belfour in the scoreless final period. Tempers flared on a couple of occasions as Butcher and Patrick Poulin fought in the center-ice area with Poulin winning a close decision. Eric Weinrich then jumped Randy Wood at the Chicago blueline less than a minute after Wood sent him flying. It was an emphatically one-sided victory for the Blackhawks and quite a demoralizing defeat for the Maple Leafs, raising many questions about the character of the visitors.

"We have a little soul-searching to do tonight," said Butcher in the deathly quiet Toronto dressing room. "The Hawks were sure fired up for the game, but we let them trample all over us and there really is no excuse for that."

Dave Ellett left the Leaf dressing room looking not too bad for a guy who had blocked a pass with his kisser. There was a small bruise on his cheekbone, but X-rays of the area were negative. "Oh, it's a little sore but I'm okay," he shrugged. "I should be fine for tomorrow night's game (against Calgary). I have no intentions of sitting out."

During the intermissions tonight, I walked to the area behind the press box and looked into the darkness from a window six floors up. The weather-man was calling for light snow, but none had materialized. All of that changed, however, by the time I left the United Center an hour after the game. A blizzard was raging in Chicago with snowflakes the size of cornflakes. Mark Hebscher and Eugene McEleney of *Global* TV had rented a van at the airport and offered me a ride back to the hotel. I gladly accepted, and it took almost 15 minutes for the three of us to brush the van clean of the white stuff.

The Maple Leafs headed straight for Midway Airport to charter back home and I felt relieved not to be flying on a twin-engine turboprop in a blinding snowstorm.

*   *   *   *   *   *

The Maple Leafs rebounded from their trouncing in Chicago and upset the Calgary Flames 2-1 at the Gardens. The Flames had watched the Leafs-Blackhawks game from their hotel rooms at the Marriott Eaton-Center and should have been more rested than Toronto. But second-period goals by Dave Andreychuk and Mats Sundin proved to be the difference. And Todd Gill scored an impressive one-punch decision over the much-bigger Joel Otto in a third-period scrap. Gill bloodied Otto's nose after being high-sticked by the Calgary player. Leafs improved their record to 2-2-1 with the victory.

SUNDAY, JANUARY 29th
Toronto

After skating at the Gardens this morning, the Maple Leafs took a mid-afternoon flight to Dallas for tomorrow night's opener of a four-game road trip, which continues on to Vancouver, Edmonton and Calgary. While I initially planned to attend all 48 Leaf games in this shortened season, economics mixed with common sense to keep me away from Texas. One-way flights from Toronto to Dallas, then Dallas to Vancouver, would have gouged our budget to the tune of $1,500. Conversely, the western Canada portion of the trip requires less than $800. So, I've decided to meet the club in Vancouver on Tuesday.

It was actually nice staying home today. Susan and I hosted our annual Super Bowl party for friends and relatives and, as usual, the party whipped the game by a huge margin. The turning point in the San Francisco - San Diego NFL championship was the coin toss. It gave the 49ers the ball to start, and they led 14-0 after only seven offensive plays. Had they not called off the dogs, the 49-26 final score would have been even more absurd. Thank goodness we had plenty of food.

MONDAY, JANUARY 30th
Toronto

After watching tonight's Leaf game, I tried hard to recall if I'd ever seen a goalie more blatantly responsible for an undeserving victory. Felix Potvin absolutely pilfered two points from the Dallas Stars in probably his most spectacular performance as a Maple Leaf. He stopped 43 shots, roughly 15 of which would have beaten most goalies in the NHL. Dallas held a 44-17 final edge, and if time of puck possession were a statistic, the Maple Leafs wouldn't have qualified.

Somehow, they escaped with a 2-1 victory.

"It was one of those nights when the puck seemed bigger than it really is," Potvin told reporters after the game. "You look around the league and a lot of goalies are playing very well. Tonight was my turn to come up big and it caught me by surprise. I was terrible in the pre-game warm-up... everybody was scoring."

Potvin had plenty of time to contemplate his sub-par effort in the warm-up, with the Dallas home opener preceded by a lengthy ceremony. As Lance Hornby wrote in the *Sun*: "A pre-game laser show ran overtime, as did WWF-style player introductions and two long national anthems. The Maple Leafs were going squirrely on the bench and in the press box by the time the puck was dropped almost 20 minutes late."

From that point on, it was Potvin's show as Dallas skated circles around the confused Maple Leafs. Despite being outshot 19-5, the Leafs held a 1-0 lead after the first period, as Dmitri Mironov beat Darcy Wakaluk with a low slapshot after taking Gilmour's pass in the slot. Todd Gill's fluky goal, just past the midway mark of the game, made it 2-0. Gill banked the puck in off Wakaluk from the corner to the left of the Dallas net. Otherwise, the Stars came at the Leafs in waves, only to be frustrated time and again.

They finally solved Potvin early in the third period, as ex-Leaf Russ Courtnall scored from a scramble in front of the net. But it did not faze the Maple Leaf goaltender, who continued to dazzle the sellout crowd. Potvin's best save of the night occurred with just more than six minutes remaining on the clock, when he snared a Kevin Hatcher wrist-shot from point-blank range. Hatcher's shot seemed headed for the far side of the goal just as Potvin stabbed it with his glove.

As the Leafs desperately clung to their one-goal margin, forward Kent Manderville tackled Mike Modano in the slot, and was sent off for holding with 1:08 remaining in regulation time. However, Dallas did not seriously threaten Potvin on its last-ditch attempt and the Maple Leafs skated off with a wholly unimpressive triumph.

Tonight's game marked the return of winger Mike Craig to Dallas, where he played last year. Signed as a free agent by the Maple Leafs in the off-season, Craig was one of the few Toronto skaters who showed any zip tonight. Peter Zezel was awarded to the Stars as compensation for Craig but he did not suit up against the Leafs. Zezel twisted his left knee while skating during the lockout and had it scoped. When doctors tried to drain fluid from the joint, they found an area of infection and Zezel is sidelined indefinitely, undergoing antibiotic treatments.

The Maple Leafs initially planned on flying to Vancouver on an American Airlines flight tomorrow morning. But the trip has a stop-over in San Jose that would have stretched the journey to seven long hours. Instead, the club decided to charter an Air Canada *AirBus*, and made the three-hour flight immediately following tonight's game. They arrived at the Westin Bayshore Hotel around 3:15 a.m. local time and will practice at the Pacific Coliseum late tomorrow afternoon.

TUESDAY, JANUARY 31st
Vancouver

Air Canada is starting to test my affinity for *Forrest Gump*. They showed the movie yet again on the flight from Toronto to Vancouver this morning and I wound up practically mouthing the script. It's beginning to feel like Tom Hanks and Gary Sinise are part of my family. The L10-11 was roughly three-quarters empty and it was a pleasure not having anyone seated next to me on the five-hour jaunt. The low clouds and fog so typical of Vancouver this time of year made for a rough approach to the airport, but we landed on schedule after 1 p.m.

The cab ride from Vancouver airport to the downtown core can often be a monotonous experience. Route 99, or Granville Street, is the only road connecting the two focal points, and much of the drive is through a residential area replete with stoplights every two or three blocks. If the taxi driver gets into a bad rythym with the lights, you can grow a full beard along the way.

Though it was raining out, today's ride was mercifully quick and it was a comforting sight to come upon one of my favourite hotels in the world: the Westin Bayshore. Perched on a secluded point, the Bayshore (with an accompanying marina) protrudes into Vancouver Harbour at the far west end of downtown, adjacent to the 1,000-acre Stanley Park. It has a large outdoor pool and sun deck, and offers breathtaking views of the north-shore mountains on a clear day. Comprised of a main building and a tower, the hotel's Harbour-view rooms have balconies overlooking the Burrard Inlet and the nearby peaks of Grouse Mountain. Susan and I arranged for such a room in the tower during our summer vacation last July, and we had difficulty pulling ourselves away from the window.

Sea planes take off and land in the Inlet, with *Esso*, *Petro Canada* and *Shell* re-fuelling stations perched in the water. The famed Lions Gate Bridge connects Stanley Park to North Vancouver, and the bridge is a sight unto itself when illuminated at dusk. The weather had been very pleasant during the Maple Leafs week-long visit here in the Stanley Cup playoffs last May, but low clouds and fog hovered over the mountains on this mid-winter day, obscuring the area's natural beauty.

While checking into the Bayshore, I tried to con the lady at the front desk into letting me have a Tower room, but she firmly declined, explaining that the Maple Leaf rate of $77 per night didn't qualify me for up-graded accommodations (Tower rooms are $200/night in the summer). My suite is hardly shabby, though — overlooking the outdoor pool down below, the coveted Tower across the way, and beautiful Cypress Mountain several miles to the west.

It was still raining quite hard when I took a cab to the Pacific Coliseum late this afternoon. The Coliseum has been the Canucks' home since they joined the NHL as an expansion team (along with Buffalo) for the 1970-71 season. It was only five years old at the time, and one of the more modern arenas in the league. But, the years have since passed it by, and the Canucks will move into a brand new home, General Motors Place (across from the B.C. Place football stadium), next season.

Located on the grounds of the Pacific National Exhibition — in a residential area about three miles east of downtown — the Coliseum is a circular facility with vertical slabs of concrete around its facade. It shares the P.N.E. with Hastings Park Racetrack and it used to be up the sidewalk from old Empire Stadium, where the B.C. Lions played their home football games until 1982. The Lions moved into B.C. Place in '83 and their vacated den survived as a CFL monument until roughly a year ago, when the wrecking ball materialized.

Any long-time fan of the Toronto Argonauts will remember Empire Stadium as the site of Leon McQuay's infamous fumble in the 1971 Grey Cup. And as I entered the Coliseum today, it brought to mind a rather ghostly experience I had while here in Vancouver for the '86 Grey Cup. The night before the game, columnist Jim Proudfoot of the Toronto *Star* arranged media passes for he and I to see the Canucks play Winnipeg.

In the late-60s and early-70s, Jim covered football for the Star and he saw many important games at Empire Stadium — including the '71 championship. The Argonaut teams he followed back then were my all-time favourites, with characters like Leo Cahill, Bobby Taylor, Mel Profit, Dick Thornton, Jim Stillwagon and Jim Corrigall. When I think back to my youth, those names evoke nostalgic sentiments every bit as strong as Punch Imlach, Johnny Bower and Frank Mahovlich. So, I wanted Proudfoot to show me Empire Stadium when we arrived at the P.N.E. for that hockey game back in '86. He obliged, and I had a wondrous time circling the old yard and listening to Proudfoot reminisce about his moments there.

At the north end of the stadium, I noticed an unshackled entrance that led down a little slope and onto the field. Jim said he'd meet me at the Coliseum and I went through the opening and found myself in the north end zone. The artificial turf beneath me was practically worn to the cement but I could see the faint yard markings and orange numbering of days gone by. Dusk had began to settle over Vancouver and I remember how eerie it was standing alone in the middle of that historic stadium, where football hadn't been played in four years. The structure seemed so fragile, with its interior comprised almost solely of decaying wood. The early winter breeze whistled through timeworn cracks in the upper rows and the entire stadium made a spooky creaking noise.

It was almost dark when I walked to the south end of the field and stood on the 11-yard line, where one of the sporting dreams of my youth had been shattered 15 years earlier. It was on that very spot that Leon McQuay dropped the football in the dying moments of the 1971 Grey Cup. I could feel the ghosts of the Calgary defenders signalling wildly with their arms that they'd recovered the most ill-timed fumble in Argonaut history. And I recalled how I threw an old shoe at my television set in Toronto. Who says there is no such thing as a time machine?

Walking into the Coliseum today, I felt momentarily saddened that Empire Stadium was now just a memory, but time suddenly raced forward a quarter of a century and there I was standing outside the Maple Leaf dressing room. After arriving in Vancouver in the middle of the night, the Leafs had all enjoyed a lengthy rest and were now suiting up for a late-afternoon practice. The mood seemed up-beat after the miracle win in Dallas, and the players sprinted enthusiastically towards Pat Burns when he blew his whistle to begin the workout.

Sitting in the Coliseum, it's easy to comprehend why this arena has outlived its economic viability. It has only 14 private boxes: all of them suspended above the goal at the south end. The seats in the lower level are a bright rust colour, while the upper-level chairs are turquoise-blue. They all have hard, wooden back-rests and it seems like years since they've been re-upholstered. The ceiling of the Coliseum is a myriad of wooden planks and beams with a suspended walkway connecting the press box to the radio booth on the opposite side. The broadcasting gondola is like something you'd see at a Junior 'B' rink in a far rural outpost. Also constructed of wood, it dangles from the rafters, and has two small compartments. The visiting radio crew sits on the right, with the Canucks' broadcasters in an enclosure on the left, above the call-letters CKNW: the club's flagship station.

Suspended above the north end of the rink is a small banner that honours former Canucks' captain Stan Smyl, the only Vancouver player to have his sweater-number retired by the club. The Steamer played for the Canucks from 1978 to 1991 and his number-12 jersey will never again be worn. He is currently an assistant on Rick Ley's coaching staff.

During today's practice, coach Burns had plugger Bill Berg skating on the second-line unit with Mike Ridley and Mike Gartner. In his two-plus seasons with the Maple Leafs, Berg has been a rambunctious checker with a penchant for causing mischief. Despite his lay-back demeanour off the ice, he is universally despised by the opposing wingers he molests. With the puck, however, Berg would have trouble hitting the lake from a dock. He has more cement in his gloves than it took to build SkyDome. Yet, today, he was skating with a 70-point-a-year centerman, and the NHL's fifth all-time leading goalscorer.

"It was kind of hard to keep up to those guys," he smiled. "But, it'd be nice to play with Rids and Garts. Y'know, Pat is experimenting with many different line combinations now and I know what he expects of me. I'll just go out and provide it, hopefully."

Meanwhile, Felix Potvin seemed none the worse for wear after his exhaustive effort in Dallas last night. Rather than practising with the club, he should have been lounging in the hotel jacuzzi, but the Cat wouldn't buy that kind of talk. "No, not at all, I feel fine," he said. "There will be many times when the guys will come up big for me and win 5-4 or 6-4. Last night was my time to come through for them and it was definitely one of my best games in the NHL."

After the Dallas victory, a reporter asked Burns if he planned on resting Potvin in the near future.

"Do you think I'm stupid?" he replied. "Felix will play till I see there's a problem. He's used to getting a lot of ice time and like the other guys in the league, he had a nice long summer (with the lockout). Until we get things sorted out around here, he's the guy I'll go to."

Which was music to Potvin's ears. "If Pat wants me to play all 48 games, I will," he shrugged. "I don't feel tired or anything. We did have a long flight from Dallas last night and it actually felt good to go out and skate today. I'm sure I'll feel better tomorrow."

After fielding a spate of questions about his "new look" team from the Vancouver media, Burns seemed to be in a chipper mood. He turned a corner into the dressing room and hollered, "Bus in five minutes, guys" before looking up to see that he was talking to four walls. "Where the hell *is* everybody?" he mumbled, at which point Mats Sundin wandered in. Burns stuck his nose in the big Swede's face and repeated, "BUS IN FIVE MINUTES, MATTY!" Unfazed, Sundin smiled and continued on to his locker.

There was a serious outbreak of truancy here this afternoon. With no sign of security in the Pacific Coliseum, about 60 pubescents chose to play hookey and attend the Maple Leaf practice. Armed with binders of cards and colour photos, the young entrepreneurs gathered by the team bus in search of autographs. Accommodating even half of them would have incurred the wrath of Burns, who shows a singular lack of patience when sitting on the bus: after practice or before a game. With that in mind, most of the players scribbled a signature or two before scurrying onto the vehicle. Todd Gill was one of the stragglers.

"If the other guys aren't out in four or five minutes, they say to go ahead," announced the defenceman.

"Okay, Giller, it's your decision," replied Burns.

Seconds later, the players sitting at the rear of the bus started howling with laughter over something and Burns looked back with a smile to see what was going on. Mike Ridley and Mike Gartner were the last to leave the Coliseum, and Ridley was wearing a dark grey trench-coat that the others apparently found comical. "That coat's a fine," deadpanned Dave Ellett, prompting Burns to erupt with laughter. Ridley boarded the bus unsuspectingly and paused for a moment to figure out the commotion. After a couple of wisecracks, he shook his head and sat down near the front. Gartner then got on after signing more than a few autographs and realized he was last man.

Burns gave him a stare.

WEDNESDAY, FEBRUARY 1st
Vancouver

Felix Potvin sat by himself in the coffee-shop of the Bayshore at 9:15 this morning, ordering breakfast. His teammates — decked out in blue-and-white Maple Leaf sweatsuits — soon arrived, and Potvin joined Todd Gill and Doug Gilmour at a larger table. Within 10 minutes, almost the entire upper level of the restaurant was filled with hungry hockey players, most of them carrying the local morning newspapers.

Both Vancouver papers had front-page sports stories about the new-look Maple Leafs. The tabloid *Province* had a photo of Pat Burns leaning on his stick at yesterday's practice, with a headline PAT DOES THE SLOW BURNS, and a sub-title TRADE RAISES EXPECTATIONS MONSTROUSLY.

"The problem is the Leafs can't win big enough," said Burns in the story. "So now, we have to try and win by six or seven goals. We can't win 2-1 or 3-2 anymore... that's not acceptable it seems. We created a monster in Toronto the past two years (by advancing to the Stanley Cup semifinals) and now the monster's alive and everyone expects a lot from it. Having coached in Montreal, I'm used to that kind of pressure, but with all the changes we made this past off-season, I think our fans are going to have to be a little patient."

While the Maple Leafs were chowing down, NHL referee Bill McCreary walked in and gazed around somewhat uncomfortably. He noticed the group of players eating breakfast, and several Leafs glanced over and noticed him. But, greetings were not exchanged.

McCreary will officiate tonight's game between the Maple Leafs and Canucks, and I wondered if the cold-shoulder atmosphere was part of the business. I introduced myself, and he quickly denied feeling awkward in front of the Leaf players. "I guess our eyes just didn't meet," he explained. "I've never had a problem staying in the same facility as a team I'll be officiating. The players and coaches in this league handle themselves professionally, and I haven't encountered any trouble."

McCreary, 39, is a native of Guelph, Ontario, and has been a referee in the NHL since November, 1984. He is not the Bill McCreary who played for the St. Louis Blues in their early years, nor is he the Maple Leaf farmhand who demolished Wayne Gretzky with a savage body check during a 1981 game in Edmonton. The latter McCreary is a younger cousin of the referee's, who played college hockey at Colgate University, and was the Maple Leafs' fifth choice (114th overall) in the 1979 amateur draft. He was called up from Moncton of the American Hockey League midway through the 1980-81 season and played only 12 games in a Toronto uniform.

But, he'll be remembered eternally for pulverizing Gretzky in the center-ice area at Northlands Coliseum during a 4-1 Maple Leaf loss to the Oilers, Jan. 3, 1981. And referee McCreary says the body check was a source of confusion during his early seasons in the NHL. "Most of the Edmonton players back then thought I was the guy who hit Gretzky," he recalls. "The fans used to boo loudly when my name was announced at the Northlands Coliseum and the Oiler players — even Gretzky, himself —treated me with some disdain. They were winning Stanley Cups in those days and Gretzky was in his prime: the best hockey player in the world. But, I never once tried to explain that I wasn't the Bill McCreary who nailed him. I guess it was a matter of pride... if he and his teammates wanted to feel that way, the hell with them, I'd rise above it."

Here's a bulletin... it's raining again today in Vancouver.

Cripes, what an awful time of year. There is no more picturesque city in Canada when the weather cooperates and all we have now are low-clouds and fog. It's depressing. Sitting on the team bus at the hotel this morning, I told Kenny Jonsson that there were actually mountains across the harbour, but he seemed to feel I was pulling his leg. Can't say I blame him, as it took *me* four days to discover North Vancouver on my inaugural visit here (for the 1983 Grey Cup). I saw the Argos defeat the B.C. Lions to win their first CFL title in 31 years, and I almost passed out the next morning when I opened the drapes of my hotel room.

Four dreary days of rain and fog had suddenly disappeared and here was this gorgeous panorama. Naturally, I was flying home that day.

Burns lumbered onto the bus this morning and complained to Mike Kitchen that he was sore from his workout. "I did the *Stair-Master* and had no energy," he griped. After shuffling impatiently for 90 seconds, he looked back, noticed a dozen of his players, and half-joked, "Okay, we have enough guys to practice... let's go driver." Reluctantly, he then waited for the entire club to emerge before the bus pulled away.

On the drive to the Coliseum, we passed by the Canucks' new arena. G.M. Place is still under construction just east of downtown, and will open in time for the 1995-96 NHL season. It seems to be wedged between two street over-passes, directly across from B.C. Place Stadium. The over-passes are at a height just beneath the arena roof and the players were wondering what road would lead down to the building. Right now, it looks like you'd have to jump off one of the over-passes to get there. If access is not a problem, the location will be much more convenient to the mainstream population than the suburban Coliseum. Of course, the Vancouver Grizzlies of the newly expanded NBA will share the arena with the Canucks when they begin play next season.

Conversation on the bus soon got around to the increase in ticket prices for Canuck games this season. Hoping to cash in on the surprise trip to the Stanley Cup final last spring, club management hiked ducats an average of 43 percent across the board. The move backfired early, as hockey fans in the area — already miffed by the lockout — stayed away in large numbers during the Canucks' initial homestand.

"Those $54 tickets are pretty expensive," said the bus driver, who then asked Burns how much tickets were in Toronto.

"Don't know, I've never bought one," replied the coach. "I have a pretty good seat already."

During the Leaf skate, it was apparent that Kent Manderville would not be able to play tonight. Manderville twisted his ankle while trying to hit Paul Cavallini in Dallas Monday night. "It feels better today than it did when we got here yesterday, but I'm not sure I can go," he confessed.

Once again, the Maple Leaf players had to fight their way through a flock of insubordinate young fans while leaving the arena. Sitting next to Mike Gartner on the bus ride back to the Bayshore, we talked about these so-called school children. "It's amazing what some of them will do to get an autograph," Mike said. "When I was with the Rangers, a kid actually showed me his exam timetable to prove he wasn't skipping school. When I looked at it, the dates were all wrong... it wasn't even close. So I told him he was lying, and all his buddies then chimed in, 'Yeah, he's lying, he's lying, don't believe him.' Some friends *that* guy had."

Much of the fog lifted after dark tonight. As we approached the Pacific Coliseum, we turned north onto Renfrew St. and could see the lights of the ski-run way atop Grouse Mountain in the distance. Of course, since we're leaving tomorrow, it'll probably be a gorgeous day.

There was quite a site at the Coliseum about 45 minutes before game time. It was Ken Daniels, my pal from CBC, who fills in for Joe Bowen on Maple Leaf radio broadcasts when Joe is doing a TV game for *Global*. Ken is not a fan of heights, and therefore has some difficulty traversing the wooden catwalk that connects the press box to the radio booth in this arena. The catwalk is close to the ceiling, about 15 feet above the sportstimer at center ice, and it makes an ominous creaking sound. Poor Ken was pinching a loaf as Gord Stellick tenderly assisted him on the journey, like he would an elderly lady crossing the street. Instructed not to look down, Ken wouldn't even look forward. His eyes were tilted slightly upward the whole way, but he did make it.

Prior to the national anthem, the Canucks held a moment of silence for Melanie Carpenter, the pretty 23-year-old from Surrey, B.C. who was murdered in a sexual assault last month... her body found riddled with stab-wounds only five days ago. The cowardly assailant, Fernand Auger, chose to commit suicide, leaving the province and much of the country abhorred by the crime. The solemn moment served to put the hockey game into perspective, albeit temporarily.

Just 1:09 into the first period, a pair of unlikely combatants got into it. Garth Butcher and Pavel Bure threw gloved fists at each other in the faceoff circle to the left of Felix Potvin. A television replay showed Butcher slamming Bure into the corner boards, and Bure reacting with a quick right jab to the face. Vancouver defenceman Gerald Diduck piled in to assist Bure and was thrown out of the game. The two main-eventers each received double-minors for roughing.

Less than a minute later, Geoff Courtnall of the Canucks elbowed a pestering Doug Gilmour to the ice in front of Potvin and was sent off by McCreary for roughing, giving the Leafs an early man advantage. And they made good on the powerplay, as Dmitri Mironov took Gilmour's pass in the slot and fired a low slapper through a screen. Dave Andreychuk was perched in front of Kirk McLean, and the goalie saw nothing of the play. A loud cheer went up from the crowd as Mironov's shot entered the net, and it was followed by chants of *"Go Leafs Go!"*

On his next shift, Andreychuk broke into the clear at center, and was blatantly hooked to the ice from behind by defenceman Jyrki Lumme. The Coliseum fell silent as Canuck fans held their breath, anticipating a penalty shot, with Andreychuk undoubtedly having been on a breakaway. Instead, the play continued with no call whatsoever from McCreary. The Maple Leaf bench went ballistic, led by Mike Gartner, who banged the shaft of his stick on the boards several times.

A few moments later, Andreychuk was back on the ice, readying for a face-off in the Leaf end. From my vantagepoint almost directly above, I noticed that McCreary skated over and whispered something to the big winger, who curtly nodded his head. "He told me he missed the call," Andreychuk later explained. "That was pretty impressive. There aren't too many guys wearing the stripes who would admit to a mistake."

Vancouver tied the score before the midway point of the opening period, and then wrested complete control of the hockey game from the Maple Leafs. Jose Charbonneau eluded Todd Gill and beat Potvin with a nifty backhand deke. It gave the Canucks their first spark of the game and they began throwing their weight around, led by big Sergio Momesso. The Leafs went into their room clinging tentatively to the 1-1 saw-off.

I was having a panic sitting in the press box next to the legendary Junior hockey coach, Ernie (Punch) McLean. Former head man of the Estevan/New Westminster Bruins, McLean was a founding father of the Western Hockey League and one of its all-time colourful characters. In the late-1970s, his New Westminster clubs won back-to-back Memorial Cup titles and were among the nastiest collections in Junior 'A' history. They featured soon-to-be NHL stars like Barry Beck, Stan Smyl and Brad Maxwell, and were Memorial Cup champs in

1977 and '78. The Bruins had also been to the Cup final in '75, losing to coach George Armstrong and the Toronto Marlboros, who won their last Junior 'A' title that year.

McLean spent much of tonight regaling me with stories of his days behind the bench. Like the incident during a 1976 playoff game against Saskatoon, in which he accidentally pulled the toupee off a linesman. "The guy missed an off-side call and I reached out to touch him on the shoulder," McLean recalled. "My hand got caught up in his hair and his damned rug came right off. I dropped it onto the ice and he picked it up and continued on with the game."

Or the night in the mid-60s, when McLean threw a tantrum and got his life-long nickname. "I was screaming for a penalty and the referee turned and said, 'Hey, McLean, who the fuck do you think you are, Punch Imlach?' I guess the name stuck."

During his tenure in the WHL (1966 - 1980), McLean coached future pros like Jim Harrison, Ross Lonsberry, Barry Gibbs, Gregg Sheppard, Lorne Henning and Ron Greschner. He became known for dabbling with the sub-conscious mind, and was able to induce his players into a hypnotic trance. He sure had me captivated up in the press box tonight.

Picking up where they left off in the first period, the Canucks completely dominated the middle frame. It was practically a replay of Monday's wild-goose chase in Dallas, during which the Leafs hardly ever had possession of the puck. Geoff Courtnall scooped in a Trevor Linden rebound to put Vancouver in front early in the period. Courtnall later scored on a two-on-one set-up from Bret Hedican, and Pavel Bure then blew past Dave Ellett and Jamie Macoun to make it 4-1. The Maple Leafs were in complete disarray behind the blueline.

While walking towards the press lounge in the second intermission, I ran into former Leaf Dave (Tiger) Williams. The Tiger is a regular at Canuck games, and has lived here in Vancouver since Punch Imlach traded him to the Canucks in February, 1980. He still looks pretty much as he did during his playing days — balding on top; the rugged, mogul-laced nose extending straight down from the middle of his forehead. I think it was Frank Orr of the Toronto *Star* who once said, "Tiger's face is so flat, he could bite a wall." Greying around the edges, Williams turns 41 on Friday (he and I share the same birth date: Feb. 3), but he still has the youthful exuberance of his Maple Leaf days in the 1970s.

"The best thing that ever happened to me was starting my career in Toronto," he says. "I got to be around great people like Johnny Bower and George Armstrong, and played with veterans like Dave Keon and Norm Ullman. They taught me how to love the game; how to treat the game and my career as a number-one priority. Unfortunately, it's not like that with most of the players in today's era."

Tiger drew great inspiration from the legends of Maple Leaf lore. "I remember talking with Conn Smythe in his house one day and I think I learned more about hockey in that 20 minutes than I had in my entire life beforehand," he says. "I just sat and listened to the man speak... it was awesome. And, of course, I loved King Clancy — everybody did. I could sit with him for hours and not get bored, and he knew exactly how to treat me. One minute, he'd be ripping me a new asshole, and the next minute, he'd be pumping me up. I couldn't get enough of him."

It doesn't take a great deal of effort to get Williams jabbering away about his Maple Leaf experience. "I just enjoyed being around the Gardens," he recalls. "I'd arrive at eight in the morning the day of a game and have coffee with the workers in the grill. The ladies would make me peanut-butter and banana sandwiches... I couldn't wait to get there. And the faces were always the same. I remember old 'Smitty' (ex-trainer Billy Smith): he carried the bricks when they built that place.

"Then there was 'Pops' — the old guy who sold ice-cream bars in the seats for so many years. When I played for the Leafs in an alumni game against Montreal a few years ago, 'Pops' came into the dressing room afterwards and we sat arm-in-arm. He was so old, he could hardly stand up, but he had a big smile on his face that day."

Tiger played for the Maple Leafs from 1974 to 1980, in the height (or depths) of the Harold Ballard era. Early in his career, he skated on a plugging forward line with Jack Valiquette and Pat Boutette. But when Errol Thompson broke a wrist early in the 1976-77 season, Williams moved to left-wing alongside Darryl Sittler and Lanny McDonald. "That was a great moment in my career, I was very lucky to be with those two guys," he remembers. "I love telling stories about the players I was with in Toronto — guys like Darryl and Lanny and Salming and McKenny. We weren't the best team in the league but we always played hard. And I'll tell you, if we had some in-put into personnel decisions, I truly believe the Stanley Cup would have been back in Toronto."

Our conversation, at that point, was heading swiftly towards the topic of Punch Imlach, and I could sense it wouldn't be subtle. "I had no use for that son-of-a-bitch and I'd say more about him if he wasn't dead," Tiger woofed. "The bastard traded us (Tiger, McDonald, Boutette) because we were friends with Sittler — not in order to strengthen the team. Poor Ballard was a vulnerable old goat by then and Imlach took full advantage of him. He single-handedly destroyed the hockey club."

Tiger is still a popular figure here in Vancouver, where he helped the 1982 Canucks to an unexpected Stanley Cup final appearance. He is heavily into sports, as chief poo-ba of the Roller Hockey International Vancouver *Voodoo*, who play their home games in the P.N.E. Agridome —up the hill from Pacific Coliseum.

Some of Tiger's reverence for the Maple Leaf uniform magically rubbed off on the current-day players during the intermission. A gritty third-period effort enabled the unyielding visitors to claw back with three unanswered goals. It started slowly for the Leafs, as Bure fired wide on a shorthanded breakaway while Greg Adams had time to cruise in front and almost convert the rebound. The Toronto players were still on the far side of Jupiter, defensively. But the game's entire momentum turned in the Maple Leafs' favour when Vancouver defenceman Jiri Slegr took an interference penalty at the 4:17 mark.

With two seconds remaining in the manpower advantage, Mike Craig tipped in Dave Ellett's slapshot from the point and Leafs trailed 4-2. It woke up the dormant Leaf supporters in the crowd of 15,312 and when Mike Gartner put a Mats Sundin rebound over McLean four minutes later, chants of *"Go Leafs Go!"* again reverberated through the Coliseum.

With the Leafs swarming the Vancouver zone, a game-tying marker seemed inevitable and it materialized with less than five minutes left on the clock. From the corner to McLean's left, Slegr mindlessly threw the puck up the middle of the rink and Mike Ridley was there to knock it down. A scramble ensued in front of the net and the puck suddenly dropped at Ridley's feet. It took seemingly forever for the Maple Leaf centerman to spot it, and he finally scooped a backhand over McLean. Again, a cheer befitting of the home team erupted from the stands.

The Leafs played cautiously in the overtime period that followed, with Mike Craig slapping a Mike Eastwood drop-pass at McLean for the club's only scoring chance. It felt like a playoff victory when the buzzer sounded, ending the match in a 4-4 deadlock.

The Maple Leaf dressing room was justifiably up-beat afterwards, and Ridley spoke to a throng of reporters about his tying goal. "I was trying to shoot the puck after it fell back to the ground, but it was bouncing and there were guys all over me," he recalled. "Bill Berg and Nicki (Borschevsky) drove to the net and the puck suddenly was at my feet. I knew McLean would probably be down (in the scramble around the net), so I tried to backhand it high."

In the funereal Vancouver dressing room, McLean confessed that he never saw the puck. "What a weird play," he said, shaking his head. "It was bouncing around in front of me and bodies were flying all over the place. I was going side-to-side and up and down trying to find it, but Ridley got a hold of it and zipped it up top. I never saw the puck till it bounced out of the net."

Burns enacted many of his coaching ploys while the Leafs were careening through the middle period. He benched Gartner for a spell and then sat Butcher during the third frame. In the end, he spoke about the club's composure. "We just didn't quit," Burns said. "We stuck to our gameplan and things eventually came together for us. I was pleased with our overall effort, despite the second-period let-down."

Several Maple Leaf players chose to put a different slant on what appeared to be a horrendous middle part of the game. "In the first two periods, they got every bounce in the book," Doug Gilmour said of the Canucks. "Every time the puck jumped over one of our sticks, it seemed like (Pavel) Bure was gone. But we were still very positive in the room at the end of the second period, believe it or not. We just said to go out and win the third and carry on to Edmonton. Obviously that approach worked very well for us."

Prior to boarding the team bus tonight, Burns had a spat with reporter Michael Kennedy of B.C.T.V. Kennedy knows his stuff well, but he's preciously short on decorum. He practically swarmed the Leaf coach with his cameraman 15 minutes after Burns held his post-game media scrum, and insisted on a short interview. Burns told Kennedy where to get off and the reporter chased him halfway to the bus before dropping the issue. "If the guy wants to talk with me, let him show up when everybody else does," said Burns. "No personal appointments."

The bus had pulled into the Coliseum basement and Dmitri Mironov shot the breeze with fellow Russian Pavel Bure prior to boarding. The Maple Leaf players already on the bus looked out the window and made some interesting observations of the Russian Rocket.

"He's sure a little bugger," said one Leaf.

"He's got big fucking ears," noticed another.

Meanwhile, Burns was appraised of Edmonton's 7-0 home-ice loss to Chicago tonight and he isn't looking forward to Friday's game with the Oilers. "I hate going in to play a team that just got waxed at home," he said, as the bus pulled away from the Coliseum.

THURSDAY, FEBRUARY 2nd
Edmonton

While having breakfast this morning in Vancouver, it was somewhat comical to notice how differently the two local newspapers treated last night's hockey game. The headline in the Vancouver *Sun* sports section said GRITTY LEAFS BATTLE BACK FOR TIE. The Vancouver *Province* headline was CHOKE JOB... LEAFS LAUGH AS CANUCKS COLLAPSE IN THIRD FRAME.

"That's ridiculous," said Doug Gilmour, gazing at the *Province*. "What team would laugh at its opponent in the middle of a tough game? I don't know how they dream up these headlines sometimes."

After checking out of the Bayshore, I took a cab to Vancouver airport with Pat Park and Gord Stellick. Park's duties on the trip include going to the airport early to arrange boarding passes for the players and coaching staff. The team bus follows about a half-hour later. I didn't mind heading out a bit early, myself, because Vancouver International has the undisputed best chocolate-covered donuts in the galaxy. Getting there 90 minutes before our flight to Edmonton enabled me to gobble one up without rushing. It wasn't exactly a breakfast of champions, but what the hell.

Another aspect of Vancouver International is far less appealing. If you want to board an aircraft, you must pay an "Airport Improvement Fee", which amounts to $10 a passenger for Domestic flights. It's one of the great Commie plots of all time and I often wonder if the policy would survive a vigorous court challenge. The airport has undergone a privatization in recent years and the money goes towards up-grading the facility. Of course, the airlines and travel agencies tell you nothing about the fee when you book your ticket and I always thought that some alternative must be provided in a free enterprise system. In Vancouver, if you refuse to pay the ten bucks, you can't go through security. And since there is no alternative airport, they have you by the short-and-curlies. The whole things smells of something unconstitutional.

The Maple Leafs gathered in the boarding lounge and several of the players were kidding Dmitri Mironov and Nikolai Borschevsky about a pamphlet on Russian phone-sex that somebody found. "Be careful Nicki —K-G-B!" joked Gilmour. The two former Soviets had a good laugh.

We flew to Edmonton on a *British Aerospace* 146 aircraft. The plane seats 83 people and has the outward appearance of a *de Havilland* Dash-8. But instead of two propellers, this craft has four jet engines. As a result, the flight northeast over the Rocky Mountains took roughly 90 minutes and it was snowing in Edmonton (big surprise) when we landed at 2:20 local time.

Edmonton has two air fields: a Municipal facility just northwest of down-town, and an International airport so far south of the city that it seems closer to Calgary. When we were boarding the plane in Vancouver, Burns asked a flight attendant which airport we'd be landing at and was told the International. He shook his head in dismay. The attendant erroneously claimed that jet aircraft are no longer permitted to fly to the Municipal field because of its proximity to downtown. She doesn't draw up the schedules, of course, so there was no purpose in arguing.

The Leaf players and coaches got their luggage and headed straight to the Edmonton Coliseum for an afternoon workout. In no such hurry, I piled into a taxi-van with Lance Hornby of the *Sun* and Paul Hunter of the Star, and we began our prolonged journey towards the city. The trip is actually about 33 kilometres north on Highway 2 (the Calgary Trail), but it always seems longer, as there are few signs of civilization along the way.

The city of Edmonton is actually perched on a bluff that ascends several hundred feet above the North Saskatchewan River. On a day less bleak than today, the approach would be rather pretty, as you climb a long, winding road into town. The Edmonton Westin Hotel, where we are staying, is located in the heart of downtown. It backs onto Jasper Ave. — the city's main drag — a street that's been famous over the past 20 years for the frequent championship parades of the Edmonton Eskimos and Edmonton Oilers. The picturesque Alberta Legislative Buildings are just down the street from the hotel.

It is only a short cab ride through residential neighbourhoods from the Westin to the former Northlands Coliseum. When Oilers' owner Peter Pocklington acquired operating rights for the Coliseum last August, he dropped the name "Northlands" in favour of "Edmonton". If Pocklington can find a major sponsor for the newly renovated building, he'll drop "Edmonton" in a hurry. On the way to the Coliseum, we passed the giant Commonwealth Stadium, home of the CFL's Edmonton Eskimos. It was built for the 1978 British Commonwealth Games, and the Eskimos moved across the sidewalk that year from tiny Clarke Stadium, which still exists.

From the outside, the Oilers' home is similar in appearance to the Pacific Coliseum. It is also a circular facility, with fewer and wider concrete slabs around its facade. Approaching the arena, it's difficult not to think about Wayne Gretzky and the incredible hockey teams that played there in the mid-1980s. I saw the Stanley Cup presented live for the first time here in Edmonton back in 1985, when the Oilers defeated Philadelphia. It's amazing to think that was a decade ago.

Both the Oilers and the Coliseum have changed drastically since then. The young Oilers have missed the playoffs the past two seasons, losing a franchise-record 50 games in 1992-93. As part of the complex deal that Pocklington negotiated with the city, more than $10 million worth of renovations are underway in the arena. Theatre-type seats with plush upholstering have been installed in the first 18 rows around the rink and are a dark mauve colour. Above the new seats is a single tier of private luxury boxes. Most of the upper-level seats remain the "sky" blue colour of years gone by and are still plastic-covered. A state-of-the-art octagon sportstimer hangs above center-ice, with four large TV screens to show fans videotaped replays.

The most dramatic renovation is in the Concourse level behind the private boxes. There is marble panelling on the walls and new blue and mauve tiles on the floor. Very chic. Thankfully, the organization has not forgotten its glory years, as 22 Oiler banners depicting division, conference and Stanley Cup champions hang in a curve above the west end of the arena: purple, orange and white in colour. The Canadian and U.S. flags are suspended above the opposite end.

After the spirited comeback in Vancouver, the Maple Leaf practice today was a cut-up. The players and coaches all piled onto the ice and had a two-puck scrimmage. It was an absolute free-for-all, with 24 men dodging and weaving to avoid a calamitous chain collision. From above, it looked like a human pinball game. There was plenty of whooping and hollering as the participants buzzed after the two pucks. Screen shots were unavoidable and Pat Burns raised his arms in triumph after banking a point-drive into the net off four or five skates. The portly coach even showed a burst of speed on a few occasions.

When the commotion ended, the players gathered at one end to work on some drills. At the other end, assistant coach Rick Wamsley flicked shots at back-up goalie Damian Rhodes. The mischievous Doug Gilmour skated over to the bench, where athletic therapist Chris Broadhurst was sitting, and whispered something in his ear. Seconds later, Broadhurst fired two pucks in the direction of Wamsley, trying to un-nerve the serious-looking coach. The first puck hit Wamsley in the left skate. The second puck missed altogether. He didn't even flinch.

After practice, Burns once again had to address the local media about the many new faces on the Maple Leafs... it's a ritual he's going through on the first visit to every city this season. "Christ, this is brutal," he groaned as we walked to the team bus. "Maybe I should make a recording or something."

During the ride back to the hotel, there was a local radio talk-show playing over the sound-system. The Maple Leafs were quietly chatting with one another and nobody was paying much attention to the program until the female host suddenly uttered the phrase "bureaucratic bullshit". It seemed to come out of nowhere and silenced everybody. "I thought you can't say things like that on radio in Canada," noted Mike Gartner, leaning forward from the seat behind me. Of course, Gartner is a Canadian, himself — hailing from Ottawa. And having spent four years in New York hearing loose cannons like Howard Stern and Don Imus, I'm surprised he even noticed the profanity.

The Westin Hotel is connected by a network of underground tunnels to the Edmonton Center Mall, and I walked there to buy some toiletries late this afternoon. As I re-entered the hotel basement, I happened to follow Gilmour into the gift-shop to buy a newspaper. Doug passed the cashier lady and said, "Keep an eye on that guy behind me — he's been known to steal things." Undaunted, I picked up the Edmonton Journal, held it at eye level, and read a mock headline.

"LEAFS NO PROBLEM, CAPTAIN STRUGGLING," I chided.

Gilmour laughed, then broke into a phony sob.

*　*　*　*　*　*

The Edmonton Oilers may have hit rock-bottom at the Coliseum last night. They were annihilated 7-0 by the Blackhawks for the worst home shutout loss in the club's NHL history, and their fifth straight defeat this season. It was perhaps appropriate that the game was played before the smallest-ever NHL crowd in Edmonton — a paltry 10,492 (capacity is around 17,000). These are troubled times here in northern Alberta, as the Oilers claim they don't have the wherewithal to compete on a level playing field with larger market teams. There is constant speculation about the club eventually moving elsewhere — most commonly, Phoenix —and interest in hockey appears to be at an all-time low.

The sportswriters in this town — most of whom covered the Oilers in their Stanley Cup years — are not prone to sugar-coating. Columnist Cam Cole of the Edmonton *Journal* penned a reaction in today's paper entitled BAD TEAM, BAD CROWDS GO HAND-IN-HAND. He wrote:

> *Peter Pocklington is absent each year at this time, golfing in the AT&T National Pro-Am at Pebble Beach, so you can't say he was missing because he can't stand to watch his own hockey team play.*
>
> *But thousands of others stayed away, some no doubt arguing that the 1994-95 Edmonton Oilers are all but unwatchable, and it will take a brave team official, indeed, to tell the fans they are mistaken.*
>
> *The House That Puck Renovated was half empty, not half full Wednesday night, and the 8,000 empties — I don't care what the announced attendance was — got the better of the deal, by far.*

Terry Jones of the Edmonton *Sun*, at the Oilers-Chicago game after a working trip to Florida, had this to say:

> *I covered this game Sunday in Miami. It was called the Super Bowl. It was over before the fans got to their seats. The only difference was, in this one, the fans would never get to their seats. They weren't in the building. And we were left to wonder when, again, they would be.*

No wonder Pat Burns is worried about tomorrow night's game. How in the world can the situation in Edmonton deteriorate any further?

Maple Leaf general manager Cliff Fletcher joined the team out here today after attending the Canadian Hockey League (Junior) All-Star Game in Kitchener Tuesday night. And speculation is rampant that Fletcher is scouting the Oilers for some muscle. Kelly Buchberger and Louie DeBrusk are said to be on his wish list, though he denies a deal is imminent.

"We have some holes to fill, but so do most other teams," Fletcher said. "Opportunities to make trades will increase with the passage of time. One reason we're not jumping out and doing something is we want to get a better feel for our team. It's still a little pre-mature to know exactly what we have and don't have."

FRIDAY, FEBRUARY 3rd
Edmonton

Today is my 36th birthday and I'm feeling old.

George Armstrong, Tim Horton and Terry Sawchuk were around this age when the Maple Leafs last won the Stanley Cup, and everyone thought they were ancient. Oh well, it's better than packin' it in.

I laughed out loud this morning when I bought the Edmonton *Sun* before breakfast. At one point during yesterday's frolicking practice, Doug Gilmour glanced up to see me and Pat Park sitting in the stands, and he flipped us the finger. A *Sun* photographer seated at ice level happened to snap a picture of Gilmour in full flip and it appeared on the inside page of today's sports section, with the cut-line "IS LEAFS' DOUG GILMOUR CALLING SOMEONE OVER, OR IS HE GIVING SOME KIND OF SALUTE? ONLY DOUGIE KNOWS FOR SURE..." Pat and I also know.

While eating breakfast in the hotel coffee shop this morning, Doug was sitting a couple of tables away. I told him to have a look at Page 2 and he shook his head in disbelief. Then he gave me the finger again.

There was another hilarious moment after breakfast. When I left the coffee shop, Dave Andreychuk was just arriving to sit down. As he waited for a table, two Oriental men began circling and peering upwards at the big Maple Leaf. Andreychuk looked down at them curiously and one of the men finally summoned enough valour to tap him on the arm.

"Are you Cam Nee-ry?" he asked in a thick Oriental accent.

"No I'm *not*," replied Andreychuk, rolling his eyes heavenward.

On the bus ride to the morning skate, those of us sitting near the front played a game of trivia. A story in the *Globe & Mail* talked about NHL teams that have had two pair of brother acts at the same time. The New York Rangers had Lynn and Muzz Patrick, and Neil and Mac Colville in the 1930s, while Chicago had Bobby and Dennis Hull, and Chico and Wayne Maki in the late-60s. The newspaper article asked readers to name the current double-brother act and we quickly indentified the Brotens (Neal and Paul) and Hatchers (Kevin and Darien) of Dallas. But only Pat Burns got the remaining duo: Darrin and Darryl Shannon in Winnipeg.

Some big news today came out of Chicago, where the old Stadium was finally meeting the wrecking ball. All indications pointed to it being a long, drawn-out process and somebody back at The *Fan* suggested they could expedite matters by attaching Oprah Winfrey to the crane. Nice.

After the skate, I went around to various Leaf players and inquired about their memories of the Stadium. None of them were too fond. "Where do you want me to start?" asked Jamie Macoun. "There was that bloody walk up the stairs from the dressing room... the towels you couldn't dry yourself with... the cock-roaches that were in your shoes all the time... and the hard, tile floor.

"Other than that, everything was perfect."

When I asked Todd Gill for *his* memories of the Stadium (Troy Murray... last night of the 1989 season... giveaway), he swiftly told me to fuck off. And I deserved it, too.

Burns was sitting alone in his office un-tying his skates when I went in to speak with him. He looked rather irritable, so I made it quick and turned to walk out. "Hey, you don't have to be afraid to ask me a question," he said. "I'm just ticked off at that Sicinski guy for the shit he came up with today."

Turns out that Pat had exchanged words a few moments earlier with Hamilton *Spectator* columnist Larry Sicinski for what he perceived to be an asinine question. Sicinski's theory was that the Maple Leaf players were being tentative because they were afraid of making mistakes that might land them on the bench, or in the press box. When he told Burns of his brainwave, the coach blew a gasket. As Sicinski later wrote:

> *Don't suggest that to Pat Burns. In fact, don't even hint the problem might be one of his creation, whatsoever. He might throw a fit like he did before the Leafs practice at Northlands on Thursday afternoon.*
>
> *"Who told you that, Larry? Where are you getting that stuff?" said Burns, clearly not liking that theory. "...I don't have time to talk to you. Get out of my face," Burns then screamed at The Spectator, before storming into his visitor's dressing-room office in a rage that was followed by a further tirade.*
>
> *...Burns is a different number, of course. The Toronto media, at least those who he hasn't verbally browbeaten into his back-pocket, will tell you about his penchant for assessing blame for losses, and his zeal to jump in and embellish his own credit for any great points these Leafs are destined to make.*

Sicinski does not count himself among the browbeaten.

Meanwhile, Burns reiterated his apprehension about having to play the Oilers after their embarrassment here against Chicago.

"Beware of the wounded bear... sometimes, if you wake him up, he gets awful grizzly," the Maple Leaf coach told reporters with perhaps his best quote since arriving in Toronto almost three years ago.

Surrounding the bus after thes workout was a group of people claiming to be close relatives of Mike Eastwood — not exactly a prime target for autographs on this Maple Leaf team. When Eastwood emerged from the Coliseum, several teammates implored him to pose for pictures with his "family."

"I've never seen these people before in my life," insisted the confused centerman, who hails from Ottawa.

"At least *somebody* knows you, Easty," chided one Leaf.

The bus was parked near a rather odd sign on the Coliseum that said: NO PARKING WITHIN 20 FEET 0 INCHES OF DOORS. Does that mean you'd be towed if you were 19 feet 11 inches away?

The Edmonton Coliseum is located across from a field of huge grain elevators and next door to an eight-story hotel called the Forum Inn. The Oilers have shifted their offices to the seventh floor of the hotel while the Coliseum is being renovated and the players were housed there during training camp. From what I recall of the Forum Inn, the Oiler decision confuses me. Back in the 80s, when I was last here, the hotel had the seediest strip-joint on this side of Okotoks. The place still advertises an "establishment", but I suppose it's been cleaned up a bit to accommodate the hockey club.

I kept an eye on the crowd tonight as the people filed into the Coliseum. By all accounts, half the place was empty for that Chicago debacle the other night, but there were whispers of a possible sellout with the Maple Leafs in town. As the puck was dropped, there were large patches of empty seats in the upper-level blues, behind the net and in the corners. Also in the lower-level seats at both ends.

Tonight's Leaf-Edmonton game proved that Larry Sicinski might have a point. Facing second-year goalie Fred Brathwaite, making his initial start of the season, the Maple Leafs appeared frightened to test him in the first period. This was an Edmonton club that had fallen behind 3-0 to the Blackhawks after only 5:52 of play Wednesday night, with starter Bill Ranford between the pipes. Two days worth of coal-raking followed in the papers and one might think the Oilers would've been vulnerable to a similar early assault by the Maple Leafs. Obviously, nobody in the Toronto dressing room felt that way.

The boys in blue were greeted by cheers when they skated onto the ice and they grew more and more likeable as the evening progressed. Instead of throwing some heavy artillery at the young Edmonton netminder, they dawdled through the opening minutes. An early giveaway by Garth Butcher set the tone, and Jason Arnott missed from point-blank range. Seconds later, Mike Ridley threw what would turn out to be the hardest Leaf bodycheck of the night. Unfortunately, linemate Mike Gartner was on the receiving end. During his next shift, Ridley was crushed by a Leaf-seeking missile named Bryan Marchment. At the halfway point of the period, Edmonton held a 10-3 edge in shots and the frame ended in a scoreless tie.

While the visitor's lollygagged through the opening 20 minutes, the beleaguered Oilers were at least skating. By doing so, they created a few good scoring opportunities. The improved effort must have warmed the heart of general manager Glen Sather, whom I visited in the first intermission. Sather has been very concerned about the smallish crowds attending Oiler games and has flat-out said it will be impossible for the team to survive in Edmonton under these circumstances.

"It's sure not like it used to be," he lamented from his private viewing area in the press box. "If the people don't start coming back soon, hockey will be a dead issue in this city."

Looking fit and tanned while chomping on his omnipresent cigar, Sather glanced out at the string of Oiler championship banners. He was, of course, the celebrated coach of Edmonton's four Stanley Cup teams in the '80s. With mega-stars like Wayne Gretzky, Mark Messier, Grant Fuhr, Glenn Anderson, Jari Kurri and Paul Coffey all playing in the prime of their careers, the Oilers were likely the most talented collection in NHL history. I asked if Sather — in hindsight — comprehended the uniqueness and glory of that era.

"It sure was a lot of fun... they were great years," he mused. "I don't think you ever fully appreciate a situation while it's happening, but I knew that fabulous era had come to an end the day Mr. Pocklington sold Wayne to Los Angeles (Aug. 9, 1988). And I still dream about how many more of those banners might be hanging in this arena had we kept that club together. We did win a surprise Cup with the kids (in 1990) before it all came crashing down."

Sather may gush with sentimentality now and then, and who can blame him? But he is also a man of exceptional business acumen and he understands why that remarkable group of Oilers could not have remained in Edmonton. "We were too good a team for this market," Sather admits. "As the NHL economy went up, this city's economy went down. When that happened, it simply became a matter of dollars and cents."

The veteran G.M. spends nowadays enjoying the fruits of his past, while promising to fashion another contender. "I think my job was more fun back then because hockey wasn't as much of a business to me," he says. "When you have players like I did, you wake up every morning and pinch yourself. I don't know if a coach will ever again have that much talent to work with. But, I'd like to do it all over.

"With the calibre of young players we have, you never know."

The Maple Leafs came out stronger in the second period and could have put the Oilers in a deep hole if they were sharper around the net. They did open the scoring early in the frame when Randy Wood backhanded Mike Eastwood's pass high into the net. Drake Berehowsky skated hard to keep the puck inside the Edmonton zone on the play. One of the ultimate turning points in the game occurred less than a minute later, when Dave Andreychuk took a pass from Doug Gilmour and beat Brathwaite through the legs. Sadly for Andreychuk, the puck ricocheted off the right goal-post and stayed out. Had the Leafs made it 2-0 so quickly, the Oilers may have succumbed to the horrific memories of Wednesday night.

As it was, they survived the Toronto flurry and quickly tied the score themselves. Dmitri Mironov failed to even budge Louie DeBrusk from the front of the net and DeBrusk shovelled Scott Pearson's rebound under Felix Potvin. Two former Leafs — Pearson and Len Esau — earned assists on the play; Esau recording his first point as an Oiler.

Undaunted, the Leafs took the lead again less than a minute later. Gilmour beat Jason Arnott on a draw to the left of Brathwaite and Mats Sundin blasted the puck into the net. But, Bryan Marchment brought the Oiler crowd back to life a few moments later by decimating Mike Gartner with a bone-jarring hit. Gartner stepped over the Edmonton blueline and sent a long slapshot towards Brathwaite. But he watched the puck a little too long and Marchment nailed him. Gartner's stick snapped in half and he floundered towards the Maple Leaf bench — his body listing awkwardly to the left. He would not return.

As it turns out, tonight's game was decided in the final five minutes. Like in Vancouver, chants of *"Go Leafs Go!"* echoed through the Edmonton Coliseum during a stoppage in play with about seven minutes to go. And the visitors responded with the tying goal. Nikolai Borschevsky made a nifty play to keep the puck in at the Edmonton blueline and sent a shot towards Braithwaite. Bill Berg took a couple of whacks at the rebound and scored with 4:43 left in regulation time to make it 4-4.

But tonight was simply not meant to be for the Maple Leafs.

Only hours after Chicago Stadium began its demolition, defenceman Todd Gill reenacted the single-most horrifying moment of his NHL career — the notorious giveaway to Troy Murray of the Blackhawks on the final night of the 1988-89 regular season, that gave Chicago an overtime win, and eliminated Toronto from the playoffs. Ironically, it was another NHLer with the initials T.M. who victimized Gill tonight. Oiler rookie Todd Marchant went around the Leaf defenceman like he would a practice pylon to score the breakaway winner with 3:18 left. All Gill felt was a breeze as Marchant blew past him inside the Toronto blueline.

Burns felt it best that Gill get right back on the horse, and he sent him out again with Mironov on the very next shift. But the damage was done and Shayne Corson cemented the Oiler triumph — scoring into an empty Maple Leaf net with 13.1 seconds left on the clock. After coming back from the dead in Vancouver on Wednesday, the Leafs couldn't take advantage of an Edmonton club reeling both on and off the ice.

To his credit, and as per the norm, Gill did not try to duck away from reporters after the game. Neither was he in the mood for a dinner-type conversation, but he answered the obvious question. "Yeah, I made a bum play and it cost us the hockey game," he said, while drying off from showering. "It was a stupid mistake and there's no excuse for it. I went across to get the angle on him, but he cut back inside and I couldn't recover. It cost us a point, maybe two."

Marchant wasn't certain who he had victimized on the play. "I was taking the defenceman wide — people tell me it was Todd Gill — and he turned on me, so I slipped the puck around him and went in alone," said the Oiler rookie. "I told myself I had to bury it and, thankfully, the shot beat Potvin. It sure was a great feeling after that terrible game the other night."

Burns, meanwhile, had to bite down hard to restrain himself during his post-game media session. "I refuse to be negative about this hockey club," he said, somewhat unconvincingly. "We've been out west twice now and have travelled more than 10,000 miles. I'm not going to use that as an excuse by itself, but it has been a factor. Half this team is made up of new faces and we need some practice time. We're going to get used to each other and get better. If we don't, it'll be my responsibility."

Mike Gartner was not in the Leaf dressing room after the game and nobody seemed quite sure of his whereabouts. After some digging, it was learned that Gartner had gone to hospital with Pat Park to have his rib-cage X-rayed. He apparently was having some trouble breathing after the big hit by Bryan Marchment in the second period.

Finding a cab back to the Westin was no problem after tonight's game — about a dozen were lined up on a sidestreet outside the arena. The Coliseum was bathed in blueish-purple floodlights as we drove away towards downtown. Despite Edmonton's victory, the taxi driver wouldn't stop railing on the Oilers. He kept referring to Peter Pocklington as a "welfare bum." I was quite relieved when he dropped me off.

SATURDAY, FEBRUARY 4th
Calgary

It was a pleasure this morning not having to make the long trek to Edmonton International for the flight down to Calgary. Lance Hornby and I took a cab to the Municipal airport ten minutes away from the Westin. The diminutive terminal there is about the size of a rural-Ontario bus station, providing a welcomed relief from the organized chaos of major airports. In fact, Lance and I were the only human beings at the check-in counter when we arrived at 9:30 a.m.

We flew down to Calgary on another *British Aerospace* 146 jet. The plane took off to the northwest and circled back south, providing us with a magnificent view of downtown Edmonton from about 8,000 feet. It was a perfectly cloudless morning, which enhanced the scene below us. The trip south took all of 40 minutes, and the Canadian Rockies were clearly visible when we landed in Calgary around 11:30.

Another taxi ride took us to yet another Westin Hotel and as we were checking in, the Chicago Blackhawks were heading out. What a nice little streak *they* are on. After beating the Leafs at the United Center a week ago yesterday, the Hawks left on their monster eight-game road trip. They've won three out of four thus far, including last night's 4-3 overtime victory here in Calgary, and are now going to Vancouver for a game against the Canucks tomorrow afternoon.

"It's been fun so far," said Ed Belfour as he left the hotel — a suitcase-bag strapped over his shoulder. "Hope it continues."

Pat Burns was walking through the lobby of the Westin and he held an impromptu media scrum. It was then we learned that Mike Gartner had remained overnight in an Edmonton hospital and had not accompanied the team on its post-game charter here to Calgary. Burns said that Gartner experienced breathing difficulties and may have suffered a partially collapsed lung. Pat Park stayed in Edmonton with the Leaf winger. For tonight's encounter with the Flames, Burns will dress both Terry Yake and Dixon Ward, and he has no idea how long Gartner will be sidelined.

After lunch I took a long walk through downtown Calgary. It was a sensational mid-winter afternoon today, with brilliantly sunny skies and a temperature around five degrees Celsius — absolutely perfect conditions for a long walk. The downtown area, quite lively on a normal business day, was practically deserted. I haven't been here in Calgary since the 1986 Stanley Cup finals, so I walked over to the mid-town apartment building I briefly resided in on 7th Ave. S.W.

I lived here for a time in 1982 when I came out to work as a sportswriter at the Calgary *Sun*. Gary Loewen was the sports editor at the time, and he hired me to cover Junior hockey and golf. Loewen covered the Leafs for the *Globe & Mail* in the late-1980s, but he's back out here now. Having lived in my parent's house all of my life, it was quite an experience leaving home and the city at the same time. I was only 23 years of age and had never been to western Canada. But I overcame my homesickness by diving into the Junior 'A' hockey scene, which was bustling here in the Foothills. So was the city, itself, as Calgary was at the tail-end of an economic boom unparalleled in Canada.

The Calgary Wranglers of the Western Hockey League were almost as popular as the Flames back in 1982. The Olympic Saddledome was under construction on the Calgary Stampede grounds and the two hockey teams played their home games next door at the Calgary Corral. The old barn held around 7,500 people and the Flames were always sold out. The Wranglers, however, weren't far behind — attracting crowds in the vicinity of 5,000 for most games. Mike Vernon was the Wranglers' star goalie back then, and I'll not soon forget the long bus trips to places like Winnipeg, Brandon, Regina and Saskatoon. Traversing the Prairies in the middle of the night during winter was often a precarious adventure.

Looking up at the sun-baked apartment tower, it seemed like I had lived there in another lifetime. I then walked under the 9th Ave. bridge, where the railroad tracks are, and up to where the old *Sun* offices were located on 10th Ave. Incredibly, the building is long gone. All that remains is a parking lot which backs onto the railroad.

I continued walking east along 9th Ave. and decided it was an ideal day to visit the Calgary Tower. Built in 1967-68, the 60-story edifice is Calgary's signature landmark, rising above office buildings a few blocks north of the Stampede grounds. For a paltry $4.75, an elevator takes you up to the observation deck and on a crystal-clear day like today, the view is mind-boggling.

To the west are the snow-capped Canadian Rockies, rising above the famed resorts of Banff and Lake Louise. On the plains to the northeast sits Calgary International Airport, about 10 miles in the distance: its control tower sticking out of the brownish terrain. Much closer, and to the south, is the Calgary Stampede grounds — featuring the Saddledome, the Corral, and Stampede Park Racetrack. From up in the Tower, you can easily comprehend why the name Saddledome is a misnomer. The arena is, in fact, anything but a dome, with a concave roof design curving inward from its edges. Obviously, it dwarfs the old Corral across the yard.

On the way back to the Westin, I walked along the 8th Ave Mall: an outdoor shopping area walled off to traffic. The entire afternoon was enjoyable and nostalgic for a guy who briefly called this place "home".

While waiting to board the team bus early tonight, a taxi pulled up and delivered Pat Park to the hotel. The Leafs' p.r. director was just arriving from Edmonton, where he remained throughout the day with the ailing Mike Gartner. Moments earlier, we had learned that Gartner did indeed suffer a partially collapsed lung and would not be able to fly back to Toronto. Instead, he will board a *VIA Rail* train tomorrow night in Edmonton and make the 48-hour trek by land.

Ol' Parksy had a look of relief on his face. "I really didn't want to go home by train," he smiled. "I put a call in for Cliff (Fletcher) earlier today, asking for some direction. When he phoned back and said to come to Calgary, I kissed the ground beneath me."

Joe Bowen was standing alone in the hotel roundabout and we began chatting about his relationship with the Maple Leaf players. Joe has been the radio voice of the Maple Leafs since the 1982-83 season and is also a popular sportscaster at The *Fan-590*. He's not a big man, but his voice can boom with the best of them, and while only in his mid-40s, he has a thatch of snow-white hair. During the lockout, Joe took a decidedly anti-NHLPA stance while broadcasting his mid-day updates on The *Fan-590*, and there had been some backlash. As an example, union vice-president Ken Baumgartner refused to voice a promotional I.D. for the radio station that had Bowen's name on it. "No chance... I'm not mentioning that guy," Bomber said when approached by a *Fan* employee during the post-lockout training camp. Other players openly bristled at the mention of Bowen's name and the animosity went public as part of Bill Houston's *Truth & Rumours* column in the Jan. 21 edition of the *Globe & Mail*. Houston wrote:

> *After the lockout, Bowen gave the labour issue all his attention and after deep thought, came to the conclusion that the players were a bunch of greedy, misguided, pathetic ingrates. He subsequently gave regular rants, er, talks to his listeners on the subject during his weekday sportscasts.*
>
> *Two examples of Joe's (tasteful) commentary: he called Wayne Gretzky's travelling 99's tour "a farce." When the owners submitted a proposal to the players, Bowen warned them: "Vote no and drink the Kool Aid" — in other words, turning down the offer meant committing suicide.*
>
> *Understandably, the Leaf players won't have anything to do with Joe now. They even refused to mention his name when they were asked by the station to promote the (Maple Leaf) games.*
>
> *Question: How long can a station employ a play-by-play man who is intensely disliked by the players?*

During the season-opening trip to Los Angeles and San Jose, Bowen appeared to keep his distance at times from the Maple Leaf players: an unusual move for someone who openly enjoys partaking in the camaraderie of such occasions. In L.A., for example, he was not on the team bus for the pre-game ride to the Forum and Joe almost always goes with the club to practices, morning skates, and games.

The following night in San Jose, I went down to the hotel lobby to board the bus, and Joe was sitting in a corner by himself while a group of players cavorted nearby. He seemed unusually reticent.

"I don't think I was *that* conscious of it," he countered during our chat. "The only tangible evidence of any backlash was from Ken Baumgartner. He refused to do that promo item, then he came up to me in Los Angeles and said he wanted to chat at some point. I said okay, but then Bomber had his shoulder surgery and we never got together. As far as the other players are concerned, I haven't heard a peep."

Bowen said he felt a bit uncomfortable around the team only as a result of Houston's *Truth & Rumours* item. "Oh, he's so full of crap," Joe said of the *Globe* writer. "But the story came out in the middle of the first road trip and I reacted more to that than anything personal with the players. I felt there was no sense rushing in and becoming buddy buddy with the guys until it blew over a bit.

"But no one came up to me and said 'Fuck you' or anything."

Bowen and Houston have been going back and forth at each other for several months now. Houston frequently jabs at the Maple Leaf announcer for broadcasting with an elevated tone, while Bowen refers to the Globe as "Canada's national fish-wrap." The by-play often takes on a comical flavour, but it's clear the two men are not enamoured with one another.

The Maple Leaf players with high ranking in the NHLPA were not at all hesitant to comment on Bowen's overt stance.

"I like Joe Bowen as a person and he's an outstanding radio man," said union president Mike Gartner, perhaps the most easygoing member in the Leaf dressing room. "But I didn't agree at all with the position he took on the air. It seemed like every comment he made had a bit of an edge to it and I guess that's simply the way he felt. Everybody has a right to his opinion and Joe certainly expressed his.

"I'm not one to hold a grudge, however, and I think I can say the same for most of the guys. Some players took his comments to heart, but there were a lot of hard feelings in different ways during the lockout and there has to be a mending process. Joe's situation is definitely a part of that."

Added former Leaf player rep Todd Gill: "That was Joe's stance and there's nothing I can do to change it. Everybody has a way of thinking, and his was pro-owner. He thought the players weren't doing the right thing and he talked about it. Obviously, being against me, I didn't feel very good about him, but I suppose he has the right to say and do what he wants. We live in a society with freedom of speech.

"As far as my feelings towards Joe, I'm not going to let a 10-year relationship go out the door because he didn't believe we were doing the right thing. That's not the kind of person I am.

"Do I agree with the way he treated some of the guys? No, I don't. But like all of us, Joe has to live with the things he says and he knew from the beginning he'd have to work with us after it was all over. If he japped a few guys, he has to accept the consequences."

Bowen remembered that his primary target was not the individual players, but rather the NHLPA's executive director.

"I took a anti-Bob Goodenow stance," he said. "I felt they got bad advice from him and he painted them into a difficult corner. But even Bob didn't have a negative reaction when we came into contact. Our sons played immediately after one another in the MTHL during the lockout and I'd see him at the local arenas. I understood that he took a number of reporters to task over the phone, but he never once said anything to me about my on-air stance, which I found rather interesting."

Goodenow might dispute Bowen's claim that the players were not among his targets. Joe repeatedly criticized union vice-president Marty McSorley for travelling to Europe with Gretzky's all-star tour, calling him the "chancellor of the ex-checker." Bowen also vehemently disputed Gretzky's claim that a chartered *Boeing-727* jetliner was fuelled up and ready to return at a moment's notice in the event of a settlement. Joe understood (as did others) that Gretzky had committed to tournament and TV officials to play the overseas event in its entirety.

"Besides, Howard, you wouldn't believe the number of players who privately came up to me during the lockout and told me I was bang on," he concluded. "Nothing I've heard in the interim makes me feel like anything I said was out of order."

The Maple Leafs lost 4-1 to the Flames here in Calgary in spite of putting forth unquestionably their finest 60-minute effort of the season. Everybody in that Toronto dressing room now realizes how the Dallas Stars felt last week about Felix Potvin. Tonight, the Leafs were victims of a similarly astounding performance by Trevor Kidd. The Calgary goalie made at least a dozen remarkable saves, while Potvin was comparatively mortal at the other end.

The Flames had the Leaf bench a bit wide-eyed when Robert Reichel beat Potvin with a routine shot just more than a minute into the hockey game. Was it going to be Edmonton all over again? The Leafs took up the challenge, however, and got stronger as the opening period progressed. Kidd heisted Doug Gilmour from point-blank range seconds after the goal and he became stronger with every save. Terry Yake, Dmitri Mironov and Kent Manderville all had quality scoring chances, but were thwarted by the Calgary netminder. The frustration got to Mats Sundin, who rudely shoved Gary Roberts into the Calgary bench from behind on a late line change. The Flames led 1-0 after 20 minutes.

During tonight's game, I sat on the broadcast side of the press box, opposite from the team benches. Bowen and Stellick were 15 feet to my right, providing me with a running account of the action. The media vantagepoint in the Saddledome is terrific, as the highly elevated press box hangs directly over the boards. The arena seats are a kelly green colour at ice level and they gradually become a deep blue as the rows expand upwards. The players turn into miniaturized dots from the high-level seats that were installed for the 1988 Winter Olympics.

Sitting to my left was the Maple Leaf executive contingent of Cliff Fletcher, Pat Park and assistant coach Rick Wamsley. Wammer views every game from the press box while in radio contact with fellow assistant Mike Kitchen behind the bench. And like most coaches, Wamsley has a tendancy to become rather frenzied at times during the course of a hockey game. As an enamoured spectator would, he loudly exults Maple Leaf players to properly execute their assignments and I'd like to have a nickel for every time he instinctively hollered "Fuck you, Andy" at referee Van Hellemond during tonight's match. He's sure into the game.

Wamsley had reason to be upset early in the second period when Mike Ridley coughed up the puck behind the Maple Leaf net. Robert Reichel pounced on it and set up German Titov in front for a 2-0 Calgary lead. It then became Potvin's turn to stymie the opposition, and he kept the Leafs within reach by making a series of excellent stops. As they have on several occasions thus far, the Leaf players lapsed into an annoying rut for a lengthy spell in the middle frame and Calgary had a 10-2 edge in shots by the 8:53 mark. The Leafs were also out of sync offensively, as Sundin passed behind Dixon Ward on a two-on-one break.

Toronto finally got on the board just past the midway point of the game when Ridley backhanded in a loose puck from the tip of the crease. Kidd had stopped Terry Yake on the initial shot. The Maple Leafs then had four tremendous opportunities to tie the game, but Sundin, Mironov, Gilmour and Macoun all failed to connect. Kidd's stop on Sundin was the best, as he kicked away a hard shot from 20 feet in front.

During the second intermission, I looked up and saw a moustache coming at me from beyond the press box. It took only a second to recognize that Lanny McDonald was behind the furry batch, as he made his way across the catwalk that extends between the two media holdings. Lanny put his arms around Cliff Fletcher, the man who rescued him from the Colorado Rockies in 1981. Colorado G.M. Billy MacMillan (a former Maple Leaf) made every bit as absurd a deal as Punch Imlach had when McDonald was traded by Toronto two years earlier. Nepotism played a role, as MacMillan acquired his younger brother, Bob, and veteran forward Don Lever from the Flames. The Rockies packed up and moved to New Jersey a year later and Billy lost his job the following season.

Lanny, meanwhile, pumped in a career-high 66 goals for Calgary in 1982-83 and finished his brilliant career by captaining the Flames to their only Stanley Cup triumph six years later. He is now the club's vice-president of marketing and broadcasting and he remains one of the most popular and recognizable sporting figures in Canada.

Kidd was again spectacular in the third period tonight, and when he made an amazing save off Ridley at the 8:30 mark, it was obvious the Maple Leafs were not going to do any business. Andreychuk fired a shot from 25 feet that Ridley deflected. Kidd made the save but the rebound went back to the Leaf centerman standing alone at the side of the net. The Toronto players were already celebrating on the bench when Ridley one-timed the puck towards the yawning Calgary cage, but Kidd somehow extended his goalstick clear across the crease and kept it out. It was totally a reflex action and the type of miraculous save you might see once or twice in a season.

Two minutes later, Kidd performed his magic on Gilmour, who would have converted Nikolai Borschevsky's rebound against any other goalie on any other night. A later stop on Dave Ellett was merely difficult, and hardly noticeable in this game.

Van Hellemond was involved in a couple of peculiar incidents late in the game. He had his arm up for a delayed slashing penalty against Gary Roberts of Calgary. While following the play up ice, Van Hellemond accidentally bumped into Roberts, who figured it was a Leaf player, and instinctively swung his stick in response. Luckily, Roberts stopped inches short of chopping down the referee.

With ten seconds left in Roberts' minor, Gilmour was called for a hooking infraction and a Calgary fan began harassing him from several rows behind the penalty box. Gilmour stood up and turned around to face the man, while the Maple Leaf players loudly banged their sticks on the boards in front of the bench to get Van Hellemond's attention. Finally, the ref called the play and ordered security to deal with the heckler.

The Flames put the game on ice with 1:42 remaining in regulation time, when Titov re-directed Steve Chaisson's shot past Potvin to give Calgary a 3-1 advantage. A minor controversy ensued after Burns yanked Potvin for a sixth attacker. Calgary defenceman Dan Keczmer purposely raised his own net off its moorings with 35.4 seconds left. The NHL rulebook states rather succinctly that a penalty shot be awarded in such a circumstance, but Van Hellemond chose merely to assess Keczmer a two-minute delay of game infraction. Burns briefly went nuts behind the bench while Andreychuk and Macoun pleaded with Van Hellemond on the ice. The effort would have been more worthwhile had Calgary been up by only a goal, but it seemed like a futile waste of time with the Flames leading by two. Titov completed his hattrick with an empty net goal in the dying seconds and the Leafs skated off the Saddledome ice sporting a less-than spectacular 1-2-1 record on this four-game road-trip.

After the game, much of the chatter surrounded Kidd's remarkable performance, and his head-spinning rejection of Ridley early in the final period. "I still can't believe I didn't score," moaned the Leaf centerman. "The rebound came right back to me and I was a little off balance. But I saw only empty net and he somehow got his stick back and took it right off the goalline. What a hell of a save."

Kidd modestly attributed his bit of larceny to good fortune. "I was totally out of position and it was pure luck," he said. "I stuck my stick out in desperation hoping that maybe he would hit it and he did. I don't know if it was the turning point or not, but it would have tied the game up and who knows what might've happened after that."

It had to be an entirely satisfying experience for Kidd, who was chosen in the same 1990 amateur draft as Felix Potvin. Kidd went in the first round, 11th overall (from Brandon of the WHL), while Toronto took Potvin in the second round, 31st overall (from Chicoutimi of the Quebec Junior League). Obviously, Potvin has made an earlier impression at the NHL level but with Calgary having traded veteran Mike Vernon to Detroit last summer, Kidd seems to be answering the club's vote of confidence.

"I was just glad to do my part tonight," said Kidd, refusing to gloat about his performance against Potvin and the Leafs.

Meanwhile, Burns reiterated that his objective was for the Leafs to play .500 hockey through their first 10 games and the club is right there at 4-4-2. "If we had gotten a point tonight, it would have been a great road trip," he said. "But, we're hanging in there and it'll be nice to get home now and start working on some things."

A few moments later, on the team bus, Burns and Joe Bowen scoured the rulebook to see exactly what type of infraction Dan Keczmer should have gotten for knocking off the net. After squinting at the book under a dim reading light, Burns said, "I thought Andy blew the call at the time and now I *know* he did."

The Maple Leafs headed back to their hotel, with one of their key performers, Mike Gartner, still laid up back in Edmonton. "I'm feeling better now but it's still uncomfortable at times," Gartner told Lance Hornby of the *Sun* from his hotel room. "I've never done a two-day train trip before, but there's no way around it (it's the only direct train to Toronto). I guess I'll get a good look at the Prairies."

SUNDAY, FEBRUARY 5th
Aboard Air Canada Flight
From Calgary

I don't consider myself to be a nervous flyer, but neither am I perfectly comfortable with air turbulence. Having assumed this season-long project, I immediately calculated almost 40 separate plane trips and realized there would come a time when I'd wish I had not accepted the assignment. That moment arrived on our approach to Pearson Airport early this afternoon.

After a wonderfully smooth takeoff in calm and clear skies from Calgary, the Air Canada pilot radioed Toronto's weather-forecast and he emphasized how windy it was back home. I didn't pay much attention to his announcement until he repeated it during the final moments of the trip. We arched out over Lake Ontario and turned left to come in from the south. The *Boeing*-767 jetliner was quivering rather severely, but it wasn't anything I hadn't previously experienced.

However, the final approach was altogether new.

As the aircraft staggered through the skies over Etobicoke, it dipped and rose with gusts of wind hammering it top and bottom. Several passengers actually screamed with horror, and only Dave Ellett — his nose crammed into a book two rows behind me — seemed unaffected by the whole thing. My knuckles were the colour of fresh snow when we finally settled onto Runway 33 and the captain radioed an apology to us for the rough ride (like it was *his* fault).

While gathered around the luggage carousel, I decided to check with a few veteran Maple Leafs to see if I may have been over-reacting. The macho among us, like Joe Bowen, shrugged it off as an every day experience, but more introspective people like Garth Butcher and Jamie Macoun admitted they could hardly recall a more bumpy approach to any airport — especially on such a large jetliner.

*　*　*　*　*　*

The Maple Leafs continued to play well at home early in the season, earning three out of four points against San Jose and Dallas. Kenny Jonsson made up for his gaffe in San Jose last month by tying a Leaf team record in the return match with the Sharks. Jonsson recorded three assists in the first period of the 7-3 romp — his first points in the NHL. It equalled the most helpers in one period in Leaf history. Dave Andreychuk and Mike Gartner had two goals apiece in the lop-sided triumph. Leaf plugger Bill Berg suffered damage to his right knee in a first-period collision with Sandis Ozolinsh and could be sidelined for a few weeks.

Mats Sundin came through two nights later against the Stars, *scoring with 1.6 seconds left in regulation time for a 3-3 tie. Dallas had gone in front 3-2 on Dean Evason's goal at 17:34 of the third frame but Sundin sent the Gardens crowd into hysteria by flipping the rebound of Dmitri Mironov's point shot over goalie Andy Moog. The Leaf record was 4-4-3 after the dramatic tie.*

FRIDAY, FEBRUARY 10th
Detroit

Boy, did I luck out today.

Driving from Toronto to Detroit in the middle of winter can be a harrowing experience, thanks to a potential variety of weather-related obstacles on route. Particularly on the stretch of Highway 401 between London and Chatham, where storm systems develop and blow southward off the bottom tip of Lake Huron. Many times, I have driven beneath crisp and cloudless skies while approaching London, only to be enveloped by a weather holocaust moments later. Blankets of gusting snow-flurries create instantaneous white-outs and nothing beyond good fortune enables you to avoid a crisis. Unpredictability is the norm.

I became privy to such conditions on my very first trip to Motown, and almost lost my life in the process. A friend of mine from Toronto, Ron Dale, studied at the University of Windsor in the late-70s, and he acquired three tickets for the final Maple Leafs-Red Wings game at the old Detroit Olympia — a Sunday matinee: March 25, 1979. I got up early that morning and drove uneventfully to Windsor with my close pal, Jeff Spiegelman. We met Ron at his apartment and went across to Detroit for the game. It was a cold, grey afternoon, with perilous weather in the forecast for the greater Detroit area.

With Joe Louis Arena under construction along the city riverfront, I knew this would be my first and last visit to the historic Olympia. I sat right behind the corner glass during the warm-up and gazed about the building in wonderment. Like the old Madison Square Garden in New York, the Olympia had a balcony that encircled the entire rink and our seats that afternoon were in the upper level, around the blueline. Many of the current-day NHL arenas have state-of-the-art features that were unfathomable in the late-70s, but none are blessed with the magnificent viewing positions of the old building at Grand River and McGraw.

Lanny McDonald scored the only Maple Leaf goal in a 2-1 loss that day and it was an absolute privilege to see a game in the Olympia, less than a year before it was razed. Driving home that night, however, Jeff and I came within a couple feet of being decapitated.

An ice storm was ravaging the area and the highway between Windsor and London had the consistency of a curling rink. It was dark, and all the vehicles on the eastbound 401 were inching along with their two-way hazard lights illuminated. Even at the slow rates of speed, cars would periodically slide off the road and into the quagmire of slush and ice in the median. Having done so, they were stranded for the night, and I desperately concentrated on avoiding that predicament.

About an hour into the trip, I was proceeding cautiously in the middle lane of the highway. Ten or eleven car lengths ahead of me were a pair of flat-bed trucks in the middle and inside lanes. They also had their hazards on. For some reason, the guy in the middle decided to try and pass the truck on his right, only to change his mind halfway into the manoeuvre. On a dry road, he simply would have jerked back into the mid-lane without consequence. On that precarious sheet of ice, however, he lost control of the vehicle and his long trailer-bed swung backwards across the full width of the highway. Like a sling-shot, it then began recovering, and was moving towards my car like a giant sledge-hammer. Had I not instinctively veered left, the back end of the trailer would have smashed directly through my windshield. It missed the car by about 18 inches. Somehow, I was able to avoid both the on-coming flat-bed and the slushy median, but I was shaken beyond control for several minutes.

That horrific memory resurfaces every time I drive between Toronto and Detroit, and it has forever cured me from attempting the journey at night. Thankfully, I was able to dodge all but a very brief snow-squall this morning and I made the 370-kilometre trip without incident. There were ominous clouds in the sky the whole way, but the weather Gods held back their unpredictable fury.

Coming from Toronto, the quickest way to enter the U.S. is through the Windsor-Detroit Tunnel: a mile-long passageway that burrows beneath the Detroit River. Traffic moves slowly at times in the Tunnel and I've often had a fear of carbon-monoxide extinction. Fortunately, I've made it to Detroit alive each time, as I did today. The only dilemma I face when proceeding through Customs at the Tunnel is the constant stream of agents who want to talk sports. You see, I have a radio station logo on my company car, which is a dead giveaway.

It provides me with a strange mix of emotions.

On one hand, I'm relieved not to be the random choice for an anal drug search; on the other, I'm usually in a bit of a hurry and I don't have time for a lengthy conversation. Most of the agents at the Tunnel seem to be energetic young men who love to debate whatever sports topic comes to mind. Occasionally, however, it's a blessing to come upon the portly woman agent who has no desire to talk to anybody. The one I had today looked like Dick Butkus and she sent me through without a word.

Once in Detroit, getting to Joe Louis Arena is fairly easy. A left turn onto Jefferson Avenue takes you westbound, but the street abruptly ends at the Cobo Hall convention complex. It requires another left turn and a detour through the front driveway of the circular Cobo Arena onto a narrow road that runs parallel to the Detroit River. J-L-A is roughly a half-mile up on the right side and cannot be missed.

Cobo Arena might ring a bell for long-time basketball fans, as the Detroit Pistons played there in the 1970s before moving to the Pontiac Silverdome and, ultimately, the Palace of Auburn Hills. Named after the former mayor of Detroit, Albert E. Cobo (1950-57), it also served ever-so briefly as home of the WHA's Michigan Stags — originally the Los Angeles Sharks — who re-located unsuccessfully in Detroit for part of the 1974-75 season, before moving on to Baltimore.

As a wrestling fan, I remember Cobo Arena for the meteoric rise of The Sheik in the late-60s. Reputed to be from Syria, the hated Sheik (real name: Eddie Farat) actually sold used cars in suburban Detroit (or "used camels", as the late Dick Beddoes would say) and began his fire-throwing reign of terror at Cobo. Of course, he was the marquis villain at Maple Leaf Gardens for wrestling shows in the early '70s — wreaking havoc on formidable good guys like Bobo Brazil, Whipper Billy Watson, Lord Athol Layton, Tex McKenzie and The Mighty Igor.

Wow, does that bring back memories!

Joe Louis, the great heavyweight boxer, was still alive in those days, but no arena had been named in his honour. That changed when the Red Wings decided the Olympia had out-lived its usefulness and the new 20,000-seat facility on the banks of the river became the hockey club's home just after Christmas, 1979. On December 15th of that year, the Red Wings and Quebec Nordiques closed out hockey at the Olympia, playing to a 4-4 tie. Twelve days later, St. Louis beat the Wings 3-2 to open the Joe Louis Arena. And on Jan. 12, 1980, 51-year-old Gordie Howe returned to Detroit as an NHLer, playing for the Hartford Whalers.

Howe's famous No. 9 jersey is among five that have been retired by the Red Wings and they all hang from the rafters at Joe Louis Arena. In fact, Howe's retired uniform dangled overhead the night he came back to play with the Whalers. He had originally retired from hockey after the 1970-71 season, only to return two years later and play with sons Marty and Mark with Houston of the WHA. His Detroit jersey had long been put to rest when he made his NHL farewell fling with Hartford in 1979-80.

The great "Production Line" of the 1950s is commemorized in J-L-A, as the uniforms of Sid Abel (#12) and Ted Lindsay (#7) join Howe in the rafters. Alex Delvecchio (#10) and the incomparable Terry Sawchuk (#1) have also been eternalized by the Wings. The predominantly red jersey replicas hang together in a row at the north end of the building. There are a number of banners at the other end depicting club achievements, beginning with the 1942-43 NHL regular-season title. The older ones — those which hung for years in the old Olympia — have clearly faded and portray a genuine sense of history.

Otherwise, Joe Louis Arena is unremarkable from the inside. It's your typical oval-shaped cavern with padded red seats surrounding the rink. The arena was built not only for the Red Wings, but in plenty of time to host the 1980 Republican National Convention (Ronald Reagan was nominated). The press box seems not to have been in the initial blueprint and is therefore inaccessible by conventional means. Reporters and broadcasters have three options — none of which are particularly enamouring. We can take an elevator to the concourse and ascend through the upper level of seats. We can take an elevator to the fourth floor and walk around to the box in the upper rows of seats. Or we can climb 96 stairs straight up. Most of us choose option two, providing the fans haven't yet streamed into the building. Otherwise, we must repeatedly excuse ourselves as we squeeze by.

When I arrived at J-L-A this morning, the Red Wings were finishing up their day-of-game skate. Coach Scotty Bowman was on the ice, wearing a Red Wings jacket and a pair of beige business slacks. He spent much of the workout leaning on the shaft of his stick, watching his players. At his feet, surrounding the center-ice circle, were the words "DETROIT RED WINGS: 69th SEASON." Overhead, the ceiling of the expansive arena is painted chalk-blue. Private luxury suites encircle the upper portion of the building and are bursting to capacity each game night.

In the basement lobby, near the corridor that leads to the Maple Leafs' dressing room, is the green reflective highway sign that used to hang above Interstate 94 — guiding motorists to the old Olympia. It is mounted on a brick wall and reads: OLYMPIA STADIUM — EXIT WARREN AVE.

Defenceman Bob Rouse will skate against his former Leaf teammates for the first time tonight. Rouse played a key role in the success of the Maple Leafs the past two seasons, but he opted to finish his career in American dollars and jumped to the Red Wings as a free agent during the summer. The defensive acumen of Rouse and Sylvain Lefebvre has not been replaced by the Leafs and it could prove damaging as the season progresses. Veteran leadership along the blueline is a must in the NHL.

"It will be a special feeling for me tonight," Rouse admitted as we yakked in the Detroit room after the skate. "I made a lot of friends in Toronto over the years and enjoyed my time there immensely. It's not the first time I've left a team (he previously played for Minnesota and Washington), but it was the toughest departure. The bonds we made while advancing so far in the playoffs the past two years were very strong and I miss some of those guys."

The greatest personal moment of Rouse's career occurred in this building almost two years ago. It was his sliding shot from the right-wing boards that Nikolai Borschevsky tipped into the net in overtime, as the Leafs beat Detroit to win their 1993 Norris Division semifinal. "I still glance at that spot on the ice in practice now and then," he confessed. "To upset the Red Wings and come back from a 2-0 deficit in that series was a great moment for myself and the Leaf organization. That's what we're trying to do here in Detroit. This team has been an underachiever the past few years. We now want to be overachievers."

Rouse admitted it was initially strange to enter a dressing room full of players with whom he'd developed such a rivalry. The Leafs and Red Wings have gone at each other tooth-and-nail the past few years and Rouse said it was weird to suddenly have the pesky Dino Ciccarelli as a teammate. "I spent three years trying to keep that little bugger away from Felix and now I'm rooting for him to cause havoc in front of the net," he laughed. "But, that's the way it is in hockey. When you bounce from team to team — as I have — you realize that the guys are all the same throughout the league. I was made to feel very welcomed here."

An even stronger aspect of the Maple Leaf-Detroit competition will be non-existent tonight. For almost a decade, the underlying sub-plot of this rivalry has been the personal warfare between Wendel Clark and Bob Probert. The physical leaders of each team have engaged in constant harassment of one another, and the prevailing club has often been the beneficiary of that battle. The Clark vs. Probert feud usually dictated the climate of games between Toronto and Detroit, but Wendel is now in Quebec, and Probert is under a league-imposed drug suspension. He inked a free-agent contract with the Chicago Blackhawks prior to the season.

"We won't miss having to play against Wendel," admitted Scotty Bowman in his coaching office after today's workout. "It's pretty clear what he's done to this team over the years. He was a constant thorn in our side, not so much with his fighting ability — we've had guys who could handle that — but with his penchant for scoring timely goals. He beat us with a big overtime goal here in Detroit last year and we never found a way to combat him properly.

"By mentioning this, I'm not taking anything away from Mats Sundin — he's a superbly talented player and will be the focal point of the Maple Leafs for many years to come. But he's a different type of player than Wendel, who always seemed to save his best efforts for us."

There was a noticeable absentee from the Leaf skate this morning. Doug Gilmour was not on the ice and Pat Burns had a concerned look on his face afterwards. "He's got a pinched nerve in his neck or something and I don't know if he'll be able to go tonight," Burns told me while untying his skate-laces. "He said he woke up with it this morning and I probably won't know his status until game time." With Felix Potvin back home in Toronto — Burns has decided to rest him for this one-game trip — the loss of Gilmour would remove two key elements from the Leaf line-up for a road game against the league's best team. No easy task.

Speaking of Burns, he and his assistant coaches dress here at J-L-A in a small room next to the Maple Leaf quarters. It also serves as a dressing room for pick-up hockey games, with wooden benches, hooks for clothing, and toilet facilities at the back. The ante rooms obviously aren't maintained quite so diligently, as Burns discovered on a prior trip here. Apparently, someone left a monstrous deposit in one of the toilets several days earlier and the Leaf coach nearly passed out when entering the room. An arena worker was summoned to freshen things up.

While in Detroit, the Leafs stay at the Omni International Hotel, directly across Jefferson Ave. from the Windsor-Detroit Tunnel. A high room facing south provides you with a dandy view of the Detroit River and the city of Windsor on the other side. The hotel is connected to a shopping complex known as the Millender Center, and it features a superb Chinese restaurant called *Foo Wah*. I look forward to coming here as much for my lunch special as I do the hockey game. For about $7, you get a hearty plate with a main course (the szechuan chicken is superb), fried rice, and a jumbo eggroll. It's sensational. I chowed down with Mark Hebscher this afternoon and he's now a *Foo Wah* convert.

The Omni International is also connected by a series of walkways to the giant Renaissance Center across the street, which features the 73-story Westin Hotel. The three-pronged, glass-enclosed complex is the signature landmark of Detroit's riverfront restoration and can be seen for miles. If you approach Windsor on a clear day along the westbound 401, you can see the Ren-Center rising in the distance above farmlands north of the highway. It makes for quite a visual contrast.

Going from the Omni Hotel to Joe Louis Arena is a snap thanks to the *People Mover* — an outdoor monorail system that encircles downtown Detroit. You catch it upstairs in the Millender Center and it takes you to a station directly across the road from the west entrance of J-L-A. A one-way ride costs just 50 cents and the only fear you must overcome is the fact the three-car trains are fully automated — not operated by human conductors. If one should break down between stations, you might need a shaving kit and food supply. Otherwise, the system is convenient for travellers in the downtown area who don't have a car.

Pre-game meals for the media at J-L-A are a delight, if you enjoy pizza. Red Wings' owner Mike Ilitch is the founder of *Little Caesar's*, and press room workers serve one pizza pie after another. You must be sure not to over-stuff yourself, or you're liable to barf it all up on the arduous trek to the press box. It requires discipline.

With Ken Baumgartner now confirmed to be sidelined for the season while recovering from his shoulder operation, the Maple Leafs' need for a greater physical presence may have been answered tonight. Prior to the game with Detroit, a press release was circulated announcing the acquisition of left-winger Warren Rychel from the Los Angeles Kings for a fourth-round draft choice. I recall Rychel in the playoffs two years ago, when he played an integral role in L.A.'s march to the Stanley Cup Final. In 23 playoff games that spring, he equalled his 70-game regular season total of six goals and became popular with the Forum fans.

His 322 penalty minutes *last* year was the third-highest total in the league (behind Tie Domi and Shane Churla) and no player had more fighting majors than the 6-foot, 200-pounder from nearby Tecumseh, Ontario. He'll be sought to fill a specific role with the Maple Leafs, beginning tomorrow night, when the Kings are in Toronto.

"I think we know what we're getting in Warren," said Bill Watters before tonight's game. "He's a feisty winger who will score between six and 12 goals... we're not acquiring him for his offensive skills. Maybe the best description of him is that he fits somewhere between Bill Berg and Ken Baumgartner. I'm not sure there is anyone tougher than Bomber, pound-for-pound, and I don't think Warren hits as hard as Bergy. But he certainly is not afraid to mix it up, and he'll keep some people honest on the other side of the ice."

While the Maple Leafs play in Detroit tonight, the Kings will be resting at the Marriott Eaton Center in Toronto and Rychel will have to make a move. "Boy, this is weird," he told reporters via the phone. "I practised with my L.A. teammates at St. Mike's Arena this afternoon and now I've got to change hotel rooms and play *against* them tomorrow. I suppose it'll be a monkey off my back right away.

"I don't really know what to think," he continued. "It's a great opportunity for me to play on a winning team and I feel I'm the type of player Pat Burns appreciates. But, then, I thought I made the same impression with (L.A. coach) Barry Melrose, so who can tell? You just go with the flow in this game."

The Leafs took to the ice tonight without Doug Gilmour, who spoke about his sudden ailment in the press box. "I woke up in the hotel this morning and went to the elevator, and when I pushed the button, my neck spazzed out on me," he said. "I have no idea how it happened. I pinched a nerve lifting weights one summer, but that was about 10 years ago. It loosened up from treatment and medication today and hopefully, it'll be a 24-hour thing. We'll find out tomorrow against L.A."

With their captain and starting goalie out of the line-up, the Leafs came up with their grittiest effort of the season. They suddenly reverted to the choking, defensive system that made them so successful on the road the past two years and upset the fully armed Red Wings 2-1. Mats Sundin and Damian Rhodes did a great job filling in for the absent stars — Sundin scoring the Maple Leafs' first goal, and Rhodes making 34 saves, as Detroit outshot Toronto 35-18.

Keith Primeau opened the scoring for the Red Wings early in the first period when he banked a centring pass from the corner off Jamie Macoun's skate, and it seemed like the predictably long evening for the Maple Leafs was underway. But big Sundin answered for the visitors less than two minutes later, eluding defenceman Paul Coffey and beating Mike Vernon with a low shot through the legs. Despite the tie score, Detroit had a wide territorial advantage, out-shooting the Leafs 12-2 in the first eight minutes. After failing to score on their initial powerplay, however, the Red Wings were held to only three shots the remainder of the period, as the Leafs settled into their strong defensive posture.

In fact, had Vernon not stopped Sundin on a shorthanded breakaway at the 16:18 mark, Toronto would have taken the lead.

The Leafs did jump in front — as it turns out, for good — when Terry Yake scored early in the second period. Garth Butcher's shot from the right point bounced off Coffey's skate and Yake slammed the rebound past a helpless Vernon. The Maple Leaf checking continued to bottle up Detroit and the fans lustily booed the Red Wings when Mike Ramsey iced the puck just past the midway point of the game. The Red Wings held a 22-8 shots advantage at the time, but they trailed by a goal. Rhodes stretched his left pad across the goalcrease to make a marvellous save on Ray Sheppard with 44 seconds left and the Leafs led 2-1 after two.

In the second intermission I saddled up alongside Matt Pavelich, who was watching the game from the press box. Pavelich was a linesman in the NHL between 1955 and 1979 — becoming one of hockey's longest-serving officials.

During that time, he worked more than 1,700 regular-season and 240 playoff games, and was a staff supervisor for 15 years after his on-ice career ended. Pavelich was essentially dismissed by the league last August and he currently does some freelance work for the Ontario Hockey Association in the Windsor-Sarnia corridor. But he has found retirement to be difficult.

"After 40 years in the NHL, it's a bit of a come-down and I miss working in the big league," he admitted. "But, I suppose I had a pretty good career and nothing goes on forever."

Hockey officials, like baseball umpires, should all sit down and write books before their memory banks diminish. There are few things I enjoy more than reminiscing with a former NHL referee or linesman, and Pavelich, now 61, is among the best story tellers of them all. A game he always talks about is the Montreal at Boston slugfest on New Year's Day, 1958. The Canadiens edged the Bruins 4-3 to take over first place and there were seven major penalties called that night.

"It was just after Henri Richard came up with Montreal and the Boston players were giving him a hard time," Pavelich remembers. "The Pocket and Fernie Flaman were pushing along the boards and Fernie said to him, `You're only up here because of your brother (Maurice).' Well, Pocket obviously felt he had to do something real quick and he ended up picking on two of the toughest players in the league.

"Leo Labine jumped off the Boston bench a few seconds later and Henri just corked him: opened him up for 20 stitches. Then, Jack Bionda came after the Pocket and he also wound up bleeding all over the ice. Richard wasn't big, but he handled himself very well that night and I don't think many players took advantage of him the rest of his career. He wanted to stop the talk about being Rocket's brother, and he sure quieted a few people that night in Boston."

Ironically, the most noteworthy 60 minutes of Pavelich's career in the NHL was not among the 2,000 or so regular-season and playoff games he worked. It was the Philadelphia-Red Army encounter at the Spectrum in January, 1976 — when the Soviets left the ice after a crunching hit by Ed Van Impe on the late Valeri Kharlamov.

"I worked that game with (referee) Lloyd Gilmour and a Russian linesman," Pavelich recalls. "The Soviets had a player named Alexandrov who spent much of the afternoon yapping away in Russian. Well, you see, I'm of Croatian descent and I understand a lot of the Russian language. At one point, Alexandrov swore at me and I gave him the sign for a two-minute unsportsmanlike conduct penalty. You should've seen his jaw drop when I answered him in his native language!

"After Van Impe hit Kharlamov, I was standing over by the Soviet bench and I heard (coach) Viktor Tikhonov say in Russian, `This is crazy! We have to play in the Olympics next month. We're not going to play anymore against these animals!' I skated over and told Gilmour and he said, `Nah, you're crazy.' Just then, the Soviets began leaving the bench for the dressing room. I saw Alan Eagleson and Clarence Campbell jump out of their seats and rush downstairs.

"We were sitting in our dressing room, just waiting it out, when Mr. Campbell came in and said the Russians were told that if they didn't go back onto the ice, they wouldn't be paid. When I heard that, I knew they'd be out there again very soon." Indeed the Soviets did re-appear and wound up 4-1 losers in a game Flyers' coach Fred Shero called the brightest moment of his career —better even than winning the 1974 and '75 Stanley Cups.

Pavelich always found the most intimidating NHL arenas to be among his favourite places to work. "The old Chicago Stadium, Boston Garden, and the old Madison Square Garden in New York had the best atmospheres for hockey," he recalls. "The upper balconies would hang right over the ice and you could practically feel the fans breathing on you. I had fun with a guy in Boston. He'd lean over in the balcony and say, `Pavelich, where's your seeing-eye dog?' and I'd reach out like I was holding a leash. Then we'd both laugh. The new arenas aren't built the same way and it's a bit of a shame. The old ones had great character."

During the third period tonight, a wild rumour circulated through the press box that the struggling Vancouver Canucks were about to trade Pavel Bure to New Jersey for Scott Niedermayer and Scott Stevens. After checking it further, the story was found to be the product of someone's fertile imagination. But it sure took our attention away from what was happening on the ice for a few minutes.

When we re-focused, we noticed that the Leafs were strengthening their choke-hold on the Red Wings. The Detroit players seemed shocked to be in such a life-and-death struggle with their under-manned rivals and they almost appeared to give up. Their passing was abysmal and they stopped attacking the Toronto net like they had earlier in the game. It looked quite similar to the Red Wing capitulations in the playoffs the past two years, when it was easy to discourage the multi-talented club with diligent checking and soft, timely goals. The Leafs were lining up across their blueline and thwarting Detroit's attack time and again.

This was supposed to be a different Red Wing team: one that could overcome opposition strategy with its own guile and determination. But tonight, it wasn't working out that way and the players and fans seemed haunted by visions of the past.

Conversely, the Maple Leaf confidence grew boundless in the third period. At no time in the first three weeks of this season has the club shown either the capacity or ambition to get its "hands dirty" and play the gritty, smothering hockey that has been its hallmark. Wendel Clark, Sylvain Lefebvre and Bob Rouse are no longer part of the mix, but their absence doesn't account for a lack of willingness. The Leafs wanted this game tonight, and nobody was going to take it from them.

Martin Lapointe hit the crossbar behind Rhodes early in the period but the Leafs prevailed defensively and skated off with a nicely earned 2-1 triumph.

Burns appeared quite relieved afterwards to pull out a victory with such a shorthanded line-up. "With Gilmour, Gartner and Berg out tonight, I was searching a lot on the bench for the right combinations to use," he said. "The penalty killing and powerplay units all had to be mixed up but I thought the guys hung in there together real tough."

The Leafs don't play another road game for almost two weeks and it will be another one-day trip here to Detroit. "I thought Damian Rhodes played great tonight and if we can keep Felix at home for our next game here, he'll have gone the better part of a month without travelling," Burns explained. "It should really help him in the second half of the season, being able to sleep in his own bed for an entire month. It's the only luxury we have in this shortened schedule of ours."

Meanwhile, Rhodes returned triumphantly to the site of his first NHL start — a 3-1 victory over the Red Wings at Joe Louis Arena, Mar. 22, 1991. "That game was so long ago that it really isn't a factor in my mind anymore but I do remember Vincent Damphousse clinching the win with an empty net goal in the final minute," Damian recalled. "Tonight was a real confidence booster for me because it showed that I can beat one of the upper-echelon teams."

And Rhodes insisted he wasn't thinking about the so-called battle with Pat Jablonski to be Potvin's regular back-up. With three NHL-calibre goalies at every Leaf practice, there's a constant threat hanging over Rhodes. But he has so far held off the challenge of Jablonski — a starter previously in Tampa Bay. "I'm glad for myself that I was able to go in and help the team win tonight, but it's not my decision whether we have two or three goalies," he said. "The important thing is we were able to give Felix a rest tonight and we still came away with two points. It was a very big victory for us."

Detroit *Free Press* hockey writer Keith Gave echoed the sentiments of the Detroit fans when he began his game story by saying, "Who were those guys wearing the Toronto sweaters Friday night at Joe Louis Arena? Doesn't matter, they did a splendid job impersonating the Maple Leafs."

*　　*　　*　　*　　*　　*

There were a lot of negative signs for the Maple Leafs during a five-game homestand that produced a 2-3 record. The players held a closed-door meeting after a ghastly 5-2 loss to Los Angeles in which Kelly Hrudey stoned the Leafs (he seems to save his best efforts for the Gardens). Toronto had 43 shots — 19 in the second period — but couldn't master the Kings' veteran goalie. To try and generate more offence, Pat Burns again switched Mats Sundin back to right-wing on Doug Gilmour's line. New Leaf acquisition Warren Rychel sat out against his former teammates 24 hours after being acquired from L.A. as part of a reciprocal agreement by both teams. L.A. sat tough guys Matt Johnson and Troy Crowder.

Leafs followed up with a much more thorough effort in a 4-2 victory over Chicago. Sundin had two goals on his 24th birthday and Rychel almost scored on his first shift as a Leaf. The fans booed a five-minute Leaf powerplay in the first period that produced only one harmless shot. Jeff Shantz had been tossed from the game with a major for slashing.

Edmonton came in a couple of nights later and embarrassed the Leafs 4-1. Unanswered goals in the third period by Scott Thornton and Jason Arnott put the game on ice for the Oilers. Emotions ran high in the second period. Pat Burns blew a gasket when Bryan Marchment felled Rychel with one of his typical submarine checks and the Edmonton player later suckered Doug Gilmour into a retaliatory penalty. Arnott went after Dave Ellett late in the period and a wild scrum erupted in front of the Edmonton bench. Ellett then tried to scale the penalty box to get at Doug Weight and Arnott before tempers cooled.

Continuing the roller-coaster trend, Toronto earned a tidy 3-1 victory over St. Louis. The Blues had played in Winnipeg the previous night and the Leafs capitalized on the fatigue factor by out-gunning St. Louis 15-4 in the first period and taking a 2-0 lead. Kenny Jonsson scored his first NHL goal and Brett Hull ruined Felix Potvin's shutout bid with a powerplay goal at 14:45 of the third period. It was the 800th game of Jamie Macoun's NHL career.

The homestand ended with a 4-2 loss to Detroit. The Red Wings scored three unanswered goals in the third period for the victory, as the Maple Leafs collapsed amid a 16-shot attack. Martin Lapointe's game winner with 5:48 left in regulation time was hotly disputed by Burns, who felt the Red Wing player had prematurely come off the bench on a line change. After Detroit's first goal — by Ray Sheppard at 7:01 of the opening period — Burns benched the Gilmour-Andreychuk-Craig line, marking the first time Gilmour has been so disciplined in a Toronto uniform. Leafs were 7-7-3 after the homestand.

WEDNESDAY, FEBRUARY 22nd
Detroit

The fates were kind to me again this morning, as weather was not a factor in the 3 1/2-hour drive here to Detroit. This is the last time I'll have to attempt the trip this winter and I couldn't possibly have lucked out any better. In fact, I made today's drive 15 minutes faster than the one here 12 days ago, but I was disappointed when I arrived at Joe Louis Arena around 10:20 a.m.

It was 15 years ago today that the most famous hockey game in the history of the Winter Olympics was played. I remember watching from a friend's condominium in Hallandale, Fla. as the up-start U.S.A. squad tamed the mighty Russian bear at Lake Placid, N.Y. on route to the most improbable gold medal of all time. Mike Eruzione's winning goal that day was the American equivalent in every way of Paul Henderson's shot heard around the world eight years earlier. And it was scored against the same goalie — Vladislav Tretiak. A member of that incredible U.S. team still plays for the Red Wings and I was hoping to interview him today. But, defenceman Mike Ramsey decided not to show for an optional morning skate and I was out of luck.

While watching the dozen or so Detroit players go through their paces, I leafed through a copy of today's Toronto *Sun* that I picked up before leaving the city. There was a rather explosive column on Page 99 by corporate sports editor George Gross — a man not inclined to take the poison-pen approach very often. Gross covered the Leafs for the old Toronto *Telegram* during their Stanley Cup dynasty of the '60s. In those days, the hockey club frequently looked after the travelling expenses of beat writers, and the resulting coverage was astonishingly biased towards the men in blue. Gross, and his Toronto *Star* counterpart Red Burnett usually called it as Punch Imlach saw it back then. It was an entirely different era of sportswriting and Gross proved today that he can lay it on the line, but-good, when he wants to.

A column entitled WHAT'S WRONG WITH DOUG GILMOUR provided the most blatant criticism so far this season of the struggling Leaf captain. It began by rehashing that Gilmour and Dave Andreychuk had been benched by Pat Burns during Monday night's 4-2 Detroit victory at the Gardens, and got nastier from there. Some excerpts:

> *What's wrong with...Wendel Clark's successor as Maple Leaf skipper? Does he think the NHL lockout is still in existence? Or did he do too much muscle-weakening mountain-*

climbing in the Swiss Alps during the NHL rest period?

(El) Capitano, once the heart of the Leafs, has certainly not been overworked this season. Not on the ice, anyway. Perhaps Gilmour is involved in too many off-ice activities, which are affecting his play.

Oh yes, I mustn't forget that his goals total in the last four games is zero, zilch, nada.

I've never been a student of logarithms, but $3 million seems to be an awfully high price to pay a player who can't score even one goal in four games. Not even on powerplays. In the last four games, the $3-million man has a grand total of one assist, and three goals against.

I'm glad he's not making $6 million a year, because at $3 million, his one assist in four games has cost the Maple Leafs something like $300,000.

(Maybe) Don Cherry's kiss (on Hockey Night In Canada two years ago) turned out to be the kiss of death for Gilmour and the Maple Leafs.

Gross's column made the rounds of the Toronto media contingent at Joe Louis Arena this morning and afterwards, in the Leaf dressing room, I asked Gilmour if he'd seen the article. "Nah, I'm staying away from the newspapers this season," he said. Meanwhile, many of his teammates clamoured after my copy of the *Sun* and scoured the column in groups of four or five before passing it on. It sure had a bite to it.

Speaking of an edge, former Leaf Mike Krushelnyski had some rotten things to say about Pat Burns when I yakked with him this morning in the Detroit room. He asked me not to repeat any of them, so I won't. But, suffice to say, he's not exactly enamoured with his ex-coach. The Kruiser signed as a free agent with the Wings in the off-season after playing a mostly support role in four seasons with the Leafs. To be quite honest, his overall performance level during that time — with the exception of the 1993 playoffs — did not warrant a regular shift and a plausible argument can be made that the Maple Leafs extended a career in the final stages of decline. However, Krushelnyski obviously believes otherwise and feels that he and fellow ex-Leaf Mike Foligno were — in essence — Burns' whipping boys.

The Maple Leaf coach didn't attend the skate this morning. He's battling the flu and was resting back at the hotel. With a fever over 100, it's possible he won't be behind the bench for tonight's game.

Detroit is off to an excellent 10-4-1 start this season, and the Wings are doing it at both ends of the ice. They've scored 58 goals so far — one behind Chicago and St. Louis for the Conference lead — and are tied with the Blackhawks for fewest goals allowed at 32. Like an explosive baseball team with a lousy bullpen, the Red Wings of recent ilk have been strong offensively, but blatantly unsure of themselves in their own zone. Had the Detroit playoff clubs of 1993 and '94 been more adept at protecting leads, the Stanley Cup might be currently residing here in MoTown. Without that skill and its accompanying confidence, the Wings — to the dismay of owner Mike Illitch — have twice been kayoed from the opening round by inferior opposition.

But it seems like Detroit has finally addressed the problem this season. The acquisition over the summer of veteran goalie Mike Vernon from Calgary was a smart move, and Vernon has been ably supported by his stand-in — Chris Osgood — who has a 1.34 goals-against average in six games. The addition of former Maple Leaf stalwart Bob Rouse has had a settling effect on the blueline, and Paul Coffey is performing with renewed vigour; at 33, he's still the most fluid skater in pro hockey.

All of these elements are being nurtured by the NHL's winningest all-time coach — William (Scotty) Bowman. If Detroit can maintain its command of both ends of the ice, Bowman will seriously contend for the seventh Stanley Cup title of his marvellous career behind the bench. He won five championships with the Canadiens — four consecutively between 1976 and '79 — and another with Pittsburgh in 1992. He has control of player personnel here in Detroit and is putting his indelible stamp on another potential champion. The Stanley Cup drought in MoTown is in its 40th year — longest of the original six teams.

Bowman is a man I've been intrigued with since grade school. After toiling as a junior coach in the Montreal system, he made it to the NHL in the 1967 expansion as an assistant to head coach and general manager Lynn Patrick of the St. Louis Blues. The Blues floundered at the start of their inaugural season, going 4-10-2 in their first 16 games, at which time Bowman was handed the head coaching reigns by the aging Patrick. On the evening of Nov. 29, 1967, the Blues beat Los Angeles 3-2 at the old St. Louis Arena and Bowman has, quite simply, never looked back.

In the years after expansion, the established six teams (Montreal, Toronto, Chicago, Detroit, Boston and New York) comprised the NHL's East Division, while the new clubs (St. Louis, Minnesota, Pittsburgh, Philadelphia, Los Angeles and Oakland) formed the West Division. The East and West champions met for the Stanley Cup in a terribly lop-sided format that served as more-or-less a welcoming bonus from NHL president Clarence Campbell for the $2 million admission fee. The Blues of Scotty Bowman made it to the Cup final in each of the first three years after expansion and never won a single game: losing four straight to Montreal in 1968 and '69, and to Boston (and Bobby Orr) in 1970. But they still were tops among their peers, and provided the hockey world with a mere preview of the Scotty Bowman genius.

In eight seasons with Montreal (1971-79), Bowman won five Stanley Cups and his teams finished first overall in the NHL six times. Critics of the veteran coach — and there are a few — have long suggested that a blind, deaf man could have stood behind the bench of those wonderful Canadiens teams and been just as successful. How could anyone have lost with Guy Lafleur, Jacques Lemaire, Larry Robinson, Guy Lapointe, Serge Savard and Ken Dryden all in the prime of their careers? Bowman's lack of playoff success in six years with Buffalo underscored that criticism and even though he copped another championship with Pittsburgh in 1992, it's often been said that he won Stanley Cups with teams that simply could not have done otherwise.

Universally disliked by the vast majority of his players, Bowman has nonetheless put up numbers better than any coach in the game's long history, and during his almost three decades in the NHL, he's been one of hockey's most enigmatic personalities. My own few encounters with the man have been mostly pleasant, including a rather surprise meeting this morning. As I stood idly in the Red Wings' dressing room after the skate — waiting for Paul Coffey to materialize — Bowman strode out of his office, noticed me leaning against the wall, and asked who I was waiting for. When I told him Coffey, he voluntarily turned around and poked his neck into the trainer's room. "He's in there, he'll be right out," said the coach, walking casually past me.

This type of benevolence flies in the face of Bowman's legendary shortness with the media, and makes you wonder even more about the man. The best article I've ever seen on Bowman was penned recently by hockey writer Jeff Jacobs of the Hartford *Courant*. In one page, he brilliantly portrayed the veteran bench boss.

> *(He) isn't a hockey coach. He is an enigma, a paradox. And he likes for all of us to think of him in such a way. He seems convinced it has given him an edge in life. He wants you to believe that matching lines with him is harder than solving Rubik's Cube.*
>
> *(He) is a loner. He is known to stay at Joe Louis Arena all day and half the night watching games on the satellite dish.*

113

(Some) call him a genius, always three steps ahead in the chess match. Some call him paranoid, the kind of guy who would ask his players for a pack of matches even though he didn't smoke. It was a way of finding out where they were spending their late hours. Some call him cold, demanding. There's a story that he once told a player to go to the airport, and by the time he gets there, he'll figure out where to trade him.

(We) love the "Rainman" post-game press conferences, where he has four topics going at once without finishing a sentence on any of them.

He is a puck savant.

(Scotty) Bowman is what he is. And we aren't sure what he is. You can't explain him; he likes it that way. So just stand back and admire what he has done.

Beyond all else, Bowman is simply a winner, and he proved it again tonight here in Detroit. The Red Wings cruised past the Leafs for the second time in three nights, prevailing 4-1. The Maple Leafs botched up five powerplay opportunities and have scored only seven goals in their past four games. The loss dropped them a game below .500 on the season.

"We'll take some heat," Pat Burns told reporters afterwards. "We talked about it. We'll just have to stick together."

It was a strange affair, highlighted by a fruitless investigation early in the first period. Vladimir Konstantinov appeared to score for Detroit at the five-minute mark when his shot bounced into the net off the skate off Toronto defenceman Dave Ellett. But referee Paul Stewart immediately waved off the goal, believing it was directed in by Detroit forward Doug Brown. What followed, was an interminable delay while the referee checked upstairs with the video replay official. After almost 15 minutes of haggling — with the sellout audience growing restless — Stewart finally upheld his decision to disallow the goal... but for a rather bizarre reason that was outlined by supervisor John D'Amico in the following dispatch to the media:

"The video goaljudge (Bill Clements) felt that he should review (the play). He phoned downstairs to verify Paul Stewart's decision... and he turned to the technician to watch it. The technician pressed the recorder to bring it back and did something in his recording that put everything a blank, completely a blank, on the video replay machine.

"Unfortunately, it was a technical error by the technician (Rob Rancour). The decision then had to go down to the ice, (where) Paul Stewart did make the decision, disallowing the goal, feeling the puck went off the Detroit player's skate into the net.

"Unfortunately, it was a technical error and it was the technician who made the error. This is the first time I've seen this happen."

Unable to be reviewed, the play stood as called, but did little to inspire the Maple Leafs. Three minutes later, Viktor Kozlov scored a legitimate goal and the Red Wings were on their merry way. The Leafs did tie the game before the end of the period, when Dave Andreychuk snapped in a rebound off Mark Howe's skate, but that was the extent of Toronto's attack. Shawn Burr's tally at 47 seconds of the middle frame turned out to be the winner as the Red Wings were finally able to solve Leaf goalie Damian Rhodes at Joe Louis Arena.

I watched the final moments of the game from the Zamboni entrance behind the Toronto goal and the building frustration of the Maple Leafs was quite apparent. Dmitri Mironov threw his stick in a futile attempt to thwart Greg Johnson's empty net goal with 22 seconds left, and Mats Sundin slammed his lumber over the crossbar after the puck went in. As the Maple Leaf players sombrely dressed, the lame excuses and promises continued to roll forward.

"Because it's a 48-game schedule, people are ready to push the panic button and want us to make trades," moaned defenceman Todd Gill. "We have 11 new faces now. If we make trades, that's more new faces."

Added Mike Gartner: "Look, we know we're better than a .500 team and when we turn things around, we'll be able to look back and say we still played .500 hockey when things weren't going well. And believe me, this team *will* turn it around. There's too much talent in this room to keep playing the way we are."

Mark Hebscher and Eugene McEleney of *Global* offered me a ride back to the hotel afterwards and I waited for them on the sidewalk outside the media entrance of Joe Louis Arena. While chatting with Harry Neale, a drunk staggered over and began lecturing us on the virtues of alcohol consumption. Harry tried to humour the guy, but he wouldn't go away. Wobbling, the man looked around and lunged clumsily at the beer in the hand of a *Molstar* employee standing next to Neale. He missed, and nearly fell flat on his face.

"Nothing like a couple of minutes in beautiful downtown Detroit," Harry sighed.

*   *   *   *   *   *

The Leafs came home after their one-game trip to Detroit and defeated Anaheim 3-1 in a real snoozer. The not-so Mighty Ducks were outshot 18-3 in the first period as the Leafs took a 2-0 lead on goals by former Duck Terry Yake, and Doug Gilmour. Anaheim failed to generate any consistent attack and Shaun Van Allen counted the visitor's only marker in the third period, when Felix Potvin was late coming across the goalcrease. Ducks' rookie Paul Kariya — in his first game at the Gardens — had an apparent goal waved off after a video replay review in the third. He actually hit the post.

Dave Ellett scored two goals against his former team as the Maple Leafs breezed past Winnipeg 5-2. His second marker was a killer for the Jets, occurring on the powerplay with only 2.7 seconds remaining in the opening period. It gave Leafs a 2-0 lead. Sundin continued to look good on right wing with Gilmour and a struggling Andreychuk. The big Swede got involved in a fracas with Stephane Quintal of Winnipeg, who checked him low at the knees in the second period. Sundin responded later with a forearm to the noggin and Quintal fought with Jamie Macoun. Winnipeg trailed only 3-2 in the second period when Felix Potvin made a fabulous pad save on Teemu Selanne. Sundin and Mike Eastwood later scored. The Leafs had a 9-8-3 record after the victory.

MONDAY, FEBRUARY 27th
St. Louis

The travel dilemma I encountered this morning was inevitable. The only question is: how many more times will it happen this season?

A forecasted winter storm conveniently held off until the moment I stepped out of my Thornhill home at 6 a.m. Large, heavy snowflakes were silently descending through the still air and it was so quiet, I could practically hear them settling onto the roof of my car. Driving to Pearson Airport along Highway 401 progressively became a chore as the snowfall intensified, and was a veritable crisis towards the end.

Most travellers in this setting will activate his or her "fight-or-flight" response. Anxiety prevails when a mid-morning deadline looms two stops away, and since there are no non-stop flights between Toronto and St. Louis, a connection must be made in either Detroit or Chicago. I was scheduled to change planes at O'Hare, and could only imagine what the weather might have been doing off the shores of Lake Michigan.

Now, United Airlines frequently boasts about its "friendly skies", but the company is obviously less concerned with harmony on the ground. Only one of four check-in positions at Terminal 3 was open at 6:45, despite a line-up of close to 50 passengers. Maybe it explains why the ticket agent wore a scowl you'd see on a bottle of Iodine. Whatever the case, I was *told* in no uncertain terms by this lady which gate to proceed to, and when I summoned the temerity to ask whether the Chicago flight was on time, a terse "I don't know!" came back at me. I thought to myself 'who shit in *her* cornflakes?'

Once seated on the *Boeing*-757, I could almost sense this St. Louis trip going "*pfffft!*" The left wing of the aircraft was covered with at least an inch of fresh snow from the raging blizzard. An airport worker braving the ghastly conditions atop a cherry picker pelted the jetliner with rust-coloured de-icing fluid. But by the time he finished spraying the opposite side of the plane, snow had re-formed on the wing. Moments later, the first officer emerged from the flight deck and observed both wings out the aircraft's windows. He then returned and, surprisingly, we began pushing back for our taxi to the runway.

It seemed, however, like too optimistic a scenario, and when the plane stood motionless at the end of the ramp, I knew we weren't going anywhere in a hurry. This was painfully confirmed by the captain, who informed us that too much snow had once again gathered on the aircraft to ensure a safe departure. He also explained that de-icing procedures at Pearson could take place only at the gate, and that we were heading back there to wait out the storm. Terrific.

I watched helplessly out the window for 35 minutes as the snowfall continued to mount. With a 9:45 a.m. scheduled connection to St. Louis, I figured that covering the morning skates were out of the question and began to merely hope I'd make it in time for tonight's game. Just then, the captain came up with a brainstorm. He decided to have the aircraft towed to the end of the Canadian Airlines departure ramp, thus reducing the length of our taxi. The plane would then be de-iced once again, and the captain would make a mad dash to nearby Runway 33.

Sounded like a plan!

After the second de-icing, both the captain and first officer came back for another look at the wings and announced we'd be leaving. They drove the plane out to the runway and snow again began to accumulate on the wing. I don't mind confessing that I had a death-grip on my armrest as we lifted off into the clouds roughly 90 minutes after our scheduled departure time. But, as they say, better late than never.

A quick mathematic calculation revealed that if there were no air traffic delays in the Chicago area — and *that's* never a guarantee — I might have enough time to leap from the jetway on to my connecting flight to St. Louis. And that's pretty much how the situation unfolded. The trip to O'Hare took 70 minutes and I was thankful we parked at the same concourse as the St. Louis plane. An all-out sprint from Gate C-21 to C-29 enabled me to board the *Boeing*-737 at the last possible moment. It was so close, the flight-attendant nearly walloped me in the ass as she pulled the door shut behind me. Whew!!

The flight was full and I excused my way into my window seat. The trip down to St. Louis took only 45 minutes and we arrived at Lambert International Airport on schedule at 10:50 a.m. — with the Maple Leafs set to begin their morning skate 40 minutes later. Once again, I had to nervously endure a delay, as ground control held the plane short of the ramp long enough to allow four other flights to leave. St. Louis is a hub for Trans World Airlines and the red-and-white TWA jets were taking off one after another. We finally made it to the gate at 11:05.

During one of the intermissions of the Leaf-Winnipeg game Saturday night at the Gardens, I was chatting with Boston Bruins' pro scout Bob Tindall, a man I've known for many years. Bob had recently been to St. Louis and he informed me that a new rail link between the airport and downtown was fully operational and it stopped right at the Keil Center: brand new home of the Blues. He recommended I take it, on the grounds of convenience and economics, as a quick 35-minute trip cost only $1. A taxi ride, conversely, would last a few minutes longer and could fetch up to $30. I remembered his advice as I entered the Lambert terminal this morning, but the train station was way at the other end of the airport. "Just another delay," I thought. After dragging my suitcase behind me for seven or eight minutes, I came upon the *Metro Link* station and bought a ticket.

Thankfully — and it was my only break this morning — the next train downtown was waiting with its doors open and I hopped on board. I glanced at the route map and was impressed at how thorough the system appeared to be. *Metro Link* has 11 stations between the airport and the banks of Mississippi, serving key downtown attractions like Union Station, the Keil Center, Busch Stadium, the Convention Center and the Gateway Arch. Cab drivers must hate this thing.

The train left at 11:13 and proved to be as comfortable and handy as Tindall suggested. Along the way, it passed through an area of west St. Louis that must have once been a thriving industrial community. A massive, three-winged factory known as *Wagner* Electric stood abandoned, like an historical museum. The small windows of the three buildings had all been shattered and the machinery of this once-flourishing business could be seen through the broken glass. Other vehicles, like trucks and ramp loaders, were scattered about the main yard of the complex: all in various stages of rust. It's as if something happened — like a fire

— that caused the factory's employees to flee the site... and no one has seemingly returned to remove the debris.

As per the *Metro Link* schedule, my train arrived at the Keil Center station around 11:50 and I knew I had to hustle, with the Maple Leafs already 20 minutes into their morning skate. There was one small drawback to the train ride: the station is actually a long block from the new hockey arena and it was pouring rain when I stepped outside. I had no other choice but to shlep my suitcase through puddles along the sidewalk, and the teeming rain thoroughly destroyed my coiffed hair-do: I looked like Moe Howard by the time I reached the Keil Center.

Then came another crisis.

I was directed to three different entrances before discovering an unlocked door. Once inside the facility, a security guard named Jim took one look at me — hair matted down; dripping water all over the arena concourse — and refused to believe I was a radio reporter from Toronto. I pulled out my wallet and showed him media credentials that would get me into the Kremlin, but he wouldn't budge. Desperately, with the clock ticking down on the morning practice, I explained to him why I looked so cruddy, and he relented. He took me to another door and showed me the way downstairs to the dressing room area.

Seven hours and 10 minutes after stepping out of my house in the snow this morning, I had finally reached my destination!

After towelling off in a bathroom, I climbed up into the stands of the Keil Center and looked around this wonderful new building. Like the United Center in Chicago, it is absolutely enormous. The colour scheme in the seating area is rather unique: almost pastel in appearance. The first 29 rows are light blue, with dark pink seat-backs and arm rests. Then comes a "Club" level ring of private luxury suites that surrounds the entire ice surface. The 20 rows of upper-level seats are purple and are positioned just beneath the "Penthouse" private boxes that ring the top of the arena. There are 80 suites in total.

A giant Blues logo envelopes the entire center-ice faceoff circle with the words "Keil Center: Inaugural Season 1995" painted around the circle. Overhead, there are seven St. Louis Blues division championship banners, including the three from 1968-70 that I mentioned earlier.

Banners representing the club's four retired jerseys hang from the rafters: in honour of Brian Sutter (#11) and Bernie Federko (#24), and in memory of Bob Gassoff (#3) and Barclay Plager (#8). There is also a banner with a green cloverleaf and the initials D.K. commemorating the late Dan Kelly — long-time voice of the Blues and one of hockey's all-time great radio and TV broadcasters. Kelly died of cancer in 1989.

Not to be outdone at the Keil Center is the St. Louis Ambush of the North American Indoor Soccer League. There's a banner depicting the Ambush's 1993-94 NAISL division championship and another one that says: "SLOBO ILIJEVS-KI 30" — honouring the club's all-star goalie and a fan-favourite who retired two years ago. St. Louis University's involvement through the years in the N.I.T. and NCAA basketball tournaments is also memorialized with a series of pennants at the other end of the arena.

When the Maple Leafs finished their skate, I went into the dressing room in search of Pat Burns. The visitor's quarters here are nothing to write home about and Burns was not at all enamoured with his little office, particularly the bare cement walls. The Leaf coach has come under fire lately for his perceived impatience with the media, and was taken to task by columnist Steve Simmons in last Friday's Toronto *Sun*. Simmons reacted to the general atmosphere around the Leaf dressing room following Thursday night's victory over Anaheim. In his column, he noted the not-so-subtle differences between this year's underachieving Maple Leaf team and the previous two that Burns coached. Simmons wrote:

> *The tension around Maple Leaf Gardens is so thick these days, Garth Butcher couldn't cut it with his stick. The tension is almost everywhere,* starting with the guy in charge.
>
> *Pat Burns, the coach who once walked around the Gardens in all his splendour — leaving little doubt as to who was in control — now bolts from press conference to corridor to office like a frightened rabbit. His post-game question-and-answer session lasted all of 52 seconds last night before he chose to end it in a childish huff. The old Burns' volatility remains; the sensibility is now open to debate.*
>
> *Burns, as much as anyone, was responsible for the rise of the Maple Leafs these past two seasons. But now you can feel it... from his tension (that) he also feels responsible for the team that struggles in search of some kind of identity.*
>
> *...Burns is running, rather than facing the music: a curious attitude that's been passed on to his players. Burns is full of excuses, but not answers. Or patience.*

When I read Steve's column on Friday and saw Burns referred to as a "frightened rabbit", I winced at the probable reaction of the Maple Leaf coach. Knowing Burns, he'd accept that description as heartily as the Pope would a charge of sacrilege.

"I don't know where Steve's coming from with that one," he told me as we chatted in the visitor's coaching office. "I've always been open to that gentleman and now he's accusing me of being distant. What he probably doesn't realize is that I had a temperature of 101 after the game the other night and didn't feel too well. So, sure, there are times when you go into a press conference and want to get it over with.

"After the Anaheim game, the questions weren't coming that quickly so I said, 'That's it' and I left. But, the next day, I felt better."

The image of Burns "running" from his media responsibilities in this difficult season is one he simply does not accept.

"I've never run from anything in my life and I don't intend to now," he insisted. "When you're a cop for 16 years in a tough area like I was, you can't run from any situation. I always stood up to the media challenge during my years in Montreal, and it was a lot tougher in that city. So, I don't believe I'm ducking the press in Toronto."

What Burns *is* doing rather frequently this season is answering one question with another. And, as such, he appears to be on the defensive. For instance, when asked why he feels Doug Gilmour is struggling, he'll reply, "Well, why are other top players around the league — like Mark Messier or Sergei Fedorov — also having bad years?" Or, if somebody points out the obvious fact that the Maple Leafs aren't living up to expectations, he'll say, "With the exception of Pittsburgh, Quebec and Detroit, who is? Sure, we want to win the Stanley Cup but there are 25 other teams that have the same idea. I'd like to know how many teams are going to finish four, five or six games over .500? I don't think there'll be too many. We're not the only inconsistent club in the NHL."

Considering that tone of conversation, when a writer like Simmons implies that Burns is lacking for answers this season, he's not too far off the mark. Problem is, nobody seems to have any solutions.

The rain had subsided when I walked outside after practice and I was able to get my first detailed look at the Keil Center. Dominating the northeast corner of 14th St. and Clarke Ave., the exterior of the new arena is magnificent — its 80-foot-high main entrance, composed of 600 panes of glass, stretches for an entire block. The arena rests on the former site of the Keil Auditorium, built in 1932 as the Municipal Auditorium, and re-named 11 years later in honour of ex-St. Louis mayor Henry W. Keil. The new hockey palace came in close to budget at $135.3 million and is adjoined to the soon-to-be-renovated Keil Opera House.

The Maple Leafs are staying in the Hyatt Hotel at Union Station on this trip. Located three blocks west of the Keil Center, the former St. Louis train station has been renovated and converted into a three-level atrium of shops and restaurants. The hotel is right in the mall and its inner rooms — like the one I have today — actually look out onto the shopping concourse. The cavernous Grand Hall of the old train station, six stories in height, is now the main lobby of the hotel and it has a cathedral-like appearance. The station opened in September, 1894, and during the "golden age" of train travel (1920s through the early '50s), 100,000 passengers a day would pass through its grand bastioned gates. Train travel inside the building ceased in October, 1978.

This is my first trip to St. Louis since April, 1990, when the Maple Leafs hooked up with the Blues in a first-round playoff series. They played again in the 1993 post-season but I missed that round while recovering from abdominal surgery. The 1990 match-up was terribly lop-sided, as the Blues breezed to a five-game triumph. It became secondary when Maple Leaf owner Harold Ballard died in Toronto the day before his club was eliminated. I'll never forget the phone ringing as I closed my overnight bag for the return trip to Missouri. It was our news director Scott Metcalfe calling from the radio station to inform me of Ballard's demise. We debated whether or not I should go back to St. Louis before agreeing, quite sensibly, that the now-stilled Leaf owner wouldn't have much to say. And the players were already in the Gateway City — having chartered out earlier in the afternoon.

The entire debacle in the immediate months before Ballard's death is something I'll always remember covering for the radio station. While the formerly bombastic proprietor of Maple Leaf Gardens lay weakened in a Miami hospital — his circulatory system nearing complete arrest — there ensued a triangular legal skirmish involving his three children, several Gardens' directors believed to be the rightful executors of his estate, and Ballard's pretentious female companion, Yolanda MacMillan. Inherent control of Maple Leaf Gardens and all its riches was said to be at stake during the frequently bizarre court battle.

I'll not soon forget dashing after silly Yolanda with my tape machine rolling as she fled the courthouse in various stages of manic-hysteria. Upon confronting her in the underground parking facility, she would launch into melodramatic homilies about the blasphemous treatment of her Harold. The Ballard children — Mary Elizabeth (Flynn), Bill and Harold Jr. — all of whom had been bitterly estranged from their father at one time or another, would then lay *their* claim on his millions. Mary Elizabeth once broke into a sobbing fit outside the courthouse as she extolled the paternal virtues of a man who often wanted nothing to do with her. It was *all* about money... and much of it outrageously so.

In many ways, it was also a fitting conclusion to the most inept and frightful ownership tenure in Maple Leaf history. My gosh, when I think back to some of the shlock this hockey club unloaded on Toronto's indulgent fans, it makes me wonder why I ever embraced the team so seriously. The other day, I was thumbing through a Leaf program from the 1981-82 season and all I could think to myself was, "Oy vay!" Apart from a duo of legitimate stars — Rick Vaive and Bill Derlago — that club relied on skaters like Don Luce, Rene Robert and Billy Harris (all five years past their prime), plus Rocky Saganiuk, Normand Aubin, Fred Boimistruck, Jim Korn, Ron Zanussi and Barry Melrose (none of whom ever *had* a prime). Is it any wonder the '81-82 Maple Leafs failed to qualify for the playoffs — winning only 20 of their 80 regular-season games?

The Hall of Fame parade continued the following year with notables like Frank Nigro, Russ Adam, Ken Strong, Reed Bailey, Viteslav Duris, Serge Boisvert, and the ever-lovable Paul Higgins.

I still crack up when I put on a videotape I made of a late-night sportscast in December of that season from CFTO-TV (Channel 9). While the Leafs were being trounced in St. Louis to extend a club-record 27-game winless streak on the road, Fergie Olver launched into a rambling, incoherent denunciation of the team that lasted almost four minutes. As was his custom back then, Fergie threw the script out the window and went off on a tangent. The easiest job in the CFTO building some nights belonged to the auto-cue operator, who often had time for a nap.

During this particular diatribe, Olver began by chatting with news anchor Ken Shaw. If ever there was an illustration of the general discontent felt by Leaf fans during that era, this was it. Here's what transpired — word-for-word:

OLVER: Mike Nykoluk popped off and called us a few names, but so what... that's nothing.

SHAW: And you've been quiet since then.

OLVER: So we've been quiet. But, y'know, I've watched the Leafs now for the past 14 years, and 13 of those years, they have been in a rebuilding program... and they'll be in a re-building program I think for another 13 years. But, really, these past couple of weeks, I think I've let my feelings get carried away because I want the Leafs to do well and I thought what the heck, we're sitting here, we're knocking the Leafs consistently every night... let's just forget about knocking them. Let's just sit back and let them go out and try and play hockey and see what they can do. And, uh, we didn't do anything.

So, um, I'm not going to knock them tonight... all I'm gonna tell you is that they're losing 7-3 in the third period in

St. Louis. I did say on the early show tonight that I thought that if the Leafs were to snap that 27-game (winless) streak on the road, tonight would be the night, because the St. Louis Blues were a struggling hockey club as well. As a matter of fact, the Leafs led 2-1 after the first period and then in the second period, St. Louis came out and scored three goals and the rest is history... they've never looked back in that game, and they are leading 7-3.

But, um... we're not going to criticize the organi... y'know, it's ridiculous to go on about the Toronto Maple Leafs... it's a sad, sad situation that we have to, as sportscasters and sportswriters... and then Ballard, if you say something wrong about the Toronto Maple Leafs, or... I noticed Nora MacAbe wrote a story in the *Globe* criticizing Paul Higgins... I'm not saying that story was called for; Paul Higgins really, and I don't mean this to be a personal thing, is a nothing on the hockey club... he is an enforcer. But, uh, really, to write a story like that on Paul Higgins... I can't blame Ballard for getting upset I suppose, but nevertheless, he shouldn't be barring sportscasters or sportswriters from Maple Leaf Gardens... but it's the old story: he's the majority shareholder down there... I guess he can allow anyone that he wants into the Gardens.

But it is unfortunate: the whole Toronto Maple Leaf situation. And he did say, Harold Ballard, that, uh, he was going to keep Mike Nykoluk till the end of the season. And I really think that in order for this hockey club to turn around — and I mean this sincerely — uh, Mike Nykoluk... I think he's a great guy, I've always said that... heck, I used to go to the races the odd time with Mike as a matter of fact... but, I don't think he's a hockey coach. I really mean that. He's just too nice with these guys, and they need somebody in there... and I was a firm believer that Punch Imlach should be the guy... uh, I thought that when Punch was there and, of course, Punch had the problems with Darryl Sittler and some of the other players on the club... they didn't like him because he was too tough.

All Punch wanted to do was win games... and he didn't have the talent there... he tried to make some changes, and Sittler and the rest of the gang didn't like it, uh, they didn't like

Imlach... they thought he was 98 years old, that hockey had by-passed him a long time ago. But the truth of the matter is, hockey did not by-pass Punch Imlach... I think that the Toronto Maple Leafs by-passed Imlach when they shouldn't have... he was the one guy — I think, personally — that could've turned that hockey club around. And they really didn't stick with him and give him the chance to continue in the building... re-building program that, uh, he was doing.

I thought he made a great trade in getting Vaive and Derlago... ah, he made a couple of bad ones... you take a guy like Boutette, what the heck, he didn't play before Imlach got here and, uh, he went to Hartford, scored a lot of goals... y'know, who's to predict that?

But, um... ahhhh, it's ridiculous even talking about the Toronto Maple Leafs.

An all-time Fergie classic!

In 1983-84, the Maple Leafs sported luminaries such a Pat Graham, Rich Costello (the phenom acquired from Philadelphia in the Darryl Sittler trade), Fred Perlini and Greg Britz. Yech!

It puts the word "struggling" into some form of perspective when referring to this year's edition of the Leafs. Parade routes would have been cordoned off by this stage of the season had one of those dreadful squads of the early '80s been a legitimate .500 team. Dividing wins and losses nowadays, of course, is tantamount to failure.

So, St. Louis reminds me of Harold Ballard and I suppose it always will. On those two playoff trips in 1990, the Maple Leafs stayed at the downtown Marriott Pavilion Hotel, which is comprised of a main building and a tower. I arrived at night on the first trip and was given a room high up in the tower — on the 17th or 18th floor. The next morning, I pulled open my curtains and gasped in amazement. Down below and across a narrow road was giant Busch Stadium, home of the St. Louis Cardinals. With a running start, I could have practically leapt out of the hotel and into the bowl of the enormous ballpark.

It started raining again here in St. Louis today so there wasn't much to do other than visit some of the shops and relax in the hotel. I walked over to the Keil Center around 5:30 and had a bite to eat in the media lounge, then went up to the press box on this mammoth freight elevator. There are actually two of these enormous lifts in the hallway outside the lounge; 60 or 70 people could probably pile in at the same time. Keil Center architects didn't plan on using the media as freight, it just worked out that way. Public elevators are on the opposite side of the building from the press box.

The media location here is similar to that of the San Jose Arena. It's way up in the rafters, but the sightlines are good, and the radio and TV booths are overly spacious.

St. Louis won tonight's hockey game — literally — during a near-record scoring outburst in the first period. The Blues came out flying and stormed Damian Rhodes in the Maple Leaf goal, building an early 11-2 advantage in shots. But Rhodes was brilliant on a couple of St. Louis powerplays, stoning Brett Hull and Esa Tikkanen in particular, and the game somehow remained scoreless. The dam, however, could not withstand the ongoing force and it finally caved in on the Maple Leafs.

Brendan Shanahan, ex-Leaf Glenn Anderson, and Brett Hull scored in a 58-second splurge near the midway mark of the period — inciting an eruption of noise at the Keil Center — and the Blues bolted to a 3-0 lead. The fans hadn't sat down from cheering the previous goal when the next one went in. The scoring spree came within two seconds of tying the St. Louis team record for fastest three goals — a 56-second binge against Atlanta at the old Arena, Dec. 19, 1978. Brian Sutter, Bob Hess and Jack Brownschidle did the damage on that occasion.

The Maple Leaf defence — easily penetrable — was reeling after the quick-strike attack which inflated the St. Louis shot advantage to 14-2. It was the fourth consecutive game in which the Blues have scored the first three goals and the Leafs appeared dreadfully vulnerable to further damage. Could the bleeding be stopped?

In this case... yes. And it took a similar quick strike from the Leafs to do it. Dave Andreychuk converted Mike Ridley's centring pass to put Toronto on the board, and Doug Gilmour tapped in a Mats Sundin feed 44 seconds later, silencing the St. Louis crowd. In spite of being overwhelmingly outplayed, the Maple Leafs were back to within one of the Blues with 7:34 remaining in the first period.

"That was Toronto's fastest two goals ever at the Keil Center," cracked a press box comedian after Gilmour's tally.

All five markers had been scored in a 5:57 span.

Maple Leaf defenceman Garth Butcher hammered on Ian Laperriere of the Blues during a one-sided slugfest in the last minute of the period. Butcher rubbed Laperriere into the end boards then came back at him with fists flying. It was the sort of nastiness we used to witness from Butcher when he played for St. Louis *against* the Leafs a few years ago. But, there hasn't been a lot of it so far this season.

*   *   *   *   *   *

Back in the 1983-84 campaign, my first in possession of a Maple Leaf media pass, I remember sitting in the press box at the Gardens and observing as former Leaf publicity director Stan Obodiac tormented this highly agitated visitor from St. Louis. The mostly bald man wore iron-rimmed glasses, and his face was the colour of ripened tomatoes. At the time, I wouldn't have known Ronald Caron if I fell over him, but I soon discovered that Obodiac was teasing the general manager of the Blues.

This made little sense when considering the impeccable decorum of other hockey executives I'd observed that year. If an opposing G.M. got mad at something that happened on the ice, he might rise from his chair and stomp quietly back and forth in the press box. Occasionally, a G.M. (like Lou Nanne of Minnesota) would storm onto the steel loft extending from the press box to confront an NHL officiating supervisor. But never would someone launch into a profanity laced conniption like this person from St. Louis. It was absolutely unreal.

As time went on, I grew accustomed to the Caron tantrums and would sit next to him during games in Toronto to try and keep him away from our radio broadcast location. He had an impulsive penchant for sticking his neck between Joe Bowen and Bill Watters to voice his disapproval in the middle of the play. Our listeners along the *Telemedia* network would be subjected to this raving maniac frequently interrupting the action.

What made Caron's outbursts all the more unusual was his immediate return to normalcy after the game. Within mere seconds of the final buzzer, and often regardless of the outcome, his blood-pressure would regulate... normal flesh tones would re-appear, and Caron would become the engaging gentleman he truly is. A remarkable metamorphosis.

But, man, could he fly off the handle!

He'd become annoyed at a supposed indiscretion that went unnoticed by the referee and would instantly want to maim everyone in the Toronto organization. "I'll beat the shit out of all of them!" he'd yell. Then he would fix his eyes on Ballard and King Clancy sitting in Ballard's famous bunker at the north end of the Gardens and say things like, "Look at the two seniles down there." It was extremely difficult not to fall over in hysterics.

On one occasion, however, I *did* lose it.

In the late-summer of 1984, just prior to his first training camp with the Leafs, defenceman Al Iafrate got into an automobile mishap on the 401 in which he knocked over a light standard. Luckily, he was not seriously injured and during a game with the Blues later that year, he became involved in a shoving match with a St. Louis player. Angry, Caron rose from his seat in the press box, leaned out over the glass, and shouted, "Iafrate, go break some lamps!!" I thought my insides would burst.

Along with providing unintentional humour, Caron could get wild. I'll never forget strolling through the Gardens press box during a St. Louis visit in the late 80s and noticing the Blues' G.M. chatting with Steve Simmons, apparently oblivious to the action down below. Suddenly — as a cheer erupted from the Toronto crowd — Caron bolted out of his chair, grabbed it, and slammed it down in front of him, almost killing Simmons. The Leafs had scored a gift goal on a St. Louis defensive zone turnover and Caron believed his player had been hooked to the ice.

During the 1990 playoff series with the Leafs, Caron's private box at St. Louis Arena was right next door to our radio broadcast location: providing the Blues' G.M. with quick access to Bowen and Watters. Once again, I left my own seat in the press box and stood guard between the radio booth and Caron. Every time he'd become upset at either the Leafs or the officiating, Caron would lean forward from his seat and give us the choke sign through a window that separated our booths. He looked like an absolute mad-man, and Bowen would just shake his head.

Finally, something happened on the ice that prompted Caron to get up and storm out of his booth and I quickly moved over to our broadcast entrance, knowing full well what he was up to. As Caron tried to enter, I made myself rigid, but he threw me out of the way and stomped towards Bowen and Watters, screaming at the top of his lungs. Bowen got up from his seat in the middle of the action and tried to shoe away the unruly G.M., and it seemed like they might come to blows. I then had no other choice but to intervene physically and remove Caron from the premises myself. It was no easy chore, as he continued going berserk, and tried to resist my efforts. I remember thinking, "What do I need this for? I'm supposed to be covering the hockey game." It was unreal.

During the 1991 playoffs, Caron lost his temper and kicked a hole in the back wall of the Chicago Stadium press box. And in the '93 post-season series between the Blues and Maple Leafs, *Hockey Night In Canada* cameras made a point of focusing on Caron every time something weighty happened during the action. Usually, they got the desired results, as the St. Louis G.M. would be standing up and gesticulating. A movement among various NHL teams to have Caron banned from their press boxes gained momentum in his latter years as G.M. and he was positioned in a private holding elsewhere in the arenas. Towards the end of his tenure, he curtailed his travel plans to other NHL cities.

I'm told that Caron's hysterics did not coincide with his appointment as G.M. of the Blues in 1983-84. In fact, he was every bit as maniacal in the

Montreal Forum press box during his long association with the Habs, for whom he served 28 years as chief scout and assistant to long-time G.M. Sam Pollock.

"Oh, that's true, but Sam liked it that way," Caron laughed as we chatted during the first intermission at the Keil Center tonight. "It's hard to be involved with the game so closely and not be emotional... at least it was for me. Even though I was the G.M., I watched the game as if I were the coach. I felt very much involved in the action."

Caron's job as the ultimate decision maker on the Blues changed last summer when Mike Keenan came aboard as G.M. and head coach. He was assigned to the ancillary position of executive vice-president — more-or-less a consultant's role. During his 12-year stint in charge of the organization, the Blues made it as far as the Stanley Cup semifinals on one occasion (1985-86), losing a dynamic seven-game series to Calgary. Otherwise, it's not unfair or inaccurate to say that Caron's St. Louis teams underachieved for the most part. Particularly when you consider the number of drastic personnel changes he made. Admirably, he never stood pat after a disappointing season, but his frequent rolls of the dice turned up snake-eyes more often than not.

Caron made a great deal acquiring Brett Hull from Calgary in 1988, even though the Flames won the Stanley Cup the following year. He also looked good in several other moves — swapping aging veterans Bernie Federko and Tony McKegney to Detroit for Adam Oates; signing free agent goaltender Curtis Joseph, and trading Tony Hrkac and over-the-hill Greg Millen to Quebec for defenceman Jeff Brown.

But his trade-deadline deal in March, 1991 spelled the beginning of the end for Caron. He swapped Geoff Courtnall, Sergio Momesso, Cliff Ronning and Robert Dirk to Vancouver, for Garth Butcher and Dan Quinn.[1] All but Dirk continue to play instrumental roles for the Canucks, while Butcher and Quinn are long gone from St. Louis. Later in 1991, he took a chance by signing Brendan Shanahan as a Group 1 free agent from New Jersey and lost Scott Stevens — perhaps the NHL's best defenceman — to the Devils as compensation.

Caron's trading of Rod Brind'Amour to Philadelphia for Ron Sutter and Murray Baron, and the contract squabble that sent Oates to Boston for Craig Janney were big mistakes. As was the free agent signing late in 1993-94 of enigmatic Petr Nedved from Vancouver that ultimately cost St. Louis Jeff Brown, Bret Hedican and Nathan LaFayette. Really, the Canucks owe Caron a profuse debt of gratitude for their unexpected trip to the Stanley Cup final last season.

---

[1] Ed. note: During the '95 NHL draft in Edmonton, July 8, Momesso was traded to the Maple Leafs for Mike Ridley. Courtnall re-signed with the Blues as a free agent the following week.

"There were ups and downs during the years," Caron acknowledges. "But, for an organization that didn't participate in the draft my first year (1983), we fared not too badly."

Caron refers to the bizarre circumstance in which the pet food company Ralston Purina divested itself in ownership of the Blues just prior to the '83 entry draft. With rampant speculation the franchise would be moved to Saskatoon (with Don Cherry as head coach), the Blues were essentially non-existent for a short time, and did not staff their table on the draft floor at the Montreal Forum. When NHL executive vice-president Brian O'Neill — following due process — called for them to select, the Blues, of course, did not answer and their draft position was passed on to the next team in line. Had they participated, they'd have been in line to select players the calibre of Tom Barrasso, John MacLean and Cam Neely. Instead, St. Louis wound up with nothing.

Now 65, Caron is under contract to the Blues as a consultant for the next four years and he currently spends much of his time scouting prospects in the organization. For his milestone birthday in December, the club bought him a motorized golf cart with a Blue note on the side. His decreased workload will enable him to participate in his two other favourite pastimes: golfing and watching baseball.

With a lesser role in the organization, Caron insists he no longer becomes frenzied while watching the Blues play. "I don't have the final responsibility for winning or losing anymore so it's much more relaxing during games," he explains. "I maintain the right to be rationally disappointed if the team loses, but I don't fly off the handle."

However, when I relayed this information to hockey writer Dave Leuking of the St. Louis *Post-Dispatch* tonight, he rolled his eyes and suggested I poke my head into Caron's booth during the second period. I did so and wouldn't you know it, the former G.M. was bouncing off the walls just like always. "Chasse, don't be stupid! Look, he's too high, did you see that?" he thundered to a hapless person seated next to him as the Blues' rookie committed an error.

Some things will simply never change.

* * * * * *

Incredibly, neither the Blues nor the Maple Leafs scored another goal tonight after their five-goal outburst in the first period. Leafs had two glorious opportunities. Kent Manderville could not find the puck at his feet with a wide open St. Louis goal staring at him in the second period. And Dave Andreychuk tipped a Todd Gill point drive just inches wide of the net in the third. Otherwise, the lasting moment of tonight's game was probably Warren Rychel's pitch-forking of

Denis Chasse early in the final frame. Rychel speared Chasse in the chest as the St. Louis player circled in his own end and got a five-minute major and game misconduct. After writhing in apparent agony for a moment or two, Chasse made a miraculous recovery and was back on the ice for his next shift. No, he is not Russian.

Pat Burns pulled Damian Rhodes for a sixth attacker with 1:04 left on the clock, but the Maple Leafs didn't threaten to tie the score.

Had Rhodes not been so sharp, the Blues would have mounted a lop-sided victory. St. Louis poured 41 shots at the Toronto net. The loss snapped the Maple Leafs' mini two-game win streak and prevented them from climbing into a second-place tie with the Blues and Chicago in the Central Division. Leafs are now a paltry 2-6-2 on the road this season.

After the game, Leaf coach Burns half-joked that his players were distracted by the surroundings. "We were impressed by the Keil Center in the first 10 minutes, I guess," he said, tongue-in-cheek. "We just stood around and watched, and you can't be absent in the NHL for that long a time and expect to win a hockey game. It was disappointing."

Meanwhile, Damian Rhodes continues to draw speculation that he'll be dealt to Edmonton as part of a package that would bring the Leafs coveted defenceman Bryan Marchment. "I don't know if they're showing me around, or what," the netminder mused after the game. "You look around the league, and it doesn't seem like a lot of teams need goalies.

"I can't fathom being traded because I really don't want to play anywhere else."

*　　*　　*　　*　　*　　*

Another five-game homestand began with a sloppy 4-3 loss to San Jose, in which the Maple Leafs blew a 2-0 second-period lead. The good old "period of death" reared its ugly head once again, as the Sharks scored three times in the middle frame and outshot Toronto 15-9. Leafs were slapstick at times, as Doug Gilmour's drive at an empty net wound up hitting teammate Mike Gartner in the back. Ulf Dahlen scored the game winner with only 4:33 left in regulation, as Leaf defenceman Todd Gill fell down in his own zone while trying to corral a high flip pass. Dahlen had a breakaway and bounced the puck in off the post. After the game, an annoyed Pat Burns talked about blowing the two-goal lead. "I don't know if we sit on our laurels and think we're the cat's ass," he said. "But, we're the donkey's ass right now."

A couple of nights later, the Maple Leafs won for the first time this season when trailing after two periods. Unanswered goals by Randy Wood and Dave

Andreychuk in the third frame lifted Toronto past Calgary 3-2 in one of the better games at the Gardens this season. Wood tipped in Garth Butcher's point shot while the Leafs were shorthanded, and Andreychuk scored on a powerplay deflection of Todd Gill's drive midway through the period. Sandy McCarthy came close on two occasions to tying the game for Calgary. He was robbed by Damian Rhodes' glove, and later missed an open net. Andreychuk had the other Leaf goal in the first.

The Maple Leafs went up 3-0 on Dallas in their next home outing, then held on for a 3-2 victory. The match came down to a battle of faceoffs in the Toronto zone between Mike Eastwood and ex-Leaf Peter Zezel. With Andy Moog on the bench for an extra attacker in the final minute, Eastwood beat Zezel on the draw three consecutive times to help preserve the triumph. Zezel had missed a tremendous opportunity to tie the score only moments earlier, when Jamie Macoun deflected his shot at a wide-open net. The popular former Leaf whizzed a slapshot under the crossbar for Dallas's first goal early in the second period. Kenny Jonsson showed great confidence by coming off the boards with the puck and cutting in on Moog to give Leafs a 3-0 lead. A lucky bounce prevented Mike Ridley from putting the puck in his own net in the dying moments. He inadvertently cleared a rebound directly off the left goalpost behind Felix Potvin. Dixon Ward of the Leafs had a dandy scrap with Dallas rookie Todd Harvey in front of the Stars' bench late in the middle period. Both players landed numerous punches.

Banners honouring former Maple Leaf goaltending greats Turk Broda and Johnny Bower were raised to the rafters in a pre-game ceremony on March 11. The Leafs and Chicago then played to a 2-2 tie, thanks mainly to Blackhawk goalie Jeff Hackett. Subbing for the injured Ed Belfour, Hackett stopped 38 of 40 Leaf shots in a tremendous performance. In the final minute of regulation, Dave Andreychuk found himself all alone in front of Hackett, but the Chicago goalie brilliantly snared his attempt at winning the match and sent it into overtime. Doug Gilmour converted Mats Sundin's pass from the corner to tie the game midway through the third period. Sundin had the other Leaf goal — his 12th of the season.

MONDAY, MARCH 13th
Toronto

At least one of the six hockey playing Sutters has been in the NHL since 1976-77, when Brian joined the St. Louis Blues. Not one of the famed brothers from Viking, Alta. has ever been a Maple Leaf, however, until today. Cliff Fletcher gave Tampa Bay future considerations for 31-year-old Rich Sutter, a veteran of 13 NHL seasons and six NHL teams. Rich had been a first-round draft choice of Pittsburgh in 1982 — the same year his twin-brother Ron went in the first round to Philadelphia. Generally regarded as the least-skilled of the Sutters, Rich should nonetheless provide the Maple Leafs with the touch of veteran tenacity Pat Burns has been looking for.

"I was surprised and excited when I heard about the trade," Sutter acknowledged. "I never expected to be playing with the Maple Leafs: the team I grew up idolizing."

Sutter will join the Leafs tomorrow in San Jose for their west-coast trip and he didn't see tonight's 4-1 loss to the Kings. Playing one of their most energetic games of the season, the Maple Leafs could not solve their nemesis, Kelly Hrudey, who was both good and lucky in goal for L.A. In yet another fabulous game at the Gardens, Hrudey had Leaf shots ringing off goalposts and crossbars all night long, while he flopped around innately to make a variety of terrific saves. The Leafs outgunned Los Angeles 41-20, but had nothing to show for it.

It's uncanny how the Kings can't play worth a damn at home this season but are able to constantly out-spook the Leafs here in Toronto. Really, it began during Game 7 of the Campbell Conference championship in 1993 when the Leafs buzzed the L.A. zone much of the night but were victimized by sudden, transitional attacks. Ultimately, the Kings wrapped up the Conference title with some magic, as Wayne Gretzky — marvellous all night long — banked the winning goal off Dave Ellett's skate while attempting a pass-out from behind the net.

Another such oddity occurred early in the third period tonight, with Los Angeles clinging precariously to a 2-1 lead. Dmitri Mironov fired a slapshot at Hrudey that caromed off the inside of the goalie's right pad, changed directions, and clanged off the left goalpost. If you cleared the ice and asked Mironov to try and duplicate that carom, it would probably take six days. The moment, however, was a microcosm of the Maple Leafs' enduring struggles tonight.

"A lot of those shots would beat (Hrudey) and the guys said it was like they were turning around in mid-air," Burns moaned after the game. "It's very, very frustrating but we just have to bear with it and hope we get enough points to make the playoffs."

There was plenty of irony at the Gardens tonight, and none of it favourable to the Leafs. Back on Oct. 3 — two days after the lockout began — Cliff Fletcher and Kings' G.M. Sam McMaster swapped minor-leaguers in a seven-player deal. The Leafs acquired Dixon Ward, Kelly Fairchild, Guy Leveque and Kerry

Toporwoski, for Yanic Perreault, Eric Lacroix and Chris Snell. All three L.A. acquisitions were in the line-up tonight, and Lacroix scored the Kings' first goal, his fourth of the season. Meanwhile, Ward, the only Los Angeles castoff to crack the Leaf roster, was placed on waivers early today to make room for Rich Sutter.

A diligent worker who earned respect and popularity in the Maple Leaf dressing room, Ward has chipped in with a mere three assists in 22 games played. The club originally signed him to a minor-league (or two-way) contract, meaning his NHL salary would apply only if he played for the Maple Leafs. He could be assigned to St. John's for far less money, and as the only player with such a contractual provision, he became the odd man out. With his repute among the players, you wonder if the club might have eaten someone else's major-league salary had Ward struck for six or seven goals. As it stands, however, the Leafs were able to make a justifiable financial decision.

Burns made a somewhat questionable remark after practice yesterday when asked about third-year winger Nikolai Borschevsky. With Sutter not arriving in time for tonight's match, the coach noted that Borschevsky would dress in his place and see some action on the club's top line... "because he's all we've got." The less-than enthusiastic remark surely couldn't have thrilled Fletcher, and wasn't exactly an emotional boost for the little-used Russian.

Meanwhile, flooding in northern California forced the Leafs to make a controversial schedule change today. To accommodate the Detroit Red Wings, whose game was postponed Friday night in San Jose, the Leafs flip-flopped Detroit's Apr. 5 visit to the Gardens with a game against St. Louis, originally slated for Apr. 7. The rub, however, is that fans must use their tickets for the game-night indicated, meaning if someone has intentionally purchased seats to watch Detroit, they will now have no other choice but to see the Blues. The re-scheduling allows the Red Wings to play a make-up game in San Jose on Apr. 5, play in Toronto two nights later, then in Chicago on Apr. 9.

It does nothing for the loyal ticket purchasers at the Gardens.

With the entire Leaf organization in somewhat of a snit, the team will now embark on its longest road trip of the season — a four-game, eight-day journey to San Jose, Anaheim, Los Angeles and Vancouver. It will mark the first time the Leafs will play four consecutive games in the Pacific time zone, and will likely have a huge bearing on the rest of their season.

TUESDAY, MARCH 14th
San Jose

For several days now, those of us around the Maple Leafs have been wondering what we might encounter when we land in San Francisco to begin this road trip. Incessant rain-showers have deluged northern California and television news reports are depicting the Silicon Valley as a latter-day Atlantis. Somehow, I can't imagine snorkling from the hotel to the San Jose Arena.

My concerns weren't tempered any by a radio news up-date on my way to Pearson Airport this morning. Two more inches of rain are apparently expected in the San Jose area before tomorrow, and the recent flooding has contaminated much of the city's drinking water. Wonderful. Here in Toronto, we've been basking in an Indian summer the past ten days, with brilliant sunshine and temperatures well above normal. My friends and relatives are actually pitying me for having to travel to California in the middle of March. Imagine.

I made the unintentional mistake of lining up behind Pat Burns at Immigration this morning. The female officer appeared to be grilling the Leaf coach about something that caused Burns to dig into his carry-on luggage. After a moment of prodding, Burns retrieved a colour photo of himself and signed it to the gushing officer. Standing in the line next to me, Damian Rhodes looked over and we both smiled. Ol' Burnsy had that lady so enchanted, he probably could have smuggled half-a-pound of cocaine across the border.

A few moments later, I was standing in front of Burns in line at the refreshment counter. Having obtained my usual airport breakfast —a chocolate donut — Burns smiled and said he had seen an article in the newspaper that claimed donuts are a male aphrodisiac. Obviously, then, I was purchasing one at the most inopportune time.

The Leaf coach said he was happy about the acquisition of Rich Sutter, but that he felt badly for Dixon Ward. "It's just a matter of dollars and cents," he explained in reference to Ward's demotion. "I really like that kid. And I'll tell you, there are a couple of other guys I would've rather shipped out of here if all things were equal." Burns is clearly frustrated with several underachieving players. Nikolai Borschevsky and Terry Yake would likely have been unloaded before Ward, if Burns was general manager.

Practically all of the Maple Leaf players were clumped together today near the back of the Air Canada *Boeing*-767 and I initially sat next to Mike Craig, whose left index-finger was wrapped in a splint. Craig said he injured the finger late in last night's game. Hoping to fall asleep during the 5 1/2-hour journey to

135

San Francisco, Craig exchanged seats with Mike Eastwood prior to takeoff. Easty had a window seat a couple of rows ahead of us and nobody was in the chair next to him. Craig went up there and spread out, lapsing into never-never land at once.

A card game almost got going among a group of players, but several of them passed out with no warning. As the jet taxied into position for takeoff, Randy Wood sat a row in front of me with his head tilted back, snoring like a foghorn. "That's what happens when you have kids at home," winked an un-married Eastwood.

Once airborne, Eastwood seemed anxious to commence the card game, but his teammates had all been rendered senseless with fatigue. It was quite a scene, as these brawny athletes were falling over one another in various directions, snoring like a pack of lambs. With no other recourse, Eastwood took to chatting with a lowly member of the media: inquiring as to how this book was coming along. We talked about the new NHL arenas this season and he emphasized how terrible the ice had been at the Keil Center in St. Louis two weeks ago. "You'd think that after spending that much money on a new building, they'd find a way to make reasonable ice," Eastwood griped. "I loved that old building there (the St. Louis Arena). It was definitely my favourite place to play."

The Maple Leafs' fifth-round selection in the 1987 draft, Eastwood has played more-or-less a support role with the club until this season. Adept at winning faceoffs, and with good size (6-foot-3, 205 lbs.), the square-jawed "Easty" is developing into a reliable third-line centerman and is one of the more likeable members of the team. Rumours persist he was born wrapped in a red and white flag, as he made his earthly debut in the nation's capital (Ottawa), July 1, 1967 — Canada's 100th birthday.

A couple of hours into the flight, the aroma of airplane food gently coaxed the Maple Leaf players back to consciousness and when the meal ended, the card game finally got started. Eastwood moved up to the vacated aisle-seat next to Craig, who was still passed-out cold. He, Dave Andreychuk, Jamie Macoun and Drake Berehowsky then got into it and their card encounter lasted the remainder of the flight — almost 3 1/2 hours. Things became a bit heated at one point, as Andreychuk appeared to accuse Berehowsky of trickery, but the young Leaf defenceman voiced his innocence and the game continued.

A bit later, Bob Stellick passed through the cabin from his seat in *Executive Class* and distributed per-diem envelopes to the players. Each Maple Leaf receives $55 per day in the currency of the country where the team is staying. From that, the players must purchase food and incidentals. The stipend is slightly less on game days, when the club convenes for a team-lunch in the hotel. It was quite humorous to watch as practically every player tore into his envelope and counted the money, as if someone in the front office had planned a rip-off.

The movie on the flight was *The River Wild* — starring Meryl Streep — a suspenseful film about a family being terrorized on a white-water rafting expedition. The irony didn't escape me, as I envisioned us careening through flooded San Jose in similar fashion. All the Maple Leafs, except the card sharks, were engrossed in the movie with intense expressions on their faces.

When it ended, we had been flying for almost five hours, and many of the players began to grow restless. Kenny Jonsson rose from his seat a row behind me and briefly watched the endless card game before pacing up and down the aisle. Mike Gartner pulled out coloured action photos of himself and answered a stack of fan mail. Doug Gilmour was stretched out on the opposite side of the plane, listening to music on a portable C-D player. We were all quite ready to land.

The approach to San Francisco was breathtaking once again. Skies in the area were partly cloudy — a relief when considering the gloomy weather forecasts. The aircraft swooped northward over the hills of the East Bay, which were brilliant with emerald foliage after the constant rainshowers. If you've flown over the British Isles in springtime, you have an idea how strikingly green the landscape below us appeared. The captain turned the plane westward over Alameda County, and the Oakland Coliseum was visible out the left side.

We then made our final approach directly over the waters of San Francisco Bay, which can be a somewhat harrowing experience. The east-west runway at San Francisco International protrudes into the Bay and doesn't come into view for passengers until the plane is less than 50 feet above the ground. "Can you swim?" quipped Pat Jablonski, sitting in the window seat behind me. Indeed, it appears certain the aircraft will make a water landing until the very last second.

Jamie Macoun must have been faring rather well in the card game, as he enthusiastically suggested it be continued on the bus ride to San Jose. Not doing quite so well was Drake Berehowsky, who wanted it over with. The two had a mild spat. Moments later, while dawdling around the luggage carousel (San Francisco has the slowest baggage handlers in the civilized world), Dave Andreychuk reached into his pocket, pulled out a Canadian quarter, and placed it on the conveyor belt. With upwards to 75 people crowded around, the mischievous Maple Leaf wanted to see if anybody would go for it. No one took the bait on the first rotation and the coin disappeared through the opening in the wall. However, it did not return the next time around, which perhaps might explain why the luggage takes forever here — the handlers are earning wages so meagre that a prank quarter becomes precious.

When the bags finally arrived, the Leaf players headed outside and were greeted by Bob Landry of *Royal Coach* Bus Lines. A big, husky man with a full beard, Landry drives the Maple Leafs around the Bay Area when they travel out here to play the Sharks. He's an engaging fellow with a thorough knowledge of the region, and the Maple Leaf management and coaches enjoy chatting with him. As the bus approached San Jose 40 minutes after leaving San Francisco airport, Landry pointed out the areas that had been flooded less than a week ago. The Guadalupe River swelled to four or five times its normal level and had the water risen just two feet higher, Landry said it would have spilled over into the terminal and runways of San Jose International Airport, shutting down the facility.

By this afternoon, the river had recessed to near-normal levels, with more rain expected tonight. Streets that had been flooded in the downtown area were still damp, but open to traffic. The surface around the Fairmont Hotel was dry and after checking in to a room on the 17th floor, I was happy to discover that the drinking water was just fine.

The fact San Jose received more rainfall in a four-day period last week than it usually does in an entire year, was still the hot topic in town today. The San Jose *Mercury News* ran a front-page headline about the relentless storm, asking WHY DID IT HIT US SO HARD? The front page of the San Francisco *Chronicle* warned, STORM'S WRATH NOT LETTING UP. Even the local cabbies were in the spirit. The driver who took me to San Jose Arena for the Maple Leaf practice this afternoon went by way of China, showing me the areas that were flooded near the rink. Having not requested the circuitous route, I nonetheless enjoyed the voluntary sojourn and did not complain about the inflated fare.

The Leafs were put through a typical off-day workout at the Arena, beginning around 1:45 p.m. The players began by casually skating around the ice and firing pucks at the two empty nets. Ten minutes later, Pat Burns stopped at the blueline and blew his whistle to officially begin the practice. The Leafs did four laps of the Arena ice at a high rate of speed then turned around and skated in the opposite direction. After slowing, they were led through their stretching exercises by assistant coach Mike Kitchen. Resting their sticks on the back of their shoulders and rotating from side to side, the players loosened their upper-body muscles. They followed up with toe-touches and groin-stretches — all done while skating slowly around the ice. Afterwards, the players went through a series of line rushes and shooting drills.

While viewing the workout with other members of the Toronto media, I was further appraised of the disastrous flooding by Ken Arnold, the Sharks' affable director of media relations. Arnold said it rained so hard last week that a popular restaurant near the Arena called "Henry's High Life" was in ruins. A staple in San Jose for more than 30 years, "Henry's" had been a frequent hangout for the Shark players. "The owner of the place (Lois Reynolds) always took good care of the guys, but her restaurant is all packed with mud," Arnold said. "When it was pouring out last week, her car was washed right out of the parking lot. It got picked up by the tide and carried down the street."

A rumour appearing on wire services in Toronto this afternoon has Burns apparently considering offers from the Ottawa Senators and Los Angeles Kings. Expanding on speculation that started back home a few weeks ago, *SportsTicker* hockey writer Tim Moriarty in New York said Burns might jump to Ottawa next season in the dual role of G.M. and coach, or L.A. as head coach. Burns still has a year remaining on his Maple Leaf contract and would have to be released from that obligation to move elsewhere.

"There's nothing to that... at least, I hope not," Burns said after practice. "But those kinds of things usually happen when a team is struggling like we are this year; a coach either gets fired or he moves down the road. I'd like to stay in Toronto for another year, and then longer if they want me. But again, you've got to win. Everybody gets impatient — the media and the fans — and that's what happens in high-profile hockey towns.

"I went through it in Montreal and I told you guys that when I signed (with the Leafs). I said, 'It's all nice and fine now, but three or four years down the road, if things aren't working, you guys will be campaigning to get someone else in here.'"

So, I suggested that after the prosperity of his first two seasons in Toronto, a Pat Burns-coached team can no longer be satisfied playing .500 hockey. "Oh, for sure... *I'm* not satisfied," he said. "We've got to turn it on here in the second half or it'll be a lost season."

After chatting with Burns, I walked into the Leaf dressing room and it seemed like I had entered a movie theatre. A group of seven or eight players, including Doug Gilmour, Damian Rhodes, Mike Eastwood and Mike Gartner, were sitting at their stalls absolutely mesmerized by a television set mounted high on the wall. They were intently watching the O.J. Simpson murder trial as defence lawyer F. Lee Bailey cross-examined Los Angeles Police Department detective Mark Fuhrman. Bailey accused the officer of planting a blood-stained glove at the murder scene and was trying to establish a discrediting racial theme. The Leaf players were engrossed by Bailey's dramatics and seemed not at all interested in chatting about hockey. Thankfully, Dave Andreychuk walked in, said he could care less about the Simpson trial, and gave me a few moments of his time, discussing the importance of faring well on this four-game western swing.

Around 7:15 tonight, I went down to the hotel lobby and sat in a chair near the main entrance. A few moments later, a yellow cab pulled up and out stepped Rich Sutter, having arrived in San Jose within the previous hour on a flight from Chicago. Strangely, no one from the Toronto organization, including Business Operations Director Bob Stellick, was there to greet the newest member of the team, who had a stack of hockey sticks resting on his shoulder. After checking in, Sutter paused for a few minutes and talked about his trade to the blue and white.

"Obviously I wasn't in Tampa Bay's plans so this move sits very well with me," he said, somewhat annoyed.

Sutter was traded to the Lightning by Chicago last month as part of a five-player deal. He dressed for just four games in a Tampa Bay uniform and was demoted to Atlanta of the International Hockey League a week ago. "This gets me back in the NHL," he said. "I don't know what happened in Tampa, or why the Lightning even traded for me. I sat on the bench for a few games and was shipped out of town. But, I can still play in this league and I plan on contributing to the Maple Leafs."

Moving around is nothing new for Sutter, as the Leafs will be his seventh NHL team. Pittsburgh, Philadelphia, Vancouver, St. Louis, the Blackhawks and Tampa are also on his NHL log.

Many hockey observers have wondered how he felt being traded from Chicago, where his older brother Darryl is head coach. "Well, I'm going stop that talk right there," Rich snapped. "Darryl was not part of the trade and he's tired of hearing about it. In fact, all of my brothers are tired of hearing that story. Darryl and his assistants (Paul Baxter and Rich Preston) had no idea what was going on. They were told about the deal after it happened and were instructed to tell the players. We all realize that hockey is a business, but we're human beings as well, and I think it's obvious how Darryl felt about the trade."

Most of the Sutters were fans of the Maple Leafs while growing up in Viking, Alberta and Rich is looking forward to pulling on a blue and white sweater tomorrow against the Sharks. "It's a big thrill, there's no doubt about it," he said. "As a youngster, I watched Darryl Sittler captain the Leafs and then had the opportunity to play with him for a couple of years in Philadelphia. Probably the happiest member of the family is my oldest brother, Gary, who was a huge Leaf fan growing up. In many ways, it's a dream come true."

I'm finding it increasingly difficult to avoid drunks while on the road these days. When looking for a place to eat tonight, I ran into Mark Hebscher and Eugene McEleney of *Global* outside "Original Joe's" —one of the busiest restaurants in San Jose. They were waiting in line for a table (at 8:15 p.m.) and invited me to join them. As we chatted on the sidewalk outside, a thin black man wobbled over and asked me for 50 cents. This guy was so crocked, he wouldn't have known half-a-buck from half-a-grapefruit and I declined to add to his whisky arsenal. We went into the restaurant and turned around to see our inebriated friend dodging through traffic in the middle of the intersection.

The whole scene was rather sad.

WEDNESDAY, MARCH 15th
San Jose

In spite of ominous warnings, there was not a cloud in the sky above San Jose this morning and the temperature had warmed up to a comfortable 65 degrees. While standing outside the Maple Leaf bus at the hotel, Bob Landry talked about driving professional sports teams around the Bay Area. On our last trip out here in late-January, Landry made two journeys to San Francisco airport. He dropped off the Maple Leafs early on a Sunday morning, then picked up the San Francisco 49ers in nearby Santa Clara for their Super Bowl flight to Miami.

"Generally speaking, the hockey teams are pretty good," admitted Landry. "In fact, I enjoy the Maple Leafs more than anyone else and I'm not just saying that because you're standing here. I'd drive this team anywhere because I'm always made to feel comfortable by the coaches and players. On the other hand, I don't really enjoy the Los Angeles Kings. The players have an arrogance about them that starts with Wayne Gretzky and filters on down. And there's no pleasing that coach (Barry Melrose) either. It seems like I pull up 15 minutes too early or 15 minutes too late. I guess you can't make everyone happy."

Mike Gartner walked by and stepped up onto the bus, saying "Good morning, Bob, gorgeous day out, huh?"

"See what I mean," Landry smiled. "These Maple Leaf players even remember my name from one trip to the next."

Burns got on the bus and glanced over at me with a weighty look. "I think Garth (Butcher) might miss the whole road trip," he lamented, shaking his head. Butcher suffered back spasms at home the other night and could not make the 5 1/2-hour flight out here yesterday. He spent several long hours undergoing therapy with trainer Chris Broadhurst, but was still unable to board this morning's non-stop to San Francisco. After his typically slow start, the veteran defenceman has been playing much better in recent games and the Leafs will miss him if he's out for any length of time.

Another calamity arose last night when Mike Craig's bruised index finger began throbbing with pain. The Leaf training staff took him to hospital for an X-ray and the finger turned out to be broken. So, Craig went back to San Francisco and returned home this morning; he'll likely be out of action for about three weeks. Unfortunately, nothing seems to be bouncing for Craig in his first Maple Leaf season. Playing very well *against* the Leafs while in Minnesota/Dallas, Craig caught the attention of Cliff Fletcher, and the Leaf G.M. took a chance by signing him as a free agent last summer. But the 23-year-old winger — a member of the 1990 Canadian World Junior Hockey champions — seems not to be a Pat Burns type. He hasn't yet played with nearly the tenacity he showed in Minnesota and Dallas and, more importantly, he isn't scoring.

Fletcher lost Peter Zezel to the Stars in compensation for Craig and right now, that swap isn't favouring the Leafs. Apart from being a premier faceoff man, Zezel was quite popular in the Maple Leaf dressing room and he centred a stable checking unit with Mark Osborne and Bill Berg. Osborne is now playing in New York, and Burns has yet to discover a facsimile of that forward line. The Leafs did gain six years of youth in the transaction but it simply will not benefit Toronto unless Craig finds his scoring touch later this season.

On the bus ride to the Arena for today's morning skate, the talk once again surrounded the O.J. Simpson trial. As a former cop, Burns is having trouble accepting what the defence is trying to do with Fuhrman. "How do you just come out and call somebody a racist?" he asked. "It's all so much bullshit. If the trial wasn't on TV, the judge wouldn't even bother to hear such ridiculous charges. He'd say to hell with it."

While the Maple Leafs were getting ready for their skate, I went into the San Jose dressing room, hoping to talk with Craig Janney. He became a Shark last week when St. Louis traded him here for defenceman Jeff Norton. Blues' G.M./coach Mike Keenan had no use for the 27-year-old center, whom he felt played with a scarcity of focus and desire, despite accomplished numbers as a playmaker. Since breaking into the NHL with Boston after the 1988 Winter Olympics, Janney has been a bit of a wing-nut in his dealings with the media, and my expectations weren't exactly soaring before today's encounter.

He was working on his sticks for tonight's game in the trainer's room as I patiently awaited for him to emerge. When he finally did, Ken Arnold asked him if he had a few moments for me.

"No, I'm busy," he barked, storming past the two of us.

Arnold looked over and shrugged his shoulders. However, just as I turned to leave, Janney re-appeared and said, "Okay, *now* I have time."

Maintaining his relative silence on the Mike Keenan issue, Janney said, "I'm tired of thinking about that situation; it's in the past and I obviously didn't enjoy my time in St. Louis. Now I'm in San Jose, and I think I'll prove that I can still be an effective player in the NHL. One man shouldn't be able to ruin another man's career."

Janney's former linemate in St. Louis, Brett Hull, didn't concur with Keenan's assessment. "That's the coach's comment, it's not coming from us," Hull told The *Hockey News* during Janney's exile. "As players, we are right behind Craig. We know what he has done in the past and we know what he can still do. I wish he was here. He's a good friend, a good teammate and a quality person."

Janney accumulated 180 assists in two-plus seasons with the Blues, including a career-high 82 in the 1992-93 season.

Pat Burns had a little fun with the media during his post-skate session this morning. Burns, Harry Neale, myself and Mark Hebscher all wound up doing Paul Morris imitations. Morris is the P.A. announcer at Maple Leaf Gardens and something of a fixture at hockey games. The coach still can't believe (as can any of us) that Morris — an electronics engineer — is unable to pronounce the word "SONY". One of the most prominent sound and video companies in the world is often referred to as "Sawny" by Morris during his Maple Leaf Gardens promotional announcements. Mind boggling!

Doug Gilmour was at it again after today's skate. "Killer" may not be having the best season of his career, but he hasn't slacked off in the prankster department. He's in the habit lately of making me out to be homosexual in the presence of the other players. All in good fun, of course. For instance, if I'm standing near the shower room waiting for a player to emerge, he'll yell out, "Stop looking at our asses, Howie." I'll shake my head and he'll stand there buck-naked with that toothless grin. Today, I was interviewing Rich Sutter in the hallway outside the Maple Leaf dressing room. Sutter talks so quietly, that I practically had the microphone pressing against his tonsils. Gilmour was standing about 15 feet away, working on one of his sticks for tonight's game, and he barked "Get that microphone out of my butt Howie" loud enough to fuck up the whole interview. He then cackled with delight when I played back the tape and realized it was unusable. Somehow, though, it's impossible to get mad at the little varmint.

For the first time this season, however, Gilmour's performance came under question from Pat Burns in a public forum. Responding to a query from Sharks' radio colourman Chris Collins, Burns replied, "Well, there's not much I can do... I can just keep putting him out there. He has all the skill and talent available and he's working hard. If he wasn't working, I'd have to address it, but that's not a problem. And, like I keep on saying, there's a lot of good players around the league who are also struggling.

"So, the reason for it (Gilmour's problems), nobody seems to know. We're going to keep on putting him over the boards and hope he breaks out of it. Dougie's a pretty conscientious guy when it comes to effort and as long as he's working, I'm sure the goals and assists will come."

Returning to the Leaf line-up tonight will be winger Bill Berg, who has missed the past 16 games with the knee injury he suffered when the Sharks were in Toronto, Feb. 6. The slight ligament damage in his joint has healed faster than initially expected and Berg will skate on a line with Mike Eastwood and Rich Sutter. "The doctor's cleared Bergy to play, so he'll be back in there," Burns confirmed.

Berg is very pleased. "Originally, they said I might be out for the season and then I was upgraded to six to ten weeks," he recalled. "But, it's come along so well that I'm back before the six-week mark. So, I'm obviously very happy with that."

Berg and Sutter had many a battle when Sutter played with Chicago and St. Louis, and both players are looking forward to being united. "Bill's a hard worker and I always knew what to expect when I played against him," Sutter said. "He's the type of player you want to have on your side. Players that lack in talent usually try a little harder and that's what I like about Bill."

Added Berg: "Yeah, I know all about Richie. Our paths crossed now and then on the ice. And I think he'll add some feistiness to our team. Hopefully, I can blend in with he and Easty like I did with Zez (Peter Zezel) and Ozzie (Mark Osborne)."

Funny how times have changed here in San Jose. It was less than a year ago that hockey observers in this area were praising goalie Arturs Irbe for leading the upstart Sharks to within a crossbar of the Stanley Cup semifinals. Now, with the team more resembling its modest capacity, the tune is altogether different.

The sports headline in today's *Mercury News* read IRBE ON THIN ICE, with a sub-title, BENCHING GOALIE MIGHT BE NEXT MOVE FOR SHARKS. Wrote columnist Bud Geracie:

> *In view of last season's performance, benching Irbe would seem to be the Sharks' greatest sacrilege yet... far worse than dumping Bob Errey or trading Jeff Norton and Johan Garpenlov. But, it's a new season and, sadly, a different Irbe in net.*

Hockey fans here are upset with the Sharks for divesting in three of their most popular players. Errey, the former captain; Norton, the club's most solid defenceman, and Garpenlov, whose slapshot in overtime of Game 6 last May rang off the crossbar, almost eliminating the Leafs, were all instrumental in the Sharks' remarkable playoff renaissance —coming only a year after the team lost 71 regular-season games. During the past month, however, management has seen fit to trade the trio of players, and the Sharks have yet to improve one iota.

In fact, none of the replacements, including Craig Janney, were particularly visible during tonight's ghastly 2-1 loss to the Maple Leafs. The Sharks could muster only 13 shots on goal — just six during the first two periods.

Despite a 14-3 edge in shots, the Leafs scored only once in the opening frame: on the first-ever penalty shot called against San Jose. Mats Sundin sped past Sharks' defenceman Mike Rathje and in alone on Arturs Irbe. As Sundin shifted to his forehand, Irbe spun around and released his stick at the puck. Referee Paul Stewart immediately blew his whistle and pointed to center ice.

Stewart, however, was not nearly as spontaneous when Sundin's shot clearly beat Irbe to the upper part of the net. Sundin moved to his backhand and scooped the puck under the crossbar, bulging the back of the twine. Incredibly, Stewart waved off the goal and skated towards the timekeeper's bench with a horde of celebrating Maple Leafs on his tail, wondering if this could possibly be another marathon botch-up like last month in Detroit. But, after checking with the video replay official upstairs, Stewart confirmed what everyone else in the Arena already knew and called for the faceoff at center.

Sundin's goal was a numerical oddity as the Maple Leafs' No. 13 scored his 13th goal of the season with 13:13 remaining on the clock. When will we see something like that again?

Sundin had another breakaway chance less than two minutes later when Sharks' defenceman Vlastimil Kroupa fell while carrying the puck in his own zone. But Irbe stuck out his right pad and blocked Sundin's attempt at making it 2-0 for the visitors. Big Mats would have enough quality chances later on to threaten Darryl Sittler's single-game mark for goals and points. Ultimately, though, it wouldn't be his night.

The second period featured some exceptional play by veteran Maple Leaf defenceman Jamie Macoun. Just past the two-minute mark, Macoun crunched Jeff Odgers into the end boards in the Toronto zone, drawing gasps from the San Jose crowd. It was a savage bodycheck — the type that's been missing for much of this season from the Maple Leafs. Later in the period, Ray Whitney of the Sharks got behind Macoun and skated in on Leaf goalie Damian Rhodes. But

Macoun sprawled flat out on his belly and pokechecked the puck off Whitney's stick.

The Maple Leafs had an ungodly 22-4 edge in shots on goal at the midway point of the game, but still led by the slimmest of margins. It took a typically unrelenting advance by Randy Wood to give them a bit of breathing room. Mike Ridley feathered a pass to Wood in the San Jose zone. The Leaf winger stubbornly fought off defenceman Ilya Byakin, who was draped all over him, and scored on a nifty forehand deke.

The Sharks showed a bit of life while on a powerplay late in the period — awakening after a seven-day hiatus. Thanks to the Detroit postponement, San Jose hasn't played a game since last Wednesday's 5-2 loss here against Edmonton. With Mike Eastwood in the penalty box for boarding, the Sharks buzzed the Maple Leaf zone for the first time, but were unable to set up a quality scoring chance. They were loudly booed off the ice at the end of the period, trailing by two on the scoreboard and by 24-6 on the shot-clock.

The press box here in San Jose stretches across the north end of the Arena, opposite the players benches, and way up in the rafters. A number of seats are obstructed by steel beams extending downwards from the ceiling. The unobstructed positions offer an excellent view of the ice down below, but are not recommended for the faint of heart. At each end of the press box, a narrow catwalk extends roughly 20 feet towards a loft that hangs directly over the corner boards. Players that aren't dressed and visiting NHL scouts usually occupy the two locations, and are clearly subject to nosebleeds.

One of those scouts tonight was Ken Morrow: undeniably, the player with the most fortuitous timing in NHL history. After helping the U.S. hockey team to that astonishing gold medal at the 1980 Winter Olympic Games in Lake Placid, Morrow joined the New York Islanders and won four consecutive Stanley Cups. He tasted the sourness of defeat almost half-a-decade later, when the Islanders lost the '84 Cup final to Edmonton, but had an entire hand-full of championship rings by then.

"Everyone mentions how fortunate I was early in my career, and who can argue?" Morrow smiled as we chatted during the second intermission. "When I was drafted by the Islanders in 1976, I never imagined I would come to the NHL at the beginning of a dynasty. But the club had been through some losing experiences in the playoffs the previous couple of years and was ready to bust out. It was great timing for me."

Morrow recalls with immense warmth and pride the euphoria that swept practically all of western civilization when the Americans beat the hated Soviets in the 1980 Olympics. At the time, a large group of U.S. citizens were being held hostage before a world stage in Iran and the Cold War was once again heating to the boiling point. With their fellow countrymen helpless at the hands of the sadistic Ayatollah, the American people were in the market for an emotional upsurge... and the unheralded hockey players provided it.

"It was obvious how our victory impacted on the political climate back then," Morrow acknowledged. "We all felt a part of what was going on in Iran and I believe it made us play even harder. Seeing those U.S. hostages on the news every night — blindfolded and humiliated — was a heart-wrenching experience, and I'm glad we were able to lift the spirits of the American people. It was very gratifying."

On reflection, Morrow says he had few problems gearing up for his NHL debut so soon after the Olympic triumph. "It was the best thing that could have happened because I didn't have time to cool down," he explained. "After two days to myself, it was right back into the same type of nervous excitement. Besides, the business aspect of the game was upon me. I knew I had to start making a living."

The top personal moment of Morrow's career occurred in the first round of the 1984 playoffs. Shooting for their fifth consecutive Cup, the Islanders went the distance with the cross-town-rival Rangers in a best-of-five Patrick Division semifinal. Don Maloney sent the deciding match into overtime by scoring for the Rangers with less than a minute to go in regulation. The two clubs then skated through what broadcaster Dick Irvin described as "the greatest stretch of hockey I've ever seen." Working the telecast with Bob Cole that afternoon at the Nassau Coliseum, Irvin watched the Rangers and Islanders trade a plethora of glorious scoring chances during almost nine minutes of breathtaking action. Goaltenders Billy Smith and Glen Hanlon took turns extending the series, and the Rangers seemed to have it in the bag when Bob Brooke — Morrow's U.S. Olympic teammate — broke in alone on Smith.

But the Islander goalie stuck out his right pad to make a fabulous save and Morrow won the series on the follow-up rush. His slapper along the ice from the right point eluded a screened Hanlon and sent the Coliseum into a tizzy. I can still hear the puck clanging off the iron at the bottom of the net... and so can Morrow.

"It was the greatest moment of my career, no question," recalled Morrow with a beaming smile. "The Rangers outplayed us that game and probably would have won by three or four had it not been for Smitty. I was on the ice when Don Maloney tied the score in the dying seconds and it was quite a bummer. On the winning goal, Pat Flatley was standing in front of Hanlon and I just shot towards the net. I like to tell people it was an Al MacInnis-type boomer, but they know better. I was never a threat to be among the scoring leaders, that's for sure."

Morrow is currently the Islanders' director of pro scouting. He travels around the league keeping books on the other 25 NHL teams.

San Jose scored the only goal of the third period tonight on its 12th (and second-to-last) shot of the game. Drake Berehowsky got caught out of position along the boards, allowing Jamie Baker to whip Gaetan Duchesne's pass through the legs of Damian Rhodes with just more than six minutes left in regulation time. But the Sharks did not seriously threaten to tie the score and the Leafs won for only the third time this season away from home.

Meanwhile, the Maple Leafs' next opponent — Anaheim — came up with perhaps the most impressive victory in its short history tonight, as Paul Kariya scored twice in a 5-0 whitewash at Calgary.

As I was standing outside the Leaf dressing room moments after the game, a TV type whisked Mats Sundin down the hall for a live interview. The big Swede looked at me, rolled his eyes, and said, "Great game huh? I need nine chances to score one goal." Indeed, Sundin could have had the biggest night of his hockey career had he been sharper around the net. Time and again, he found himself on Irbe's doorstep, but he scored only on the first-period penalty shot. When he returned to the dressing room, Sundin expanded on the subject.

"I'm very happy we won tonight, but I can't go on needing eight or nine shots to score one goal," he said. "I've got to start burying my chances a little more often."

About the penalty shot, Sundin recalled: "I kind of wondered where the puck went. I had gotten around (Irbe) and was looking at the net and all of a sudden, the puck was in the corner. So was Irbe's stick. I was happy when (Stewart) called for the penalty shot."

Sundin scored with a high backhand on Irbe and couldn't figure out why he abandoned that strategy later in the game. "I kept shooting low on him in the third period and you're not going to beat Irbe that way," he said. "He's down on the ice a lot and he covers the area from post to post. You have to either deke him or go high. On the penalty shot, I faked like I was going to shoot, and he backed into his net. I then had lots of room to go upstairs on him."

It was the third penalty shot of Sundin's young career. While with Quebec, he scored on Tom Draper of Buffalo in a 4-4 tie at the Colisee, Mar. 3, 1992. He was then stopped by Kelly Hrudey of the Kings, also in Quebec, Feb. 2, 1993. But the Nordiques won the game, 3-2.

Apart from San Jose's offensive inadequacy — only 51 goals scored in 23 games — Pat Burns felt his new checking unit played a key role in stifling the

Sharks. The line of Eastwood, Sutter and Berg handled San Jose's few legitimate attackers, and the coach was quite pleased. "A line like that makes so much of a difference," he said. "It's easier to shut down the other team's best line and it makes our other two top lines an inch taller. I wish I had three more players like that."

A number of Maple Leafs took their time dressing after the game, and Bob Landry had to make two trips to the hotel. Eastwood was standing on a loading platform outside the Arena, waiting for the second bus, and he still couldn't believe a penalty Stewart gave him in the third period. Streaking towards the net, Eastwood looked over his left shoulder for a pass from Kenny Jonsson and he collided with Irbe, who came out to cut down the angle. Stewart nailed him for charging — a correct call based strictly on the rulebook — and Eastwood jumped up and down in a fit of rage behind the net. He skated after the referee and had to be restrained by Berg.

"God, what an awful time to take a penalty," he said, as we waited for the bus to return. "What's a guy supposed to do in a situation like that? We're told over and over to be aggressive and go to the net, but if the goalie comes out, we get called for interference. You gotta have eyes in back of your head with all the rules today."

Landry arrived about two minutes later and the second wave of Leaf players boarded the bus. Sitting in the front seat, Kent Manderville asked the driver, "How far is Reno from here?" Told it was a trip of several hours, he playfully replied, "Wanna make some extra money?"

"You mean *lose* some extra money," Landry chuckled.

Berg got on and said his injured knee held up well. "I felt a bit of a twinge in the first period and got a little nervous but the pain went away as I was sitting on the bench," he told me. "The rest of the game was just fine."

Dave Andreychuk then walked out of the Arena and towards the bus. Sitting on the right side, Terry Yake said, "Okay, Bob, shut the door on this guy." Landry smiled and pulled the door half-closed. Andreychuk slithered in between the narrow opening — gave Landry a dirty look —and sat down next to Berg. The players began razzing the winger about his new maroon sportjacket, purchased earlier today. Noticing a loose thread, Berg reached over to pull it and Andreychuk yelped, "Don't, Bill... the fucking arm will fall off!" Everybody cracked up.

The players then gave Jonsson a sinister look as they discussed the defenceman's rookie initiation. He was given the choice of either footing the bill for an elaborate team dinner, or losing all of his bodily hair. Staring at Jonsson, Jamie Macoun deadpanned: "I got a 25-thousand-dollar signing bonus and half of it went to taxes. You got not ten, not 20, but 32 times that amount ($800,000). Is that fair?"

Smiling sheepishly, the freshman looked over at Damian Rhodes, hoping for a little support from his stoic teammate.

"Either pay up or get shaved," Rhodes winked.

The decision was easy.

THURSDAY, MARCH 16th
Anaheim

The O.J. Simpson trial is everywhere.

After taking a cab to San Jose Airport this morning with Bob and Gord Stellick, I went into the Departures lounge and noticed about 75 people watching the familiar scene on TV. Mark Fuhrman was no longer on the stand, but it didn't seem to matter. Passengers pulled themselves away when they heard the final boarding call for their flights. Another TV showed early round action from the NCAA basketball tournament.

The Maple Leaf players arrived about half-an-hour later and they showed no mercy as Jim Carey got fleeced by security. Standing in the lounge, a bunch of them mimicked the lanky trainer — throwing their arms in the air and rotating. Carey just smiled and shook his head.

Pat Burns sat on a window-sill and happily confirmed that Garth Butcher was healthy enough to fly out to Los Angeles today. The coach is hoping his veteran defenceman will play tomorrow night in Anaheim.

We flew from San Jose to Orange County on Southwest Airlines this afternoon and several of us had a laugh at the expense of Ken Daniels. Prior to boarding the plane, Daniels poignantly informed us that he heard Southwest had the nicest looking flight attendants of any airline. It was open seating on the *Boeing-737* and we perched ourselves near the front, anxious for an up-close look at our stewardess.

Seconds later, an old hag emerged from behind the flight deck. This battle-axe would have made Phyllis Diller look like Julia Roberts.

"Nice tip you got there, Kenny," cracked a disgusted Bill Watters, as the lady went through her safety demonstration.

Once airborne, the flight down the coast took just over an hour, and the captain put the old hex on all of us. About 15 minutes in, as we were still climbing over the hilly regions of northern California, his voice came across the intercom. "Folks, we're expecting a smooth ride down to Orange County today, so I'm going to switch off the seat-belt sign." Not more than 15 seconds later, the plane was rocked by a pair of ferocious wind gusts, staggering the flight attendants.

"Get the whisky out," quipped Joe Bowen.

Happens every time.

On the flight today, the Maple Leaf players held their annual NCAA tournament pool. They were all obliged to get involved, although some were completely in the dark. Mike Gartner walked by and said, "Howard, you know anything about basketball?" Glancing at *USA Today*, I noticed the national rankings and told him to take U.C.L.A. (he owes me).

John Wayne Airport is situated about 40 miles south of Los Angeles International — just off Interstate 405 (San Diego Freeway). It serves the densely populated communities of Orange County, including Anaheim, Santa Ana, Costa Mesa, Newport Beach, Irvine, and Fullerton. Our flight soared directly over Anaheim before turning around and landing to the west. Out my left-hand window, I could see all of Disneyland from about 5,000 feet. At that height, the amusement park itself is dwarfed by the acres and acres of parking lots surrounding it.

The runway at John Wayne Airport begins just west of the San Diego Freeway and the wheels of landing aircraft are no more than 100 feet above passing motorists. You can almost see their facial expressions as the plane cruises over the north-south artery, seconds before touching down.

While surrounding the luggage carousel, the Leaf players gave Felix Potvin an unmerciful ribbing when his bright pink garment-bag arrived on the conveyor belt.

"Got your hair-pins and rollers, Cat?" chided a teammate.

"Does that come with a matching purse?" asked another.

Potvin smiled weakly and walked towards the bus: his wise-cracking mates in tow. The ride north to the Westin South Coast Plaza took about 40 minutes in L.A.-type traffic, and the conversation on route centred around yesterday's news that National Football League owners had vetoed the proposed transfer of the Los Angeles Rams to St. Louis. Explaining to Pat Burns how Georgia Frontiere became owner of the Rams, Bill Watters recounted that Frontiere's late husband, Carol Rosenbloom, had been found floating on a raft... "deader than Kelsey's tits." Burns got the drift, and he burst out laughing at Watters' uncouth metaphor.

The Westin South Coast Plaza is located in the town of Costa Mesa, just off — and clearly visible from — the San Diego Freeway. The 17-story hotel is part of an up-scale shopping and entertainment complex that includes the giant South Coast Plaza Mall, roughly a dozen movie theatres, and the Orange County Performing Arts Center. We arrived at the hotel around 2:40 this afternoon and the Leafs had a 4 o'clock practice scheduled at the Arrowhead Pond.

Before getting off the bus, however, Burns asked the driver how long it might take to get to Anaheim at this time of day. He was told roughly 45 minutes, and the driver estimated the return trip could take twice as long at the tail-end of rush-hour.

The coach had done enough travelling.

As the players crowded around the reception area getting their room-keys from Bob Stellick, Burns informed them he had cancelled the practice. Predictably, there were no arguments, and most of the Maple Leafs hurriedly changed into summerwear and made a bee-line for the shopping mall. Priortites seemed out of kilter, but nobody complained.

As I was checking in a few moments later, Mike Gartner came back down to the desk, smiling and shaking his head.

"Someone else is in my room," he said. "I walked in, and there was luggage and stuff hanging in the closet. Thank God nobody was in bed."

The Leafs aren't the only sports celebrities at the Westin this weekend. Members of the P.G.A. Seniors Tour are in town for the annual *Toshiba* Classic at the nearby Mesa Verde Country Club. I was working in my room late this afternoon when the phone rang. I answered and some guy said, "Al, how 'ya doing?"

"Al who?" I replied.

"Isn't this Al Geiberger?"

"No, but you got part of the name right."

I went on to chat with this stranger for about five minutes, and his accent quickly became familiar. Damn if I wasn't talking to Chi Chi Rodriguez! After inquiring as to why I was in southern California, he apologized for bothering me and I wished him luck in the tournament.

FRIDAY, MARCH 17th
Anaheim

Yesterday's warm sunshine was blanketed by a thick cloud-cover this morning. The main lobby of the hotel was buzzing with golfers and hockey players, as the Maple Leafs prepared to leave for their game-day skate. Lee Trevino and Gary Player signed autographs at the entrance to the coffee-shop and the star-struck fans then pulled out binders full of hockey cards. What a bonanza!

The bus ride to Anaheim took about 25 minutes in light traffic and the Leaf players discussed their NCAA basketball pool on the way. Seems that Drake

Berehowsky was the big loser last night, as Colgate and Ball State were both eliminated in the first round of the tournament.

"What a joke, I'm already out of it," Berehowsky moaned.

The Arrowhead Pond is located on Katella Ave. in Anaheim, directly across the Orange Freeway from Anaheim Stadium: home of the California Angels and Los Angeles Rams. As mentioned, the football team is trying to re-locate in Missouri and as we passed the Big 'A' on our left, Dave Andreychuk and several other Leafs talked about how the sport may never again be played here. The Pond then came into view across the road and my first glance convinced me why so many people are calling it the most immaculate and luxurious arena in the NHL.

This is Disney in all its splendour.

The facade of the building is made up of large granite walls, red-brick in colour, and is accented with pine-green trim and panelling. It features green-glass archways over cathedral-like windows that comprise the main entrances, while clusters of tall palm-trees have been planted on the sidewalk around the entire circumference of the building.

The place just exudes class.

Our bus driver today had us all holding our breath as he actually backed the vehicle down a long, winding ramp into the bowels of the arena. The concrete wall was mere inches from the right-hand side and Kenny Jonsson, seated behind me, leaned in-wards away from the window. One slight miscalculation would have totalled the entire bus, and quite likely the Maple Leafs as well.

With the Leafs having played here only twice since the arena was built — both times last season — no one seemed to remember where the visitor's dressing room was located. The team hesitantly trailed its coach into the building and everybody came to a halt.

"We're following you, Burnsy," said Mike Gartner.

"Oh, don't be doing that," replied the coach.

Mike Eastwood came upon a door that was labelled "Dressing Room C" and he said, "Guys, I think we're in here." But the tiny room consisted of three or four stalls and a small toilet.

"Way to go, Easty," chided Burns.

The Leafs continued walking and a few of the guys began to lose their patience when we ended up back where we started. Finally, someone made a proper turn and we found the dressing room corridor.

The players went to get changed for their skate and I walked into the rink through the Zamboni entrance in the northwest corner. The Pond is just as handsome inside as it is on the exterior. Like in San Jose (and unlike the new rinks in Chicago and St. Louis), the two levels of seats here rise quite vertically, providing excellent sight-lines. All of the 17,250 chairs are a rust colour, while the ceiling and its steel girders are painted the same pine-green as the outside panelling. There are the customary two levels of private luxury suites, encircling the middle and upper portions of the arena.

This building, however, is most famous for its elegant corridors. More than 250,000 square feet of marble panelling and tile-work adorns the concourse level. The floors and walls are tiled in brown and beige marble, while support-columns in the hallway are pine-green. The mid-level private boxes feature chairs made of pure green-coloured leather. The entire place is sparkling clean and even the concession stands are up-scale. Comparing this arena to Maple Leaf Gardens is like comparing a Rolls Royce to a Geo Metro.

The Mighty Ducks' dressing room is similarly luxurious and is made up of four separate areas. Surrounded by wooden stalls, the main room is all trimmed in the Ducks' primary colours: concorde grape and teal. An air-hockey game sits in the middle for recreational purposes. Like in the basement corridor, finding your way around for the first time can be a trifle confusing. While waiting to talk with a player or two this morning, I accidentally walked out of the main room and right into the damned showers. Thank goodness none of the heads at that end were on. But, hell, did I get some strange looks.

The subject of my interest this morning was Mighty Ducks' rookie Paul Kariya (he wasn't in the shower, nor was I looking for him there). The first draft choice in Anaheim team history, Kariya was taken fourth overall in the 1993 lottery at Quebec City and is considered one of the brightest prospects in the NHL. He gained valuable front-line exposure playing for Canada at the 1994 Winter Olympics in Norway, and helped the team to a silver medal. Two months later, he was part of Canada's first global champions since 1961 and was named top forward in the world tournament. An exceptional skater, many observers are certain that he'll develop into one of pro hockey's most dominant players.

Despite all of this, however, there has been a down-side to Kariya in his rookie NHL season. Clearly the focal point of the Mighty Ducks' marketing strategy, he has been less-than cooperative when it comes to self-promotion. Kariya begrudgingly attends team-sponsored events and has repeatedly refused to appear as an intermission guest during local hockey telecasts. In that vain, he swiftly blew off Mark Hebscher when asked for a between-periods interview on *Global* later tonight.

His critics say he's developed an attitude un-becoming of a hockey player in his freshman campaign, and has made life extremely difficult for the Mighty Ducks' marketing and publicity staff.

As a result, I figured to be not-so politely dismissed when approaching Kariya for an interview after the morning skate today. As he passed me, I attempted to introduce myself, but he curtly said, "Not right now," and disappeared into the trainer's room. Figuring that I had nothing to lose, I waited interminably for him to re-appear (more than 40 minutes), and was rewarded for my patience. I broke the ice by reminding Kariya that I was the first reporter to speak with him after he'd been drafted by the Ducks — waiting in the bowels of the Colisee when he arrived at the interview area. He flashed a pleasant smile and proceeded to answer all of my questions in a patient, low-key manner.

I thus experienced first-hand the not-so-subtle contrast in his disposition. Kariya had been a veritable puppy dog during that draft-day chat in Quebec City, having yet to be touched by the bright lights of international hockey exposure. He was congenial and thoughtful... entirely devoid of temperament. Almost two years later, though, it's clear that he's developed an attitude. He wasn't impolite during our chat this morning, but there was an unmistakable edge to all of his answers. Had this been a baseball interview, I wouldn't have noticed. But, hockey players are generally more receptive.

The Maple Leaf goaltending situation will not be altered for this evening's game with the Mighty Ducks. Damian Rhodes hardly had to shower after Wednesday's victory in San Jose and he'll be the starter again tonight. Burns has said, in fact, that Rhodes will continue to start as long as the Maple Leafs avoid losing. That must obviously leave Felix Potvin with some mixed emotions. "They told me I wouldn't be playing after the game in San Jose so I'm not surprised," said the Cat. "Of course, I'd rather be in net but I didn't see too many shots in my last game (Monday night against Los Angeles) and we still lost. With Damian playing well, I've got to be patient and do better when I get back in there."

Rhodes, meanwhile, is going with the flow and trying not to become too philosophical. "It's nice to get back-to-back games, but I think Burnsy is just hoping to string something together," said the goalie. "We haven't had too many win streaks this year and the coach is staying with whatever is working. I'm just taking it a game at a time."

By late afternoon, the blanket of clouds over Orange County had burnt off and given way to warmth and sunshine. The Leaf players went into a meeting room on the second floor of the hotel at 4:15 p.m. to review a videotape and strategy for tonight's game. The team bus waited outside the main entrance, across from a small and hilly park rimmed with jogging trails. A young gentleman ran with an awkward gait reminiscent of the *Forrest Gump* character, and Joe Bowen found humour in the comparison. The players and coaching staff got on the bus a few minutes later with Burns decked out in his St. Patrick's Day special —a kelly green sportjacket — and we left for Anaheim at 4:50.

As we approached the Arrowhead Pond 35 minutes later, those of us on the right side of the bus noticed some guy standing on the sidewalk in front of a portable TV camera, wearing *Mickey Mouse* ears. "Look at that poor shmoe," Bob Stellick laughed, as we drove towards the man from behind. When we got closer, the players let out a roar. The "poor shmoe" was, in fact, Mark Hebscher — taping his opening for tonight's *Global* telecast. After briefly losing his concentration, Hebsy waved at the passing bus and resumed his shtick.

I took one of two elevators directly up to the press box after eating dinner in the arena and noticed the only drawback at The Pond. Typically, the media holding is secondary to all of the amenities. It's located on the side wall of the structure — on top of the second level of seats — and as far away from the ice as you can possibly be. While the Mighty Ducks make it entirely pleasant up there — with drinks, and pretzels, and popcorn, and doughnuts, and free programs, etc. — you do need a good set of eyes to see the action down below.

While waiting for the game to begin, I watched a TV monitor that had Vancouver at Detroit on ESPN. Dino Ciccarelli scored a big goal for the Red Wings in the third period, then got into a fight with Canucks' goalie Kay Whitmore. It was quite a scene.

The pre-game revelry here is like none other: a Disney production in every sense. The lights in The Pond are all extinguished and the Ducks' mascot, *Wild Wing*, is lowered from the ceiling by a tether in front of the goal at the east end of the building — a floodlight illuminating his dramatic descent. Then begins the performance of *Wild Wing and The Decoys*. Amid a kaleidoscope-enhanced laser show, the mascot and half-a-dozen scantily clad cheerleaders perform a dance routine at center ice, with loud rock music blaring over the arena sound system. Two enormous Mighty Ducks logos are illuminated high above the seats each end of the rink. The "Entertainment Extravaganza" (as the hockey club calls it) is unquestionably geared towards the young. Elderly fans are likely to suffer chest pains before the first puck is dropped.

Tonight's game had a nondescript start, a nondescript middle, and a decent ending. On an excitement scale of one to ten, it registered a decimal-point higher than zero... roughly the same as when these two teams cured insomniacs at the

Gardens last month. The final score was 3-3 and the highlight for the locals was Bob Corkum's game-tying goal with 34.5 seconds left in regulation time.

Anaheim coach Ron Wilson pulled netminder Guy Hebert for a sixth attacker with 1:20 to go. The Ducks buzzed around the Maple Leaf goal and Jamie Macoun failed to clear the zone. Paul Kariya took the puck off the right-wing boards and slapped one towards a phalanx of bodies in front of Damian Rhodes. Corkum planted himself near the goalcrease and Kariya's shot deflected in off the shaft of his stick — sending the Anaheim audience into a frenzy.

Dave Andreychuk and Dmitri Mironov had decent scoring chances in overtime, but neither club scored.

It appeared the Leafs would win the game when Andreychuk potted a lucky powerplay goal with 6:38 left on the clock. Gary Valk was in the penalty box for holding and Andreychuk banked a centring pass in off the skate of Ducks' defenceman David Karpa. Less than a minute later, Mats Sundin almost did the same off Mike Gartner's skate. But the Leafs couldn't put it away.

Ironically, tonight's match may have been decided in the scoreless second frame. The good old "period of death" reared its ugly head once again, with the Leafs either unable or unwilling to expend much energy. Watching the Mighty Ducks control the game, a thought occurred to me that there simply is no such thing as an easy night for the Leafs this season. Every game seems to be like the previous one... low-scoring, with either a tie or a one-goal separation well into the third period. It used to be in the past couple of years the Maple Leafs would enjoy a blow-out every so often against an inferior team. They were capable of winning 6-2 or 7-3 now and then. But such has not been the case in this peculiar, lockout-shortened season.

And it has to be disturbing for general manager Cliff Fletcher, as his exhaustive re-tooling during the summer was geared towards curing the offensive blahs. The Maple Leafs couldn't put the puck in the ocean against Vancouver in the Cup semifinals last spring, with Burns opting to triple-shift an ailing Doug Gilmour. Acquiring Mats Sundin and Mike Ridley was supposed to alleviate the problem, but the Leafs are having even more trouble finding the net than a year ago. Obviously, Gilmour's enduring struggles are contributing significantly, but they cannot be blamed for the club's general malaise — particularly in second periods this season. It happened again here at the Pond and likely cost the Leafs a valuable point.

An unusual event did occur early in the third period, as perhaps the most unlikely duo of Maple Leafs combined to put the club ahead of Anaheim. Kent Manderville sent Warren Rychel in on a clear breakaway at center ice and Rychel beat Hebert low to the stick side, giving the Leafs a 2-1 lead. It was Rychel's first goal of the season (also first in a Toronto uniform)... and Manderville's long-awaited first *point* of the year. "At least now I'm one up on Felix in the scoring race," Mandy quipped after the game.

Sundin had the other Leaf goal while Bobby Dollas and Stephane Lebeau also scored for Anaheim. Lebeau had a potential second marker negated by referee Rob Shick at 11:53 of the middle period when the official correctly ruled that he batted the puck in with a high stick.

Apart from Anaheim's late comeback, the evening here at The Pond featured silly duck-whistle calls during each stoppage of play — the kind that hunters utilize to attract bait. The Mighty Ducks sell more than 2,000 of them on some game nights and though funny sounding, they seem grossly out of place inside a hockey arena — particularly one as magnificent as this.

While I was standing in the hallway outside the Leaf dressing room after the game, the security man who guards the room told me Pat Burns was screaming at the top of his lungs in the second intermission. "He kept on telling them they were playing with no intensity," recalled the guard. "I'm glad I was here and not in there."

In that vain, Burns merely repeated himself during his post-game media scrum. "There's no use in even talking about it anymore," he said about the abysmal second period. "We seem to have a lot of difficulty staying awake in the middle part of the game and we did again tonight."

Dave Fuller of the Toronto *Sun* pointed out the delicate, yet valid issue that the top players on the Maple Leafs continue to have problems creating offence.

"They're definitely struggling, yup," replied the coach, seemingly uninterested in expanding on the subject.

"Can you put your finger on what it'll take to get them going?"

"Nope. No idea."

"Is effort the problem?" pressed Fuller.

"Nope. Effort's there."

Burns then swivelled around and walked back into the dressing room with Fuller and several other reporters in tow. Before he entered his office, he glared at Fuller and accused him of trying to lead a "hate campaign" in the newspaper. It was the latest in a running feud between the coach and the veteran sportswriter.

"In more than 20 years in this business, he's the only coach I've not gotten along with," Fuller said later. "I've gone back and checked what I've written the past few days and I can't see where he gets this hate campaign thing. I quoted him as saying that (Edmonton defenceman) Bryan Marchment is overrated and I think Cliff (Fletcher) got mad at him (the Leafs may be interested in acquiring Marchment). Maybe that's why he feels I'm out to get him, but he's completely wrong."

The problems between Burns and Fuller date back to Dec. 3, 1992, when Bill Berg was acquired on waivers from the New York Islanders. The Leafs were in Chicago and Fuller wrote about the transaction in the *Sun* the following day, using the most infamous quote in Burns' Maple Leaf tenure. "I wouldn't know Bill Berg if I ran over him with my car," the coach quipped. Fuller remembers it well.

"The night before, Frank Orr (of the Star) and me were having a drink with Burns in the Drake Hotel and Pat said over and over again how upset he was that the Leafs were carrying so many extra bodies; I think they had 29 players on the roster," Fuller recalled. "The next morning — at Chicago Stadium — Orr was down in the dressing room area and I was watching the practice from the stands. Bill Watters came over and informed me the Maple Leafs had acquired Berg. Burns was sitting a few rows behind me and I went up there to ask him about it, and that's when he made the comment about not knowing who Berg was.

"I thought it was kind of a crummy thing to say about a player who was coming to the team, and I wasn't sure I would use it. But then Orr came up from the dressing room and Burns told him the same thing. So, now, the opposition had the quote and I had to go with it. They chopped other parts out of my story and the quote really stood out.

"Later on, I was told that Fletcher was furious when he read the comment and he apparently scolded Burns in a one-on-one meeting. Since then, Pat has rarely had the time of day for me."

Fuller believes that Burns dislikes him because of the manner in which he handles the coach. "I just don't let him bully me like he does his players and other members of the media. He's a very suspicious man who doesn't like any obstacles. In his eyes, you're either a good guy or a trouble-maker and there's nothing in between.

"Our lack of a relationship affects me at times because he's not likely to give me the same quality of answers as he does other people. So it makes my job a bit more difficult.

"Actually, I don't really mind the guy, but I can see through him. There have never been any hard feelings on my part and I'm just sorry he can't take a little justifiable criticism now and then."

Losing a point in the final minute tonight weighed heavily on the Maple Leafs. There was a funereal atmosphere in the dressing room and on the team bus afterwards. The players munched on pizza and submarine sandwiches during the 50-minute drive northwest to Santa Monica. As we passed downtown Los Angeles in the middle of the night, the illuminated buildings and skyscrapers were shrouded in smog.

We arrived at the Loews Santa Monica Beach Hotel just after 1 a.m. and the players quickly scurried to their rooms, hoping to sleep away the night's sorrow.

SATURDAY, MARCH 18th
Los Angeles

Today was exactly what you dream of when you know you're going to have a day off in southern California.

The ocean fog dissipated by mid-morning and the rest of the day was spectacular. Our location here on Santa Monica Beach is almost too luxurious for the circumstance: that being a one-day stopover in the middle of a lengthy road trip. Nothing about the ambience of this place is even remotely connected to hockey, but it was perfect timing for the Maple Leafs to clear their heads and shut it down for an afternoon.

Even a few hours of *work* at this hotel was delightful. My room is on the second floor — not quite high enough to be termed "ocean front" — but nonetheless facing in that direction. The white sandy beach and deep-blue Pacific are across a narrow street and the calming sound of ocean waves fill the air with the window open. It made for a wonderful atmosphere while sitting at my hotel-room desk this morning.

The sun poked through the fog just before 10:30 a.m. and I took a slow walk along the ocean shore with the Maple Leafs' video coordinator Paul Dennis, who's on this trip. Paul is a phys-ed teacher at Henry Carr Secondary School in Etobicoke and I've known him for a number of years. On game nights in Toronto, he sits in the coach's office at Maple Leaf Gardens and breaks down the action on video for Pat Burns. He has a satellite dish at home and is thus able to tape and assess out-of-town games for the Maple Leafs. A pretty valuable guy.

After getting back from the beach, I sat in the hotel lobby and read the Los Angeles *Times*. Burns was strolling around, waiting for a camera crew from CBC to arrive and tape a segment for *Hockey Night In Canada*. The Leafs-Kings game at the Forum will be the second half of the Saturday night doubleheader. Burns sauntered over to where I was sitting and we shot the breeze for about ten minutes.

"This place is incredible," he smiled. "I have an ocean-front room and I slept last night with the window open, listening to the waves. There's not too many places you can do that during the hockey season." Burns is going with Damian Rhodes in goal again tonight, which I found a bit surprising. The coach, however, feels he's committed to Rhodes until the team loses a game and the Leafs have picked up three out of four points so far on this western trip.

"Besides," Pat reasoned, "Damian has been really patient playing behind Felix all of this time, and now I think it's Felix's turn to be patient behind Damian. I mentioned a couple of days ago that we need some kind of streak and he hasn't lost a game yet. Perhaps I'm thinking it'd be bad luck to make a change now, but I don't see any reason to go away from Damian."

Indeed, Rhodes has maintained a praiseworthy attitude as Potvin's stand-in the past two seasons. During his brief moments in the sun, he has proven capable of playing regularly in the NHL, but that chance will not come in Toronto unless the Cat suffers a prolonged disability.

"I give a lot of credit to Damian," Burns continued. "He's taken on a personal trainer and worked very hard at his conditioning. I'm not taking anything away from Felix because he's been terrific for us ever since he came into the league. But maybe things have gone *too* well for him. At some point in every athlete's life, there comes a time when he has to be shown he's not invincible... that there is somebody who could take his place. And maybe Felix is learning that lesson this week."

Burns and I then segued into a more general discussion about the team and it's clear he's been thrown for a loop by this unpredictable season. The subject of Doug Gilmour came up and Burns grew even more confused. "I don't know what it is, Howie, but I see Doug working just as hard as he has the past two years," the coach sighed. "He and I have had some long talks and neither of us can pinpoint why he's struggling. The only solace I can find is that so many other top players around the league are also having problems. You look at guys like Mark Messier and Steve Yzerman. Or even Sergei Fedorov (last year's Hart Trophy winner). They're all playing below their normal standards for some reason."

Mike Ridley then walked over and wondered where the team would be having lunch. "Tell those CBC guys I'm in the restaurant if they show up," Burns asked me, clearly unwilling to sacrifice his meal.

A few moments later, I walked out in front of the hotel to wait for my mother-in-law, as we had made lunch plans for this afternoon. As I loitered in the parking circle, Gilmour came over in a golf-shirt and shorts. We took a brief walk up the street and he seemed anxious for someone to talk to. Now, I must say that I truly love my mother-in-law, but our timing for this lunch date couldn't possibly have been worse. Here was the captain of the Toronto Maple Leafs — arguably the city's most revered athlete and a man whom I've grown to admire and respect

—actually requesting a few moments of my time, and I simply didn't have any. We strolled a few hundred yards up the road and Gilmour leaned on a Los Angeles *Times* newspaper box.

"It's been a tough season and I'd feel better if somebody would take down that wall in front of the net," he sighed.

The game of hockey has suddenly become mental warfare for Gilmour. In two-plus seasons with the Maple Leafs, he has been the league's best reactionary player. It's the aspect of the game that has elevated Wayne Gretzky to unprecedented heights... executing the proper move without thinking. Such a rare intangible — the ability to assess and react by nature — has been Gilmour's forte since arriving in Toronto. Combining innate playmaking skills with tenacity and chutzpah unmatched by any smallish player in recent history, he almost singlehandedly lugged the Maple Leafs out of a generation-long quagmire.

Suddenly, now, the magic has disappeared, and Gilmour doesn't know where to turn. "I'm in a rut this season and it's tough to keep my mind off it," he confessed. "You miss two or three good chances in a game and that feeling hits you like a tidal wave. You start thinking, 'Here we go again' and every shift becomes a mental battle. It's awful. But, you have to plug away and hope your next time out will be better."

Just then, my mother-in-law's red Acura pulled up to the curb and I shook hands with the troubled Leaf warrior. As we drove away, Gilmour continued walking, fully immersed in his anguish.

The latter part of this afternoon was so California! I laid out on the hotel's magnificent pool patio, which rises four stories above the beach, and yakked with Mike Gartner, whose right ankle was the size of a grapefruit. Gartner blocked a shot last night in Anaheim and will not play against the Kings. He stretched out on a lawnchair with the ankle wrapped in ice and bemoaned his injury plagued season. The cool breeze wafting in off the ocean was a bit much for him and after Leaf trainer Brent Smith examined his enlarged foot, Gartner hobbled back inside.

I then took my *Walkman* and strolled along the boardwalk of Santa Monica Beach for 40 minutes. Rollerblading is a pastime in these parts and dozens of young, athletic types breezed past me on either side. In one corner of the boardwalk, a chess tournament was in progress, while a sign affixed in the sand proudly proclaimed that I was walking on the original site of the 1960s movie "Muscle Beach." A monstrous ice cream sundae looked horribly tempting, but my uncommon self-discipline kicked in, realizing that dinner was only two hours away.

The downside to staying at this paradise in Santa Monica is the long bus ride to the Great Western Forum. It took us almost 40 minutes to arrive in Inglewood late this afternoon, whereas the trip would have been about 15 minutes from one of the Los Angeles airport hotels. There is always traffic on the freeways of this enormous city and travelling on a weekend provides little relief. It's simply a factor of life that Angelenos learn to anticipate and plan around.

Nobody said much on today's ride to the Forum until we exited the San Diego Freeway at Manchester Blvd. Sitting a row behind me, Randy Wood suddenly announced, "Hey guys, there's my restaurant." Several of us glanced out the right side at a place called "Randy's Doughnuts." Unimpressed, rookie Matt Martin rolled his eyes as Wood flashed him a toothy grin. "Actually, a doughnut place would be more appropriate for a goalie than a winger, wouldn't it?" Randy asked. Nobody answered.

The Forum audience let out a cheer tonight when Warren Rychel was announced in the Leafs' starting line-up. "It's going to be exciting and a bit nerve-wracking," Rychel predicted last night about his return to the Forum. "I spent two years with that team and we had some success in my rookie season (the Kings went to the Cup final in 1993 and Rychel scored six goals in the playoffs). I think the fans enjoyed the effort I gave them and it'll be neat going back."

A pre-game ceremony honoured former Kings' captain Bob Berry, who played here in Los Angeles from 1970 - 1977. "Who's next, Don Kozak?" asked Gord Stellick, seated behind me in the press box, and obviously anxious for the game to begin. An attractive young lady named Karen Springer strolled out to center-ice to sing the national anthems, but the Forum sound people forgot to turn on her microphone. As a result, the first half of O Canada was practically inaudible. Springer handled it well, though — smiling and pointing to her malfunctioning equipment until someone finally got the message.

The electronic kink set the tone for one of the strangest periods of hockey I've ever seen. Neither the Maple Leafs nor the Kings scored a goal, but both teams had numerous can't-miss opportunities. How the puck stayed out can only be attributed to the full moon hanging in the sky tonight over the Forum. Some examples:

* On the Leafs' first powerplay, Dave Andreychuk sent a pass to Mike Ridley across the goalcrease. With Kelly Hrudey flat on his back, Ridley had the entire net to aim for, but he somehow shot wide.
* Ridley and Kent Manderville broke out of the Maple Leaf zone on a two-on-one minutes later, only to have Manderville abruptly put on the breaks and head to the bench for a line change.
* With Matt Martin off for holding late in the period, Jari Kurri defied physics. From behind the net, Wayne Gretzky fed Kurri a perfect pass

at the front edge of the goalcrease. All Kurri had to do was tap it behind a beaten Damian Rhodes. Instead, he somehow flipped the puck not only over the net, but clear over the end-glass into the crowd. How he managed *that* while standing so close to the goal was astounding.

* In the final two minutes, Manderville gobbled up a loose puck in the center-ice area and started in on a breakaway. Rick Tocchet of the Kings already had some momentum and could have easily caught the Maple Leaf winger. Tocchet, however, decided to peel off on a line change, leaving Hrudey to deal with Manderville all by himself. Mandy's futile backhand attempt rolled wide of the net.

* With 30 seconds to go, Mats Sundin had Hrudey at his absolute mercy. Lying on his right side, Hrudey extended his left pad into the air and distracted Sundin, who somehow flipped the puck over top the wide--open net.

Incredibly, the period ended scoreless.

There was a disturbing incident midway through the opening frame that left Bill Berg's face looking like a road map of Amsterdam. A scuffle ensued behind the Los Angeles net after Rich Sutter piled into defenceman Darryl Sydor on an icing call. Kings' behemoth Troy Crowder took exception and tried to get at Sutter, only to be intercepted by Berg and Mike Eastwood. Crowder and Berg jostled briefly, but linesmen Brad Lazarowich and Mark Wheler quickly intervened. Crowder nodded at Wheler, indicating the tussle was over, but when the linesman loosened his grip on the mammoth winger, he lurched forward and sucker-punched Berg over the left eye. Berg got up with blood trickling down his face and Crowder was excused from the remainder of the match by referee Andy Van Hellemond.

The Leafs were awarded a five-minute powerplay but it was negated by a monstrous hit from Randy Wood. With 2:40 left in Crowder's major, former Leaf Eric Lacroix raced towards the area in front of the penalty box to corral a loose puck. Wood took a few strides, caught Lacroix off balance, and launched him into the boards head-first. The Forum crowd gasped, and then let out a collective sigh when Lacroix immediately got to his feet. Wood was sent off for charging.

The spooky trend of this game continued into the early moments of the second period when Hrudey made a trio of miraculous saves on Dave Andreychuk, Kenny Jonsson and Mats Sundin. On a Toronto powerplay just past the six-minute mark, Wood found himself alone in front of Hrudey. He spun around and beat the goalie with a shot to the far side that hit something — perhaps the crossbar — and ricocheted wide. Burns threw his hands in the air behind the Leaf bench in obvious exasperation.

It came as no surprise whatsoever that the first goal of the game was a cheapie. Just as the powerplay ended, Sundin took a rebound from Jamie Macoun in back of the net and while fending off Darryl Sydor, he stuffed the puck into the far side on a wrap-around. It was the Leafs' 21st shot of the hockey game.

Shots No. 22, 23 and 24 should also have counted, but Wood and Rychel (twice) had clay in their gloves. It proved costly and the Kings took advantage by tying the score. Tony Granato tapped Gretzky's behind-the-net feed through the five-hole on Damian Rhodes — the goal coming just after the Maple Leaf offensive surge. It could have been deflating for the visitors had Doug Gilmour not gotten a rare break less than a minute later. Like Sundin on the first goal, Gilmour snuck around from behind the Kings' net and attempted a wrap-around. This time, however, the puck bounced off defenceman Michel Petit's skate and fluttered into the goal over Hrudey's outstretched glove.

It would prove to be the evening's turning point.

During the second intermission, I looked down one row in the press box and noticed Kings' general manager Sam McMaster sitting by himself. A heavy-set man with glasses, he was leaning on his elbows in apparent dismay, and I could understand why. A front-page sports story in today's Los Angeles *Times*, co-authored by hockey writers Helene Elliott and Lisa Dillman, indicated that former Boston Bruin defenceman Mike Milbury had recently spurned an offer to become the Kings' general manager and coach. According to the article, had Milbury accepted, McMaster would have been reassigned to a lesser role and Barry Melrose would've been fired.

The story also opined that the promotion yesterday of Rogie Vachon to president of the hockey club was a move made out of desperation.

Hoping to obtain a reaction from McMaster on tape, I inadvertently walked into a maelstrom of emotion. The beleaguered rookie G.M. poured out his spleen in an intense, rambling interview that lasted the entire intermission. It took minimal prodding to unleash his fury.

"My reaction to that story is disbelief that a newspaper like the *Times* would print things that aren't true," he began. "It's really easy to write 'sources say' but unless you go on record with information, I don't think anyone should take it seriously. It's all a bunch of crap."

Adding to the speculation was the fact that Milbury chose not to deny the story, even though Elliott and Dillman gave him an opportunity to do so. Neither did he confirm the Kings' offer, and his aloofness served only to credit the rumour.

"It's just bad journalism," McMaster snapped. "I can't speak for Mike Milbury but I can tell you that at no time was anybody offered the job to coach the Los Angeles Kings. As far as the G.M. is concerned, I suppose that's something you'd have to ask the owner."

McMaster has been under seige here in L.A. for the Kings' woeful record, especially at home in the Forum, where they've won just two of 13 games thus far. Last month, McMaster sent talented young defenceman Alexi Zhitnik to the Buffalo Sabres in a deal that brought goalie Grant Fuhr to the Kings, and Fuhr has been an unmitigated disaster so far in a Los Angeles uniform. The Kings are rapidly falling out of realistic contention for a playoff spot and the hounds are baying.

"It's difficult to accept all the criticism," McMaster admitted. "Some of it's fair, but a lot of it is unfounded. We're trying to build this organization back up to standard and I read stuff that makes me think those who write it haven't got much of a life."

McMaster's life didn't improve any in the third period tonight, as the Maple Leafs actually carved themselves a bit of breathing room. I mentioned last night in Anaheim how lop-sided games have been foreign to this year's Leaf team, but that all ended for a spell here tonight. Mike Ridley and Dave Andreychuk scored in the first six minutes to put the Buds ahead, 4-1. The luxury of a three-goal cushion must have been overwhelming and the Leafs decided to slack off for a few moments. They paid for it as Eric Lacroix banged a second rebound past Damian Rhodes, shaving the lead to a pair of goals with still 12 minutes remaining.

But the Maple Leafs settled down and the Kings did not pose a serious threat the rest of the way. A television image of Barry Melrose was flashed on the Forum sportstimer with four-and-a-half minutes to go in regulation time, drawing a noisy spate of boos from the dwindling L.A. audience. Amazing how times have changed in this building. During the Kings' surprise march to the Stanley Cup finals less than two years ago, Melrose could have run for mayor of L.A. and won by a landslide. Now, the fans are campaigning for his scalp.

Melrose pulled Hrudey for an extra attacker with 1:02 left on the clock, but Sundin scored into the empty net to make it 5-2 Leafs. John Druce potted a meaningless goal for L.A. with 10.8 seconds remaining and the Kings lost for the ninth time in 14 outings here this season.

In direct contrast to last night, the post-game mood in the Maple Leaf dressing room was virtually party like. Having spent much of the day in the sun, the fair-skinned Paul Dennis came into the room looking like a freshly boiled lobster. I was yakking with Mats Sundin at his locker when a collective

"WHOOOOOAH!!" erupted. Not expecting such an intense reaction, the Maple Leaf video coordinator flashed a big smile, but any embarrassment would have been masked by his charred complexion.

"Get the *Noxema* out!" bellowed Dave Andreychuk.

"This was just a great team win," said an enthusiastic Sundin. "We have been trying to put a streak together all season and it's finally happening. It feels really good to be winning on the road."

About 15 minutes later, I was sitting on the Maple Leaf bus in the Forum basement with Paul Dennis and Gord Stellick. The first player to board was Randy Wood, who comfortably stretched out across Pat Burns' exclusive territory — the two front-row seats on the right side. Wood talked about his crushing bodycheck on Eric Lacroix, admitting, "I've been trying to get that guy for awhile."

Seconds later, I looked out my right-side window and noticed Burns walking towards the bus. Initially, I was going to alert Wood about the coach's imminent arrival, but my preference was to see Burns' reaction.

Climbing the stairs, he looked to his left, paused, then playfully barked, "Hey, 'Big Balls,' go find your own seat!" He shocked the hell out of Wood, who quickly bolted from the front row.

"Fucking guy... scores a couple of goals lately and thinks he can take the coach's seat," Burns continued with his mock tirade.

Having fun is so much easier when you win.

To the sheer surprise of the uninitiated, there was bumper-to-bumper traffic on the southbound San Diego Freeway during our post-game ride back to the hotel. We were on the opposite side of the road, but it was still an unusual scene. "Look at the cars at 11:30 at night," marvelled a Maple Leaf player seated a few rows behind me.

Welcome to L.A.

*   *   *   *   *   *

Art Hindle is a Canadian-born actor of some renown, and a rather avid fan of the Maple Leafs.

His entertainment credits include the character Mike Fennell on the acclaimed Canadian drama series *ENG*; the good-guy cop who took on Alex Karras in the popular 1980s spoof *Porky's;* and the one for which I'll eternally associate him — rough-and-tumble Billy Duke in the 1971 hockey love-story *Face Off* (also a Canadian production).

I've known Art for several years now and I ran into him outside the Maple Leaf bus prior to leaving the hotel for tonight's game at the Forum. He came over to Santa Monica to visit close friend Doug Gilmour. When I finished my post-game work tonight at the hotel, Art called the room and invited me down to the lobby bar for a drink. We sat there for an hour, and I revelled in his stories about the filming of *Face Off*.

If you've seen the movie, you'll recall that Art played a hot-shot rookie on the Maple Leafs, who was torn between his obsession to make it big in the NHL and his ever-growing love for drug-addicted rock star Sherri-Lee Nelson (played by actress Trudy Young). The film features actual footage of Maple Leaf games from the 1970-71 season, and cameo appearances by members of that year's team (including George Armstrong, Paul Henderson, Rick Ley, Jim Dorey, and trainer Joe Sgro). Art's character in the authentic footage is portrayed by former Maple Leaf defenceman Jim McKenny, and a bus scene shows a thin rookie named Darryl Sittler all decked out like a priest in his Neru suit (it *was* fashionable at the time). Former Boston star Derek Sanderson also has a prominent role at the beginning of the story.

Hindle made a west-coast trip with the Leafs that winter to film scenes for the movie. Footage appears from a game in Oakland with the California Golden Seals, and there's a memorable fight scene from Los Angeles that I recall listening to on radio when it actually happened. Bill (Cowboy) Flett of the Kings bowled over Maple Leaf goalie Jacques Plante in the crease and defenceman Bob Baun pummelled Flett in a brawl that emptied the benches. Jim Dorey fought with Paul Curtis of L.A. and Jim McKenny jostled former Leaf teammate Bob Pulford. The Kings were resplendent in their old uniforms — gold jersey, pants and socks, with purple trim and a crown logo. The Leafs had changed that season to the uniforms they would wear throughout the 70s and much of the 80s, with shoulder-piping that extended from the neck to the sleeve.

The mock fight scenes in the movie were filmed during a day-long shoot at Maple Leaf Gardens on Victoria Day, 1971. Fans were encouraged to come down and fill the seats, and I was among those in attendance. More than a dozen NHL players wearing their predominantly coloured road uniforms were part of the cast, as were NHL officials John Ashley, John D'Amico and Matt Pavelich. The entire afternoon of filming was a cut-up, as the players could not avoid uproarious laughter during the fake brawls. Former Chicago defenceman Doug Jarrett had the most trouble and even in his actual movie appearance, he can be seen straining to avoid breaking up. Virtual reality took a beating.

"Ed Giacomin and Rod Seiling were playing for the Rangers at the time and I remember how much trouble we had filming their scene," Art laughed as we sat in the bar tonight. "I had to take Eddie out in the corner as he scrambled after a loose puck, and Seiling was supposed to come in and fight me. Well, Rod just couldn't do it without laughing. We must have filmed six or seven takes, and I finally got fed up.

"On the next try, I went into the corner and really socked Eddie in the kisser. He was wearing a mask by then, but I gave him a heck of a wallop and then peeled away and ran for my life. I locked myself in the Maple Leaf dressing room and opened the door only when Seiling came over and insisted that Giacomin wasn't out to kill me.

"I let Rod in and he said he understood why I reacted that way... it was my profession and the players weren't taking it seriously. Eddie came over and we apologized to each other."

Art sat with me and told stories until 1:15 a.m. and we were both falling on our faces by then. Since *ENG* was cancelled last season, he spends most of his time here in Los Angeles with his son, Zeke, and has appeared in a number of television series — including *Matlock,* with TV legend Andy Griffith. It was great seeing him again.

On the way back to my room, I noticed Leaf assistant coach Rick Wamsley sitting alone in the hotel lobby, still in the suit he wore at the Forum tonight. "Just part of the routine I had when I was playing," Wammer explained. "I'm kind of hyper for a few hours after a game."

I wished him pleasant dreams and went to bed.

SUNDAY, MARCH 19th
Vancouver

The focus of the sporting world was Indianapolis this morning, as Michael Jordan made his celebrated return to professional basketball. I went down to the hotel lobby in Santa Monica at 9:45 to buy a muffin for breakfast, and the Chicago at Indiana game was on television in the same bar I had left nine hours earlier. Having discarded his familiar No. 23 jersey in favour of No. 45, Jordan seemed incapable of hitting the broad side of a barn with a tractor. His early game shots fell astray more often than they would have in an entire week during his first go-around.

Mike Kitchen lumbered into the bar after his morning jog, dripping sweat all over the floor. We watched Marv Albert say *"Yesss!"* for about 10 minutes, then went to get organized for the trip to Vancouver.

While waiting in line to check out 20 minutes later, Rich Sutter was settling his incidental charges at the front desk.

"Hey, Howard, come here," he said, summoning me with a jerk of his head. "I have to apologize. I've been calling you Damien Cox for the past two days. No offence intended, okay?."

"None taken," I replied, unsure if Richie felt he was offending me by forgetting my name... or confusing me for Damien.

I went to Los Angeles International Airport with Dave Fuller, who rented a car on this leg of the trip. Bob Stellick and Larry Sicinski were also aboard. We were driving peacefully in light traffic along the Santa Monica Freeway when an ominous legion of motorcycles enveloped us on either side. A surly looking gang of roughly 75 members went zooming by at break-neck speed and though they meant us no harm, we were happy when they continued on towards downtown Los Angeles. Pat Burns would've been far more impressed (the Leaf coach owns a Harley-Davidson).

Arriving at L-A-X just behind us, the Maple Leaf players had some time to kill before the flight. Warren Rychel lined up at the gate to ensure tabulation of his Delta Airlines points, while defenceman Matt Martin attempted fruitlessly to change locations aboard the aircraft. The *Boeing*-727 has a seating configuration of three-and-three and all windows and aisle positions were taken.

"Me and Kenny (Jonsson) have the only middles, but that's what you get for being a rookie," he shrugged.

Several of the players visited a *Burger King* outpost in the Delta terminal for a nutritious lunch, while others — including Mats Sundin, Kent Manderville, Pat Jablonski, Rich Sutter and Bill Berg — took the opportunity to catch up with family members abroad. They monopolized a row of pay phones and Sundin actually telephoned Sweden to speak with his relatives. "It's Sunday, so the rates are cheaper," he smirked.

Hoping to appease my fetish for a window seat, I then waited for Manderville to finish his conversation and he generously switched with me — an aisle more appropriate for his long legs.

I sat with Sundin on the 2 hr. 20 min. flight up to Vancouver this afternoon. Actually, we were separated by a young, blonde-haired woman in the middle seat, but she was engrossed in Danielle Steel's *Accident* and seemed immune to us leaning forward and talking over her. At one point, Sundin asked if we were being a nuisance. The woman looked up and tersely replied, "Not yet, but I'll let you guys know if you start bothering me." Mats gave her a sideways glance and turned his head forward momentarily.

Later on in the flight, he told me the rather amusing story of the immediate hours following his trade last summer to the Maple Leafs. It required another 15 minutes of constant chatter without admonition from our indulgent seat partner. Sundin had travelled north in Sweden to Borje Salming's home-town of Kiruna, and was a guest instructor at the former Leaf defenceman's hockey school. With trade rumours swirling about the up-coming NHL draft meetings in Hartford, Sundin expected to be moved by the Quebec Nordiques, but he had no idea where.

"My agent (Mark Perrone) and me had some verbal agreements with the Nordiques that didn't work out," he explained. "Basically, we were told that if I attained certain numbers offensively, they would pay me a bonus. But, we didn't have it in writing and they refused. There was a stalemate between us and Quebec said if we didn't like the contract, the team would move me elsewhere. So, I knew two or three weeks before the draft that I'd probably be traded. Toronto, the Islanders, and San Jose were the three teams we heard they were talking to."

The deal with the Maple Leafs came together around suppertime in Hartford, which was the middle of the night in northern Sweden. Sundin got a phonecall around 5 a.m. from Bengt Lundholm, a former NHLer with the Winnipeg Jets, who works with Perrone.

"When I found out that Wendel Clark was the player Toronto traded for me, I got a little nervous," Sundin recalled. "But, I had a fishing trip planned with my brothers and cousins and decided to go ahead with it. Around 8 o'clock that morning, we got on a helicopter and flew for about half-an-hour to a remote area in the bush — right in the middle of nowhere. There weren't any roads leading in or out of the place and we set up a little camp with three or four tents. I was looking forward to a couple days of peace and quiet."

Sundin was under the impression that nobody else in the world even realized his fishing spot existed.

"That's what I thought," he smiled. "But, later on that morning, I heard a helicopter approaching from the distance and I figured one of our guides was coming back with some food. It landed right next to my tent and out stepped a crew from Swedish television, wanting to talk to me about the trade. I wasn't very happy about that, but I decided to go ahead with the interview and get it out of the way.

"The next morning, I was fishing when another helicopter flew in from the distance. This time, a Swedish newspaper reporter got off. The whole thing was crazy but the biggest surprise happened when I got back to Kiruna later that day and a reporter from Toronto was waiting for me (Paul Hunter of the *Star* had flown to Sweden). That blew me away.

"I returned home to Stockholm the next day and there were about 70 messages on my answering machine; media people from all over the world were calling. And that night, I had to go to Johan Garpenlov's wedding. It was the wildest two days of my whole life."

While initially apprehensive about the trade, Sundin has obviously adjusted well to his new environment. With Doug Gilmour struggling for points, he's been the best Maple Leaf performer and has grown to enjoy Toronto immensely. "I was a bit scared right after the trade because I knew how popular Wendel was," Sundin remembered. "I figured I was going to have to score three goals a night to keep everybody happy. But, the fans and the media accepted me right away and were very fair. It was a big relief to be treated so nicely by everyone."

The 3 1/2-month lockout was probably a blessing in disguise for Sundin, as it provided healing time for Wendelmania. "There would have been a bit more pressure if the season had started on time, but I tried not to let it bother me," Mats recalled. "I went back home and played for Djurgarden (of the Swedish Elite League) and it helped me to stay focused on the game. I was able to come back in pretty good mental and physical condition after the lockout."

Of course, Sundin left the Nordiques just as they were poised to become one of the NHL's best teams. Having drafted in the top three or four positions for the past half-decade, Quebec ultimately had to show some dramatic improvement, and the Nords have developed this year into a legitimate Stanley Cup contender. But Mats ended the story by telling me his isn't kicking himself.

"No, not at all," he insisted. "I had a great time in Quebec but I don't miss the organization. Things are more stable with the Leafs and we have a lot of good, experienced players. Dave Ellett was really helpful to me when I arrived in Toronto and he found me a place to live in his apartment building. I'm enjoying myself and I think our team has a lot of ingredients to do well again in the playoffs."

Neither Mats nor I knew if our inconspicuous seat mate was paying attention to his story, as she kept reading and never uttered a peep. We landed in Vancouver at 3 o'clock this afternoon and with the airport undergoing a facelift, we endured a ridiculously long, winding trek to the baggage-claim area. "Cripes, what did we do, land in Seattle?" Mike Kitchen groaned as we trumped through the construction site.

Once the players had emerged from Customs and claimed their bags, they were forced to wait outside awhile. For the first time all season, the team bus was late and Bob Stellick immediately got on the phone to find out why. The Leafs stood around in two groups outside the terminal and were greeted by the ubiquitous autograph seekers. It was overcast and quite a bit cooler than Los Angeles. A white stretch-limo, wedged along the curb between two parked cars, attempted to pull away, and Dave Andreychuk graciously helped the chauffeur negotiate the tricky manoeuvre. I admired how calmly the Leafs accepted the inconvenience and could only imagine the spectacle that would have unfolded had this been a group of baseball players.

It reminded me of an absurd moment during a west-coast trip I was on with the Blue Jays in the summer of 1987. After a Thursday afternoon victory in Oakland, the team took a commercial flight to Orange County for a series with the California Angels and bussed to the Anaheim Marriott. Baseball players are a different breed because they simply do not lift a finger away from the field all season long. A typical example of the pampering they're accorded occurs after every game. Whereas hockey players will gather their undergarments and place them in a container, ballplayers simply disrobe and drop everything at their feet. A clubhouse worker is left to do the dirty work and appealing for some humanity is out of the question. Combining this mandatory coddling with outrageous amounts of compensation, it's easy to see why baseball types believe they stand alongside the Almighty Himself.

Still, watching them carry on at times can be mind-boggling. As we checked into that Anaheim hotel almost a decade ago, outfielder Lloyd Moseby requested an adjoining room for he and his family (many of the players had their wives and children on that late-summer trip). When a front-desk attendant explained that the hotel was full and such a room was unavailable that night, Moseby launched into a tantrum befitting of a petulant school-child. "I don't care if other people are in that room — I'm a baseball player," he moaned with astounding temerity.

While Moseby carried on, outfield partner Jesse Barfield could be heard ranting at another employee, "Aw, how could my room not be ready, I play baseball." A chap named Michael Murray was the Blue Jays' travel secretary back then and God only knows how he survived such immaturity.

When the Leaf bus finally arrived at Vancouver airport today, the driver disembarked and asked, "Have you guys been waiting long?"

"Yup, over an hour... where ya been?" grumbled Pat Burns, feigning hostility. "Somebody's gonna pay for this, big time."

Mike Gartner then deadpanned, "Watch, now he'll say, 'You guys *are* the men's choir, right?'"

I loaded my suitcase on the underbelly of the bus, along with the heavy duffel-bag that contains my electrical equipment. "Howie, are you away from home for six months or seven?" Burns chaffed. I've received that type of wisecrack many times over this season. Why, just moments earlier, while gathered around the conveyor belt, Bob Stellick noticed my purple-and-black luggage and blurted, "Howard, here comes one of your six bags." Having to drag two tape recorders, a microphone and a telephone wherever I go, it does seem like I pack for a European vacation. But it's better than having a pink garment-bag, (right Felix?).

Maple Leaf team unity began to dissolve on the ride downtown. Dave Andreychuk circulated through the bus, trying to collect $40 per player for the team's NCAA basketball pool. And the pains he endured were just comical. It began with Gartner's ignorance of the tournament progress.

"Is Toledo still in it?" he asked.

"Was Toledo ever in it," replied someone behind him.

Andreychuk had further trouble with Gartner when he received a $50 bill from the veteran Maple Leaf winger.

"Don't you have the correct change?" he inquired.

"No... if I did, I'd give it to you," came the terse reply.

"Just asking, Garts."

Bill Berg forked over his payment and bugged Andreychuk for a receipt. Andreychuk went up and down the bus with great purpose, and finally sat down. "Shit, he isn't that intense during games," noticed someone at the back. After a few moments of relative serenity, the real turmoil began.

"Alright, fifty dollars is missing, dammit!" Andreychuk snapped, prompting the entire bus to explode with laughter.

"Did you take math in high-school?" asked Warren Rychel.

"Not funny," Andreychuk grumbled — head down — shuffling through the wad of U.S. bills one more time. His ledger still unbalanced, he conducted an exhaustive player-by-player search in a desperate attempt to locate the defrauding party. Unsuccessful, he angrily sat back down: his features twisted in strife and discontent.

Seconds later, though, he erupted again.

"Alright, the guy who has it... it'll be on your mind. You have to sleep tonight," he warned. Once again, teammates began to fall out of their seats in hysterics.

"Did you check your sleeve, Chucky?" asked Todd Gill.

"C'mon guys, this is serious!" Andreychuk pleaded.

"I think we're going to have to fly in Max Offenberger," said Bob Stellick, referring to the team psychologist.

Finally, Gartner grew fed up and pulled all of the American money out of his wallet. "Chucky, look at this," he said. "In my hand, I have six $50 bills. Is it impossible for *me* to have the extra money? And if so, how in the world are you going to find out?"

That served to end the debate, as a perplexed Andreychuk stared at Gartner without reply. Seconds later, the team bus mercifully puled up to the Westin Bayshore Hotel.

MONDAY, MARCH 20th
Vancouver

This was a good-news/bad-news day for Kenny Jonsson.

Happily for the Maple Leaf defenceman, he still had some hair to comb when he awoke this morning. Sadly, it cost him 5,000 dollars.

As mentioned earlier, Jonsson's rookie initiation encompassed two choices: take out the entire Maple Leaf road show (media excluded) for an extravagent dinner... or receive a close and not-too comfortable shave free of charge. Without even a moment's hesitation, Jonsson chose Door No. 1 and is thus on a budget for the remainder of our western journey.

The Leafs showed precious little mercy for the well-to-do freshman last night, mounting an outrageous stipend at The *Tea House* in Stanley Park. "There were bottles of wine on that table from the 1960s," joked defencemate Jamie Macoun. The players stuffed themselves with culinary delights and their host simply went with the flow, downing a mixture of shrimp, mussels, crab cakes, and a New York steak, all by himself.

"Really, it wasn't too bad," Kenny admitted when the team arrived at the Pacific Coliseum for practice this afternoon. "St. Louis had its rookie dinner four nights ago and it came to $18,000. But, they had six guys to split it up. The food was okay and I made sure to order lots of it for myself. I wanted to enjoy the evening if I was going to pay."

Actually, no one should pity the youngster from Sweden. Earning a first-year salary of $700,000, Jonsson pulls in $13,461.54 per week, or $1,923.08 per day. Therefore, last night's meal cost him roughly 2 1/2 days worth of compensation.

"Like I said, it was easier than losing my hair."

Leaf assistant G.M. Bill Watters almost lost his lower lip today. Wilbur took a shave in the Coliseum dressing room before practice and emerged looking like a crime victim. Blood was pouring from a gash on his lip and he observed the workout while constantly dabbing the wound with a Kleenex. "Just went a little too far up my chin, Howie," Watters explained when I inquired about the carnage.

The Vancouver players were just getting off the ice when the Maple Leafs arrived and Pat Burns wandered through the narrow passageway to the visitor's bench. "Jyr-kee Lu-may... Jyr-kee Lu-may," he called out with a fake Scandinavian accent to the Canuck defenceman he coached in Montreal. Burns and Lumme had a brief chat before the coach went into the dressing room to change for practice.

Getting to the ice in the Coliseum requires the visiting team to turn left out of its dressing room, turn right past a draped partition, make another left behind the low-level portable stands, then one more right through the narrow passageway to the bench. While walking under the stands, players and coaches are protected by a low-hanging piece of rubber, onto which a pair of messages have been inscribed.

"WATCH YOUR HEAD!" says the most obvious one.

In case you miss it, though, there's a smaller notation above the warning that says "READ THIS."

Burns was not at all pleased with the substance or pace of today's practice session. At one point about 20 minutes in, he abruptly skated to center ice, blew his whistle, and said, "Make your minds up what you want to do (with the puck)... you're not working out here." Then, after a very short pause, he bellowed, "GET THE FUCK TO WORK!" so loudly and angrily, his words echoed through the empty arena for several seconds.

Meanwhile, Bill Watters had changed back into his sportjacket and shirt and was sitting with myself, Dave Fuller, Larry Sicinski and Bob Stellick about 20 rows above the Leaf bench. In accordance with the media sideshow on this trip, there was a lot of pissing and moaning — some of it real; some contrived. Fuller talked about how Burns hates him; Sicinski talked about how he hates Burns, and then Larry went toe-to-toe with Stellick, who tried to wear him down with wisecracks. The two swapped verbal indignities to the amusement of the rest of us.

"Everybody hates you. I like you the most and you're shitting on your only ally," Stellick told Sicinski.

"If you were a concern of mine, I'd pay attention to that remark," replied the Hamilton reporter.

Several minutes later, some character known on the radio talkshows out here as "The Pause" came down from the upper seats and leaned on a concrete divider behind Watters. He began prophesizing about how he'd make the Leafs an improved team, but he did so with a self-deprecating sense of humour that dulled Watters' agony.

"You gotta move Sundin back to center," he insisted, whereupon Stellick quipped, "Yeah, the poor guy's struggling on a 45-goal pace."

"Doesn't matter," said The Pause. "And you know, Mr. Watters, if you want to make the team better, you should pick up Rob Brown (from Los Angeles). He's a character guy who can score you a few goals."

"Hold 'er there Pauser," Bill shot back. "You were doing okay till that suggestion. I think it's time to go back and re-load."

Brown had 49 goals with Pittsburgh in 1988-89 but hasn't scored 49 since, while bouncing between the NHL and the minor leagues.

Joe Bowen stopped by towards the end of practice and noticed the predominantly red Kleenex in Watters' hand.

"Cut yourself, Wilbur?" he queried.

"Yeah Joe, but it's starting to subside... I'm only down a quart."

Even Sicinski laughed at that one.

The focus after practice again today was Damian Rhodes, who makes his fourth consecutive start tomorrow night against the Canucks. Half-a-dozen TV cameras surrounded the bemused netminder as he approached the dressing room. "My goal has always been to play in the NHL and I think my break will come one of these days," he told the inquisitive group of reporters. "This week has been a little break for me but I think there's going to be a bigger one down the road."

When the television mob dispersed, I asked Damian is he's merely riding the wave on this road trip, or pinching himself to see if it's all a dream. "You know, that was just running through my mind as one of the quotes to tell the TV reporters, but I decided not to use it," he laughed. "I like all the positive attention I'm getting this week, but I feel like people are just waiting for me to have a bad game so they can shoe me off. I don't want that to happen, even though it has in the past. I think about it, then I forget it."

I asked Damian about Felix Potvin, and how he perceives the club's number-one goalie is reacting to his back-stage role on this trip. "You know, Felix has always been great to me," Rhodes said. "There isn't a hurting bone in his body and I think he'll ultimately benefit from this experience. I can see him coming back and playing better than ever.

"I said before that my big break will come down the road. I can't imagine it being in Toronto, as long as Felix is here. But there has never been any animosity between us and I've never felt bad or envious playing behind him. I'd like to remain a Maple Leaf for the rest of the season, even though I realize my role will be as a back-up."

Potvin, as you might expect, isn't showing any outward signs of distress, even though the inactivity must be knawing away at him.

"Well, it's tough not playing but the most important thing is the team is winning right now and they're doing it with Damian in goal," he reasoned. "It's not like I'm sitting out and he's playing badly. Damian is earning these starts. I just have to continue to be patient and win back the starting job when I get the chance."

Pat Burns came out into the hallway to do his post-practice media scrum and I saw warning lights when Michael Kennedy of B.C.T.V. barged forward with his cameraman to ask the first question. Kennedy and Burns had a minor altercation, you may recall, after the Leaf game here last month when Burns declined a follow-up interview. Today, Kennedy seemed determined to make up for lost time.

"Can I have some room please," Burns asked, extending his arms to push back the aggressive reporter.

"At this point in the season — two games over .500 — how are you describing the Maple Leafs?" Kennedy began.

"We're doing alright. Why... what are you getting at?"

"Well, does the word mediocrity fit?"

I immediately moved back a few steps, sensing an outburst, but the Leaf coach calmly replied, "Who isn't a bit mediocre this season? With the exception of Detroit, just about everybody's hovering around the .500 mark... aren't you paying attention?"

Burns then scurried away from the camera.

"What an ars-hole," he groused.

A few moments later, I headed towards the team bus about 15 feet behind Burns. The Maple Leaf coach was walking with a man who seemed to be appealing for something. As I got closer, Burns desperately tried to inform the man he was crazy. Regarding what, I wasn't sure. A security officer finally arrived and pulled the stranger out of the building.

Annoyed, Burns turned to me and said, "What is it with this place? You can't walk to the damn bus without some loony coming over. That guy actually wanted to put on his skates and play for us tomorrow. And he got mad at me when I said no."

Once again, the Coliseum was devoid of security, and roughly 25 supposed school-children had the run of the place. Among them, was a shapely blond-haired girl who seemed rather attractive from the rear. When she turned around, though, her left eye was just above her chin.

"Whoo, she's got the bad alignment," noted Rick Wamsley.

The bus driver wanted to back the vehicle out of the arena and on to a ramp outside, but his path was blocked by the kids.

"I don't want to run over any of these nose-pickers," he said.

"It's alright," Burns replied. "We'll scrape 'em off the tires."

Burns then stood beside the bus chatting with Bowen and Watters. He idly reached over to a maintenance cart, retrieved a whisk-broom, and practised his golf swing. The players began to arrive and Burns got onto the bus and sat in his spot in the front row. Mike Eastwood came towards us in his usual hurried manner. The Maple Leaf centerman moves quickly from place to place — slightly bent over, with a pigeon-toed walk. "Easty always looks like he has to have a piss," Burns noted, as the player approached the bus.

After waiting for 15 minutes, several players were missing and the coach wanted to leave. Mike Kitchen voluntarily left the bus and walked back to the dressing room to fetch the stragglers. He came back about three minutes later and Burns said, "What's the matter with you, Kitch, you getting all soft?" The Leaf assistant responded by grabbing Burns in a headlock and flailing away with mock punches.

"Get off of me you little rat," Burns yelled.

The late-comers arrived and we left for the hotel.

*　　*　　*　　*　　*　　*

The Maple Leaf player whose off-ice demeanour I admire most is Mike Gartner. In fact, there are times when I downright envy his mellow, unobtrusive nature.

Gartner has been a professional hockey player since 1978-79, when he skated as a 19-year-old rookie for Cincinnati of the WHA. He came to the NHL with the Washington Capitals a year later — the same season as Wayne Gretzky in Edmonton — and 16 years hence, only four players in the storied annals of hockey (Gretzky, Gordie Howe, Marcel Dionne and Phil Esposito) have scored more goals. Heading into tomorrow night's encounter with the Canucks, Gartner has 621 career markers: more than hockey legends Bobby Hull, Guy Lafleur, Maurice (Rocket) Richard, Stan Mikita, Frank Mahovlich and Jean Beliveau.

He is unquestionably on the downside of his career and his critics claim, somewhat accurately, that his benign character off the ice has transcended his play. A front-office employee in the Leaf organization complained to me recently about Gartner's aloofness around the club —how, for instance, he chooses to sit near the front of the team bus and not engage in the frivolity of his younger mates. The employee feels it is condescending on Gartner's part, and that the veteran may be alienating himself from his co-workers.

If so, there is little outward evidence to support that claim. It is true that Gartner separates himself from the group-mentality, but he does so without any hostile intent. He emits the laudable impression of a man who is supremely proud of his career achievements; content with his place in hockey history; his family life; and is not the least bit interested in fashioning artificial airs about himself. He's a learned man with interests that extend beyond the game. His interpersonal skills come in handy as president of the NHL Players' Association and he's always heavily involved with charity work. Simply put, Gartner has abundant self-confidence: to the chagrin perhaps of others less secure. And I can tell you, first-hand, that he's one of the friendliest and most genuine people you'll ever meet... a complete antithesis of the snob-like character defined by that Gardens' employee.

"Oh, I'd hate to be perceived that way," Gartner said as we talked early this evening in the lobby of the Westin. "That's the worst insult anybody could hand me and I truly hope it's not accurate."

Gartner does not deny, however, a certain distancing from the team but he believes it's all part of a natural process.

"I guess after you've played 16 or 17 years, you develop a certain confidence in what you've accomplished and what you hopefully can do in the future. I still love playing the game and all that it encompasses. I enjoy the camaraderie with the guys and sometimes, it's just as much fun observing it as being part of it. I'm playing with guys now who are almost young enough to be my children and it's a great experience. If I seem a little different than some of them... well, I am. But I never try to put myself above them in any way."

Averaging 41 goals per season during his NHL career, Gartner has steadily ascended the all-time ladder and overtaken many of the immortal figures in hockey. His place in history is secure — even if he never scores another goal — and he finds that to be a bit fantastic and somewhat comforting.

"I do give myself a pinch now and then," Mike admits. "If someone had suggested I would play this long — let alone be considered in the company of legends like Hull, Lafleur and Mikita — I would've told him to get his head examined. I don't even consider myself in that type of category even though, statistically, I know I'm there. Really, it's all very humbling to me.

"Fifth place on the goalscoring list has a nice ring to it, but all I have to do is look at the stats *this* season and it brings me back to earth. I haven't been doing much lately, and professional sports has always been fashioned around that motto. I'd like to be contributing a little more right now."

TUESDAY, MARCH 21st
Vancouver

While I waited to board the bus for today's morning skate, five fire-trucks pulled up to the hotel roundabout — their sirens wailing. Nothing seemed too urgent, however, as the fire-fighters disembarked and strolled casually into the lobby. Moments later, Burns got on the bus and shivered from the dampness. "There was too much moisture in one of the kitchen fire-detectors," he explained about the hotel scene.

As we descended the ramp outside the Pacific Coliseum 15 minutes later, there must have been an all-time record of autograph seekers standing in the rain.

"It's March break around here," explained the bus driver.

"Nosepickers!" Burns replied, staring out the window.

When the Canucks came off the ice from their morning skate, I went into the dressing room and asked goalie Kay Whitmore about his impromptu fight with Dino Ciccarelli Friday night in Detroit. Moments earlier in that game, Ciccarelli had intercepted an errant clearing attempt by Whitmore to put the Red Wings ahead 3-1. I wondered if the fight was a result of frustration on the goalie's part, or something else Ciccarelli did.

"I was pissed off at screwing up but that's not why I fought," he said. "Dino and I hacked each other, then he skated through the crease and punched me right in the face. I said, 'I'm not going to take this shit,' so I dropped the blocker and went after him. When the linesmen broke us up, he was screaming at me. The guy's fighting a goalie and he's whining. Everyone is asking me if I'll be in goal for the rematch with Detroit here on Saturday. It's like the WWF."

I went up into the stands to watch the skate and, incredibly, Bill Watters' blood-stained Kleenex was in the same place that he dropped it yesterday. Now, it was a ghastly brown colour. Mike Gartner was back on the ice, skating without any apparent discomfort from the bruised ankle he suffered Friday in Anaheim. Defenceman Todd Gill was also back after missing the Los Angeles game on Saturday with a shoulder injury. During one of the drills this morning, Gill caught his skate in a rut and went crashing into the side-boards near the penalty box. Everyone held their breath for a moment, but he regained his feet almost immediately.

Damien Cox of the Star and Bob Stellick had a little set-to this morning as a result of something Damien wrote in yesterday's paper. Cox does a column on Page 3 of the sports section each Monday called LEAF LIFE — at the top of which, he expresses an opinion. The headline on yesterday's column read

WINGS-BLUES TICKET SWITCH RIPS OFF FANS. Damien criticized the Maple Leaf organization for randomly exchanging the St. Louis and Detroit home games of Apr. 5 and 7. He wrote:

> *There's a certain arrogance to the way the Leafs have handled, or mishandled, this one. The fans — already stuck without the chance to see the Habs, Quebec, Boston and Pittsburgh — get burned, and the club seems to shrug.*

When Cliff Fletcher saw the column, he almost went through the roof of his Gardens office. The article was faxed to Stellick here in Vancouver and the Maple Leaf employee had it out with Cox. Just another example of the verbal retching on this trip.

When I arrived back at the hotel from the Leaf practice yesterday afternoon, there was an envelope at the front desk addressed to me from the Vancouver Grizzlies. The NBA expansion team will begin play along with the Toronto Raptors next season and the Grizzlies' communications director, Tom Mayenknecht, arranged a private tour of the city's new arena — General Motors Place — for Toronto media in town with the Leafs.

Mayenknecht resigned from the Raptors' top communications job at the beginning of February to take a more all-encompassing position here in Vancouver with the umbrella company that owns both the Canucks and Grizzlies. While he's careful not to admit it publicly, it's clear that he grew tired of the janitorial role he had to play with the Raptors' tarnished image. The basketball club's two primary figureheads — owner John Bitove Jr. and president Isiah Thomas — made some rookie mistakes (to be kind) in their dealings with the public, and Mayenknecht rode to the rescue each and every time. Too many times, it turns out, for the sharp-minded executive, who leapt at the opportunity to jump ship.

At mid-afternoon, I drove along with Dave Fuller, Joe Bowen, Bob Stellick and Larry Sicinski to the Grizzlies' new office across the main sidewalk from B.C. Place Stadium. We went next door to borrow some construction hats and boots, then walked down the stairs and across a narrow street to the makeshift entrance of G.M. Place. My boots were three sizes too big and I was swimming in them. Every time I lifted my foot to take a step, the boot stayed on the ground and I had to do knee lifts the whole way. It made for a dandy heel blister.

The structure of G.M. Place is finished, and workers are putting the initial touches on cosmetics both inside and out. As I mentioned earlier, the arena fits snugly below two main-street overpasses, and access routes are being fashioned as we speak. The building will open in time for the Canucks' first pre-season hockey game next September.

We went up a temporary construction elevator on the north side of the arena and found ourselves standing where the upper-level private luxury suites will be located. We looked down and saw the distinct outline of the hockey rink, as workers laid the vast network of piping for the ice-refrigeration system. Two large floodlights at each end of the rink illuminated the surface. The inside of G.M. Place is just a mass of concrete right now but it's quite simple to envision what the arena will ultimately look like. It should undoubtedly be a dandy place to watch hockey and basketball, as the side walls had to be constructed tightly to fit between the overpasses. The seats will thus rise steeply and provide favourable sightlines: much like the new buildings down the coast in San Jose and Anaheim.

At 2:45 this afternoon, I walked through a narrow passageway and down a short flight of stairs to the concrete platform that'll be the hockey broadcast gondola when the arena opens. Using my cellular phone, I went on the air back to the radio station in Toronto with Bob McCown and Jim Hunt, thus becoming the first reporter to do a live interview from G.M. Place. I knew I'd make history if I waited long enough. Steve Frost of the Grizzlies p.r. department accompanied me and couldn't find the construction elevator. So, he and I carefully climbed our way back down through cracks and openings in the concrete structure.

Back at the hotel 90 minutes later, the sun finally broke through a ridge in the clouds, brilliantly enhancing the North Shore mountains. Ironically, however, a cloud-burst erupted overhead, producing a lovely rainbow to the west. I felt empathy for a lone kayaker in the waters beyond the hotel marina.

The Maple Leafs should have had their way with the Canucks tonight at the Pacific Coliseum. Five players — all of whom enacted key roles in the playoff elimination of Toronto last spring — were out of action for Vancouver, including the explosive Pavel Bure. Joining Bure on the sidelines were defencemen Jeff Brown, Jiri Slegr and David Babych, and roughneck Gino Odjick. With so many critical elements of the Vancouver club missing, this was a splendid opportunity for the Leafs to enhance their puny road record, as they iced a relatively healthy line-up.

Not!

Offensively anaemic once again, the Maple Leafs didn't score until there was only 1:13 left in regulation time. By then, the Canucks were up 2-0 and Vancouver added an empty net goal to seal a 3-1 victory. If it weren't for Dave

Andreychuk backhanding a third rebound past Kirk McLean with Damian Rhodes on the bench for an extra attacker, Toronto would have drawn a blank. Leafs finished their west journey at 2-1-1.

"It was a good road trip, but we can't get overly excited," said Burns after the game. "Tonight, one team was desperate (Vancouver) and one team was content. We started playing for keeps in the third period but it was too late by then."

Vancouver opened the scoring midway through the first period when Geoff Courtnall emerged from the penalty box and stole the puck from Randy Wood in the neutral zone. Courtnall motored down the left side and blew a high slapshot past Rhodes from 20 feet. The Leafs fanned on their best scoring opportunity with 2:50 to go in the period, when Mike Gartner and Kent Manderville both whiffed at a nice set-up in front by Doug Gilmour. It was an entertaining, fast-paced period that saw the Maple Leafs come on strongly after a dreadfully slow start.

The Leafs were lethargic early in the second period as well, but they came close a few times during a Vancouver bench penalty for too many men on the ice at the 6:00 mark. Gartner, once again, could not solve McLean despite shooting the puck from point-blank range. On a later Canuck penalty (Dana Murzyn was off for tripping), Wood tipped a Mike Ridley set-up just over the crossbar. The Canucks got a break with 4:45 left in the frame when Courtnall was awarded a penalty shot by referee Dave Jackson, as Jamie Macoun pulled the Vancouver player down from behind on a breakaway. But Courtnall shot wide on his solo journey against Rhodes, trying to go high on the glove side. The period ended with Vancouver still in front, 1-0.

During the second intermission tonight, I ran into NHL officiating supervisor Dave Newell outside the press lounge. Whenever I see Newell, I think back to the wildest Maple Leaf game I ever attended. He was the referee during the Philadelphia at Toronto quarterfinal playoff game of Apr. 15, 1976 — the night Joe Watson, Bob Kelly and Don Saleski of the Flyers were issued criminal charges by the office of Ontario Attorney General Roy McMurtry. They were accused of weapons offenses after using their hockey sticks in a dangerous manner during an ugly altercation in the second period. Watson swung his stick over the glass at the penalty box to scatter fans who were harassing teammate Dave Schultz. Watson's stick wound up clubbing a Metro policeman on the shoulder, which likely had something to do with the follow-up charges.

That was also the night Flyer rookie Mel Bridgman showed how truly brave he was by singling out placid Leaf defenceman Borje Salming for a fight that started the melee. The game took 3 1/2 hours to complete.

"Yeah, I remember they tag-teamed Salming... first Kelly and then Bridgman," Newell recalled tonight. "That game definitely ranks among the three toughest I ever handled — it was out of control pretty much from beginning to end. But you had to expect that when you officiated games involving the Flyers back then. They weren't called the 'Broad Street Bullies' for nothing, and intimidation was a big part of their success. The Leafs were one of the few teams who could match them when things got rough with guys like Tiger Williams, Kurt Walker and Scott Garland. That's why we had such a long night."

It was Game 3 of the best-of-seven series and Philadelphia came in with a 2-0 lead. Newell worked the match with linesmen John D'Amico and Ray Scapinello, and the trio foresaw a difficult night. "John lived in Rexdale and the three of us went over to his house for a barbecue that day," Newell remembers. "D'Amico was always intense, and he really knew how to prepare himself mentally. While he cooked our lunches, he played loud rock music to get us pumped for the game.

"And apart from the incident with Bridgman and Watson, I'll always remember that night for the Philadelphia player — to this day, I'm not sure who — that took my feet out from under me. I just remember I was standing beside the Toronto net during the play and someone flipped me on my backside with his stick. It was certainly no accident but there were several Philadelphia players in the same area when I recovered, so I'm not certain who did it. But it never happened to me again."

The officials stayed that evening at the Holiday Inn near Toronto International Airport and Newell remembers not getting a wink of sleep. "We were up writing reports till 5 in the morning. The people who ran the hotel knew us pretty well and when we arrived back after the game, they had a special room set up with telephones and note-paper. Clarence Campbell, the league president back then, was at a playoff game in Los Angeles, and his rules stipulated we had to let him know if there was an incident off the ice, regardless of when it happened.

"So we phoned him in his hotel room at 4 a.m. Los Angeles time and filled him in on the details. He always wanted to be informed."

The Leafs beat Philadelphia, 5-4, in that wild game and then tied the series with a victory at the Gardens two nights later. But, Philly prevailed in seven. The Flyers were two-time defending champions, and they went on to lose the Stanley Cup final that spring to Montreal. The late Fred Shero coached Philadelphia and Newell remembers him well.

"The Flyers had willing combatants but I think all of us in the league realized that Fred was behind their intimidation tactics," he opined. "Fred would stand behind the bench and almost challenge you to call a penalty, but he rarely argued when you did. Many of us remember those Philly teams for their rough-house antics but I'll tell you, they had fantastic penalty killing. They never would have won without it."

You can't win without scoring goals, either, and the Maple Leafs proved that once again tonight. Mike Eastwood came close to putting Toronto on the board in the opening minutes of the third period, only to be stopped on a breakaway by the impenetrable McLean. Later on, Dana Murzyn slid on his belly to pokecheck the puck away from Mike Gartner, who was breaking into the clear. But the Maple Leafs couldn't bury any of their scoring chances, leading to Vancouver's administration of the lethal blow with 7:09 remaining in regulation time. Martin Gelinas dug the puck out of Dmitri Mironov's skates in the crease and slid it past Rhodes to give the Canucks an apparently insurmountable 2-0 lead.

McLean made difficult stops on Todd Gill and Bill Berg before Dave Andreychuk finally beat him from a scramble in front with Rhodes on the bench for sixth attacker. Rhodes made it off the ice a second time with 40 clicks left, and Mironov had what seemed to be an excellent scoring chance when the puck bounced off the right-wing boards. Dmitri leaned into a slapshot that might have eluded McLean had it gotten through, as the slot area was badly congested. But Dana Murzyn valiantly dropped in front of the shot and his timely block sent the puck catapulting out of the Vancouver zone. Sergio Momeso gobbled it up and fed Christian Ruuttu for the game-clinching empty netter with 1.3 seconds to go.

While he was hardly at fault, tonight's loss almost certainly ends the Damian Rhodes show. While Burns wouldn't commit to Felix Potvin for Friday's game at the Gardens against Winnipeg, the coach has repeatedly stated that his number-one goalie will return to action as soon as the Leafs fail to win. And Damian is expecting him to follow through.

"You never know this season, but I think Felix will be back," said Rhodes. "It's only fair, because I lost. All in all, I'm quite pleased with the four starts I made on this trip. Sometimes, it hard to stay sharp when you haven't played that much but, surprisingly, I felt good through the whole road trip and I'm happy about that."

The tone of Mats Sundin's voice wasn't nearly so positive. "We were lazy tonight," said the big Swede. "It's too bad we had to wind up the road trip like this. They outhustled and outhit us all night long and you can't win hockey games in this league playing like that."

WEDNESDAY, MARCH 22nd
Toronto

The Maple Leafs returned home today on an Air Canada flight that departed Vancouver at 9 a.m., ending the longest west-coast trip in the club's history. Collecting five out of eight points has enabled Toronto to remain just a point behind St. Louis for fourth place in the Western Conference and home-ice advantage in the opening round of the playoffs. The little hot streak has also opened up a five-point edge on Edmonton and Vancouver.

A minor irritation ensued when the Leafs landed at Pearson Airport around 4:30 this afternoon. An equipment failure aboard the *Boeing*-767 delayed arrival of the club's luggage for almost 45 minutes. Television crews from CFTO (Channel 9), CBLT (Channel 5), and The *Sports Network* inundated the baggage-claim area and had plenty of time to gather comments and opinions from the players and coach Burns.

A number of the Maple Leafs were met by their wives and children. Wendy Berg took one look at the combative graffiti on husband Bill's face — courtesy of Troy Crowder — and shook her head.

"You look like a racoon," she said.

Rapidly losing his patience, Burns glared several times at the men behind the luggage counter, wondering if the bags would ever arrive.

"This is great," he moaned.

Finally, the conveyor belt sprung into action — suitcases poured out of the wall — and the crowd of hockey people quickly dispersed.

SATURDAY, MARCH 25th
Winnipeg

It was difficult to imagine any hockey game being more tedious to watch than the two Maple Leaf-Anaheim tilts this season, but a new all-time low may have been established last night at the Gardens.

The Leafs sleepwalked to a 3-2 victory over Winnipeg in the opener of a home-and-home weekend series and even coach Pat Burns had trouble maintaining his concentration. "Is everybody awake after that game?" he deadpanned, entering the press room.

"What about you, coach?" I asked.

"Oh, it was tough... especially that first half, there. Not only the fans were sleeping — I was about ready to pull up a pillow under the bench and have a little snooze as well. It wasn't a very exciting game, that's for sure."

A revealing element of last night's spectacle was the number of media wags who chose to watch the beginning of Michael Jordan's debut at the United Center on press box televisions. Jordan and the Chicago Bulls hosted the Charlotte Hornets and a healthy scrum of people being paid to cover the hockey game were glued to the TV images. It's a sad commentary on the Leafs and Winnipeg that the pre-game basketball show was more compelling than the live action down below.

Is the increasing number of dull hockey exhibitions at the Gardens merely a by product of this lockout-shortened season, or are the Maple Leafs simply a boring team? Columnist Al Strachan examined the issue in the Toronto *Sun* today, under the heading ANOTHER FRUSTRATING YAWNER.

Strachan wrote:

> *If you liked the game last night between the Toronto Maple Leafs and Winnipeg Jets, you'll be pleased. Games of that type are becoming increasingly prevalent in the National Hockey League.*
>
> *Unfortunately for the rest of us, however, if you liked that game, you probably like to read a book during games. You probably also drive at 20 mph in a 60-mph zone and think cleaning the bird cage is a titillating activity.*
>
> *Toronto hockey fans — and, for that matter, fans around the league — are getting increasingly frustrated with yawn-a-minute hockey, but on a lot of nights, that's all they can expect.*

While the goalscoring frequency in hockey is obviously cyclical — totals of 10 and 12 per game were commonplace in the mid-80s during the Edmonton Oiler Stanley Cup reign — it's difficult to conceive which style of hockey is more acceptable. Nowadays, NHL fans crave for higher scores and more offensive action, but a decade ago, many of us thought the goal-producing binges were parochial. For example, in the seven-day period between Jan. 13 and Jan. 20, 1986, were the following results:

> *Toronto 7, Detroit 4/ Pittsburgh 6, Islanders 3/ St.Louis 10, Toronto 1/ Hartford 11, Quebec 6/ Los Angeles 9, Vancouver 7/ Calgary 7, Detroit 4/ Calgary 9, Toronto 5*

That's 89 goals in just seven games, or 10.3 per outing.

Of course, never before or since has there been a spate of Hall of Fame-type goalscorers at or near their prime. These players were among the top 25 point-getters nearing the midway mark of the 1985-86 season:

WAYNE GRETZKY... MARIO LEMIEUX... PAUL COFFEY... DENIS SAVARD... JARI KURRI... MIKE BOSSY... PETER STASTNY... GLENN ANDERSON... MICHEL GOULET... DALE HAWERCHUK... MARCEL DIONNE... BRYAN TROTTIER

It was an era during which hockey was influenced by the European methods of rapid puck movement and creativity in the neutral zone. The Edmonton Oilers had the talent to play that style in North America and were the supreme measure of success. However, the offensive explosion was aided by another factor: a generally meager quality of goaltending in the NHL. Several of the names at the elite end of the goals-against race in 1985-86 will hardly be confused for legends. They include: Bob Froese, Doug Soetaert, Clint Malarchuk, Al Jensen, Roberto Romano and Doug Keans. If you're thinking to yourself, "Who??", you're not alone.

But, even back then, coaches around the league were beginning to understand that reverting to a more defensive style was in their best interests. The Minnesota North Stars of the early '80s were stockpiled with scoring machines like Bobby Smith, Al MacAdam, Steve Payne, Dennis Maruk, Neal Broten, Brian Bellows and Dino Ciccarelli. But defensively, they couldn't have prevented beachballs from entering the net.

In 1983-84, the North Stars scored 345 goals — fifth-highest in the NHL. But, they yielded 344 markers to rank 16th in the 21-team league. True, they advanced as far as the Campbell Conference final that season, but began to realize that a combination of scoring talents and defensive acumen would ultimately provide more meaningful results.

"Maybe it would be better entertainment if hockey started with offense and went from there, but it really works backwards," confessed Minnesota coach Lorne Henning in 1986. Speaking to columnist Frank Orr in The *Hockey News*, Henning said, "You win games by scoring more goals than the other guy, but that's only on the scoreboard. You really win games by being strong defensively, which means you start from your own zone and work from there."

That philosophy — a decade later — has hockey fans groaning from Long Island to Los Angeles. The recent trend towards expansion, and its accompanying dilution of talent, has set the game back 20 years: to an era in which the NHL and WHA struggled to stock 32 professional teams. With the growing popularity of hockey in the U.S., and the availability of players formerly restricted by Soviet and Eastern-European policies, it should be easier for the current-day NHL to provide a higher quality of entertainment. But that simply isn't the case.

At the same time, we must acknowledge that the general quality of goaltending in the league has never been higher. Somehow, the Quebec Junior League — historically regarded as pitiable defensively — has become a genuine factory for young netminders, churning out stars like Patrick Roy, Felix Potvin, Stephane Fiset, Martin Brodeur and Jocelyn Thibault. Maple Leaf draft pick Eric Fichaud is said to be capable of following in that company.

There is the European influence, with Arturs Irbe, Dominik Hasek, Tommy Soderstrom and Nikolai Khabibulin, and the impact of U.S. college hockey, with Ed Belfour, Curtis Joseph, Darren Puppa, Jon Casey, Damian Rhodes and Jim Carey. So, G.M.s and scouts around the NHL have had much less of a problem capitalizing on the worldwide availability of goalies in recent years than they have talented forwards.

The resulting conundrum was further explored by Al Strachan in his *Sun* column today:

> *An increasing number of coaches are writing off even-strength hockey as a potential source of goals. They encourage their players to sit back and wait for the powerplays, hoping they can muster something with the man advantage.*
>
> *The problem from the fans' point of view, however, is that many seasoned referees simply don't bother to call a lot of penalties. On other nights, the players don't bother to get physically involved. As a result, there are fewer powerplays, and even fewer exciting moments.*
>
> *When the teams are at even strength, more and more teams simply refuse to use the center of the ice.*
>
> *They bang the puck up along the wall as much as possible. If they get control in the attacking zone, they circle around, keeping their body between the net and the puck. Then, when pressured, they again bang the puck off the boards in an attempt to put it behind the net. There, the process begins again.*

In less complicated terms, it's called playing an effective "low" game, meaning low down in the offensive zone. Teams that have strong skaters and willing grinders usually do it well, albeit to the chagrin of entertainment seekers around the league. Teams that have only a fair amount of these qualities — like the Maple Leafs and Winnipeg — can render an audience senseless when they try and play the style. Such was the case during last night's snoozer at the Gardens.

I'm a bit anxious about tonight's return match at Winnipeg Arena, as I'll be doing colour commentary on our radio broadcast for the first time in more than four years. Gord Stellick has a prior commitment in the Maritimes. I worked with Joe Bowen on three occasions in 1990 when Bill Watters could not be available for one reason or another. I did a home game against Detroit, and road games in Hartford and Los Angeles. Fashioning a rapport with Bowen (or any broadcaster) when you do colour work so sporadically is not easy, and I'm hoping that tonight's match proves to be more of a conversation piece than last night's debacle.

My flight to Winnipeg left Toronto at 11 o'clock this morning and took roughly 2 1/2 hours. I used to spend a lot of time out here in the early 1980s, when I wrote articles for the Jets' game program. I'd come out for a week or ten days during training camp and conduct interviews for player profiles. The Jets had a pretty decent club back then, with Dale Hawerchuk, Paul MacLean, Lucien DeBlois, Laurie Boschman, Thomas Steen and Brian Mullen up front; David Babych, Randy Carlyle, Robert Picard, Tim Watters and a young Dave Ellett on defence. John Ferguson was the general manager. We'd sometimes watch practice together and he would captivate me with yarns from his rambunctious career in the 1960s with the Montreal Canadiens. Fergy played on five Stanley Cup winners.

Mike Doran was the Jets' director of player personnel back then, and the poor man died an agonizingly slow death after getting into an automobile accident near Peterboro. He was on his way to scout a Junior game and lost control of his car in icy conditions. It slammed into a Hydro pole and he suffered a horrific head injury. I'll never forget visiting him in the hospital several months after the mishap. He was in a coma, but his eyes were open. It was pathetic to see him glance in my direction with such a blank expression on his face. His relatives and friends tried to snap him out of it. They'd talk to him and he'd slowly move his head from side to side in a moribund manner. It was very sad, and Mike passed away without ever coming around.

Winnipeg isn't the most enthralling city in North America, but it still gets a bad rap. During the dead of winter, it can be one of the most uncomfortable places on earth, but so can Chicago, and you don't hear a lot of negative things about the Windy City. I remember visiting a friend here over the Christmas holidays back in 1984. Within a minute of walking outside, the hairs of my mustache turned to little needles and they would have snapped off like paint chips if I'd rubbed beneath my nose. The wind-chill is a killer at that time of year, but even when the gusts are calm, it can be next to unbearable.

As long as I live, I'll never comprehend how football fans endured three-plus hours at Winnipeg Stadium during the 1991 Grey Cup. Covering that game between Toronto and Calgary for the radio station, I ventured out to mid-field for a live radio report early in the afternoon. It was brilliantly sunny and there wasn't a trace of wind, yet I still almost froze to death while waiting for the producer to put me on the air. I walked off that field looking like the Tin Man in *The Wizard of Oz*. My joints simply wouldn't bend, and I felt like muttering, "Oil Can."

Apart from the winter conditions, however, Winnipeg is a clean, tightly knit community with some interesting night spots.

The lobby of the Winnipeg Westin Hotel was a barren wasteland when I arrived around 1:15 this afternoon. Not a human being could be found, and the only noise came from one of those self-playing pianos in the middle of the floor. Finally, an elevator swung open and Pat Burns got off for his afternoon walk. "I'm going to check out all the sights," he said. "I should be back in about ten minutes."

Rick Wamsley then appeared from around the corner and greeted me with a wisecrack. "Big night tonight, huh Howie?" he said, in reference to the colour commentary. "It'll be nice to see you earn your money for a change." Good to have friends on the road, isn't it?

While doing some homework in my hotel room this afternoon, I found it intriguing to notice the scoring imbalance of the Winnipeg club. It has frequently been referred to as a one-line team this season, and nothing could be closer to the truth. The Jets have scored 83 goals in their 29 games so far, and the unit of Alexi Zhamnov, Teemu Selanne and Keith Tkachuk has accounted for 42 of them: just more than 50 percent. Tkachuk, the emotional captain and team leader, was terribly upset after last night's loss in Toronto, which extended Winnipeg's winless streak to six games (0-5-1).

"We have to win tomorrow night's game or we might as well kiss the season goodbye," he barked at a scrum of reporters. "You say we worked hard tonight, but I don't agree. What good is working hard if you don't win the hockey game? I don't give a shit how we look. We're not here to be pretty, we're here to win hockey games. You don't make the playoffs by looking good and losing."

It was a quiet ride along Portage Ave. to Winnipeg Arena late this afternoon. The days are getting longer and it was still light out when we left the hotel, though it was heavily overcast. The chatter on the Maple Leaf bus centred around Mike Tyson's discharge from an Indiana state prison earlier today after serving his sentence for raping beauty pageant contestant Desiree Washington in 1992. The boxing warlords will surely be clamouring for his return to a nameless and faceless sport.

Winnipeg Arena is located in the southwestern tier of the city — directly across a narrow street from Winnipeg Stadium, and at the rear of the giant Polo Park shopping plaza. When the Jets joined the NHL in the 1979 merger of WHA leftovers, the roof of the Arena was raised to accommodate 5,000 extra seats. While the city requires a new, modern building to survive in the current-day NHL, the old Arena isn't a half-bad place to watch hockey. Balconies on each side hang steeply over the ice from goalline to goalline, like they do in the Boston Garden. Most of the 15,393 seats are red, but the higher chairs in the balconies and end zones are blue. The stairways are painted red and yellow.

One drawback is the seating plan in the north end of the Arena, where many of the additions were placed when the roof was raised. The blue seats extend up towards the back wall a full 42 rows, and rafter-beams extending from the original ceiling partially obstruct the view of the opposite end of the rink. The nosebleed seats are only sparsely populated on most game nights, as the Jets hardly ever sell out.

Hanging high above the south end is truly one of the most dreadful portraits of Queen Elizabeth you'll ever see. The gigantic painting is roughly 35 years old and has long been a target of abuse throughout the hockey world. 'Ol Lizzy has a crooked, almost pained expression on her face — the kind most of us make when we let out a fart. Apparently, they've had to replace several panels around her mouth over the years, as hockey players have delighted in trying to knock her teeth out during practice with high, soaring slapshots from the center-ice area.

Flanking the portrait are the flags of Canada and the U.S.A., and five hockey related banners, celebrating the Winnipeg Victorias Stanley Cup triumphs of 1896 and 1901; the Winnipeg Jets Avco Cup (WHA) titles of 1975-76, 1977-78 and 1978-79, and the retired No. 9 jersey of former Jets' star Bobby Hull, whose defection from the Chicago Blackhawks in 1972 started the ball rolling for the WHA.

Having dinner in the upstairs media lounge before tonight's game, I asked Joe Bowen if he had any pointers for me on the broadcast. "Just have some fun," was his reply, and I loosened up.

The press box here at Winnipeg Arena is perhaps the most unique in the NHL. It hangs low from the ceiling and juts out directly over the east boards.

When there's a pile-up below us, we have to lean forward and look straight down; it's almost *behind* where we sit. If I jumped out of the broadcast booth, I'd kill the penalty timekeeper. The press box would be absolutely ideal if it were moved back a few feet. We are literally on top of the action — much like in a smaller, Junior 'A'-sized facility.

The Maple Leafs and Jets played a more spirited game tonight and the Leafs showed some gumption by bouncing back from a 3-1 deficit. The game ended in a 3-3 tie, and there was plenty to talk about afterwards. The Leafs played most of the game without Mats Sundin, who suffered a freak shoulder injury in the first period. Sundin and Jets' defenceman Neil Wilkinson collided innocently along the boards in the Toronto zone early in the opening period. The two players hardly touched one another but the big Swede doubled over in pain and cruised uncomfortably to the Maple Leaf bench. Athletic therapist Chris Broadhurst massaged Sundin's shoulder under his uniform and Sundin tried to take his next shift. But he quickly returned to the bench and did not re-appear.

"It was a very soft collision," Sundin said after the game. "I was reaching for the puck with my left hand and he (Wilkinson) hit me right on top of the shoulder. It felt like something had stung me there and I went right to the bench, where Chris felt it was probably a sprain of the A-C joint. I don't know how bad it is. We'll find out more when I'm examined on Monday, but I think I'll be okay."

The Leafs survived Sundin's absence in the first period, taking a 1-0 lead on Doug Gilmour's eighth goal of the season. But the Jets then answered with three markers in the first 11:30 of the middle frame and it appeared they would gain some revenge for last night's defeat. The evening, however, turned back in Leafs' favour in a 1:20 span late in the period, when a couple of players performed wholly out of character.

To begin with, Bill Berg showed some uncustomary offensive finesse by slamming his own rebound past goalie Nikolai Khabibulin to bring the Leafs within a goal of Winnipeg. Just more than a minute later, Dmitri Mironov rammed Jets' star Teemu Selanne to the boards in the Leaf zone and began carrying the puck towards the Winnipeg end. Selanne regained his feet and raced wildly after the Maple Leaf defenceman. Just inside the Jets' blueline, he wound up with a full baseball swing and whacked Mironov across the back of his pants. Joe Bowen almost jumped out of the broadcast booth next to me. Mironov went to the ice more out of shock than in pain, and Selanne drew his first penalty of the season — a ridiculously lenient two-minute minor for slashing.

Never before, have I seen Cliff Fletcher so incensed. Joe and I were discussing the play when Fletcher walked in and closed the door. He was red as a beet. We looked over at him and he slammed the palm of his hand against the wall, then turned and stormed out. We shrugged at each other and continued the broadcast.

While Selanne served his penalty, justice prevailed when Mironov's point shot was deflected into the net by Dave Andreychuk, knotting the score at 3-3 with only 32 seconds remaining in the period.

"That may have been the worst slash I've seen in my NHL career," Fletcher seethed during the intermission. "It was a very aggressive, two-handed blow and I have trouble understanding how Selanne wasn't at least thrown out of the game. Mironov laid one of his best hits as a Maple Leaf... it was a clean check, and Selanne came off the boards in a total act of frustration and deliberately went after him. Those are the types of incidents we're trying to eliminate from the game.

"The league reviewed the play via satellite and will now conduct an investigation. So, we'll see what happens."

The attack was completely out of character for Selanne, who had only 67 penalty minutes in 164 regular-season games before tonight. "I was just mad, that's not my style," he told me afterwards. "Mironov and me had some run-ins earlier in the game and I got angry when he hit me into the boards. It looked like a bad slash but I wound up hitting him on the pants, in a padded area. That's why it sounded so loud. If I hit him higher, it would have been more serious."

Mironov was still confused about the play after the game.

"I don't know why he got so mad," said the Maple Leaf defenceman. "I hit him into the boards, but it was a good, solid check. He just got pissed off. The slash hurt me only a little. I was more surprised about it than I was injured. He's not that type of player."

The third period of tonight's game was scoreless, thanks to the rookie Khabibulin. The Winnipeg goaltender was brilliant during a two-man Toronto powerplay midway through the period. Dave Manson and Randy Gilhen were in the box and the Leafs buzzed the net in a rare display of offensive wizardry. But the 56-second advantage was to no avail.

Winnipeg had the only shot in the uneventful overtime period.

Keith Tkachuk was in a bad mood once again, both during and after the game. The Winnipeg captain took four minor penalties and he railed for the second night in a row in front of reporters.

"We're not satisfied with the tie," he insisted while pedalling through a cooldown workout on an exercise bike. "We felt we deserved more but we can't pat ourselves on the back. We didn't win the hockey game and teams in front of us continue to come out on top. We were up, 3-1, and we should have buried them. When we get momentum... when we can put a team away, we don't.

"I know I'm not satisfied, especially with the number of stupid fucking penalties we took. They're killing us."

With the tie, the Leafs remain two points up on St. Louis for fourth place and home-ice advantage in the Campbell Conference. But, the Blues have five games in hand.

*   *   *   *   *   *

A 4-3 victory over Edmonton at the Gardens was marred by a couple of Maple Leaf injuries. Eight minutes into the third period, captain Doug Gilmour was decimated by former Leaf Luke Richardson in the center ice area. Gilmour came across the neutral zone with his head down and Richardson smashed into him like a locomotive. It was the hardest open-ice bodycheck at the Gardens in several years and Gilmour left the game with a mild concussion. It rekindled memories of Richardson's belt on Tony Granato of the Rangers a half-decade ago, when the big defenceman played for the Leafs. Later in the third frame, Dmitri Mironov dove to strip Todd Marchant of the puck and crashed into the end boards behind the Leaf net, separating his left shoulder. He could miss the remainder of the regular season. Mike Ridley and Randy Wood scored goals 1:38 apart in the second period to wipe out a 2-1 Oiler lead. Shayne Corson of Edmonton went after Bill Berg when the final buzzer sounded and was assessed a gross misconduct penalty for verbally abusing linesman Scott Driscoll — an incident that'll be reviewed by NHL vice-president Brian Burke. "Everything goes under review in this goddamned league," Corson griped afterwards. "You have to play with eggs in your pocket."

FRIDAY, MARCH 31st
Chicago

There must be something about the 7:35 a.m. United Airlines flight to Chicago that screws up the weather patterns in Toronto. We haven't had a morning snowstorm since the last time I booked on this departure — on route to St. Louis, Feb. 27. But there we were this morning — my wife Susan and me — sitting on the *Boeing*-757 and gazing out the port-side window in astonishment as a blizzard whipped through the west end of Toronto. With no connection to make, another delay wouldn't matter, but I found the coincidence to be rather bizarre.

The weather system soon passed by and we were on our way only 15 minutes late. Susan is on this trip because she's never been to either Chicago or St. Louis and with the entire weekend off in Missouri, we should be able to relax and spend some time together. The Maple Leafs flew to Chicago yesterday afternoon and Doug Gilmour was on the plane, apparently of sound mind. Gilmour had his brain rattled by Edmonton's Luke Richardson at the Gardens Monday night — the victim of a classic open-ice body crunch in the neutral zone. The Leaf captain had a CAT-scan on Wednesday to see if he'd incurred any damage, and he typically found some humour in the situation, as indicated by hockey writer Frank Orr in today's Toronto *Star.*

> *When it was suggested to Doug Gilmour that the doctors had looked in his head and found nothing, the Maple Leaf captain had a quick retort.*
> *"No! No! There really is a brain there," Gilmour said. "I know, because I saw it on the machine when the doctors were looking."*

Gilmour also confessed to seeing "no brain cells, but definitely a brain," and reported that two days of hearing bird songs had finally passed. "I don't feel too bad and the doctors have said there's no risk after a slight concussion. You have to be aware at all times on the ice and I guess I wasn't for just a split second (against the Oilers)."

Gilmour suffered a grievous head injury while driving nine years ago, when he played in St. Louis. He was struck by a motorist who ran a red light and his car smashed into a parked vehicle. "I didn't have my seatbelt on and I hit the windshield very hard," he recalled. "I was conscious all the way, even going to the police station to make out the report. I played three games with the head injury before my eyes began to go out of focus. I was playing on a line with Tony Hrkac and Todd Ewen and I told them not to give me the puck.

"But as time went on, I slowly began to feel better and the CAT-scan Wednesday did show some scar tissue from the accident."

I received a letter at work yesterday from a lady named Susan Hughes, who teaches journalism at Turner Fenton Secondary School in Brampton, Ontario. Hughes is obviously an avid follower of the Maple Leafs and she wrote about helping one of her students research an article on Gilmour for the school newspaper. During a 45-minute phone interview with the Maple Leaf captain, Susan uncovered what she believes is the basis for Gilmour's difficult season. Her theories aren't completely novel, though she articulates them wonderfully, and with emotion. Here are several excerpts from her letter:

> *The characteristic of Doug Gilmour that surprised us the most was his admitted lack of self-confidence. Until this year in Toronto, he has played with such assurance that we expected self-confidence to be a major reason why he has achieved what he has. Doug was remarkably candid during the interview. He told of times when he hid behind walls in high school because he was intimidated by "bullies." He described himself as a "cocky little kid" although his brother says he was more of a prankster than cocky. We all know the type. I teach students like this all the time and they are often very insecure. He said his lack of self-confidence held him back as a junior hockey player (until his final year), as it did in his early days in St. Louis. He said that he was "put down" all his life because of his size and it had a profound effect on the way he felt about himself.*
>
> *This past fall, during the lockout, the old self doubts seem to re-surface. Gone was the "fearless" man of the past couple of years, as described by his brother. He talked about losing his edge. He talked about retiring. Doug Gilmour seems to have psyched himself into a bad season.*

Hughes did her own analysis of Gilmour's mind-set this season, and she went back and discovered similarities during his Junior career with the Cornwall Royals of the Ontario Hockey League.

> *I really believe the reason that Gilmour was able to elevate his play to the elite level in Toronto was because he felt needed here. Cliff Fletcher relied on him to turn the club around and Gilmour responded beyond anyone's wildest imagination —including Fletcher's. What a confidence booster it is to be needed.*
>
> *... Gord Wood took over as coach (of Cornwall) 19 games into (Gilmour's last season) with the club. In previous years, Dale Hawerchuk had been the star of the Cornwall Royals. Now, with Hawerchuk gone, no player stepped up to fill the*

void. That changed when Wood went to Gilmour and told him the team needed him to be (its) leader. Gilmour responded by going from 27th to first on the scoring list in only ten games! Wood gave Doug's line 45 minutes of ice time many nights. Wood says, "The more I said to him, 'You're showing them all,' the better he got. He wanted to play forever." Doug went on to win the scoring title and was selected league MVP.

When someone really believes in Doug and makes it clear that his contribution is crucial — that no one else can do the job — he responds in a remarkable way.

In continuing her thesis, Hughes explained that the trade last summer with the Quebec Nordiques for Mats Sundin has not been healthy for the Gilmour psyche.

The acquisition of Mats Sundin has quite possibly made Gilmour feel that the Leafs no longer need him the way they once did. Maybe he feels that Fletcher and Burns are beginning to doubt him just a little. To make matters worse, he is skating on a line with his future replacement. I wonder what that does to your psyche? It must be very difficult to be in the prime of your career — playing the best hockey of your life — and have your team acquire your successor, clearly labelled as such. To make matters worse, this successor is young, big, naturally gifted with tremendous skills, and has turned out to be a star.

Like the rest of us have done this season, Hughes went on to ponder whether injuries have been a factor in Gilmour's struggle, and she concluded by clearly pointing out at the bottom of her letter, as sort of a P.S.:

* I personally researched the accusations of sexual misconduct against Gilmour in St. Louis. I was not about to publish a story about a hockey "hero" in a high school newspaper if I felt there was any truth to the accusations that he had sexual relations with a very young teenager — a girl the same age as some that I teach. Quotes from St. Louis prosecuting attorney George Westfall ("The whole handling of this situation makes it suspect that a child molestation occurred"), assured me of Gilmour's innocence. It's too bad that some disgruntled

people keep dragging this issue up whenever they want to embarrass or humiliate him.

The flight down to Chicago was smooth and quick this morning and my wife somehow convinced me to take the train into town. The Chicago Transit Authority has a rail line between O'Hare and the main downtown core, and while it costs much less than a taxi ride, the trains have been rumoured to be seedy and (at times) dangerous. However, we had no difficulties on the 40-minute ride today, even though it was an arduous trek with our suitcases from the airport gate to the train station.

After checking in and getting settled at the Drake Hotel, Susan went off towards *Bloomingdale's* with our credit card (yipes!), and I walked down to catch the Maple Leaf bus to the morning skate. On the ride to the United Center, I saw a side of Pat Burns I wasn't aware of. During our travels this season, I've frequently witnessed Burns depart from his dour public posture. Away from cameras and microphones, he can be very laid back and it's actually quite engaging to share a relaxing moment with him. Today, however, I saw the Maple Leaf coach break into practically hysterical laughter... just lose it.

The bus sound system was playing Howard Stern's syndicated morning show, and no one was paying much attention to it until Stern made what sounded like a crude remark about somebody's figure. Burns was lounging in his front-row seat when he suddenly turned to Pat Park across the aisle and said, "Listen to that, the guy just called somebody 'fat.'" I informed Burns he was listening to crazy Stern, who then launched into a highly personal attack against Liz Smith: entertainment-gossip columnist at the Long Island-based tabloid *Newsday*. Smith apparently critiqued some movie role that Stern had auditioned for, and the shock jock laid into her but good.

"Liz says she wouldn't want to be like Howard Stern... well, I wouldn't want to be a fat sow like her," the D-J griped. "I wouldn't want to have rolls of blubber hanging off my sides like that whale..."

Every time Stern called Smith a "fat sow," Burns almost fell off his seat and into the aisle. He was bursting. As deplorable as Stern sounded, it *was* rather funny to hear him compare the columnist to a marine mammal and you had to laugh... albeit pitifully. Burns was beet-red and still had a smile on his face as we walked into the arena.

There are two giant holes at either end of Chicago Stadium and you can see that workers are busy shelling out the inside of the old arena before razing it. The Stadium is a thick, solid brick structure and is not going to fall easily. In fact, there hasn't been much progress in the visual aspects of the demolition since we were last here at the end of January. The sale of Stadium bricks and interior seats is starting to become big business, and will only get bigger.

Susan and I had enough time this afternoon to go for lunch, then up to the 94th floor of the Hancock Building — two blocks south of the hotel. It was overcast in Chicago today, but there was still a fabulous view from the top of the city's second-tallest building (only the Sears Tower is taller). Around the supper hour, we took a taxi to the United Center, and with the exception of New York, there is no more harrowing city to meander through during rush hour than Chicago. Especially when *your* cab driver is causing much of the chaos. Susan and I could barely watch as this guy sped through intersections with amber lights turning red — honking madly to keep right-of-way motorists from proceeding. We were very happy to arrive at the arena unscathed.

While walking around to the press box tonight, I could look down from the fifth floor of the United Center and see into Chicago Stadium through the gaping hole in its west end. There isn't much left of the interior, but the cement pad that used to be the arena floor is still intact. It seems incredible that hockey was played in that ranshackled building just 11 months ago.

The Maple Leafs came up with some late heroics tonight and escaped with a 3-3 tie against the Blackhawks in a game that featured one of the classic cheap shots of all time. Dave Andreychuk scored from a mad scramble in the Chicago goalcrease with 48.1 seconds left on the clock to produce the tie, with Leaf netminder Felix Potvin on the bench for an extra attacker. It was Andreychuk's second goal of the period. Todd Gill made a nifty play to keep the puck in at the blueline, and Gilmour and Mike Ridley had whacks at it before Andreychuk banged it home. Chicago deserved to win the game in the third, producing a 19-2 edge in shots before the late Maple Leaf rally. Goals by Hawks' Bernie Nicholls and Maple Leafs' Mats Sundin had produced a 1-1 tie after two periods. Tony Amonte and Andreychuk exchanged goals early in the third, and Chicago took a 3-2 lead near the midway mark of the frame, when Joe Murphy scored on the powerplay.

"It feels good to contribute," said Andreychuk afterwards. "At the beginning of the season, the shots weren't going in. Now they are and the team is getting points because of it."

The Maple Leafs gained the important tie with five regulars back home nursing various ailments. Dave Ellett, Dmitri Mironov, Mike Craig, Mike Gartner and Ken Baumgartner all watched the game from Toronto, and Mats Sundin was still feeling the effects of the sprained shoulder he suffered last week in Winnipeg.

"I consider this a win; that's how big we feel this point was," said Todd Gill, one of the better Maple Leaf performers tonight. "We were down with five minutes left in their building and came back to score. It's a big lift for us."

The cheap shot I referred to earlier occurred near the Maple Leaf bench at the 6:15 mark of the second period. Leaf rookie Ken Belanger and Chicago's Jim Cummins fenced with one another inside the Blackhawk blueline. Belanger dropped his gloves, but Cummins refused to meet the challenge. When Belanger turned to skate to the bench, Cummins came at him from behind and viciously cross-checked him into the boards. It was a cowardly attack from the rear and had Belanger been a little closer to the boards, he easily could have gone in head first and broken his neck. Stunned only briefly, however, Belanger got back up and went after Cummins, and was intercepted by Chicago defenceman Greg Smyth (a former Maple Leaf). The two players fought, and Cummins and Smyth were both excused for the remainder of the match.

"That was a premeditated attack and stupid," fumed Pat Burns after the game. "Things like that in hockey just can't happen. It can end a player's career."

"He's obviously a cheap-shot artist," said Belanger of Cummins. "If you can't face a guy head on, you shouldn't be playing the game."

Chicago coach Darryl Sutter was unimpressed by Cummins' attack and said, "I don't know if I'd dress him again after taking that penalty. It was very selfish."

There was lots of activity at the Leaf bench in the middle frame. A puck was shot over the boards and it conked athletic therapist Brent Smith in the noggin. Smith retired to be stitched up then cautiously viewed much of the game from the little corridor between the benches.

SATURDAY, APRIL 1st
St. Louis

Susan and I went to O'Hare Airport for our 9:45 flight down here this morning and I almost had heart failure when I stepped on board the plane. You know how they ask you to empty your pockets at security, to avoid setting off the metal detector? Well, I dropped my keys into one of those plastic containers and walked to the United Airlines boarding lounge without them. When I sat down on the *Boeing*-737, I checked my pockets and a wave of panic came over me. I ran off the plane and back to the gate and, thankfully, the United agent was very sympathetic.

She called "lost and found" and my keys were there. The flight was scheduled to leave in five minutes and she asked an airport worker to "run" the keys over to the gate. Four minutes later, there still was no sign of the worker and the lady explained two things: a) that the word "run" was a misnomer among airport personnel, and b) that she couldn't hold the flight for me. She took my hotel address in St. Louis and said she would courier the keys to me, but just as I turned to run back onto the plane, the "rushed" worker casually sauntered up to the gate. Whew!

The flight down to St. Louis took 45 minutes and there wasn't much work to do this afternoon. Pat Burns gave his charges the day off and, moments after arriving at the Hyatt Union Station, I called Bill Berg's room to arrange a short interview. Bergy is one of the most cooperative and easygoing Maple Leaf players, and agreed to meet me in the 3rd-floor lobby. I waited 10 or 15 minutes when I arrived, as Bill was chatting with Jeff Norton, his former New York Islanders teammate. Norton was traded here from San Jose on March 6th in the deal that sent Craig Janney to the Sharks, and he's temporarily living in the Hyatt.

Many of the Maple Leaf players spent today strolling through the mall area here at Union Station, doing a little shopping. Susan and I had dinner tonight at *Dierdorf and Hart's* steakhouse in the Station —the restaurant owned by former St. Louis Cardinal football players Dan Dierdorf (of the ABC Monday Night crew), and quarterback Jim Hart. We arrived and were put at a table next to Pat Burns, Bill Watters, Mike Kitchen and Rick Wamsley. I introduced Susan to the coaches, and Burns offered his suggestions from the menu. The 12-ounce fillet was awesome.

SUNDAY, APRIL 2nd
St. Louis

There was pleasant news out of Chicago today, where the long major league baseball strike finally ended. After eight months of haggling —and the cancellation of last year's playoffs and World Series — the geniuses on both sides came to a "temporary" agreement that will allow the 1995 regular season to begin Apr. 26. But no promises were made to ensure post-season competition this year. Unbelievable! At least, it'll lift the pall of death hanging over the radio station back home. Our bread-and-butter property at The *Fan* and *Telemedia* is the Toronto Blue Jays, and windows were being tightly secured on the ninth floor of our building the past few weeks. Everyone will breathe easier now.

Before attending the Leaf practice today, I took a late-morning walk with Susan past Busch Stadium and then under the Gateway Arch to the banks of the Mississippi River. It was a perfect early spring day — sunny and comfortably warm. Arriving back at the hotel around 12:45, I grabbed my tape machine and met Bill Watters and Pat Park in the lobby. We walked over to the Keil Center, where the Leaf players were getting dressed for practice at the Brentwood Ice Rink. There was a high-school all-star basketball game at the Keil Centre this afternoon and 16,200 fans were in attendance. I briefly watched the spectacle from a corner entrance and it was quite a show. With no hint of defensive play, the game was merely a series of acrobatic slam-dunks, and the crowd loved it. The match was televised here in St. Louis by the local CBS affiliate.

When I walked back to the Leaf dressing room, most of the players had already left. Jamie Macoun came out and asked me where the bus was parked and I led him, Dave Ellett and Garth Butcher back through the corridor the way we came in. After two minutes of trekking through the arena bowels, Macoun asked if I was sure where the bus was, and I said, "I think so." Finally, we came upon the vehicle and I realized that by turning left outside the dressing room, I'd guided the Leaf defencemen on practically an entire circuit of the arena. Had I turned right, the bus would have been 50 feet down the hallway.

"Howie, you trying to tire out my players?" Pat Burns asked with a smirk, as we climbed aboard.

The bus pulled out of the Keil Center and made its way onto Interstate-64 (the Daniel Boone Expressway). A 20-minute drive took us west towards the suburb of Brentwood and on the way, we passed the old St. Louis Arena: the Blues' home from 1967 to the end of last season. From the outside, it looks very much the same as it always has — with its arched entrances and dome-like roof. But the inside has apparently been hollowed out like Chicago Stadium, in preparation for the wrecking ball.

Driving by the soon-to-be demolished Arena reminded me of all the Stanley Cup playoff games I watched on TV in the late-60s, when the Blues were West Division champions the first three years after expansion. Glenn Hall, Jacques Plante, Red Berenson, the Plagers, Gary Sabourin, Terry Crisp... they were the pioneer St. Louis players who'd be greeted by standing ovations when they skated onto the ice in front of sold out crowds at the cavernous Arena. Organist Norm Kramer would play "WHEN THE SAINTS COME MARCHING IN!", and the fans would sing the lyrics in unison — substituting the word "Saints" for "Blues". Soon, the building will tumble and only the memories will remain.

The Maple Leaf players lumbered off the team bus in full equipment and walked into the Brentwood practice facility to don their skates. While they worked out, we media types watched from behind the corner glass — sipping coffee and hot chocolate to combat the artificial frostiness. Leaf practices in

Toronto are closed to the public and are secured by guard personnel, though there forever seems to be a mob of unrecognizables at the Gardens. Today's workout in Brentwood was not policed, yet only a few locals dropped by. One gentleman had a bound collection of St. Louis Blues team photos from the very beginning of the franchise in 1967-68. I was glancing at them when Bill Watters — obviously bored — challenged me to stump him with any name on any of the photographs. And he was up to the challenge, remembering notables like Ray Fortin, Myron Stankiewicz, Don Caley, Mike Lampman and Dave Hrechkosy. That's what the agent business will do for you.

Pat Burns kept today's skate mercifully short in the cold and damp arena, and afterwards, the players lingered outside the bus to warm up in the sunshine. They looked like a house-league team — wearing full equipment, with skates dangling from their shoulders. I was chatting with Randy Wood when I felt a gentle shove from behind. Turning around, Felix Potvin was standing there with a crooked grin, and he inquired as to how I was enjoying my travels with the Maple Leafs this season. It was essentially the first time I'd ever talked with Felix away from the rink, and it sort of blew me away. The "Cat" usually keeps to himself, and often has little to say during even hockey related confabs. Today, I saw a more down-to-earth side of his persona.

Arriving back at the Keil Center late this afternoon, the players showered, and someone turned on the TV in the dressing room. The Blues were playing at Detroit in a matinee on FOX and an up-date from Chicago revealed the somewhat shocking news that Jeremy Roenick will probably be sidelined for the rest of the season. The Blackhawks' best player tore up his knee in a mid-ice collision with Darien Hatcher of Dallas, and he sat on the ice practically crying with pain and frustration. You have to wonder if Chicago can hang on to its fourth-place standing in the Western Conference without its combative leader.

Susan and I went for dinner tonight at the *Mandarin House* in Union Station and our place-mats were one of those Chinese zodiac calendars. Based on the year of your birth, you are thought to be the descendant of a particular animal, and you possess a certain nature. I thought it might be interesting to apply the calendar to a handful of Maple Leafs. Determine whether or not these profiles coincide with your image of the people involved.

For example...
* Born in 1952, Leaf coach Pat Burns is a *Dragon*, about which the Chinese zodiac says: "You are passionate, but often appear distant; soft-hearted, but your stubbornness can cause others to distrust you."

* Born in 1963, captain Doug Gilmour is a *Hare*. "You work well with people and have a good mind for business."
* Born in 1961, defenceman Jamie Macoun is an *Ox*. "You have a calm, patient nature. Your need for security leaves you disdainful of failure."
* Born in 1971, center Mats Sundin is a *Boar*. "You have a quiet inner strength. You are chivalrous, gallant and intelligent."
* Born in 1972, defenceman Drake Berehowsky is a *Rat*. "You are a go-getter and are blessed with great personal charm. Your power of self-control usually restrains your quick temper."
* Born in 1969, goalie Damian Rhodes is a *Rooster.* "You are devoted to work, diligent, self-confident and conservative. You are a loner.
* Born in 1966, injured enforcer Ken Baumgartner is a *Horse*. "Your cheerful disposition and flattering ways make you popular. You have good judgement."
* Born in 1967, winger Bill Berg is a *Sheep*. "You are sensitive and refined. You can often benefit from guidance."

Having no players born in 1968 or 1970, the Maple Leafs are devoid of *Monkeys* or *Dogs*.

MONDAY, APRIL 3rd
St. Louis

If I hadn't personally witnessed what transpired in the second period of tonight's Maple Leaf-St. Louis game, I likely wouldn't have believed it. Toronto *Sun* hockey writer Dave Fuller recounted the scene in his game story, which ran under an apt headline HAUNTING REFRAIN.

> *ST. LOUIS — The Maple Leafs are starting to wonder just what wacko haunts the Keil Center.*
> *Rod Serling?*
> *For the second time in as many visits to the St. Louis Blues' fabulous new arena, the Leafs strayed into the Twilight Zone.*
> *They completely froze for 49 seconds during the second period, while the Blues pumped three goals past Felix Potvin en route to a 5-2 victory.*

The game was an eerie replay of a 3-2 loss here on Feb.
27 when the Blues scored three goals in 58 seconds.

Only in this bizarre Maple Leaf season could the Blues finish off what they came so close to accomplishing last time out. The 58-second eruption back in February came within two seconds of matching the team record for fastest three goals. Tonight — against the same club... in the very same place — the Blues shattered that mark. Ian Laperriere, Esa Tikkanen and Adam Creighton all scored in the 12th minute of the middle period, instantly reversing a game the Maple Leafs were clearly dominating. The scoring spree erased by seven seconds the St. Louis record for a trio of goals, set back in 1978.

"The thing that hurts is that we talked about it before the game," said Randy Wood. "We remembered what happened the last game in here and mentioned that the Blues are the type of team that gets pumped up and scores goals in bunches. We purposely warned each other not to let down after their first goal, and look what happened?! Again."

Up until the St. Louis outburst, the Leafs had the game well under control. First-period goals by Mats Sundin and Doug Gilmour had given Toronto a 2-0 lead. Gilmour's tally had a disheartening effect on the Blues, who were holding a 12-2 advantage in shots at the time. The home club appeared dejected at the end of the period, and the Leafs settled down nicely in the first half of the middle frame.

Even after Greg Gilbert's goal, that put St. Louis on the board at 9:31 of the second period, the Leafs remained composed, and seemed not at all on the verge of collapse. But, then it happened.

"We warned them and warned them," griped Pat Burns afterwards. "That's how the Blues play. They score and then bang... bang... bang... they come at you again. It was frustrating, because we knew it would happen. But, we weren't concentrating out there."

In the second intermission tonight, I had a chat with a player who always concentrated on the ice, and a man who kept his opponents aware. Bob Plager was a rugged defenceman with the Blues in their early years — one of the game's all-time great hip-checkers, and one of its truly funny people. He is currently the Blues' advance scout, and spends his time in other NHL arenas analyzing opposing teams.

Plager is often at Maple Leaf home games and every time I see him at the Gardens, I think back to one of the most incredible scenes I've witnessed at any sporting event. Many Leaf fans who go back to the '70s remember the night the

Plager brothers chased Eddie Shack all over the ice at the Gardens. It happened on Jan. 12, 1974, in a 4-2 Toronto win over St. Louis that was clearly overshadowed by the incident.

I was sitting in Sec. 76 of the west-side Greens that night. Shack was in his second go-around with the Leafs, having been purchased from Pittsburgh in the summer of '73. He had previously worn a Leaf uniform from 1960-67, when he established himself as one of the zaniest players in hockey history. A perennial 20-goal shooter — and a member of all four Leaf Stanley Cup teams in the '60s — Shack's unorthodox style and carefree nature earned him the nickname "The Entertainer", but it clashed mightily with the boot-camp stoicism of coach Punch Imlach, who played Shack sparingly. In 1965, the colourful Maple Leaf forward had a song written about him, called *Clear The Track, Here Comes Shack*. He was extremely popular with the fans at the Gardens, who'd often chant "We Want Shack!" when the action slowed. It was all too much for Imlach, and he traded Shack to Boston for Murray Oliver after Leafs won the '67 Cup, only to re-acquire him when he became general manager and coach of the expansion Buffalo Sabres three years later.

Shack's former Leaf teammate, Red Kelly, coached Pittsburgh when Shack played there and Kelly brought Shack to Toronto when he became Maple Leaf coach for the 1973-74 season. The veteran forward played a support role and was used far more willingly by Kelly to stir the pot when things got stale. In this January, 1974 meeting with St. Louis, a volatile combination sparked the wild eruption.

Shack became embroiled with Blues' defenceman Steve Durbano, one of the classic hot-heads in NHL annals. A former Toronto Marlie Junior, Durbano had a very short fuse and could easily be goaded into blowing a gasket on the ice. Durbano and Shack jostled and were assessed minor penalties. Shack stepped into the penalty box and continued jawing with Durbano, who passed in front of him — gripped by linesman John D'Amico — while skating to the Penguins' box. Durbano stopped and tried to get at Shack, who stood in the box taunting him with a big smile, and circling his index finger beside his head, implying that Durbano was nuts. The two players finally settled down and served their infractions.

When they stepped out of the box, they began fencing once again and a pile-up of bodies occurred along the boards. Removed from the scrum in the grip of D'Amico, Shack began grumbling with the other St. Louis players on the ice — including the Plager brothers: Bob and Barclay. St. Louis forward Phil Roberto pulled Shack away from the linesman and tried to pummel him, but the slippery Leaf broke his grip. The Plagers and Roberto then began pursuing Shack, and an unforgettable scene developed.

Skating backwards and facing the posse of enraged Blues, Shack motored down the west-side boards, around in back of the south goal, then up the east-side boards. At the first opportunity, he leapt head-first into the Toronto bench, almost capsizing a bewildered Kelly. The Gardens audience reacted with a sense of bemusement — cheering wildly, but not truly believing what they'd seen. It's been ingrained in their memories ever since.

"Shackie knew he could get Durbano to take a stupid penalty, so I went over to the box and challenged him to a fight," Plager remembers. "When we chased him down the boards and in back of the net, I recall thinking to myself, 'This has probably never happened in an NHL game.' It was almost funny to be a part of, but none of us were in a humorous frame of mind. Shack probably saved his life by jumping over the boards and into the bench."

Shack has never tried to soften the fear he felt at that moment. "Wouldn't *you* shit if you looked around and saw Inge Hammarstrom and Borje Salming on the ice?" he asks. "They were my protectors out there. In other words, I was on my own."

Plager and Shack had a run-in — literally — the previous season in St. Louis. Playing for the Penguins, Shack was belted by Plager and came away with stitches. "Shackie used to jump in the air when he tried to split the defence and I caught him with my hip," Plager recalls. "He tumbled to the ice and his stick went flying in the air, then came down and landed on his face. He was cut pretty badly. The doctors stitched him up and said it was okay for him to return. But, he said, 'No, those Plagers take this game too seriously, I'll stay in here.'"

The Leafs should have stayed in their dressing room in the second period tonight. Perhaps a doctor could develop a middle period vaccine; something that'd ward off a virus that has plagued the Toronto club for 20 minutes of practically every game this season.

The Maple Leafs had only five defencemen in the line-up tonight. Already without the injured Dave Ellett and Dmitri Mironov, Leafs lost Jamie Macoun when he developed a pulled muscle in his side. Youngsters Drake Berehowsky, Matt Martin and Kenny Jonsson saw lots of ice time as a result. In a calculated manner, several Blues' players intentionally tried to goad the healthy Leaf defencemen into taking penalties and further deplete the blueline unit. Especially in the third period, when the Blues had a two-goal lead to protect. It may not have been the most sportsmanlike manoeuvre, but it was brilliant strategy.

* * * * * *

The Maple Leafs began their final extended homestand of the season by getting physically manhandled in a 6-4 loss to St. Louis less than 48 hours before the trade deadline. "I wouldn't buy any groceries if I were them," Pat Burns warned his players through the media afterwards. The Blues out-muscled the Leafs into numerous odd-man rushes and were clearly dominant in the corners and slot areas. They even tried some intimidating tactics, like Denis Chasse running Matt Martin into the boards from behind in the second period. It resulted in a fracas that Leaf goalie Damian Rhodes entered to pull Brendan Shanahan away from the pile. Shanahan turned around and grabbed Rhodes, then fired a right jab at the netminder, which brought a cascade of boos from the crowd. Warren Rychel sucker-punched Murray Baron of St. Louis from behind to spark a third-period altercation. Rhodes replaced Potvin in the middle of a game for the first time this season after the opening period, with St. Louis leading 3-1. Potvin looked weak on Chasse's goal at the 18:11 mark, as the puck dribbled through his legs. The six goals represented the most the Leafs have allowed in one game this season.

The following day, Leaf G.M. Cliff Fletcher made a trio of trades, sending a conditional fourth-round draft choice to Montreal for center Paul DiPietro, and hotshot goaltending prospect Eric Fichaud to the New York Islanders for left-winger Benoit Hogue. He also dealt little-used Nikolai Borschevsky to Calgary for a fifth-round draft pick. The jury is out on dispatching '94 first-rounder Fichaud at such a young age. Fletcher, however, is looking for goalscoring help from Hogue, who potted 36 for the Islanders last season, but is struggling this year.

Two more deals followed at the trade deadline. Fletcher sent blossoming center Mike Eastwood to Winnipeg for tough guy Tie Domi, who began his career in a Maple Leaf uniform six years ago. He then swapped underachieving defenceman Drake Berehowsky, the club's first-round pick in 1990, to the Penguins for fellow rearguard Grant Jennings — a slow-footed but physical player. It's clear that Fletcher and Burns are tired of the Leafs getting pushed around like they were in the loss to St. Louis at the Gardens.

Domi jumped on a plane moments after the deal was announced and he arrived from Winnipeg about 20 minutes before the Leaf-Detroit faceoff. Toronto lost its third consecutive game, 4-2 to the Red Wings. For the umpteenth time this season, the Leafs were brutal in the second period, as Detroit scored three goals for the final victory margin. Martin Lapointe, Viktor Kozlov and Keith Primeau all beat Felix Potvin in the latter half of the period. Maple Leafs failed with a 41-second two-man advantage and Mike Vernon made a cluster of excellent stops late in the middle frame. Detroit then threw a defensive blanket over Toronto, and the Leafs did not generate a legitimate scoring chance in the third. In fact, they could muster only four shots on goal. Poor Doug Gilmour had yet another set-

back in this difficult season. Battling in the corner with Paul Coffey in the game's final minute, the Leaf captain took a puck in the shnoz and fell to the ice bleeding. He suffered a badly broken nose and lots of internal bleeding. He'll have to wear a face shield when he's healthy enough to get back into the line-up.

New Leaf Jennings made his Toronto debut the following night, as heroics from Damian Rhodes enabled the club to end its losing streak with a 4-3 victory over Winnipeg. Rhodes turned aside 38 shots as the Jets out-gunned the Leafs 41-29... 17-4 in the dreaded second period. Mike Eastwood made his Winnipeg debut on a line with Kris King and ex-Leaf Ed Olczyk, recording two assists in the game. But the Leafs were able to remain a step ahead of Winnipeg all night long. Three times, the Jets closed to within a goal, but they never drew even. The key moment of the game was Mike Ridley's shorthanded marker at 6:12 of the second period, giving Toronto a 3-1 lead. Benoit Hogue scored his first Maple Leaf goal from the slot in the third period.

Rhodes was spectacular once again as the Leafs closed out the homestand with a dull 2-1 victory over Dallas. The back-up goalie made a startling pad save on Dave Gagner with 45 seconds left in regulation time to preserve the win — his 29th stop of the game. Randy Wood shook off Derian Hatcher to pot the winning goal near the midway mark of the third period. He beat Andy Moog with a shot from 15 feet. The Dallas powerplay floundered in the final period, failing to record a shot in three opportunities. The goalscoring exchange in the first period was ironic as Peter Zezel scored for Dallas and Mike Craig for the Leafs. Of course, Zezel went to the Stars as compensation last summer for Cliff Fletcher signing free agent Craig. The game was overshadowed by a wild fight in the eastside Red seats during the second period. Two beefy gentlemen went at it tooth-and-nail and beer was sprayed among fans in the area. Boots and Kristy Fletcher — wife and daughter of the Leaf G.M. — were seated close by. Gardens communications director Bob Stellick went down to the area afterwards and handed out Maple Leaf hats to the spectators who were disrupted. The Leafs finished the homestand with a 2-2 record and were 17-15-7 overall.

SATURDAY, APRIL 15th
Winnipeg

The Maple Leafs have been coming here to Winnipeg since the 1979-80 season, when the Jets and three other World Hockey Association teams became part of the NHL. But, there's a good chance they'll never again be here in southern Manitoba after tonight.

Most indications point towards Winnipeg losing its NHL franchise at the end of this season. A move to Minneapolis seems more likely each day, as a May 1st deadline looms for transfer of the club's private shares from president and governor Barry Shenkarow to a group called the Manitoba Entertainment Complex. The MEC plans to build a new arena for the Jets, but only if the transfer deal is closed within the next 16 days. And a provincial election here in Manitoba — slated for Apr. 26 — will have a large bearing on the issue. It is said that only a majority Progressive Conservative government can save the Jets.

Few people in this city are convinced that NHL power brokers want Winnipeg to remain in the league. But the league's general council Jeff Pash met with the MEC group on Thursday and had some fairly optimistic points of view. "I think this is a community that can support a major-league team but it has to probably work harder to do so than larger, more prosperous markets," Pash told the Winnipeg *Free Press*. "But, if it's prepared to make the investments and prepared to provide the kind of facilities the team needs...then I think the Winnipeg Jets can be here for a long time.

"We're not looking for a short-term solution. We want a long-term solution that will keep the team here for many years to come, that will have it adequately financed, and will allow it to field a competitive team on a regular basis. We don't want a league that divides into haves and have-nots. We're at a point now for people to make some decisions."

It's against that ominous back-drop that the Maple Leafs are here for their final regular-season meeting with the Jets. The club arrived on a charter after last night's victory over Dallas and I came out this afternoon on an Air Canada flight that got in at 2:30. Tonight's game is scheduled for 6:30 p.m. as the first act on *Hockey Night In Canada's* Saturday doubleheader, which didn't leave much time for relaxation once I got to the Westin Hotel. Complicating matters was a cab driver with a dismaying affinity for the left lane of traffic — the one constantly delayed by motorists making turns. This man seemed to have all day and next week until I not-so politely suggested that he consider using the wide-open right lane. He complied, but the trip from the airport to the hotel took an extra 15 or 20 minutes.

With the Maple Leaf bus scheduled to leave at 4:15 for Winnipeg Arena, I had less than an hour to get settled. My luck, the hotel was inundated with perky adolescents from across the country competing in the national ringette championships, and the little varmints couldn't sit still. They constantly moved between floors — partying with each other — and tying up the damned elevators. I waited 15 minutes in the lobby before one arrived and figured I had to plan for a similar delay on the way down. It left me just enough time to drop my bags and glance quickly at the sports headlines in the newspaper.

I'm happy to see that Mike Eastwood is off to a flying start with the Jets. Easty had blossomed into a quality checking-line centerman by the time the Leafs traded him here last week for the brawn of Tie Domi. But he's been an offensive force so far in Winnipeg — with three goals and two assists in his first three games, including a pair in the Jets' 5-2 victory over St. Louis Thursday. He's been playing with hard-nosed Kris King on his left side and either Ed Olczyk or Teemu Selanne on his right. And the points are starting to accumulate.

"I don't even want to talk about that," he told reporters after the game Thursday, in which he beat Curtis Joseph with a burst of speed on a breakaway. "The fans who saw me play in Toronto know that I'm not a goal-scorer, believe me. I just want to play hard and do what I have to do. The points? I don't think it matters who gets them."

As I expected, Christmas threatened to come before an elevator arrived to take me to the lobby. I had to squish in between roughly a dozen frolicking ringette types and thankfully, the Leaf bus was still in front of the hotel when I got off. Another mob of about 40 autograph seekers of all ages had formed at the entrance to the bus, and most of the Leaf players were good-natured enough to pause and sign. One young lady went a bit too far, however, when she stepped aboard and asked, "Excuse me, is Doug Gilmour here?" Our horrified driver, who had been waiting outside, burst forth with a flying tackle and yanked the little red-head off. The players applauded his athleticism.

About 20 minutes later, I was sitting at an ice-level seat in the northeast corner of empty Winnipeg Arena. Looking around the building at all its nooks and crannies had me wondering if this is, indeed, our final visit here. I remember the first time I saw this place. It was in the late-spring of 1982, when I was living in Calgary. A man named Gord Coleman owned a pizza restaurant in my apartment building and we struck up an immediate friendship. He purchased the Winnipeg closed-circuit TV rights to the Larry Holmes-Gerry Cooney heavyweight championship fight and flew me here with him to see the program at the sold-out Arena.

When I glance about this place, however, two things immediately come to mind — Game 3 of the 1972 Canada-Soviet series (the 4-4 tie), and... the World Hockey Association.

*   *   *   *   *   *

Youngsters of today may not realize that the NHL had a legitimate rival less than a generation ago. Between 1972 and '79, the World Hockey

Association competed with the established league for playing, managerial and coaching talent, and it ultimately forced a merger that saw the NHL incorporate Edmonton, Winnipeg, Hartford and Quebec City.

The rival league was the brainchild of California businessmen Gary Davidson and Dennis Murphy, and was initially considered a pipedream by owners in the NHL. Hardly anybody noticed when the WHA held its first player draft in Anaheim on Feb. 12, 1972. But more than a few eyebrows were raised two weeks later when Bernie Parent, one of hockey's finest young goaltenders, announced he would leave Toronto to play for the Miami entry in the WHA the following season. Scepticism lingered for several more weeks, but was officially shattered when the Winnipeg club lured Bobby Hull away from Chicago and presented him with a $2 million cheque at the intersection of Portage and Main — forever altering the wage scale of professional hockey.

Suddenly, the flood gates opened, and established NHL players like Derek Sanderson, J.C. Tremblay, Ted Green, John McKenzie, Andre Lacroix and Gerry Cheevers signed with the new league, which began operating in 12 centers in the 1972-73 season. The East Division teams were the New England Whalers, Cleveland Crusaders, Philadelphia Blazers (originally the Miami franchise), Ottawa Nationals, Quebec Nordiques, and New York Raiders. The West Division was comprised of the Chicago Cougars, Winnipeg Jets, Houston Aeros, Los Angeles Sharks, Alberta Oilers, and Minnesota Fighting Saints. Six of the WHA clubs went head-to-head with NHL rivals and the league played an 80-game interlocking schedule.

After granting previously unheard of salaries to its top players, the WHA required a strict operating budget. Many of the original arenas were far smaller than their NHL counterparts. For example, the Alberta club played in the 5,200-seat Edmonton Gardens. Chicago's home was the 9,000-seat International Amphitheatre, and New England played half its season at the 6,000-seat Boston Arena. Corners had to be cut, and the original WHA teams endured unreasonable travel schedules.

Glancing recently at the first WHA media guide brought that predicament to light. The schedule bordered on irrationality. Ottawa would play at Los Angeles on a Wednesday night; Houston on Thursday, and Philadelphia on Saturday. The poor L.A. team was run ragged. One week, it played Sunday in New York; Tuesday in Philadelphia; Thursday at home against Houston, then Friday and Saturday in Chicago! But the league had great staying power and it lasted far longer than anyone predicted.

The first WHA champions were the New England Whalers. How many of these names do you recall?

214

GOALIES- Al Smith, Bruce Landon. DEFENCEMEN- Jim Dorey, Ted Green, Brad Selwood, Rick Ley, Paul Hurley. FORWARDS- Kevin Ahearn, Brit Selby, John Cunniff, Terry Caffery, Larry Pleau, Tim Sheehy, John French, Tom Webster, Tom Earl, Mike Byers.

Bobby Hull had 51 goals for Winnipeg that first WHA season and he finished 10 behind league leader Danny Lawson of Philadelphia. Lawson scored 29 goals in 219 NHL games with Detroit, Minnesota and Buffalo prior to joining the WHA. His Blazer teammate, Andre Lacroix, was the scoring champion with 124 points, while Quebec's J.C. Tremblay had a WHA-high 75 assists. Houston defenceman John Schella led the league in penalty minutes with 239.

The star of the 1960 U.S. gold medal Olympic team — goalie Jack McCartan — played 35 games for Minnesota, while hockey legend Maurice (Rocket) Richard coached Quebec for two games before stepping aside.

The WHA came to Toronto the second year when the Ottawa Nationals were relocated. The Toronto Toros hosted their games at Varsity Arena in 1973-74 and faced the same crazy travel log. They once played at Los Angeles on a Friday; at Chicago on Saturday, and home against Edmonton on Sunday. The club moved into Maple Leaf Gardens the following year. My father's accounting firm had season tickets in the Golds, five rows behind the Toros bench, and I recall spending many a night watching and enjoying the rival league.

The Toros averaged around 8,000 fans per game and would come close to selling out when Winnipeg (with Hull), or Houston (with Gordie Howe) came to town. I'll never forget shovelling driveways with my pal David Silverman for an entire day after a major snowstorm in 1975, so we'd be able to afford a pair of Blues to see the Jets.

The Toros had a pretty decent team with many familiar players. Ex-Leafs Frank Mahovlich, Paul Henderson and Jim Dorey were on the club. The big scorer was (Shotgun) Tom Simpson, who had 52 goals in 1974-75, and Czechoslovak expatriate Vaclav Nedomansky was a star. As the Maple Leafs became respectable in the mid-70s, interest in the Toros began to wane and the club was transferred to Birmingham for the 1976-77 season.

During its seven-year existence, the WHA also entered markets like Calgary, Cincinnati, Indianapolis, Detroit, Denver, Vancouver, Phoenix, San Diego and Baltimore. The unparalleled career of Wayne Gretzky began in the WHA with Indianapolis and Edmonton in 1978-79, its final season. Future NHL stars Mark Messier, Michel Goulet, Mark Howe, Kent Nilsson, Mike Gartner, Rick Vaive,

Craig Hartsburg and Mike Liut also started in the final years of the renegade league. It left quite a legacy.

And no place was it more prominent or successful than here in Winnipeg, where the Jets appeared in the Avco Cup final five times —winning three championships. The forward unit of Ulf Nilsson, Anders Hedberg and Bobby Hull may have been the most talented and explosive of all time, in either league. A banner commemorating Hull's familiar No. 9 jersey still hangs at the west end of Winnipeg Arena.

*   *   *   *   *   *

One man who has observed the Jets since their WHA beginning is Winnipeg *Free Press* sports columnist Scott Taylor. A dead-ringer for Canadian musician David Clayton Thomas, Taylor is one of the country's most popular and entertaining media wags and he forever recalls a scene here at the Arena in the second-last year of the WHA.

"I even remember the date: Apr. 14, 1978," he says. "The Jets were playing Birmingham in the opener of a playoff series and the Bulls had a couple of real pests — Steve Durbano, and 18-year-old Ken Linseman. Durbano may have been the craziest player in the history of hockey, and he also got into trouble off the ice, spending time in jail. There was a pile-up along the boards in that first playoff game and Durbano wound up ripping the toupee off Bobby Hull's head. He skated around the rink holding it in the air and the fans wanted to kill him... it was a scene right out of (the movie) *Slapshot*.

"Bobby came out the next period wearing a helmet and the fans gave him a standing ovation."

The anthem singer here in Winnipeg is an eye-catcher... sort of a Kelly Bundy lookalike. Blonde and busty, Jennifer Harper strolled onto the ice from the northeast corner tonight wearing a low-cut dress. Her ample cleavage was quite visible from the press box and during the anthem, many of us were watching Felix Potvin to see if he'd resist a glance to his right, where Harper was standing. Potvin had his mask on, but his neck did seem to "twitch" in that direction a couple of times, and who can blame him. What a great way for a goaltender to lose his concentration just prior to the opening faceoff. If Harper moved a bit closer to the front of the net, the Jets would probably jump in front by a couple of goals in the first minute of each game.

One of my reporter pals pointed out another Arena "attraction" in the northeast corner, where a long-time usherette has six fingers on her left hand. A set of powerful binoculars confirmed the report on the otherwise attractive lady.

The Leafs wound up getting trounced by Winnipeg tonight, and it was very much their own fault. Rarely has this offensively challenged team been so inept with the puck than in the first period of the game. The Leafs outshot the Jets 16-5 but all of their advances went for naught. Dave Ellett personified the entire 20 minutes when he somehow missed a wide-open net with 10 seconds left. Standing just off the right edge of the crease, Ellett had the entire four-by-six staring him in the face, but he shot the puck through the crease and wide left. The incomprehensible gaffe maintained a scoreless deadlock.

During the first intermission tonight, I went downstairs to the main-floor lobby and noticed a rather interesting display. Encased in glass were several artifacts from the Manitoba Sports Hall of Fame —including the green Minnesota North Stars jersey worn by the late Bill Masterton in 1967-68. A native of Winnipeg, Masterton was a centerman with the North Stars in their inaugural season and he became the first and (to date) only player in NHL history to perish as the result of an on-ice incident. Defencemen Ron Harris and Larry Cahan of the Oakland Seals decimated Masterton with a clean bodycheck at the old Met Center, Jan. 13, 1968. The rookie forward suffered a cracked skull and severe brain injuries, and he never emerged from a coma — passing away in hospital two days later.

The Minnesota club retired Masterton's No. 19 jersey and the NHL Writers' Association named a trophy in his memory: presented annually to the NHL player who "best exemplifies the qualities of perseverance, sportsmanship, and dedication to hockey." Claude Provost of Montreal was the first recipient, and players the calibre of Jean Ratelle, Bobby Clarke, Lanny McDonald and Mario Lemieux have won it since. Masterton's original North Stars jersey was donated to the Manitoba Sports Hall by his widow, Sally.

Winnipeg opened the scoring tonight early in the second period when Dallas Drake deflected in Darryl Shannon's shot. Trailing 2-0, the Leafs got their only goal of the night when Todd Gill snapped a shot past Tim Cheveldae while Garth Butcher was serving a cross-checking penalty with 1:25 remaining in the period. But the shorthanded marker didn't contribute to any momentum, and Winnipeg put the game away with three unanswered goals in the third. The Leaf defence was atrocious in the final period, getting caught up ice numerous times. All in all, it was another night of frustration for coach Pat Burns.

Having outshot Winnipeg 45-24, nobody in or out of the Maple Leaf dressing room was too sure how the club got beaten by four goals — its largest margin of defeat this season. Tim Cheveldae was fairly solid in the Winnipeg net, but the vast majority of Maple Leaf shots were of the soft variety. It marked the first Maple Leaf loss in four games without Doug Gilmour. The captain is still unable to suit up after breaking his nose so terribly against Detroit last week. Tie Domi suffered a groin injury in practice a couple of days later and hasn't been able to play either. You know it had to hurt the former Jet being in the press box tonight, especially watching Mike Eastwood set up a couple of Winnipeg goals. Heading to Chicago for a key game on Monday, the Leafs remain tied with the Blackhawks for the fourth playoff spot in the Western Conference (and home-ice advantage in the first round). But the 'Hawks have two big games in hand.

SUNDAY, APRIL 16th
Chicago

I almost had heart failure on the Air Canada flight down here from Winnipeg this morning. About 20 minutes into the trip, the captain came on and said a light had illuminated in the cockpit indicating a problem with the plane's landing gear. Terrific. He throttled the engines back to 250 nots and twice lowered the wheels, causing the DC-9 aircraft to vibrate rather noisily. After consulting with maintenance people on the ground, he came back on and announced he was "reasonably certain" the problem had been rectified.

There were only a dozen or so passengers on the plane — including last night's referee, Bill McCreary — so I wandered up to the flight deck to get a first-hand report. The captain assured me the problem was with the light and not the gear, and invited me to sit with he and the first-officer for landing at O'Hare, which was quite the experience. Indeed, the wheels did support the jetliner as it settled onto Runway 9-L and I breathed an internal sigh of relief.

There wasn't much to do in old Chi-town today. Despite the ugly loss in Winnipeg, Pat Burns gave his charges the day off to regroup and he scrummed with the Toronto media in the lobby of the Drake Hotel just after 2 p.m. The coach's 17-year-old son, Jason, is on this trip, and Burns managed to score a pair of tickets for this afternoon's Chicago-New York NBA game at the United Center. Father and son headed in that direction after the media session, both excited to see Michael Jordan in person for the first time.

I took a walk along a practically deserted Michigan Ave. today and then went up to my hotel room to watch the Chicago at Dallas NHL game on FOX. The 'Hawks are reeling without Jeremy Roenick and were beaten for the seventh consecutive time. A 2-1 loss to the Stars extended the club's winless streak to nine games since Roenick went down with a knee injury two weeks ago this afternoon.

MONDAY, APRIL 17th
Chicago

There was some pleasant news for the Maple Leafs at the skate this morning when both Doug Gilmour and Tie Domi pronounced themselves ready to return to the line-up for tonight's game. Gilmour will wear a full face-shield to protect his busted beak and he's not looking forward to it. During the skate today, he had to pause a half-dozen times to wipe the sweat and mist off the inside of the plastic mask. "I haven't much of a choice right now, so I'll try to endure it," he said afterwards.

Chicago Stadium is a pathetic sight. The inside has been hollowed out completely and the old barn is nothing more than a mangled frame of steel. Remarkably, a single stairwell in the upper northeast corner has remained intact through all the demolition. It used to take fans to the cheap seats for hockey and basketball games and the building is falling down around it. The single flight of about 10 stairs — painted red and yellow — stands out among the ruins. Both ends of the former rink have been bashed in by the wrecking ball. Standing at the west end, you can look right through the length of the building and see the giant Sears Tower in the downtown area, two miles away.

On the bus ride back to the hotel this morning, former Expos and Mets pitcher Tim Burke was sitting with Mike Gartner, which was rather odd. I later found out the two met while Gartner was at training camp in Montreal for the 1987 Canada Cup and became fast friends. Burke and Gartner were in New York together when Gartner played for the Rangers. Burke lives in nearby Indiana and has driven up to see tonight's Leafs-Blackhawks game. He still has that long mane of silvery black hair.

On route to the hotel, we passed the *Oy Vay Bagel Bakery*, which made me wonder about the quality of its food. The last thing a Jewish cook wants to hear when his patrons take a bite is, "Oy vay!"

I spent much of this afternoon roaming through the greatest book store I've ever seen. *Borders Books and Music* is a block away from the hotel on Michigan Ave. and it would take a week to thoroughly explore its three levels of material. For lunch, I walked over to *Gino's East*: "Chicago's Legendary Pizzeria" — an aptly named restaurant on Superior St., south of the hotel. Nowhere in the civilized world will you find a more delicious spicy-sausage pizza. It's well worth the long wait.

Our ride to the United Center for tonight's game was interesting, as the bus driver took the "carbon monoxide" route. He travelled most of the way along

Lower Wacker St.: a tunnel-like stretch of road, quite logically, below Upper Wacker. In the meat of Chicago's paralysing rush hour, the driver tried to find a quicker route, but cars were backed up in the tunnel and the fumes began to slowly overwhelm many of us on the bus. Thankfully, he soon emerged onto the Eisenhower Expressway and we could breathe relatively fresh air once again.

Tonight's edition of The *Blue Line* takes a run at Pat Burns. There is a full-page photo of the Maple Leaf coach — looking perturbed — in a post-game media scrum at the Gardens. The accompanying caption reads: "Can we hurry up this press conference? I have an 11:00 date with Jenny Craig." Yes indeed... a real program.

The Maple Leafs were able to escape with a giant win tonight, and prolong Chicago's interminable woes. A 3-1 Toronto victory had fans at the United Center muttering away in disbelief. Is it possible that one man can make an entire team? It certainly seems that way, as the 'Hawks are now winless in ten games — eight in a row without Jeremy Roenick. Opposing checkers are concentrating their efforts on Chicago's second-line centerman, Bernie Nicholls, and the results have been disastrous.

Frustrations have boiled over now and then. Coach Darryl Sutter blasted defenceman Gary Suter and forward Patrick Poulin after the loss in Dallas yesterday afternoon. "Gary Suter is a very, very average hockey player for us right now, Chris Chelios is carrying him," said the coach. "Deservedly or undeservedly, there are guys getting a lot of ice time, and the Poulins and these people aren't doing a damned thing for our club."

Goalie Ed Belfour set the tone tonight when he made a horrid mistake in the opening minutes. Moving out of the crease to his left, Belfour corralled a loose puck and fed it behind the net... right onto the stick of Mike Gartner. The veteran Maple Leaf said "thank you" and fed a wide-open Mats Sundin in front for a 1-0 Leaf lead. The ghastly error brought a cascade of boos from the disgruntled spectators, and though Denis Savard tied the game less than two minutes later, Chicago was again doomed to failure.

The United Center video scoreboard continuously flashed images of voluptuous females in attendance tonight — inducing the predictable response from male spectators. But the cheeky habit came to an abrupt end midway through the third period, when a blonde bombshell sitting behind the Blackhawk goal pulled down the upper part of her halter-top: exposing practically her entire bustline. Only wide-angle crowd shots were shown the rest of the way.

The Leafs scored a couple of goals in the final period to win the game. Mike Ridley whacked in a rebound to break a 1-1 tie and Gartner clinched the victory with an empty net goal. Several Blackhawk players busted their sticks in despair after Gartner's goal went in — and the winless streak was guaranteed to hit ten.

Tie Domi ran shotgun for Gilmour throughout the game, as both players made their returns to the line-up. When Blackhawk forward Jim Cummins slammed Gilmour into the side boards in the second period, Domi jumped Cummins and felled him with a barrage of punches in his first fight as a Maple Leaf. Nobody ventured too close to Gilmour the rest of the night. About three minutes after the incident, Bill Berg suckered Chicago captain Dirk Graham into taking an embarrassing penalty. The two players jostled with their sticks and elbows and Graham made the mistake of dropping his gloves. Berg turned and skated away, smiling, as referee Rob Shick called Graham for unsportsmanlike conduct.

The Blackhawk frustration also showed in the first period, and Jeff Shantz was fortunate to escape the wrath of Shick. The referee was in the way as Shantz went after a loose puck in the corner to the right of Felix Potvin. An exasperated Shantz literally threw Shick out of the way and to the ice, somehow avoiding a penalty.

Meanwhile, Gilmour had some decent jump in his first game back from his broken nose. "The face-mask is something I probably will not get used to," he explained afterwards. "It's really hot in there and a (plastic) bar across the top makes it difficult to see at times. We'll have to re-evaluate the visor before the playoffs; maybe I can go from a full mask to a half visor."

Out in Calgary tonight, Wayne Gretzky became the first NHL player to reach 2,500 career points when he set up Los Angeles teammate Rob Blake for a pow-erplay goal. He now has 650 more points than runner-up Gordie Howe, who played 26 NHL seasons.

*   *   *   *   *   *

The Maple Leafs edged Anaheim 3-2 at the Gardens in another sure-fire cure for insomnia. Damn, is it excruciating when these teams meet! Thankfully, the spectacle was confined to those on the premises, as it was not televised anywhere north or south of the border. The game was also a microcosm of this entire Leaf season — underscoring the club's inability, once again, to finish off an inferior opponent. A 2-0 lead in the second period could have grown to 4-0 or 5-0 with some focus on the jugular. Instead, the Leafs allowed Anaheim to creep within a goal on two occasions and the Mighty Ducks could have won the game in the third period if their gloves weren't full of clay. Mike Gartner gave Leafs a 3-1 lead early in the third, but Peter Douris brought Anaheim back to within one less than two minutes later. The Ducks began to out-hustle the Leafs, and had control of the puck in the Toronto zone for a 90-second stretch that forced coach

Pat Burns to look sideways at one point, in fear of the inevitable. The line of Paul DiPietro, Bill Berg and Rich Sutter floundered during that shift and would have been scored upon by a halfway decent team. Felix Potvin was forced to make a game-saving stop on Stephane Lebeau from point-blank range with five minutes left in regulation time. Todd Gill and Mats Sundin had given Leafs a 2-0 lead in the second period. Grant Jennings assisted on Sundin's goal for his first point as a Maple Leaf.

THURSDAY, APRIL 20th
St. Louis

Some lunatic blew up a federal office building in Oklahoma City yesterday, killing scores of unsuspecting people, including babies and young children in a day care center. The disturbing images were still on everyone's mind today as the Maple Leafs gathered at Pearson Airport for an afternoon charter flight to St. Louis.

"Howie, did they find any suspects yet?" asked a grim-faced Doug Gilmour, checking in at the Air Canada counter. There is speculation that the F.B.I. has zeroed in on the persons responsible for detonating the car bomb that blew apart the building, but no confirmation as yet. "How could anybody — regardless of how crazy they are — do something horrible like that?" wondered Garth Butcher as the players proceeded to the boarding lounge. It's a question everyone is asking today.

Pat Burns was sitting by himself at Gate 91 when the players began to arrive. Todd Gill approached the Air Canada agent and wondered if we'd be able to earn *Aeroplan* miles for the flight. "He's wasting his time," Burns said. "They'll never go for it on a charter." I decided to check for myself and the ticketing lady said she'd try and credit us once the flight departed. When I appraised Burns, he said, "Oh really?" and went to register his number as well. "I still don't think it will happen," he repeated, taking his seat.

My original plans were to fly to St. Louis via Chicago tomorrow morning, but I shifted gears when *Telemedia* network manager Allan Davis phoned and asked me to do colour commentary on the radio broadcast of the Maple Leafs-Blues game. Gord Stellick is staying home to attend a surprise birthday party for his mother and will join the team in Dallas on Saturday. I'll be working with Ken Daniels tomorrow night, and I'm looking forward to swapping some tales with my pal from C.B.C. Going in a day early with the team will enable me to do some additional homework for the broadcast. Daniels likes associating himself with the informed.

The Leafs rented an Air Canada *Airbus* for the three-hour trip to St. Louis and what a bonus it was not having to make a connection. The coaches, trainers and media (along with Pat Park) gobbled up *Executive Class* seats, while the players shuffled to the rear of the plane. It's a paradox that occurs on every charter — the handsomely paid athletes sit together at the back, as they do on bus rides, while us comparative paupers stretch out up front like seasoned prima donnas.

We took off for St. Louis at 4:45 this afternoon and an apparently infinite trend began to materialize. There has been only one constant of late while travelling with the Maple Leafs — turbulence. Maybe it's the time of year, with the changing seasons and all, but I cannot seem to avoid rocky plane rides. Used to be that turbulence would interrupt a smooth flight now and then but these days, it's the other way around: I'm lucky to get a moment of tranquillity. The onset of shaking and rolling today followed an even more precise script: it occurred just as our dinner trays materialized and produced, at one point, a delectable mixture of salad dressing, orange juice and tea on my supper plate.

Otherwise, the flight was uneventful. The Maple Leaf players spent a portion of it answering questionnaires from The *Sporting News* that Pat Park distributed. A dress code consisting of sportjacket and tie is in effect while the players are in public areas — like the airport — but once aboard a charter flight, many of them strip down to T-shirts and slacks. When returning the questionnaires to Park in *Executive Class*, a number of the Maple Leafs made small-talk with the coaches or trainers. Burns and Gilmour engaged in a serious-looking discussion, and the Leaf captain, noticing my relaxed posture, smacked me playfully upside the head as he returned to the back. Always clowning.

As we descended towards St. Louis between ominous layers of cloud cover, the aircraft began shuddering once again. A few moments later, the captain turned on the seatbelt sign and made a solemn announcement. "As you've noticed, gentlemen, we've had a fairly bumpy flight and I've got reason to believe it'll get even rougher before we land. So, I'll kindly ask you to take your seats and strap yourselves in. Thank you."

Why couldn't I write a book on canoeing?

True to the captain's words, the final ten minutes of our journey today were rather hair-raising. All of us at the front of the aircraft were nervously looking around at each other. Poor Jim Carey was white as a ghost as he leaned back in his seat, eyes closed. As we approached the ground, the pilot made an unusually sharp left turn and then dive-bombed the jetliner onto the runway. It was like the climactic final seconds of a long orchestral arrangement. No airport ever looked quite so beautiful as Lambert Field while our plane slowed to a crawl.

After taxi-ing, we pulled up beside a giant TWA *Boeing*-747 and got out of our seats as a stairway was rolled towards the plane. "I'm not disappointed *that* one is over," Burns confessed. When the flight-attendant opened the front exit-way, it immediately became apparent why our trip had been so bumpy. The St. Louis air was warm and unseasonably humid as I stood atop the stairwell. It felt like Toronto in the middle of July. Obviously, then, we had flown through a weather system that produced an extreme change in temperature (it had been cool and windy back home), thus causing the turbulence. Lugging our bags, we descended to the tarmac and boarded a mercifully air-conditioned bus. The trainers remained behind as they always do to load the hockey gear on an equipment truck and take it to the arena.

The bus-ride to downtown St. Louis took about half-an-hour along Interstate-70 — one of the U.S.A.'s major longitudinal arteries. The highway begins just south of Pittsburgh and winds westward through Indianapolis, St. Louis, Kansas City and Denver, to central Utah.

Seated behind me on the bus today, Kenny Jonsson put his left foot on my arm-rest and the poor boy was wearing dark-blue *Bugs Bunny* socks. "Kenny, if I were you, I'd take my foot off there before the other guys notice," warned a good-natured Mike Gartner. Jonsson complied. On the way, we passed the new domed stadium where the St. Louis Rams will play their home football games next season. The NFL initially rejected the Rams transfer here from Los Angeles, but reversed its position when the club threatened a monstrous law-suit.

Metro Link trains running eastward from Lambert Field sported St. Louis Rams logos as the city warms to the NFL's return. Of course, the Cardinals played here (in Busch Stadium) until 1988, when they moved to Phoenix. The new stadium must be almost finished on the inside because — cosmetically — the exterior still has a long way to go.

"They're going to have that place ready for *this* football season?" Gartner asked me. Based on appearance, it was a justifiable question.

We're staying tonight in the Adam's Mark Hotel at the eastern-most end of downtown St. Louis. Our usual spot, the Hyatt at Union Station, is sold out. While checking in, I requested a room with a view of the Gateway Arch — located just beyond the hotel in a grassy park between I-70 and the Mississippi River. The 630-foot-high steel Arch has become the symbol of St. Louis since being completed in 1965. It commemorates the city's historic role as "Gateway to the West" and is among the most stunning examples of architectural engineering in the world.

"This room should be nice for you," said the front-desk attendant in what might be the understatement of the century. I meandered through the enormous hotel and came upon my room at the end of a long hallway. Upon opening the door, I figured the front-desk man had made a mistake. This was a parlour suite: the type of room President Clinton would stay in if he came to St. Louis. It had a Murphy bed; separate bathroom and vanity areas; full bar facilities with a sink; a huge wooden diningroom table beneath a Victorian chandelier, and two couches. A notice on the back of the door quoted the nightly rate as $270. The Leaf rate is $67.

But the key worked, so I didn't ask any questions.

Best of all, I have a full view of the Arch and the Mississippi. My 15th-floor room literally hangs over the eastbound lanes of the I-70 and the Arch is right there, across the highway. What a sight!

The Maple Leaf players gathered in the lobby soon after checking in and went for dinner. I ate in the hotel with *Hockey Night In Canada* director Jim Marshall and we then joined Pat Burns, Rick Wamsley, Mike Kitchen, Joe Bowen and Harry Neale in the lobby lounge and watched the third period of Hartford at New York on a giant TV screen. The Rangers won a crucial game and now hold the upper hand for the final playoff spot in the Eastern Conference. The Whalers are all but harpooned.

Before going to bed tonight, I watched the late news and was happy to hear that F.B.I. authorities have arrested a suspect in yesterday's Oklahoma City bombing. It was widely believed at first to be the work of Middle East terrorism, but it now appears that some anti-government fanatic here in the U.S. planned the whole thing. After last year's bombing of the World Trade Center in New York, it wasn't unreasonable to jump to conclusions about yesterday's attack. As it stands, however, many of us owe the Middle East community a sincere apology.

FRIDAY, APRIL 22nd
St. Louis

I woke up in the middle of the night and glanced at a remarkable view out my hotel window. A brilliant half-moon was hanging low in the eastern sky at 3:30 a.m., perfectly framed by the Gateway Arch. It was the type of alluring scene that must inspire artists and painters.

Across the river — in the town of East St. Louis, Ill. — there appeared to be a disturbance, as five or six police cars had converged on an overpass: their blue signals flashing in the night. I could only imagine what might have been going on, as I once read that E. St. Louis is the most violent location per capita in the entire U.S.A. Thousands of Illinois-bound commuters pass through the town every day — crossing a bridge over the Mississippi. But, it sure doesn't sound like an ideal place to stop for the night.

I mentioned earlier that this hotel is one of the most expansive I've ever seen. It's an 'H'-shaped building with corridors all over the place, and arrows directing guests to a lone set of elevators. Finding my room last night required a fair amount of exercise as I wound my way through the maze of hallways for what seemed like five minutes. Curious as to the exact distance, I counted my footsteps while walking to the elevator for breakfast this morning and I totalled 130 — more than the length of a Canadian Football League field.

Any frequent traveller knows that hotels are notorious for grossly overpricing food and ancillary items, but this place is ridiculous. The coffee shop was jammed solid when I arrived downstairs, so I mindlessly ordered a muffin to go. The waiter brought it to me a few minutes later and it was roughly the size of a sewing thimble. The packet of butter next to it was bigger. Before I could look up and enquire about the shrunken pastry, the waiter said, "That'll be $3.95 sir." I asked him, quite seriously, if he was joking, and his guilt-ridden reply was, "I don't make the prices, I just serve the food." At which point I invited him to *eat* the food and flipped the mini-muffin back his way. Amazing.

Joe Bowen materialized a few seconds later and we decided to walk over to the Keil Center for the morning skates. This hotel is quite a bit further from the arena than the Hyatt, so the journey took about 20 minutes. But, it was sunny and crisp out today, and Joe entertained me with a story about a hockey trip here during the Harold Ballard regime several years ago. The Leafs stayed at the Chase Hotel out near the old St. Louis Arena and they apparently did not enjoy deluxe accommodations.

"The first night in there, I decided to take a bath before going to bed," Joe remembered. "The hotel had those old, deep bathtubs and I was just starting to relax when this thing plopped out of the tap and into the water. I quickly realized that a three-inch cockroach was about to go swimming with me and I jumped the hell out of there as fast as I could. The bloody thing scared the daylights out of me.

"But after the fright went away, I was pissed off. I gathered the insect up in a glass of water and slipped on some clothes, then took it down to the front desk and plopped it on the counter. The check-in man grabbed the glass and pulled it out of sight before anyone else could notice, and then sheepishly said, 'Oh, I'm so sorry, sir... what can we possibly do to make things better?'

"I looked at him and replied, 'Well, considering the size of that bug, I think it should at least pay for *half* the room, don't you?' He was very quick to agree."

Upon arriving at the Keil Center, I again encountered resistance entering the building. If the Secret Service hired the security staff there, it wouldn't have to worry about people crashing airplanes into the White House. My felony this morning is that I didn't have a general NHL media pass... of course not, why the hell would I need one when I only cover the Maple Leafs?! It was no use trying to explain that to Dick Tracy at the security desk and I had to wait 15 minutes for a p.r. type from the Blues' office to come down and offer me a formal invitation.

The St. Louis players were enjoying a leisurely skate when I made it up into the stands. Leaf winger Tie Domi was chatting with *Global's* Mark Hebscher on the visitor's bench. Al MacInnis of the Blues gathered a clump of snow on his stick and plopped it on Domi's head as he skated by. Domi smirked and shook his fist at the defenceman. Meanwhile, down in the Leaf dressing room, the players were calling Doug Gilmour "Herb Tarlick" for the navy checkered sportjacket he was wearing. Killer came back with his normal reply. "Fuck all of you!" he blurted, as the boys cackled away. Obviously, the Maple Leafs are a pretty loose bunch.

The Blues' new digs at the Keil Center are rather impressive. The fully carpeted main dressing room is gigantic, with the outline of a hockey rink embroidered in the rug. As in the United Center, there's a separate changing area with individual photos of the players above corresponding locker-stalls. A spacious, handsomely decorated coaching office for Mike Keenan is on the other side of the room.

After the skate this morning, I shot the breeze for a few moments with former Maple Leaf Glenn Anderson, who has played well in a limited role for the Blues this season. Anderson signed here as a free agent in early February and has chipped in with eight goals in 28 games. The 15-year veteran won his sixth career Stanley Cup with the New York Rangers last spring, after being swapped to Gotham by the Maple Leafs for Mike Gartner late in the season. Of course, Anderson was an integral part of the Edmonton Oiler machine that won five Stanley Cups in the late-80s.

Maple Leaf fans will have bittersweet memories of Anderson from the club's exciting playoff run two years ago. The fast-skating winger went from hero to goat in 48 hours. His overtime goal won Game 5 of the Campbell Conference Final against Los Angeles at the Gardens — shoving the Kings to the brink of elimination. However, he then took an asinine boarding penalty late in Game 6 at L.A., allowing former teammate Wayne Gretzky to score a powerplay goal in overtime and extend the series to a seventh and deciding match. Los Angeles ultimately prevailed.

But Anderson harbours only fond memories from his brief time in a Maple Leaf uniform.

"Toronto is the hockey hot-bed of North America, there's no doubt about it," he says. "And it was great to be known and appreciated in a city that understands the game so thoroughly. There's obviously a rich hockey history in Toronto and I feel privileged to have played a small part in it. I really enjoyed myself there."

Anderson says he's surprised to be playing here in St. Louis after a whirlwind tour of the hockey universe. "This is my fifth team in the past year," he explains. "From New York, to Team Canada, to Germany, to Finland, to St. Louis. But, it's been very exciting and interesting for me and that's what I enjoy most about life: unpredictability. I really did think after the playoffs last spring that my NHL career was over. I played in Europe, which is something I always wanted to do, and then I had to contemplate my hockey future.

"The passion and the love and commitment were still there, so I decided to come back for one more year. We have a young, talented team here in St. Louis and it's been a great experience so far."

Doug Gilmour and I took a cab back to the hotel after practice. As we walked out of the Keil center, the Leaf captain confirmed that he'll discard his bothersome face-shield for tonight's game. "It's driving me nuts, Howie," he confessed. "I tried to make it sound not that bad when I absolutely had to wear it, but it's awful... I can't breathe properly and it fogs up all the time. So I'm just going to take my chances. The doctors tell me the worst thing that can happen is I'll get hit in the nose and bust it again. It's not like my life is in danger."

While driving to the hotel, Gilmour appraised me about his plans to wed model Amy Cable. The duo will tie the knot Aug. 4, one day after *my* wedding anniversary. Doug's been engaged for a couple of months and is looking forward to settling down. He's purchased a lakefront cottage in his hometown of Kingston, Ont. and will spend a sizeable portion of the summer there. After his personal struggle this season, escaping the hockey environment will be good therapy for the beleaguered Maple Leaf.

"I generally enjoy living in the hockey atmosphere of Toronto, but it's been difficult this year," he admits.

It was a gorgeous afternoon today and when I finished my work for the radio station, I sat at my hotel window for several moments and enjoyed the fabulous view. The shore of the Mississippi River is dotted with a cluster of timeworn factories — some still in business; others not. *Continental Grain* and *Peabody Coal* are located across the river on the Illinois side while *Switzer's Licorice and Cherry Red Candy* is just downstream on the St. Louis side. The famed Mississippi Riverboats are docked on each shore, readying for the night's dinner/gambling cruises.

Late this afternoon, Pat Park and I walked over to the Arch and we wanted to take the inner tram up to the observation windows. I did that when I was here in 1990 and the view is phenomenal. Two-seat elevators inside the Arch piggyback towards the summit and drop off passengers in a narrow room with windows on either side. There's a gorgeous panorama of downtown St. Louis to the west, with the river and the ruggedness of East St. Louis, Ill. in the other direction. Unfortunately, there was a 90-minute wait for trams this afternoon, and we didn't have the time or patience. Instead, Pat and I saw an intriguing, 35-minute movie on the building of the Arch before heading back to the hotel.

Prior to the game tonight, I went on the air with KMOX Radio here in St. Louis. The Blues' flagship station does live remotes from the posh Keil Club: a sports-theme restaurant in a corner of the arena that overlooks the ice down below. It's the same idea as the Hard Rock Cafe at SkyDome. The hosts and I gabbed about a number of sporting topics, including today's firing of head coach Barry Melrose by the Los Angeles Kings. Boy, what a tumble from just two years ago, when Melrose and the Kings were the NHL's Campbell Conference champions.

Actually, it was quite an honour to be on KMOX. If you scan the AM dial at night from the Toronto area — like I used to as a kid — it's quite easy to pick up the St. Louis radio giant. It has a strong, clear signal on the 1120 frequency that spans a large area of the U.S. and Canada. In my teenage years, I often would find KMOX on my bedside radio and listen to the great Dan Kelly call the Blues games. He shared the microphone with several colour commentators back then — including former NHLer Gus Kyle and original Blues' defenceman Noel Picard. They are the subjects of two of my favourite broadcasting stories.

The radio signal from St. Louis would be particularly strong late at night and in the early and mid-70s, I'd go to bed listening to the Blues play on the west coast — in Los Angeles, Oakland or Vancouver. They were playing the California Seals one night and I thought I would pass out from laughing when I heard Gus Kyle commit one of the great radio bloopers of all time. The action stopped after a pile-up in the corner, and Kelly wanted to take a break. He voiced his normal out-cue — "This is St. Louis Blues hockey" — but the operator back at KMOX forgot to hit the commercial cart. Instead, listeners were treated to Kyle lamenting the fact he had stomach problems.

"Gee, Dan, I've got the farts tonight," he told Kelly.

For a second, I couldn't quite believe what I'd heard.

Noel Picard was a rugged defenceman with the Blues during their early years in the NHL and is probably best known for being the player flipping Bobby Orr in the air in the famed photograph of Orr scoring the overtime goal that won the 1970 Stanley Cup. Picard skated for the Atlanta Flames in their inaugural season of 1972-73 and after retiring, he had a brief stint as Kelly's broadcast partner. Despite an engaging personality, Picard spoke with a thick French-Canadian accent, and it likely shortened his radio career.

"Aloh again my friend, dis is Noel Picard at de San Louee Arena as de Blue lead Chicago 2-1 in de first hintermission."

Picard's achilles heal almost certainly was his accented reference to the Blues' president back then, Sid Salomon III. Salomon reportedly would go snaky listening to Picard call him "Sid de Turd." After two seasons with Kelly, the former defenceman was fired.

During the 1990 playoff series between the Maple Leafs and Blues, Bill Watters and I would walk over to the KMOX studios by the Arch and do *Prime Time Sports* cut-ins back to Toronto. Dan Kelly had been dead for about a year at that time — having succumbed to cancer — but you could almost feel his ghost in the station. Few play-by-play announcers in any sport had Kelly's perfect inflection; he made a hockey game hum. He'll be eternally remembered north of the border for his television call of Mario Lemieux's last-minute goal that beat the Soviets and won the 1987 Canada Cup in Hamilton. I remember Kelly equally as much for his Sunday afternoon telecasts on CBS in the late-60s. He worked with New York sportscaster Bill Mazur back then and the TV matinees gave the hockey world a first glimpse of the newly expanded NHL. Games from St. Louis and Minnesota were especially popular on the network.

The Maple Leafs were finally able to avoid a quick-strike attack by the Blues tonight, but they still wound up dropping their third consecutive game at the Keil Center. St. Louis rookies Dave Roberts and Ian Laperriere scored third-period goals to lift the Blues past Toronto 3-1 and the enduring moment of the game was an emotional outburst by Pat Burns midway through the final period.

For the first time in this annoying season, Burns completely lost it behind the bench. It happened at the 9:42 mark of the third. About a minute earlier, Leaf defenceman Garth Butcher had drawn what appeared to be a legitimate interference penalty from referee Don Koharski in the neutral zone, but it prompted a near-riot on the Toronto bench. Damien Cox described the subsequent episode in his Toronto *Star* game story:

With the score tied 1-1 eight minutes into the third period
of a game dominated by Koharski's dogged search for every

infraction on both sides — he whistled 16 powerplays in all — Butcher was called for hauling down Greg Gilbert in the neutral zone. While it was a half-dive by Gilbert, Butcher was beaten on the play and forced to use his stick to prevent Gilbert from breaking loose.

Still, the Leaf bench erupted, and Burns went ballistic, waving his arms wildly while the crowd roared at his image on the video scoreboard.

Blues rookie Dave Roberts scored 42 seconds later, a goal that proved to be the winner, and that just made matters worse.

With Koharski standing on the other side of the rink, the mustachioed Leaf coach spewed invective from his post behind the bench, with all the cameras in the arena focusing in tightly.

After a few seconds, Koharski had had enough and gave the Leafs a bench minor.

Ken Daniels and I, broadcasting the game on radio, had differing opinions of the incident. Ken believed the penalty call on Butcher was marginal and felt that Burns was merely trying to fire up his charges by throwing a fit. Conversely, I had little argument with the call — though I think Koharski has become an insufferable attention seeker — and I couldn't fathom Ken's point about the firing up strategy. I mean, the Leafs were only down by one goal at the time, and weren't playing all that badly. There have been many occasions this season when they've needed a spark but, in my view, this wasn't among them.

To me, Burns just lost his temper. Plain and simple. I've seen it coming all season. The combative Maple Leaf coach has managed to suppress his emotions through repeated failure and disappointment. A full-scale tantrum like tonight's was bound to happen.

But, back to Koharski for a moment. The mark of a quality official in any sport is his ability to be somewhat predictable. The over-used synonym for what I've just described is consistency. It seemed to be different when I was younger. With the NHL full of veteran referees in the '70s, you pretty well knew what type of game to expect before the opening faceoff. Wally Harris, for example, wasn't known as "Last-Call Wally" for nothing. Players had to practically attempt murder before he'd send them off. As a result, his games were usually shorter than others, enabling him to make "last call." Bruce Hood, on the other hand, was more inclined to call a spate of penalties evenly on both sides. Then there was Bob Myers, who was indecisive and unsure of himself in almost every situation.

So, you had good and bad. But the bottom line was, you pretty well knew what to expect from just about every official on a given night. There was consistency.

Now you fast-forward to a referee like Koharski, who is considered by his superiors to be among the best in the business. And if you're a follower of the Maple Leafs, you compare tonight's game to the seventh and deciding match of the Detroit playoff series two years ago. Varying situations, I agree, but were these games really officiated by the same person? Koharski called one measly penalty in a lively and passionate winner-take-all situation back then, and he couldn't pull the whistle out of his mouth in an entirely more docile circumstance tonight. Does it make sense to you? Obviously it does to the tall foreheads in the officiating office, as Koharski continues to draw the most significant playoff assignments each spring. And likely will again this year.

Then there's Koharski's temperament. He seems to have been on a personal crusade for law, order and respect ever since Jim Schoenfeld called him a "fat pig" during the infamous "doughnut" incident in the 1987 playoffs. Whereas most referees will grant an agitated coach the decency of a quick bench visit, Koharski likes to be different. It was typical of his style tonight to stand defiantly across the ice from a fuming Pat Burns and let the Maple Leaf coach hang himself in front of more than 20,000 people. I'm not in any way condoning Burns' outbreak, but there are ways in which a truly competent official can repress such commotion. Koharski seemed to draw pleasure from Burns' predicament, while ensuring that he'd be front-and-center in the story line.

Vengeance may have also entered the equation. Four minutes after the bench-minor penalty, Maple Leaf winger Randy Wood was tripped as he tried to crash the Blues' net. Both Wood and the puck crossed the goal line, but Koharski immediately waved off the apparent tally and refused to call upstairs for a video review of the play, even though it begged for a second look. This time, he was taken off the hook by attending supervisor (and officiating director) Bryan Lewis, who somehow deduced that the goalpost mooring had been dislodged prior to the puck crossing the line. Daniels and I squinted at frame-by-frame replays of the goal in our broadcast location, and at no time did the net appear to budge even a millimetre. I removed my head-set and walked to a neighbouring booth to ask Lewis about it, but he held firm on his optical analysis.

Did Koharski make a rash judgment based on his contempt for Burns' tantrum minutes earlier? And did Lewis then concoct a video ruling to merely quell any further demonstrations? Both are legitimate queries. In any event, Koharski was once conspicuous by being inconspicuous. He quietly called an efficient game, time and again, early in his career. Then the doughnut incident occurred at the Meadowlands, and he's been a spotlight-grabbing egomaniac ever since. It's a denouncement of his work that I've just used up more than a page discussing him.

The Wood controversy occurred with the Maple Leafs trailing by two goals, as Laperriere had given St. Louis its victory margin by slapping the puck off Damian Rhodes' glove seconds earlier. Benoit Hogue scored the Leafs' only marker on a powerplay early in the second period, re-directing a perfect goalmouth feed by Mats Sundin past Jon Casey. Glenn Anderson answered for the Blues later in the middle frame.

Burns had calmed down after the game, as he stood outside the Leaf dressing room talking to reporters, but his disdain for the officiating was more than evident. "There was no flow to that hockey game at all — it was a special teams game," he grumbled. "It couldn't have been very interesting for the fans to watch."

I asked Burns if his third-period outburst was more the result of his simmering emotions than it was Koharski's penalty call on Butcher. "No, it's not frustration, it's my opinion," he said. "The bench minor was a legitimate two-minute penalty... it happens."

About the video ruling on Wood's apparent goal, Burns emphatically said, "It was the wrong call. When I look up (to the press box) and see (Blues' assistant coach) Bob Berry talking to the video replay official (Lewis) — in my mind, something is real weird. I watched the play five times on video after the game and it was a goal. No doubt about it. But what am I going to do? I'm just a coach."

Randy Wood was also shaking his head over the play. "I was just going to the net and I couldn't tell whether or not the moorings came off," he said. "But I thought there was a rule in place that states if the net is dislodged by the force of an attacking player being pushed, a goal still counts. And I certainly wasn't the cause of me flying into the net... I was tripped from behind. So, it was a curious decision."

Meanwhile, Butcher could only shrug off the third-period penalty call by Koharski. "I just stepped up and hit (Gilbert). My stick was still tangled up with him and we both went down to the ice. He had the puck when he was hit, so I don't know how you could call interference. I was doing everything I could *not* to take a penalty on the play, but I guess (Koharski) saw it differently."

Fellow defenceman Jamie Macoun was even more outspoken than Burns when discussing Koharski. "Let's clear up one thing first: if our darn powerplay had been hot, we would've won the game easily," he said. "To be honest, how-

ever, the refereeing was brutal. This St. Louis team has players who are known
to jump around and take dives: guys like (Glenn) Anderson and (Esa) Tikkanen
who are looking for the cheap penalty all the time. And tonight, the referee called
everything. It was awful. I think the supervisors up top must be too busy eating
hotdogs and pizza because they don't seem to be doing shit."

As the Maple Leaf players got changed and the trainers loaded the equipment on a bus bound for the airport, I had a some time to reflect on tonight's
broadcast. There seemed to be more chemistry with Daniels than there was with
Bowen a few weeks back in Winnipeg, because Ken and I are friends away from
the rink. Joe made me feel very comfortable — don't get me wrong — but we
aren't socially acquainted in any way. My familiarity with Daniels enabled me to
relax a little more. I also enjoyed the presence of *Hockey Night In Canada* executive producer John Shannon, who spent much of the game in the booth with me
and Ken. I tried ardently to concoct a trivia question that would stump Shannon,
but he gunned me down every time. It loosened things up, though.

On the bus afterwards, Burns sat in his usual front-row location waiting for
the players and stewed over Koharski's performance tonight. In fact, he may
have broken John Brophy's Leaf coaching record for most fucks uttered in a 30-
second span. The man was hot. So, apparently, was the weather outside, as a
storm system had developed over the area. The bus was packed with hockey and
media personnel heading for a charter flight to Dallas and though it wasn't raining out, flashes of lightning were snapping off in the darkened skies above St.
Louis. Would it make for yet another bumpy plane ride? The answer seemed too
obvious.

Tomorrow's Leaf-Dallas game is on *Hockey Night In Canada*, thus the overflow media throng. Bowen, Harry Neale, John Shannon, Ron Harrison, Jim
Marshall, Mark Askin... they were all joining us on the charter to Texas. After a
30-minute bus journey to Lambert Field that took us past the old St. Louis Arena,
we pulled up beside a *Boeing*-737 aircraft with an insignia of the San Antonio
Spurs on the fuselage. The jet is owned by the NBA club, but with the Spurs
playing at home tonight against the Los Angeles Clippers, it was available for
lease. Tomorrow, the plane will be flown back to San Antonio and will take the
basketball team to Minneapolis for a Sunday afternoon game against the
Minnesota Timberwolves.

Upon boarding the aircraft, it's primary function was obvious. All the seats
were *Executive Class* width — two on each side of the aisle. And there was one
row for every two on a normal jetliner, to facilitate leg room for the elongated
basketball types. Each individual chair was also built higher than usual, and my

feet could barely touch the floor in front of me while seated. It was extremely comfortable. The flight attendants had a buffet of munchies laid out for the players on a table in the middle of the plane while a large-screen TV was moulded into the bulkhead at the front. Seats near the back of the plane were positioned to face one another, with card-tables in between. Luxury all the way.

Tonight's take-off through the storm clouds over St. Louis is something I might remember for the rest of my life. By comparison, it made yesterday's flight to Missouri seem like a canoe trip down a soft pond. There is air turbulence, and then there's the tide of motion we faced tonight. About five minutes into the trip, we entered the clouds and the plane began bucking like a wild bronc. Not only was it swaying from side to side, but it was climbing and then dropping in massive air pockets. When you're in the clouds and lightning is nearby, it doesn't look the same as when you view a storm from the ground. Instead of a quick flash of electricity, you are enveloped by a constant brightness; it's as if somebody has turned on a big floodlight outside the plane. That's exactly what happened to us tonight and we were hanging on for our lives it seemed as the plane careened through the weather.

Seated two rows up on the other side, a wide-eyed Pat Burns kept looking back at me with an uncomfortable smirk. You could tell he was trying to be brave, but deep down, I knew he was no longer deliberating the performance of Don Koharski. When the brightness appeared outside the window, Burns looked at me and mouthed, "Is that lightning?" I nodded affirmatively and we both rolled our eyes heavenward.

"Get Howie a drink," jibed Rick Wamsley from across the aisle.

His humour escaped me.

"Wow, this is even worse than last night," said one of the flight-attendants, in a reference I had no desire to explore.

One row ahead, poor Jim Carey seemed to be deep in prayer.

All we could wonder is, "When will this stop?"

Seconds later, the plane burst through the last clump of clouds and into clear sky. And it was like someone had pulled the plug on one of those weight-reducing machines. We went from tumult to tranquillity in the snap of a finger. The captain, who had wisely spared us warning of the situation (what you don't know can't hurt you, right?), switched off the seatbelt sign and many of us took a long, deep breath.

The flight attendants came around with boxes of food, but anything eaten would have ended up on the person in front of me. I asked for a carton of chocolate-milk and just relaxed.

About halfway through the flight, Burns came by and glanced at me with that sinister expression of his.

"You turned white on us, Howie," he smiled.

I thought to myself, "Look who's talking?!"

We flew for almost an hour-and-a-half and the plane again started to shudder as we made our descent. I could see lightning snapping off in the distance, but it was clear down below. Back in his seat, Burns looked over his shoulder and we did the eye-rolling routine again. Thankfully, this episode was short and the remainder of the flight was routine.

On final approach, the captain made a right turn over the center of Dallas. The downtown skyscrapers shone brilliantly in the night with the giant sphere atop Reunion Tower clearly visible. We landed roughly three minutes later, supposedly at Dallas/Fort Worth International Airport. However, when the flight-attendant opened the front door of the aircraft, Burns stood atop the stairwell and looked at the nearby skyline of Dallas. "There's no way this is the International airport — not with the city that close," he said.

Following Burns into a small, empty terminal the size of a bus station, I asked an airport employee where we had landed. And his reply sent shivers down my spine.

We were at Dallas Love Field. The same place where President and Mrs. Kennedy landed on their fateful trip here — November, 22, 1963. And where the President's body departed for Washington aboard Air Force One later that day after the most notorious political assassination in American history. I stood outside in the stilled night air and thought about the films so many of us have seen of the citizens who greeted the President and First Lady at this air field. It was eerie beyond words.

Walking through the tiny terminal, we exited through a door on the opposite side and were assuming we'd come upon a team bus. However, no such vehicle had yet materialized at 1:30 a.m. Pat Park ran back inside to make a phonecall and you had to see this dishevelled group of hockey players sprawled out on an airport sidewalk in the middle of the night.

"Ahhh, I love the smell of this warm, humid air," Burns said to no one in particular. "It's just like being by the lake in summertime."

After a 20-minute wait that seemed like three hours, a motor-coach pulled into the parking lot beyond us, and Park said, "That's probably it." With another game later tonight, and having grown somewhat annoyed by the delay, Burns scornfully replied, "Well, I don't think any *city* buses are coming out here at this fucking time!" As Park smiled weakly, the coach laughed out loud and we all climbed aboard.

With our proximity to downtown, we were at the Hyatt Regency hotel within ten minutes. For the first time this season, my room key wasn't with the others and I had to wait half-an-hour to be registered. Quite by accident, I wound up with the room originally reserved for assistant coach Mike Kitchen. When I entered the suite, there was a lovely fruit arrangement on the desk with bottles of beer and mineral-water chilling in an ice-bucket atop the television unit.

And, Kitch, I want you to know I enjoyed every bit of it!

SATURDAY, APRIL 22nd
Dallas

Dealey Plaza. Finally.

For more than 30 years — like so many of us — I've studied with intrigue the assassination of John F. Kennedy and today, for the very first time, I saw the infamous site in person. Pulling back the drapes of my 22nd-floor room at 8:30 a.m. and looking down to my left, there it was... the former Texas School Book Depository building; the grassy knoll; the white picket-fence, and the triple-underpass leading to the Stemmons Freeway. What an awesome and ghostly sight. And, to think I'm here on the 22nd of the month.

After sitting with Jamie Macoun and Mats Sundin at breakfast this morning — we talked in the hotel lounge about last night's frustrating experience in St. Louis — I did some pre-game reporting work for the radio station, then went back down to the lobby. I ran into Tie Domi, who has visited the Kennedy assassination site on previous trips to Dallas, and was told to expect a metaphysical experience. He wasn't kidding.

Leaving the hotel, I walked under the train tracks of the triple-underpass and up Commerce St. to Houston. I made a left on Houston and walked two blocks north to Elm, passing Main St. along the way. It was at the corner of Houston and Elm that J.F.K.'s motorcade turned sharply left in front of the Texas School Book Depository; and halfway down Elm towards the triple-underpass that Kennedy was shot.

Looking up at the old Book Depository was a bit spooky. The seven-story, red-brick building is unremarkable in appearance, but it has an unmistakable aura. The textbook brokerage firm that leased the building moved out in the early '70s and preservation of the historical landmark was threatened by potential buyers who wanted to raze it. But, the city refused to issue demolition permits and the government of Dallas County exercised an option to buy the building in

March, 1981. It's been known as the Dallas County Administration Building ever since.

The County took immediate measures to assure preservation of the sixth floor, where Kennedy was determined (by the Warren Commission) to have been shot by Lee Harvey Oswald, and a lasting exhibit was created by the Dallas County Historical Foundation. The *Sixth Floor* — as it's known — opened to the public on President's Day (Feb. 20), 1979. At a cost of $4, visitors enter the north side of the building and take an elevator to the exhibit.

I went up today and found it quite fascinating. The actual window where Oswald was said to have fired at Kennedy is cordoned off by panes of plexiglass and the alleged sniper's nest has been reconstructed with boxes of schoolbooks. However, the window next to it is available, and it presents an almost identical view of Elm St. through the clump of trees that Oswald supposedly shot both Kennedy and Texas Senator John Connally. Taking a first-hand glimpse at the angle and distance of Elm from the window makes the Commission theory all the more reprehensible.

The first *Associated Press* wire reports of the assassination are mounted in a glass encasement — reflecting the moment's utter chaos.

While watching a video documentary about J.F.K., I heard somebody call my name and turned around to find Mike Gartner at the exhibit. He and I glanced about for 15 minutes before he returned to the hotel for an afternoon nap. When I left the building, it was lightly raining in Dallas and I walked down Elm St. to the grassy knoll. Standing on that patch of soil blew me away. It was like a movie you've seen all your life suddenly coming true. I suppose if there was a real wicked witch of the west somewhere, I'd have a similar feeling.

An entrepreneur selling J.F.K. memorabilia showed me the cement pedestal upon which Abraham Zapruder stood while filming the tragedy. We are all familiar with his exclusive images of Kennedy slumping over in the limousine and being fatally (and graphically) shot in the head.

What struck me about the whole of Dealey Plaza was how small it is. The concentrated images we've seen through the years have evidently had a distorting effect, as the entire assassination site is no larger than a suburban block. It takes about a minute to *walk* from the corner of Houston and Elm to the triple-underpass, and the grassy knoll is roughly one-third the size of a typical front lawn.

But the entire experience was mind-boggling, and a definite must-see for a first-time visitor to Dallas. At all times of the day, people young and old stand at the Elm/Houston intersection and gaze wistfully at the former Book Depository building. There are few locations in the world more preeminent than this tiny annex of downtown Dallas.

The Hyatt Regency Dallas is a reflective glass building situated to the southwest of Dealey Plaza, on the opposite side of the railroad tracks. The hotel guests could all be flashing moons out their windows and nobody looking at the building would realize it. The flat-topped Reunion Arena (home of the Dallas Stars and Mavericks) is just south of the hotel — across a hilly street and a man-made pond. Located between the two buildings is the 50-story Reunion Tower.

Approaching the arena about 90 minutes before tonight's game, I noticed Maple Leaf defenceman Grant Jennings *leaving*. Our eyes met and I asked him where he was headed. He broke into a queer smile and said, "I've got a bit of an injury." I found that to be rather odd, as Pat Burns had earlier confirmed that all of his charges for tonight's game with Dallas were healthy. It was only when I entered the media lounge that Pat Park informed me about Jennings' "groin injury". Upon further investigation, it was revealed that the newly acquired defenceman had been hoofed in the nether regions by Esa Tikkanen last night, and that his left testicle was roughly the size of a cantaloupe.

No wonder he smiled at me like that.

The interior of Reunion Arena is similar to most of the newer NHL rinks, with one major exception — there is nary a private box. It was built in the late-70s (and opened in April, 1980) — just prior to the luxury-suite boom. Two levels of dark-green seats rise from the ice, but there is no medial walkway between them and, therefore, no apparent room to add private boxes like they've done in Edmonton. Otherwise, it is a handsome and clean facility, and no team in the league makes more effective use of its video scoreboard. The press box is, typically, at the top of the second level, but the sightlines are fairly good.

Sitting in the press box during the warm-up tonight, and munching on mini-pizzas, were a pair of former Leafs now playing for Winnipeg: Mike Eastwood and Ed Olczyk. The Jets played in Chicago last night and are here for a game tomorrow with the Stars. On my way back to the hotel from Dealey Plaza this afternoon, I walked by Winnipeg coach Terry Simpson, who was on his way to the Kennedy site. Eastwood hasn't been away from Toronto for three weeks yet, but he had a season's worth of questions to ask. I filled him in on all his old Maple Leaf buddies, and he mentioned how happy he is playing in Winnipeg. Contentment and success couldn't come to a better guy.

The Maple Leafs were able to achieve neither of the above tonight against the Stars. In perhaps their sloppiest defensive effort of the season, they were beaten, 6-4, and have taken a huge step backwards on this weekend jaunt to St.

Louis and Dallas. After taking early 2-0 and 3-2 leads tonight against a shaky Darcy Wakaluk, the Leafs folded up like a cheap suitcase. They fumbled around in their own end like be-headed chickens and received only marginal support from Felix Potvin. And all members of the hockey club had difficulty hiding their consternation.

Cliff Fletcher watched the debacle three seats to my left in the press box. Cliff rarely displays any emotion in public but he may have left a palm print on the table in front of him tonight after repeatedly slamming his hand down in frustration. Pat Burns was criticized for his abruptness in post-game media sessions earlier this season, but nothing compared to tonight. The coach stopped by long enough to say, "This was horseshit!" and off he went. And even the players, while they continued their hollow analyses, were less-convincing than ever before. This team has been in trouble all season and I think it began to sink in tonight, as they made a slow-footed Dallas team look like the late-70s Montreal Canadiens. That isn't easy to do.

The loss also prevented the Maple Leafs from securing a playoff spot in the Western Conference, though it should be a formality.

The stars of the game were southern-Ontario natives Todd Harvey and Mike Torchia. And their timing couldn't have been better, with a nationwide TV audience watching the game back home. With abundant help from the Maple Leaf defence, Harvey produced his first career hattrick, while Torchia shone in the Dallas goal after replacing Wakaluk at 12:13 of the opening period. Harvey is from Hamilton; Torchia from Toronto.

"We were all singing the *Hockey Night In Canada* theme song in the dressing room before the game," Harvey said afterwards. Torchia entered the match after Dave Andreychuk scored the Maple Leafs' third goal and he nearly yielded a fourth. Mike Gartner rang one off the right post on the first shot at Torchia, and the youngster said afterwards, "I told myself to wake up or this thing could get real ugly." Wake up he did — permitting only one goal on 27 shots the rest of the way.

Five of the six Dallas goals came from within ten feet of the Leaf net as the defence failed miserably in its coverage assignments.

Once again, a failed Maple Leaf powerplay contributed mightily to defeat. Former Leaf Peter Zezel chopped Randy Wood across the arm late in the second period and was given a slashing-major and game misconduct by referee Dan Marouelli. Gord Donnelly of the Stars was already in the penalty box for boarding, providing the Leafs with a two-man advantage for 1:39. But a goalpost dinger by Benoit Hogue was the only legitimate scoring opportunity and a tripping call on Dave Andreychuk at 19:37 of the period nullified the remainder of Zezel's sentence.

On the bright side for Toronto, Todd Gill had a pair of assists for his 15th and 16th points in the last 14 games. And Garth Butcher scored his first goal as a Leaf, taking Mike Ridley's pass and sending an unscreened slapper through Wakaluk's legs from the right point. It gave the Buds a very brief 2-0 lead in the first period.

SUNDAY, APRIL 23rd
Dallas

Without planning it, I was treated to the other half of my Dallas sightseeing adventure this morning.

I took a shuttle-van to Dallas/Fort Worth International Airport and the driver got on the westbound Stemmons Freeway right behind the hotel. Along the way, I saw the opposite side of the triple-underpass from where Kennedy was killed — with the signs ELM, MAIN, and COMMERCE above the corresponding street entrances. A few miles up on the right was the Dallas Trade Mart building, where J.F.K. was headed to deliver a speech. And then Parkland Hospital — also on the right — Kennedy's ultimate destination. Once again... like a movie coming to life.

Before arriving at the airport, we passed by one other Dallas landmark: Texas Stadium, home of the Cowboys, was on the left-hand side in the town of Irving.

It was quite an emotional contrast to the other buildings.

*   *   *   *   *   *

The Maple Leafs' final home game was unquestionably their best 60- minute effort of the entire season. A thorough 5-2 pounding of Vancouver sparked hopes for a sudden revival in the playoffs. All four lines contributed to the scoring as the club played a strong, physical game in the Canucks' end. And Felix Potvin made some difficult, timely saves for one of the few occasions since early in the season. The club was sparked by Doug Gilmour, who pounded Pavel Bure with a clean, hard bodycheck while Leafs were shorthanded in the opening moments. It set the tone for the entire evening. And for once, the Maple Leafs actually enjoyed a dominant second period. Bure had given Vancouver a 1-0 lead in the first, but Gilmour, Dave Andreychuk and Todd Gill wiped it out in the second as Leafs had a 16-12 edge in shots. Bill berg and Benoit Hogue added goals in the third period. "Everyone in this room believes in himself but a game like tonight only adds to that," said Gill. NHL commissioner Gary bettman and actress Whoopi Goldberg were in the crowd for the game. Leafs finished with a 15-7-2 home record.

FRIDAY, APRIL 28th
Calgary

Terminal 2 at Pearson Airport was unusually quiet for a Friday afternoon as the Maple Leafs gathered to begin their season-concluding road trip out west. Rich Sutter and Paul DiPietro wandered through the Departures level seeking the group check-in area but there was no sign of any of their teammates. Nor were there any Leaf players at Gate 78 when I arrived there 20 minutes before the scheduled Air Canada flight to Calgary. Finally, Matt Martin and Mike Craig materialized and Martin was nice enough to exchange my aisle seat for a window.

Once aboard the *Airbus,* seating had to be arranged to accommodate the unavoidable Dave Andreychuk-Jamie Macoun card game. Andreychuk had an aisle seat in the middle of the aircraft, while Macoun was stuck near the back. Wielding his power of seniority, Macoun moved up and sat across from Andreychuk, causing a nebulous chain reaction that threatened to delay the flight. Kenny Jonsson was removed from his pre-assigned spot and shuffled to a window seat in row 22, displacing Darby Hendrickson, who moved up to an aisle seat. Hendrickson then got the boot from Craig, who had a middle position three rows back. "Happened to me on every flight in Minnesota," said Craig, when asked about his malevolence. Macoun then shuffled himself again, prompting Mats Sundin to occupy the seat originally assigned to Jonsson.

Meanwhile, French-Canadian pals Felix Potvin and Benoit Hogue were putting an elderly woman through quite a workout. Complying with their request to be together, the unsuspecting woman got up and moved to the window, but was then re-shuffled to the aisle when Potvin decided he wanted to sit inside. She looked haggard after the exchange.

A stunningly attractive brunette excused herself and sat in the middle seat of Row 18 between Mats Sundin and Rich Sutter. Both players gave her the once over, but *Don Juan* Sundin fell asleep before the plane left the runway — prompting looks of astonishment from many of his teammates. "He must be nuts conking out on her," lamented an envious Maple Leaf sitting behind me.

The flight to Calgary left windy and overcast Toronto at 3:30 this afternoon and took about three hours and 20 minutes. The plane was full, and with only one aisle on the A-320 aircraft, there wasn't a lot of room to move around. Most of the players read for the first part of the trip. Mike Craig, seated next to me, was engrossed in the *National* Star tabloid. It's lead story, entitled FORREST DUNK, featured clandestine photos of Tom Hanks and family on a surfing vacation. Potvin and Hogue were leafing through copies of the french-language newspaper La Presse.

Many of the passengers were disappointed when the aircraft's video equipment malfunctioned, cancelling the in-flight movie. Warren Rychel left his seat next to Todd Gill and walked up a few rows to observe the Andreychuk-Macoun card game. Moments later, a flight attendant made her way up the aisle, prompting Rychel to climb upon the arm rest of Garth Butcher's seat like a linesman would the side boards in a hockey game. It was an unusual sight, and Rychel was fortunate the aircraft did not encounter any turbulence. Butcher and Tie Domi were also involved in the card game and Domi — obviously prevailing — wore that in-your-face smile he often gets after winning a fight.

"These guys are my victims," he boasted, pointing to the solemn trio of fellow card-sharks.

Mike Ridley and Dave Ellett were sitting next to Domi on the left side of the plane and I engaged in a lively conversation with them on the future of hockey in Winnipeg.

Financial stipulations imposed by the NHL yesterday will almost certainly force the Jets to re-locate in the U.S.: likely Minneapolis. Ridley hails from Winnipeg and he played hockey at the University of Manitoba before turning pro with the New York Rangers in 1985. Ellett was chosen by Winnipeg in the third round of the 1982 draft and played the first six-plus years of his career in a Jets uniform. And Domi, of course, left Winnipeg just three weeks ago in the trade-deadline deal for Mike Eastwood. So, all three are notably intrigued by the probable transfer of the hockey club.

"(Gary) Bettman is sure good at starting fires and then trying to put them out," said Domi, in response to Bettman's planned meeting with hockey and government officials tomorrow in Winnipeg.

Ridley and I both agreed that the NHL appears contradictory in its stance on small-market teams, whose well-being was the focal point of the league's propaganda during the lockout. Revenue sharing was viewed as essential for smaller outposts like Winnipeg, and such a plan was loudly trumpeted by Bettman and his foot-soldiers. Only three months later, however, they have put forth conditions that seem purposely incompatible for a small-market franchise.

Ellett looked up from his book long enough to grunt something miserable about Barry Shenkarow and went back to reading.

A few rows behind the Winnipeg crew, Todd Gill was entertaining fellow passengers at the expense of teammate Randy Wood. Sitting across the aisle from Wood, who was sound asleep, Gill rolled up a small piece of tissue-paper. He then reached across and carefully inserted it into Wood's left nostril several times, prompting the sub-conscious player to involuntarily twitch his nose, and drawing muffled hysterics from those seated nearby. Gill followed up by getting down on his hands and knees and tying Wood's shoes together.

Meanwhile, assistant coaches Mike Kitchen and Rick Wamsley were seated among the players in the *Economy* cabin, while Bill Watters and Pat Burns enjoyed the comforts of *Executive Class*. Kitchen didn't mind being back with the real people but he disdained his middle seat. "You think with all the business we give this airline, they might be able to reserve windows and aisles for us," he groused.

As the aircraft swept over the farmlands of southern Alberta on its descent into Calgary, it seemed as if patches of brownish terrain were lightly dusted with snow. This was confirmed when we appeared through low fog on final approach... it was actually snowing rather heavily on the 28th day of April, more than five weeks since the onset of spring. "It looks like Sweden," noticed Kenny Jonsson in the seat behind me. "They just had six inches in Stockholm the other day."

Once inside the airport, the snowfall was clearly visible through windows at the end of the Arrivals corridor and Burns lit into Wamsley, a former Calgary Flame. "Great place, huh Wammer?" he chided. "Anybody would love to live in a Paradise like this." As the players boarded the team bus, many of them tossed similar barbs at ex-Flame Jamie Macoun, who does real estate work out here in the summertime. "Bring your golf clubs Cooner?" asked a teammate. Macoun just smiled.

By the time we approached downtown, 20 minutes after leaving the airport, the city was ravaged by a full-scale blizzard: the type you'd see in mountain elevations during the dead of winter. The huge office buildings and the 60-story Calgary Tower were barely visible through the thick sheet of snow. Hockey weather was obviously hanging in for the balance of this prolonged regular season.

SATURDAY, APRIL 29th
Calgary

The snow had stopped, but it was overcast and dreary in Calgary and I spent much of the afternoon ambling through the downtown Eaton's store in search of a cheap sweater. The outside temperature was hovering just above the freezing mark and I had packed for spring.

After taking a cab to the Calgary Stampede grounds for tonight's game, I walked over to the entrance of the old Corral across the street from the

Saddledome. The building was locked up, but I was able to peer through the door-windows and see a number of the historical photographs that line the corridors (much like in Maple Leaf Gardens). It brought back memories of my brief time covering Junior hockey out here 13 years ago, when the Corral was my second home.

On my way into the Saddledome, I ran into Ed Whalen, a man who has long been synonymous with the media here in Calgary. Whalen is the play by play voice of the Flames' local midweek telecasts, but he's equally recognized for being the long-time host of *Stampede Wrestling*.

During the early 1970s, the CBC affiliate in Barrie, Ont. (CKVR) used to air *Stampede Wrestling* shows from the mid-60s after its late news package on Tuesday nights. The hour-long black-and-white films would begin at 11:50 and I always stayed up to watch starry names like Sweet Daddy Siki, Abdullah The Butcher, Angelo Mosca and Archie Goldie (known as The Stomper). The bouts were filmed next door at the Victoria Pavilion and were promoted by Stu Hart (Bret The Hitman's father), who often found himself grappling with one of his wrestlers in the post-bout interviews Whalen conducted. In fact, Whalen himself showed little concern for the villains of the ring, and it got him into trouble now and then. He remembers one incident in particular.

"Abdullah The Butcher hailed from Khartoum in the Sudan, which I believe is 30 miles south of Detroit," Whalen winked as we ate dinner in the press room. "One night in the late-60s, he was wrestling a good guy from Britain named Billy Robinson and we were in the Corral with an overflow crowd of 10,000 on hand. At one point during the bout, the two wrestlers fell outside the ring and broke the announcer's table I was sitting at. I got chunks of it in my leg and became annoyed.

"Abdullah then grabbed my microphone, took it into the ring, and proceeded to club Billy over the head with it. Well, that was my mike — my Linus's blanket — and I didn't take kindly to having it removed. So, I stormed into the ring and can still hear the crowd going nuts. I hauled the microphone out of Abdullah's hands and tattooed him on the forehead, opening him up for 13 stitches: there was blood all over the place. Within a few seconds, the crowd noise disappeared. All I could hear was this voice inside my head saying, `What in the world are you doing? This guy's gonna kill you!'

"I ran like hell out of the ring and afterwards, I was embarrassed over the incident. I felt like going back and apologizing to Abdullah, but I wasn't sure if he'd accept it so readily.

"Two weeks later, we were doing a show back at our normal spot —the Victoria Pavilion — and Abdullah had a hold of a fan at ringside. It seemed like he was going to plough him and I didn't want to lose our licence. So, I tapped him on the shoulder and said, `Don't you dare!' He responded with a wallop to the side of my head that left me with a dull ache for a year-and-a-half. Stu Hart, the promoter, jumped in and grabbed me and he was laughing out loud. I said, `Why the hell are you laughing? He said, `Because, if I let you go, you're dead!'

"About six weeks later, it was just before Christmas, and I was standing in the lobby of old McCall Field here in Calgary waiting for my mother-in-law to arrive on a flight. Suddenly, I turned around and there was Abdullah coming at me from the other end of the terminal. I glanced about the place and could not find a policemen. I don't mind telling you I was shittin' myself pretty good. Abdullah walked over and handed me a beautifully Christmas-wrapped package. He said, `Here, dis for you... open!'

"Naturally, I was in no position to disobey him, so I tore into the package and pulled out a gorgeous smoking jacket he had purchased while wrestling in Japan. I was flabbergasted. Abdullah glanced at me with a smile and said, `Whalen... when you get that look in your eyes, I get nervous.' Then he walked away laughing, and that was the last time I ever saw him in person."

Embroiling himself with the wrestlers was part of the routine on *Stampede Wrestling*, but Whalen swears that clubbing Abdullah over the head with his microphone was not included in the act. "No, I used to antagonize some of those wrestlers now and then, and that was a prime example," he smiled.

It was nice seeing Ed and his story brought back some great memories from my youth.

The Maple Leafs played another decent game here in Calgary tonight and came away with a 2-2 tie. Ironically, they weren't quite as dynamic as their game here at the beginning of February, and they *lost* that one 4-1. The point moves them one up on Chicago for home-ice advantage in the opening round of the playoffs, but the Blackhawks now have a game in hand and they play Winnipeg at the United Center tomorrow. I'm sure this scramble in the Western Conference standings will continue to the final night of the regular season on Wednesday.

Each team had the lead tonight, but couldn't hold it. The Leafs came out strongly and went in front before the midway point of the first period, as Dave Andreychuk converted Mike Craig's rebound for his 21st goal of the season. In fact, had it not been for the brilliance of Rick Tabaracci in the Calgary net, the Leafs could have built a rather substantial margin, having forged a 10-2 early advantage in shots, on the way to a 17-7 first-period edge. Instead — and as per usual this season — they failed to convert a cluster of scoring opportunities, as Tabaracci, the Toronto native, flopped miraculously from post to post in a performance reminiscent of Trevor Kidd's the last time Leafs were here. Calgary tied the game when Paul Kruse banged his own rebound past Felix Potvin and the period ended 1-1.

Looking down from the radio press box tonight, I spotted Lanny McDonald sitting in the corner seats across the way. How ironic it is that the Maple Leafs are playing here in Calgary, for it was on this night 17 years ago — April 29, 1978 — that Lanny scored his famous overtime goal against the New York Islanders. Few moments in Maple Leaf history are quite as memorable as Lanny beating Chico Resch at the Nassau Coliseum in Game 7 of the Stanley Cup quarterfinals to cap a monumental upset. It was the lone triumph during the calamitous Harold Ballard era and its memory still evokes a feeling of warmth. I talked with Lanny about it.

"Next to winning the Stanley Cup here in Calgary, that was the greatest moment of my career," Lanny said. "What made it especially sweet is we were such huge underdogs in that series. Nobody in or out of Toronto gave us a chance to beat the Islanders and to hang in there the way we did was an absolute thrill."

The Islanders of that era were beginning to rev the engines that would motor them to four consecutive Stanley Cups, beginning two years later. They had it all, with Bryan Trottier and Mike Bossy leading the attack; Denis Potvin spearheading the defence, and battlin' Billy Smith about to become one of hockey's all-time money goaltenders. What they did *not* yet have was the means by which to succeed in the playoffs, and a youthful and cocky Toronto club made them pay. With McDonald, Darryl Sittler, Dave (Tiger) Williams, Borje Salming, Ian Turnbull and Mike Palmateer forming an excellent nucleus, the Maple Leafs of rookie coach Roger Neilson laid a relentless pounding on the Islanders, and the edge in physical play enabled them to rebound from a 2-0 series deficit.

Actually, Salming was not a part of that courageous comeback. The slick Swede — in the absolute prime of his career — had been felled by an accidental high-stick from Islander checker Lorne Henning in Game 4 at the Gardens and was finished for the season. His absence, however, was countered by the dazzling performance of defence-partner Turnbull, who grabbed the leading role in a drama that peaked when the decisive match went into extra time, knotted 1-1.

At 4:13 of the first overtime, McDonald saw an errant pass drop at his feet and he fooled goalie Resch with a soft but well-placed shot to the far side — winning the series — and sending Maple Leaf fans into a night-long binge of celebration.

"It wasn't exactly one of my patented wrist shots, but it did the job," Lanny chuckled about the floater that eluded Resch. "Chico and I later played together in Colorado and I used to tell him I never had to shoot hard to beat him. Actually, with all joking aside, it truly was an amazing moment for me... and the entire team. We chartered back to Toronto after the game and that plane would have flown without fuel."

McDonald played with intense pain that evening. If you recall the goal — or have seen a replay of it since — you'll notice that Lanny was wearing a football-type face shield to protect a broken nose. "It happened during Game 5 on the Island when Denis Potvin nailed me with a clean check," Lanny remembers. "I saw him coming at the last second but I couldn't get out of the way. And Denis could hit like a truck!" Lanny also had a broken wrist in that game, suffered during the Leafs' two-game elimination of Los Angeles in the previous playoff round. "It was starting to feel better, but (Isander defenceman) Dave Lewis hit me in Game 3 and hurt it again," McDonald says. "However, in a game-seven situation, you ignore the pain and play on."

His big moment on Uniondale, Long Island ranks second in Lanny's career to the goal he scored just more than 11 years later as a member of the Calgary Flames. On May 25, 1989 — a Thursday night, in Montreal — the Flames were gunning to become the first road team to ever parade the Stanley Cup around the hallowed ice at the Forum. Leading the Habs 3-2 in the '89 Cup final, Calgary needed one more victory to secure the championship and Game 6 was tied 1-1 in the second period when McDonald struck. Emerging from the penalty box, he gathered in a pass from Joe Nieuwendyk and beat goalie Patrick Roy with a hard wrist shot. Wearing a full playoff beard to compliment his utopian moustache, Lanny burst into celebration as the Forum crowd sagged. It gave his club a lead it would not relinquish, and a pair of goals by someone named Doug Gilmour cemented the Flames' first and only Stanley Cup title.

"The overtime goal against the Islanders will always be a special memory but you can't beat the feeling of winning a Stanley Cup," Lanny says. "So, the goal I scored in Montreal that night was by far the best moment of my career. It helped my team achieve the ultimate objective."

McDonald's Flames went ahead of the Maple Leafs, 2-1, early in the second period tonight when defenceman Kevin Dahl scored a bizarre goal. Racing to the right-wing boards, Dahl flipped a harmless-looking shot towards Felix Potvin that would have sailed wide had it not glanced off the shoulder of Dave Ellett and carromed downward into the net. Like the Leafs earlier, Calgary could not maintain the lead and Mike Gartner tied the score once again, finishing off a nice three-way exchange with Todd Gill and Benoit Hogue. Nothing had been decided after two.

Garth Malarchuk, the Maple Leafs' western-Canada scout, sat next to me in the press box tonight and it was difficult not to laugh at the minor predicament he encountered. Rooting vociferously for the Leafs, Malarchuk repeatedly called Calgary's Theoren Fleury a "little prick." Every time Fleury skated with the puck, or backchecked, Garth nervously exclaimed, "C'mon guys, watch that little prick" — obviously unaware that Fleury's agent, Don Baizley, was seated two chairs to his right. Early in the third period, the connection must have donned on him. He quickly turned to Bill Watters and asked, "Is Fleury Baizley's guy?" Wilbur nodded affirmatively and Garth mumbled, "Oh shit."

The entire Maple Leaf hierarchy gasped with anxiety several times during the scoreless third period tonight. Cliff Fletcher flew in for the game earlier today and was seated with Watters, Malarchuk, Rick Wamsley and Bob Stellick. That unmentionable, Fleury, had a couple of good scoring chances, inducing a collective, *"Eeeeeeee!!"* from the Leaf brass. Actually, it was Toronto that had the best opportunity to score, as Doug Gilmour deflected Kenny Jonsson's point drive off the goalpost during an early powerplay. Incredibly, the Maple Leafs were unable to register another shot during the period. Fletcher, Wamsley and Co. had a moment of near cardiac arrest with only one second remaining on the clock, when Fleury set up Robert Reichel alone in front. But, Potvin made a huge save and the match went into overtime.

The Leafs played somewhat carelessly in the extra frame — icing the puck three times as if they were protecting a lead. Again, Calgary almost won the game in the final seconds, as Joel Otto wound up from the slot with two ticks left. But, Benoit Hogue smothered Otto before he could fire and the Leafs escaped with a tie — winning the season series against Calgary by a 2-1-1 count. "The only way (Otto) was going to score is if he shot me in the net, too," Hogue joked afterwards. It was a terribly strange game when considering the Leafs had 17 shots in the first period and only eight the rest of the way (two in the final 25 minutes). But the point may prove valuable.

"We did alright, huh Howie?" Pat Burns asked rhetorically, when I passed him in the corridor outside the Maple Leaf dressing room moments after the final buzzer. The coach then turned a corner and proceeded to watch the final moments of the Buffalo at Montreal game on a TV monitor in the hallway. His old team, the Canadiens, were fighting for their playoff lives and Burns confessed to rooting for the Habs. "Oh yeah, I still have a lot of friends over there," he said. "Me and Serge Savard will always be close."

Just then, Alexander Mogilny swooped in on Patrick Roy and almost ended the game in overtime. "Boy, that Mogilny can motor," Burns said, walking back to the sanctity of his dressing room (the Canadiens wound up tying Buffalo and are still breathing... but on life support).

A few moments later, I walked into the Leaf room and Mats Sundin came up to me with an annoyed look on his face. "Can you believe the holding that went on out there tonight? Every time I got to center ice, it was this," he said, grabbing me by the shoulder part of my jacket. "I finally told (Kerry) Fraser he'd better start calling something or 20,000 fans will be asleep by the third period."

Sundin's frustration has been echoed all across the NHL the past two seasons. Be it the diminishing talent pool of the expansion era, or merely an effective way for unimaginative coaches to school their players, the so-called neutral-zone trap has become a monster. Referees are obviously being instructed to overlook much of the restraining ploys for the very reason that if they called even the majority of them, hockey games would last four hours. And it seems apparent that officiating, in general, is complicated nightly by a barrage of guidelines from supervisors.

As it stands, there are far too many rules for the men in stripes to master. Like governmental bureaucrats, NHL power-brokers seem intent on altering the game to merely justify their existence. We all realize that change — to a reasonable extent — is progress, but the endless implementation of rules on a yearly basis begs the question, "What was wrong with hockey in the good old days?" With seemingly one half of the directives now in place, the six-team NHL of the 1950s and '60s played to an audience capacity of close to 99 percent. And two thirds of the teams — like today — were based in the United States. That time in history is not referred to as the "Golden Age of Hockey" for nothing.

Over in another part of the Maple Leaf room tonight, Dave Ellett smiled weakly when discussing Calgary's second goal — the one that glanced in off his shoulder. "That kind of weird thing has happened in the past and I suppose it'll happen again in the future," he reasoned. "I thought I was an innocent bystander, but I guess you're officially part of the defence union when you put one into your own net."

I walked out of the Saddledome about 15 minutes later with Mike Gartner and we both paused in wonderment when we opened the back door. With the game having started at 5:30 p.m. locally (for *Hockey Night In Canada*), it was still light outside at 8:45 — not unusual at this pre-summer time of year. It's just that we weren't expecting it. During the dead of winter, games customarily begin at 7:35, and it's pitch-dark long before the opening faceoff. This was a surprise.

SUNDAY, APRIL 30th
Edmonton

The coffee-shop of the Calgary Westin Hotel was filled with Maple Leafs in mid-morning today, as Doug Gilmour, Kenny Jonsson, Mike Ridley and others enjoyed the $14.95 all-you-can-eat Sunday brunch. Pat Burns got off the lobby elevator in his trench-coat, all set for his morning walk. But the aroma of pancakes and smoked sausage prompted him to gaze in the direction of the buffet. "Hmmmm, that sure smells good," noticed the coach, and he made an immediate change of plans.

Afterwards, as he left the hotel for his post-*brunch* walk, Burns held open the front door for a slow-moving octonagarian. It took the elderly woman about 20 seconds to shuffle past the Maple Leaf coach, who showed limitless patience. As he turned around, he had to cut sharply to his right to avoid sending the woman flying from behind. I silently wished him a pleasant stroll.

The Leaf players brought their suitcases to the lobby for today's flight to Edmonton and piled them on two luggage carts. Kenny Jonsson sat in a lounge chair and read the Calgary *Sun*. "I have to keep reading English, it's part of the program I took back home," he told me. "It's also a lot harder than speaking the language." Matt Martin then came down and summoned Jonsson to an awaiting cab bound for the Saddledome, and a full team practice. It was partly cloudy on this final morning of April, and some light snow-flurries continued to fall.

As the team bus filled up outside the hotel, Grant Jennings got on and said to Rick Wamsley, "Scrimmage today?"

"Ask the big guy (Burns)," Wammer replied. "I'll let *you* bring it up." Jennings just smiled and continued towards the rear.

Burns got on a few moments later and Wamsley informed him that ex-Montreal coach Claude Ruel had suffered a heart attack yesterday.

"Is he dead?" asked Burns, somewhat startled.

"Nope, but he's critical," Wammer said.

"Well, it doesn't really surprise me," said Burns, as he sat down. "You ever see what that man eats? French-fries, apple pie, donuts, and about 18 Pepsis a day.

"... He's only 56, huh? Geez, I hope he's alright."

Roughly 20 minutes later, I was sitting in the empty Saddledome, 15 rows above the visitor's bench. Except for the electronic buzzing of overhead lights, you could have heard a pin drop in the deserted arena. Above me — stretching from blueline to blueline — were eight Calgary Flames banners, including the

Stanley Cup flag of 1989. Next to them: a red and white banner depicting Lanny McDonald's retired No. 9 jersey. Looking around the place brought back some vivid memories. Like the day in mid-June, 1982, when I was still living out here. The Saddledome was under construction and the Flames arranged for a media tour hosted by Jim Peplinski and a Finnish-born defenceman named Pekka Rautakallio. We climbed to the northeast corner of the still-uncovered arena (the area above my left shoulder as I sat there today), and tried to imagine what the building would ultimately look like during a hockey game. In fact, several areas of the Stampede grounds were being built or renovated for the 1988 Winter Olympics — still six years away.

Which evokes yet another vision. What Canadian sports fan can possibly think of the Saddledome and not remember Elizabeth Manley's stunning performance during the Olympic figure skating competition? An impeccable display in the long program lifted Manley to a silver medal, behind only defending Olympic champion Katarina Witt. It ranks among the top moments in Canadian sport during the past generation.

From a hockey standpoint, Montreal paraded the Stanley Cup around this building after a surprise victory in the spring of 1986. Two years earlier, the Saddledome had been home to the most enthralling Canada-Russia hockey game since 1972. It was the semifinal of the 1984 Canada Cup and Mike Bossy of the New York Islanders won the match in overtime after Edmonton's Paul Coffey — in the prime of his wonderful career —brilliantly thwarted a two-on-one Soviet rush. Only twice since the '72 series have I been overcome by a similar feeling of total exhilaration: Bossy's extra-frame goal in '84; and the silly, yet spellbinding shoot-out that decided the 1994 Winter Olympics in Lillehammer. Strangely, I never got that feeling when Mario Lemieux scored his famous goal to win the 1987 Canada Cup tournament in Hamilton... and I was *at* that game.

This building — only 12 years old — will have a fairly different look in the future. A massive renovation project will commence virtually the moment the Flames are finished in this year's playoffs. The entire lower bowl of the Saddledome will be reconfigured with the construction of 45 luxury suites. Rows 14 to 25 from ice level will be repositioned directly over top the new private boxes. The lobby and concourse areas of the arena will also be up-graded, like in Edmonton.

The Leafs took to the ice in the Saddledome at 11:45 a.m. They're practising here because of the *Stars On Ice* figure skating show at the Edmonton Coliseum this afternoon. Otherwise, they'd have gone up to Edmonton after last night's game and skated there. As the Maple Leaf players and coaches warmed up for the workout, Theoren Fleury sauntered up to the glass in the northwest corner of the arena. The Flames are in Vancouver tonight, but having clinched first in the Pacific Division — and second in the Western Conference playoff seeding — their remaining two games are meaningless. Coach Dave King has therefore chosen to rest several key players, including Fleury, and Joe Nieuwendyk, who departed last night's game in the second period with a stiff back.

As Fleury nonchalantly watched the Maple Leafs warm up, Pat Burns and Rick Wamsley fired pucks off the corner glass, inches from Fleury's nose. The Calgary player acknowledged the horseplay with a smile. The Buds went through their various practice drills, and then engaged in a spirited scrimmage that featured forwards against defencemen. I don't have to tell you which side prevailed, though it was close for awhile.

Standing outside the team bus around 2 o'clock, Burns bemoaned the fact Calgary has kept so many key players at home for today's encounter with the Canucks. "I'm not happy with them sending a fucking `B' team for a game that still means something in the playoff race," he groused. The Maple Leafs are not yet assured of finishing ahead of Vancouver in the Western Conference, and would thus welcome some assistance from the Flames later this afternoon. With two hours until the scheduled flight to Edmonton, Burns figured the club had time to stop for lunch before heading to the airport. He planned on letting the players off at the Eau Claire Market, behind the Westin Hotel, but they were slow emerging from the arena and the bus proceeded directly to Calgary International.

Along the way, several Leafs reminisced about playing in the old Calgary Corral and how the side boards were roughly eight inches higher than in other NHL buildings.

"When you jumped onto the ice for a line-change, you needed a parachute," quipped Mike Gartner. "A small guy like Paul DiPietro would have to shimmy down on a rope."

"Yeah, it was the only rink where you shot the puck over the net and still hit the boards," joked Rick Wamsley.

Gartner (with Washington), Wamsley (with Montreal and St. Louis), and Mike Kitchen (with Colorado and New Jersey) all played in the old Corral, as they were in the NHL prior to the October, 1983 opening of the Olympic Saddledome. In fact, Gartner just barely missed being able to play in the old Detroit Olympia, as the Red Wings moved to Joe Louis Arena halfway through his rookie season (1979-80). The three veterans remembered playing at the Omni in Atlanta: home of the Flames till the end of the '79-80 campaign and their move here to Calgary.

Despite the two-degree (Celsius) temperature outside, the players were apparently quite warm on the bus. "Air conditioning, please," came a request from the rear that the driver obviously didn't pick up. "Put the air on, they're dying back there," Burns repeated from his front-row seat. Arriving at the airport around 2:35, the players and coaches received their Edmonton boarding passes from Bob Stellick, then fanned out in search of some grub. A number of them holed up in a *Swiss Chalet* restaurant, while others chowed down at the food court. Burns swallowed an *A & W* hamburger.

Prior to entering the boarding lounge, Paul DiPietro and Kenny Jonsson were busy amusing themselves in the airport arcade — DiPietro playing a video game; Jonsson some pinball. Todd Gill, Mats Sundin and Benoit Hogue dropped by to watch. Most of the Leaf players got to the lounge before our plane to Edmonton arrived. Pat Burns made a marathon phonecall to somebody and much of the chatter evolved around today's matinee games in the NHL. Bill Watters had skipped attending practice at the Saddledome to watch FOX's TV game at the hotel and was annoyed that Detroit — cooled out atop the overall standings — was tanking at home against Chicago, with whom the Leafs are still battling for home-ice advantage in the playoffs. "It figures," Wilbur said.

We got on the *British Aerospace-146* aircraft and left for Edmonton in cloudy skies around 4:05 p.m. The plane took off to the south and it circled almost directly over the Stampede grounds to head north. Maple Leaf trainer Brent Smith sat next to me on the right side and we had a terrific view of the Saddledome and downtown Calgary about 5,000 feet below us. The cloud-cover dissipated nicely a short time into the trip, and we descended into Edmonton amid sunny skies. We flew directly over Edmonton International Airport, about 35 kilometres south of the city: it's two runways clearly visible in the desolate terrain. The aircraft then passed to the left of Commonwealth Stadium and its wheels almost scraped the roof of a Sears department store before settling onto the runway at Edmonton Municipal Airport 40 minutes after leaving Calgary.

While waiting at the conveyor belt for the luggage to arrive, Paul DiPietro started a "first-suitcase" pool at five bucks a head. There were few takers until the belt started moving, whereupon Mike Kitchen bolted forward and said, "I'm in!" He gave DiPietro the $5 bill and Pat Burns broke into a pitiful smile. "What a scam," he laughed as Kitchen leaned forward and plucked the first piece of luggage off the belt. DiPietro's face dropped. He looked around and noticed Burns shaking his head. Then he turned back and saw Kitchen with his arm outstretched. "I win," said the crafty assistant.

It finally donned on DiPietro that Kitchen had entered the pool only after noticing his bag poke through the wall ahead of the others. But it was far too late for an appeal.

"You slime-bucket," DiPietro whined, as he reluctantly handed over the winnings.

"Gotta be sharper than that, Pauly," said Burns, still laughing.

Stepping outside, we noticed it was warmer here in Edmonton than it had been down in Calgary (a none-too-frequent occurrence). And, for the second consecutive week, the Maple Leaf team bus was a no-show. Bob Stellick had a quick glance up and down the sidewalk then hurried back inside amid a barrage of taunts. "This wouldn't happen if Parksy was in charge," chided Burns, as the others cackled away. Of course, Pat Park had been the target of similar wise-cracks last weekend when the bus was late in Dallas. Stellick re-emerged from the terminal building about 90 seconds later and instructed everyone to take cabs to the hotel.

"The bus went to the International airport," he announced.

A collective groan ensued and there was a mad scramble as the Leaf players organized in groups of three or four. Thankfully, a phalanx of taxis was lined up at curbside.

"Which hotel are we at?" asked Grant Jennings.

"There's only *one* in the whole fucking place," cracked Burns.

I got into a cab with Jennings and Matt Martin. Our driver was an elderly man who told us he hailed from France. When he discovered that a couple of hockey players were in the car, he launched into a caustic assessment of the hometown Oilers, who collapsed in the third period at the Coliseum last night and were trounced by Winnipeg. A Maple Leaf win tomorrow will eliminate Edmonton from playoff contention.

"Put them out of their misery... please," the driver moaned. "You wouldn't believe how they crapped away that game. It wasn't hockey. If I pay money to buy tickets, I want to see some action... some hitting. Last night was like the Ice Capades."

The cabbie then turned his attention to the Maple Leafs and voiced his dis-approval of the Wendel Clark deal.

"They never should've traded that guy," he insisted, at which time I decid-ed to have some fun with the man.

"What about Drake Berehowsky?" I asked.

"Who's Drake Berehowsky?"

"The guy they traded for Grant Jennings."

"Grant who???"

Jennings looked at the floor and shook his head.

A few moments later, the cabbie turned his radio on and cranked up a station playing the Big Band sound of the '40s. "Do you always listen to music from the

War?" asked Jennings, who then noticed the dearth of humanity roaming the streets on this Sunday afternoon, and wondered if civilization still flourished in Edmonton. The cab driver thought he was serious and took great pains in showing us a well-known furniture store that seemed to be busy. However, with his thick European accent, he mis-pronounced the name, and sent all three of us into hysterics.

"Look over there... The *Prick* is still open."

MONDAY, MAY 1st
Edmonton

Pat Burns and Mike Gartner sat on opposite sides of the lobby bar in the Westin Hotel this morning, seemingly unobservant of each other. The coach appeared to be in a contemplative mood and I gingerly offered him a "Good morning, Pat" as I walked by with the Edmonton *Sun*. Dressed sharply in a sport-jacket and tie, Gartner was leafing through the *Globe & Mail* and his sartorial splendour drew the attention of Rick Wamsley. "Gee, Garts, you look like you own the place," said Wammer. "Not yet," the veteran winger smiled back.

The players began filtering down to the lobby to leave for their morning skate and when Jennings got off the elevator, he wandered over to me. "Doozie of a cab driver we had yesterday," he cracked. We then sat down and Jennings reflected on his three-plus years with Pittsburgh — a juncture during which the Penguins won back-to-back Stanley Cups.

"It was fortunate timing for me," said the big defenceman, whose name was practically ignored in the March, 1991 deal that sent he, Ron Francis and Ulf Samuelsson to the Penguins for John Cullen, Jeff Parker and Zarley Zalapaski. "Of course, the two Stanley Cups were great, and playing with Mario Lemieux is something I'll always remember. He had more natural ability than any athlete I've ever seen and the only tough part was trying not to look silly against him in practice every day."

A native of Hudson Bay, Sask., Jennings played Junior `A' hockey in nearby Saskatoon and was signed as a free agent by Washington in the summer of 1985. He appeared in one playoff game for the Capitals before his July, 1988 trade to Hartford, and his ultimate deal to the soon-to-be champions in Pittsburgh. There is limited finesse in his 6-foot-3, 210-pound frame, but Jennings is not shy about mixing it up and tossing his weight around. He appeared in 38 playoff games with Lemieux and the Penguins over a four-year span.

"Football and baseball used to be ahead of hockey in Pittsburgh, but Mario has changed all that," Jennings said. "He's a quiet man who never enjoys being in the public eye; he doesn't promote the game like Wayne Gretzky or some of the other top stars... it's just his nature. Golfing was his passion back then — it still is — and that's how he escapes the limelight. He doesn't like being in large groups of people.

"But, when we'd get together for team functions, I was able to see the other side of him. He's much more laid back and comfortable in his home and he has a fabulous wine collection. He has a big farm outside Pittsburgh and I'd go there and let my dog romp around all day."

Jennings has a couple of Lemieux stories he likes to tell.

"I got to Pittsburgh just before the playoffs in 1991 and it was awesome to see the fire in Mario's eyes," he recalls. "He absolutely dominated the semifinal against Boston and I can still see some of the moves he made on the Minnesota defence in the finals. He set me up for a goal at home in the Boston series. I pinched in from the point and he saw me coming and put the puck right on my stick. I scored only twice during the regular season and as Mario congratulated me, he said, 'What the hell were *you* doing there?'

"Another time, we were playing in Hartford a night after hammering Ottawa. Mario had five points against the Senators and during our first power-play in Hartford, (coach) Pierre Maguire, who used to be with the Penguins, put Pat Verbeek out to follow Mario all over the ice. Verbeek stood right beside him the whole shift. We all thought it looked weird from the bench and on our next powerplay, Mario left the Hartford zone in the middle of the play and went out to center ice. Well, believe it or not, Verbeek also left the zone and stood with Mario again. It was a four-on-three powerplay with two guys watching from the neutral zone. We were all laughing, wondering where Mario came up with *that* scheme."

While pulling into the Edmonton Coliseum this morning, we drove past the Forum Inn once again — the hotel where the Oilers have their team offices. And we all got a kick out of the marquee sign above the main entrance, which read: NIGHTLY ENTERTAINMENT, FEATURING PENTHOUSE CHARLIE AND MISS MICHAELS. "Well, at least we know what the Oiler staff does after they get off work," laughed Bob Stellick.

The Edmonton players were just finishing their morning skate when I arrived at the seating area of the Coliseum. Pat Burns came up into the stands to watch and Oilers' P.R. director Bill Tuele informed him that the start of tonight's game would be delayed a few moments by the club's annual awards ceremony.

"No fucking way! No fucking way!" Burns exploded, as Tuele went pale. The Leaf coach then broke up laughing and sat down. "Got you good there, Bill," he smirked.

Afterwards, in the Oiler dressing room, I walked over to the spot where Wayne Gretzky's locker used to be during the Stanley Cup years. It is one stall away from the refreshment room — in the corner — and is currently occupied by former Leaf Scott Thornton. "It's a little awe inspiring, but I suppose they had to put the same kind of player there to keep the shrine alive," Thornton cracked.

The Leafs' first-round choice (third overall) in the 1989 draft, Thornton failed to develop quickly and was traded to Edmonton in the seven-player deal (September, 1991) that brought Toronto Grant Fuhr and Glenn Anderson. He has learned to use his size effectively, but is still not an overly productive scorer.

Bill Ranford emerged from the shower-room and was surrounded by a pack of local media. The veteran goalie will miss tonight's game with recurring back spasms and rookie Fred Brathwaite will take his place. It was a year ago right now that Ranford was backstopping Canada to its first World Hockey Championship in 33 years, but he told me the memory of that triumph has become somewhat distant.

"It's kind of hard to think about last year with all the problems we have here in Edmonton right now," Ranford conceded about the Oilers' life-and-death struggle to make the playoffs.

The Brandon, Man. native is one of the few players to have toiled on World Hockey and National Hockey League championship teams — he won the Conn Smythe Trophy for his role in Edmonton's surprise Stanley Cup conquest in the spring of 1990. But he says the comparisons end there.

"The World Hockey Championship was a unique experience but nothing compares to winning a Stanley Cup," Ranford insists. "During the World tournament, you have to be at your best for roughly two weeks and you aren't necessarily playing against top-level competition. You've got to be on top of your game a lot longer in the NHL playoffs, and the tempo of every game is so much higher. The hardest challenge in international hockey is being able to overcome generally incompetent officiating. And the ice surfaces are obviously larger. But, on the whole, it's still a bigger accomplishment to win the Stanley Cup."

A few moments later, I was standing idly in one corner of the dressing room when I felt a tap on my left shoulder. I turned around to see Luke Richardson with his hand extended. "How 'ya doing?" he asked, obviously remembering my face from his years with the Maple Leafs. Luke was Toronto's first-round selection (seventh overall) in the 1987 entry draft and he spent four full seasons in a

Leaf uniform. Tall and sturdy at 6-foot-4, 210 pounds, he's never blossomed into a front-line defenceman, but has nonetheless improved dramatically since coming here to Edmonton in Cliff Fletcher's initial blockbuster as Maple Leaf boss.

On September 19, 1991, three-and-a-half months after becoming Leaf president, Fletcher dealt Richardson, Thornton, Vincent Damphousse and Peter Ing to Edmonton for Grant Fuhr, Glenn Anderson and Craig Berube. He later swapped Fuhr to Buffalo for Dave Andreychuk; Anderson to the Rangers for Mike Gartner, and Berube to Calgary in the ten-player deal that landed Doug Gilmour, so Fletcher's exchange with the Oilers wound up bearing generous returns. Having said all that, a more confident and effective Richardson would look pretty good on the declining Maple Leaf blueline right now. In fact, he'd likely be the club's best defenceman.

Of course, Luke was front and center in the Oilers' visit to the Gardens last month when he levelled Gilmour with that bone-jarring hit in the neutral zone. As mentioned, it immediately reminded me of a game on January 28, 1989, when Richardson kayoed New York Ranger rookie Tony Granato with a similar jolt at the Gardens. Granato's chin connected with Richardson's shoulder pad that night and he was knocked cold, like a boxer who gets cranked in the same spot. As it happened early in the period, the ice was still slick, and I can still see Granato spiralling uncontrollably into the corner, flat on his back.

Luke remembers it well.

"Tony was leaning forward and he tried to jump inside of me," the defenceman says. "He left his feet a few inches and slammed right into my shoulder. I could see that his lights went out right away."

Conversely, the Gilmour hit was more of a straight-on collision, with the Leaf captain having his head down coming across the center-ice zone. "That was just a solid bodycheck," Richardson explains. "Dougie had the puck and he glanced around for someone to pass it to. He looked up at the last second and saw me coming, but didn't have time to brace himself. It all happened very quickly and I had no idea he was shaken up until I got to my feet and the whistle blew.

"Then, as I half expected, the other Maple Leaf players on the ice came after me, but (referee) Paul Stewart was yelling, `Get away, it's not a penalty.' I understood what they were doing, though. I would have reacted the same way if my best player was laying on the ice. When I was a rookie with Toronto, I played very aggressively in training camp and (fellow defenceman) Chris Kotsopoulos told me that if I played that way during games, the opposition would target me. It's all part of the game, though, and the funny thing about the Gilmour check was that the same fans who cheered me after Granato were now booing me."

Another man who started his career as a Maple Leaf has been head coach of the Oilers for the past 24 days. Ron Low took over behind the Edmonton bench when Glen Sather fired rookie coach George Burnett back on April 7th and the Oilers are 5-5-1 since that time. The 44-year-old native of Birtle, Man. was an eighth-round choice of the Maple Leafs in the 1970 amateur draft and he split the netminding chores with Jacques Plante and Gord McRae during Toronto's awful 1972-73 campaign. That was the start-up year for the World Hockey Association and the Maple Leafs had lost key players Bernie Parent, Jim Dorey, Brad Selwood, Rick Ley and Guy Trottier to the fledgling league. As well, veteran defenceman Bob Baun had to retire after suffering a neck injury against Detroit early in the season. It was definitely not the optimum juncture to be a rookie Maple Leaf goalie, as Low vividly remembers.

"That was quite an awakening," he laughed as we leaned on a ping-pong table in the middle of the Oiler dressing room. "It kind of set me up for playing later on with Washington."

Low won't confess to having nightmarish visions of John Grisdale, Joe Lundrigan, Dave Fortier, Jim McKenny, Brian Glennie and Mike Pelyk, but that's the stellar defence crew he played behind in his freshman season with the Leafs. "The guys were young, but we all tried real hard that year," he remembers. "I was supposed to play an entirely back-up role to Jacques Plante, but I wound up getting into 42 games. And I'll always remember working with the great Johnny Bower in practice. He was one of the best goaltending instructors in the business and his relaxed demeanour was perfect for a nervous rookie like me.

"In those days, he would still strap on the pads for practice and he was a fierce competitor, even at that age (48)."

The 1972-73 Maple Leafs finished out of the playoffs with a dismal 27-41-10 record for 64 points — 16 fewer than the previous season, and their lowest total since 1957-58. They permitted 279 opposition scores, a colossal increase of 71 from the season before, and 37 more than they had allowed in any prior campaign. But the Leafs were veritable Stanley Cup material that year compared to the Washington club Low played for two seasons later. The expansion Capitals established futility records that have not since been matched... and may never be.

"That was the year I started smoking," Low chuckles. "I considered myself fortunate to be in the NHL and I was still young enough to enjoy just playing, even if it was with a brutal team. After about 20 games, though, the losing began to wear on me and I had no other choice but to persevere. Being a farmer's son, I think I had that inherent quality — after all, it rains on a farm every now and then."

The 1974-75 Capitals still hold NHL regular-season records for the fewest wins (8), fewest points (21), and the lowest winning percentage (.131) in a minimum 70-game schedule. Their long-standing record of 67 losses was erased by both the San Jose Sharks (71) and Ottawa Senators (70) during the 1992-93 season. And Washington's goals-against total of 446 is still 31 more than any club has ever allowed in one season.

"We had only one victory on the road that year and it happened in Oakland during the second-last week of the season," Low remembers. "We beat the California Golden Seals 5-3 and after the game, we all signed a garbage can in the visitor's dressing room. Tom Williams and Garnet (Ace) Bailey then led us back onto the ice and we paraded that trash can around like a team doing a Stanley Cup victory lap. What a sight!"

During the early to mid-1970s, those who watched Maple Leaf games on *Hockey Night In Canada* were treated to the amusing diatribes of ex-Leaf player and coach Howie Meeker. As long as my memory prevails, I'll be able to hear Meeker's vexation when analyzing the inferior Toronto defence units of that era.

"What's McKenny doing... he's on his knees looking for nickels," Meeker would often grouse during his intermission homilies.

Today, he's here in Edmonton to perform similar analysis for The *Sports Network* (TSN), which is televising tonight's Maple Leafs-Oilers game nationwide. Now in his early 70s, and living in Vancouver, Meeker is a little whiter on top and a bit more wrinkled around the edges, but he hasn't lost the fiestiness that governed his Saturday night TV spots a generation ago.

"Oh, those were great days in Toronto — with (Harold) Ballard and (King) Clancy," Meeker gushed as we watched the Maple Leafs skate this morning at the Coliseum. "Going into the Gardens was always exciting... I still consider it my second home. There's a Maple Leaf tattooed on me somewhere and it's great to see them competitive once again."

A right-winger, Meeker played in 346 regular-season and 42 playoff games for the Maple Leafs from 1946-47 to 1953-54 — winning the Calder Trophy in his rookie campaign. He was a member of the Leaf clubs that won four Stanley Cups in five years under Conn Smythe between 1947 and '51. He later coached the Leafs for one miserable season (1956-57), in which the team finished in fifth place and out of the playoffs. He was replaced the following year by Billy Reay.

The central theme of Meeker's television lectures throughout the years has been for minor-hockey coaches to teach children the skills of the game. And he hasn't changed his tune. "Kids are bigger and stronger today and they improve in spite of the system, not because of it," he says. "We live in a most intelligent generation in which kids are being taught to do things we never dreamed of in the old days... like working on computers. Yet, when you put those same kids on the ice and ask them to move the puck out of their own territory, they're brain-dead... they couldn't think their way out the Zamboni door. If you can't think, you can't be creative, and it's obvious when I see minor hockey that a vast major-ity of the kids can't think fast enough."

Meeker volunteers as a guest coach with various minor hockey teams on Vancouver Island and he finds it to be a frustrating experience.

"One of the main reasons for kids dropping out of the game is that they don't have the mental skills — it has never been taught to them," he argues. "A kid today will make an all-star team in Peewee or Bantam because of his physical abilities; he's bigger, stronger, and he shoots the puck harder. But once he advances to the Midget level, he meets his match. At that point, he's no longer capable of beating his opponent physically and has to start using his head. It's an adjustment that a lot of youngsters simply cannot make."

Meeker believes that similar obligations exist at the NHL level — and the results are often the same. "Everything that happens behind the blueline is the coach's responsibility, and once outside the zone, it's the GM's responsibility," he explains. "The G.M. has to acquire players who can score, which is a skill that cannot be self-taught. The rest of it can... but, usually, it's too late by then."

Pat Burns took a cab back to the hotel after this morning's skate, but assis-tant Rick Wamsley would not occupy his front-row-on-the-right position during the follow-up bus journey.

"Nope, that's the Captain's seat," Wammer confirmed from the second row. "See that?" he added, pointing to Bill Watters across the aisle. "He's Spock. But Kirk isn't here."

Star *Trek* lives!

The Maple Leafs accomplished tonight what our eccentric cab driver appeared to be wishing for yesterday, when they knocked the Oilers out of play-off contention. There was nothing pretty about Toronto's 6-5 win at the Coliseum, but there hasn't been a whole lot of neatness during this entire Leaf season. The victory assures the club of a first-round playoff rematch against the Chicago Blackhawks, with home-ice advantage to be determined over the final 48 hours of the regular season.

Edmonton opened the scoring in the first minute of play, as Igor Kravchuk beat Felix Potvin through the legs with a slapshot from the point. But it didn't take long for the Maple Leafs to seemingly assume complete control of the hock-ey game. An uncharacteristic offensive spurt produced four unanswered goals the remainder of the period, and a 4-1 lead at the intermission. Rookie Fred Brathwaite looked weak on three of the Toronto goals, as Jamie Macoun, Randy Wood and Mike Gartner all beat him with unobstructed shots. Wood's tally, which made it 3-1, came only 11 seconds after Dave Andreychuk's one-timer from the faceoff. And it could have been worse for the Oilers, as Mats Sundin messed up two other glorious opportunities.

However, an explicit microcosm of this entire Maple Leaf season occurred during the second period tonight. Having no other alternative, Ron Low replaced Brathwaite with third-string netminder Joaquin Gage — called up just two days ago on emergency conditions from Cape Breton of the American League. Gage had never played a minute of NHL action but he watched from the best seat in the house tonight as the Oilers roared back to tie the game in the middle 20 minutes.

How often this season have we witnessed the Leafs flub a chance to bury the opposition? A five-dollar bill for each bungled occasion would buy you a full-course meal at the fancy steakhouse of your choice. Wine included. But tonight, the Leafs went a step further. They had to know that Edmonton — requiring nothing less than a win to maintain its slim playoff hopes — would emerge with a vengeance before its restless fans in the second period. It was the ultimate nothing-to-lose situation for the home team but somehow, the Leafs were caught with their guard down.

Shayne Corson, Scott Thornton and Peter White all took advantage of Maple Leaf defensive blunders to knot the score by the 14:17 mark of the middle frame. Corson walked around Jamie Macoun and scored on his own rebound when Todd Gill failed to cover. Thornton fooled Potvin into going the wrong way and stuffed the puck in from behind the net. And the sophomore White blew past Macoun again to handcuff Potvin with a wrister from the opposite wing. Felix was weak on the latter two goals. Edmonton held a 14-5 shots advantage in a total collapse by the Leafs.

During the second intermission, I decided to check the emotional well-being of my pal Bill Watters in the Maple Leaf executive box and he seemed resigned to another disappointment. "What else can happen to us this year, Howie?" he pondered in exasperation.

Wilbur and I go back a few years to our days together at the radio station. One of hockey's top agents in the 1980s — among his clients were former Leaf captains Rick Vaive and Rob Ramage — Bill gradually began to phase himself out of player representation when he became colour commentator on the Maple Leaf radio broadcasts in 1986-87. He sold his shares of Branada Sports Management Ltd. to partner Rick Curran in 1988, though he maintained a consulting contract with Curran through '91. In the fall of that year, Bill was hired by Cliff Fletcher to be the Maple Leafs' assistant G.M.

For three years, Bill and I worked together on *Prime Time Sports*: our supper-hour magazine show on The Fan-590 and the *Telemedia* network. I produced the program, while Bill co-hosted with Bob McCown. During Bill's final year at the station, it was widely rumoured — and became almost a running joke — that he applied for every one of the myriad of hockey management jobs that came open. The speculation was fuelled in large part by Watters' friend, veteran sports broadcaster Pat Marsden, who often had some fun at Bill's expense on rival radio station CFRB.

"The truth is simple, Howie... the only job I ever applied for is the job I now have," Bill told me tonight. "I wound up interviewing for nine different positions, including three as G.M. and one as assistant G.M., but I was approached by the team on each occasion. Good old `Mars Bar' (Marsden) had me going to practically every city in North America, but he's never happy unless he's making trouble."

Bill was a candidate for several positions outside NHL management circles, including Canadian Football League commissioner in 1988 (the job went to Donald Crump). He also interviewed for the role as SkyDome president in 1989 and lost out to Richard Peddie. He was later said to be among the finalists for Executive Director of the National Hockey League Players' Association — which would have been the ultimate irony after his acerbic 1980 divorce from ex-business partner Alan Eagleson. The position ultimately went to another former agent: Bob Goodenow.

"That one stuck in my craw for awhile," Bill admits. "The firm of Price-Waterhouse conducted interviewing for the position and they told me a couple of times I was the leading candidate. I said, `I can't have that job, Eagleson would never let it happen.' But they insisted Al had nothing to do with the process. Somehow, though, I never made it to any of the final five interviews."

Similar anomalies occurred with a couple of NHL teams.

"Just prior to the 1989 draft in Minnesota, I got a call from Jack Diller (vice-president of Madison Square Garden) saying he wanted to interview me to replace Phil Esposito as Ranger G.M.," Watters recalls. "We sat down together for two hours in Bloomington and, I should be struck by lightning right now if Jack didn't say to me, `Bill, that was the most fascinating couple of hours I've ever spent with anyone in hockey. We'll be in touch soon.' I went home and told my wife (Naddie) to get ready to move to New York. But I never heard another word from the Rangers.

"A short while later, Keith Allen phoned me from Philadelphia and asked if I wanted to be interviewed with five other candidates for the position of Flyers' G.M. I said, `Keith, I've just been through a big frustration with the Rangers,' but he talked me into it. So, I went to Philly and a half hour into the interview, (Flyer president) Jay Snider said I was among his final two choices and that I should bring Naddie down to see the city. A few hours later, though — as he was driving me to the airport for my flight home — Jay said, `I might have been a bit premature in promising you anything.' So, something happened between 4 o'clock and 8 o'clock that day to change his mind."

Bill refuses to acknowledge that Eagleson may have sabotaged him with New York and Philadelphia, but it's difficult to imagine how the enthusiasm of Diller and Snider could've so suddenly waned. The Snider family, in particular, has always been close with Eagleson. And while neither Eagleson nor Watters will admit it, there has without question been deep-rooted acrimony among the two men ever since Watters left the agency partnership (along with Bobby Orr) a decade-and-a-half ago.

"The Philadelphia thing was the biggest let-down," Watters admits. "But in the end, I wound up with a pretty good job. When Lyman McInnis became heavily involved with the Leafs (in 1991), I figured he'd hire a fellow Maritimer to run the hockey operation and I heard it might be (Calgary assistant G.M.) Al MacNeil. But when I called Cliff Fletcher to ask him about it, he told me Al would be staying with the Flames and wondered why I was interested. I told him that if the right guy came to Toronto, I wouldn't mind the assistant G.M.'s position. He said that a few things could happen over the summer and we hung up.

"When Cliff joined the Leafs, I interviewed him on the radio and afterwards, he said, `Don't forget what I told you.' I was hired a few weeks later and I've enjoyed every minute of it."

Bill also enjoyed the final moments of tonight's shootout with the Oilers. The game was tied, 5-5, with less than six minutes remaining in regulation time when Edmonton's Mike Stapleton went off for hooking. On the powerplay, Mats Sundin took Dave Ellett's pass to the right of Gage and he beat the rookie goaltender with a low shot between the legs. The Maple Leafs hung on for the one-goal victory, as Potvin snared an Igor Kravchuk point drive through a screen with 1.6 seconds left.

There was a mad post-game scramble in the Maple Leaf dressing room to do everything quickly, as a charter jet was waiting to take the club down to California. As I stood outside the room moments after the game, the players were practically screaming at each other for nearly blowing it against the Oilers.

"C'mon guys, this has to be a lesson, there's no fucking way we can do that in the playoffs!" barked one player, whose voice was imperceptible amid the overall din. Pat Burns stepped out of the dressing room a few moments later and met with reporters.

"We'll take the two points and run," he said, shaking his head.

The chatter quickly moved on to the up-coming playoff series with the Blackhawks. "We've been preparing for a long time to play Chicago," the coach confirmed. "Everything is ready."

"Yeah, it should be a good, tough series," added Dave Ellett, who played well in the six-game elimination of Chicago last spring. "They like to play the same type of game we do. It'll probably be a physical, close-checking series and I wouldn't expect to see a lot of goals." Of course, three of the four Maple Leaf victories in last year's opening round were by scores of 1-0.

It wasn't 30 minutes after the final buzzer tonight that the Maple Leafs were seated on their team bus. For some reason, everyone hurries when there's a charter flight to catch — even though departure time is thoroughly flexible. I always figured that's why you arrange for a charter: so it can leave when you're ready... at your convenience. Instead, players and equipment staff hustle through their post-game routines as if they are about to miss the last *commercial* flight of the day. Half the Leafs hadn't even combed their towelled-off hair when the bus was pulling out of the Coliseum around 11:30 tonight.

Having rented an Air Canada *Airbus*, the team could not depart from nearby Municipal Airport due to the size of the plane, and noise-curfew restrictions in the downtown area. It necessitated a 35-minute drive to Edmonton International Airport. Along the way, several players began to rib Mike Gartner about his advanced years in the game.

"Garts, were you the first draft pick of the Washington Capitals?" asked Randy Wood in a ridiculous exaggeration (Gartner was only 14 when Washington joined the NHL in 1974). The veteran winger just smiled.

"You still attend Vietnam war memorials, don't you?" jibed another teammate seated towards the back. Gartner continued smiling.

"Are you just going to sit there and take that, Mike?" wondered Mats Sundin.

"I just consider the source," he replied.

The players have also been kidding Gartner about our last trip to Edmonton, when he suffered a partially collapsed lung from a bodycheck by Bryan Marchment and couldn't fly with the team. "You coming with us or taking the train home again?" they asked him.

The Maple Leaf bus arrived at the airport just past the stroke of midnight and Edmonton International was conveniently deserted. Never in cross-border relations has Customs been more of a formality than it was tonight, as we half-heartedly scrawled our names and destination on the appropriate forms while hauling our suitcases past U.S. agents who were more interested in talking hockey. We could have smuggled firearms into California had we so desired.

Once again, management, the trainers, and the media were accorded the comforts of *Executive Class*, as the players shuffled to the rear of the *Airbus*. The plane roared off the runway at around 12:20 and slumber quickly overcame most of us on board.

The flight down to Los Angeles took just over three hours and was smooth most of the way. A bit more than two hours in, the night skies were crystal clear over northern California, and we had a breathtaking view out the right side of the entire San Francisco-Oakland Bay Area — and then San Jose — from 39,000 feet. We descended into the L.A. basin above the blackened Pacific Ocean and reached land directly over Santa Monica — its illuminated pier jutting into the darkness of the sea. We then barrelled out over the vastness of Los Angeles and made a sweeping right turn to head back towards the airport. The sprawling skyscrapers of downtown L.A. and the adjacent Hollywood hills were entirely visible on this unusually clear night.

I was sitting in the first row of the aircraft, watching the final approach over Inglewood, when I suddenly felt a pillow bounce off the back of my head. Turning around, I noticed Pat Burns one row behind me, feigning sleep with a mischievous grin on his face. We descended through some low fog drifting in off the ocean and touched down at Los Angeles International Airport around 2:25 a.m. Pacific time.

John Wayne Airport in Orange County is much closer to Anaheim, but we had to land at L-A-X for the same reason we couldn't leave from the Municipal air-field in Edmonton: curfew restrictions. John Wayne is located inland, and is surrounded by the populace Orange County cities of Costa Mesa, Santa Ana, Irvine and Newport Beach. Conversely, the Los Angeles airport is situated just off the ocean shore and is sequestered from its neighbouring masses by industrial buildings and the eight-lane San Diego Freeway. Therefore, jet-airliners do not have to come in low over-top residential areas in the middle of the night, and the field is open to traffic 24 hours.

"Is that fog or is it raining out?" Burns asked me as we taxied to the terminal building. The heavy ground mist had shrouded the aircraft, forming droplets of water on the outside windows. We filed into the terminal through a portable jetway and the desolation of L-A-X at this time of night was ghostly. We were the only people in the airport. With my in-laws living here in Los Angeles, I've lost count of the number of times I've snaked my way through this bustling departure lounge during normal travel hours. Seeing it deserted was almost spooky.

Similarly, cruising unimpeded down the San Diego Freeway moments later was a unique experience. Bumper-to-bumper traffic is the norm on this busy artery during daylight and early evening hours. A 40-minute bus journey ended at the front door of the Westin South Coast Plaza and the Maple Leafs dragged their weary bodies into the hotel. Mercifully, room keys were laid out on the concierge desk and the players grabbed at morning papers from an adjacent stack of L.A. *Times.* When I entered my seventh-floor suite, the clock-radio beside my bed said 3:33 a.m.

TUESDAY, MAY 2nd
Anaheim

This was one of those do-nothing days here in southern California as Pat Burns allowed his charges to recover from the all-night travel. He called for an optional skate at the Arrowhead Pond and only those who are not playing regularly — like Kent Manderville, Damian Rhodes and Darby Hendrickson — took part in the mid-afternoon workout. Dmitri Mironov also skated after re-joining the club yesterday in Edmonton. Of course, "Tree" has been sidelined for the past 13 games after suffering that separated shoulder against the Oilers on March 27 at the Gardens. And Burns is hoping to use him against the Mighty Ducks tomorrow night so Mironov can acquire some game action before the playoffs begin.

Most of us in the Maple Leaf travelling party chose the occasion to sleep in rather late this morning. I pulled back the curtains of my hotel room at 11:30 a.m. and noticed Bill Watters and Tie Domi sunning themselves at the pool down below. As I briefly watched, Domi suddenly rose from his lounge chair and took a flying head-first dive into the deep end. Wilbur, who never passes up an opportunity to bronze himself, had his face buried in the morning paper. It was still mostly cloudy out, as the ocean-fog had not yet dissipated, but it would later evolve into a perfect California day — sunny and warm.

Several players, including Mats Sundin, Dave Ellett and Todd Gill, relaxed by playing a round of golf at the nearby Mesa Verde club this afternoon. Others, like defenceman Jamie Macoun, spent much of the day thinking about hockey.

Macoun had an awful game last night in Edmonton and was benched for most of the second and third periods. After having lunch across the road at the South Coast Plaza Mall today, I came back and noticed Burns and Macoun sitting alone in the hotel lobby.

"Yeah, we had a little chat," Jamie smiled when I asked him about the one-on-one session. "Listen, being benched is something that has happened to me before and it's really no big deal. I've been around too long to start dwelling on a bad game. The coach felt I made a wrong decision while killing a penalty last night (getting beat in the neutral zone on Edmonton's second goal) and he chose to sit me down. It's not a big deal... unless he keeps on using me in that manner."

Burns, Watters and Bob Stellick took the Maple Leaf training and equipment staff out for dinner tonight in appreciation of their hard work this season. I went for supper with the other Toronto media guys at *Legend's* sports bar just down the street from the hotel. Joe Bowen ordered a bucket of chicken wings that our entire party of six couldn't finish. We all chowed down pretty good and watched on a jumbo screen as the Kings remained alive for a playoff spot in the West by downing the Jets in Winnipeg. None of us at the table could help but wonder if we were seeing the last-ever NHL game at the Winnipeg Arena.

WEDNESDAY, MAY 3rd
Anaheim

It was beautiful from the get-go this morning and many of the Maple Leaf players ate breakfast on a courtyard patio outside the hotel coffee-shop. About an hour later, just prior to leaving for the morning skate at The Pond, I rounded up Pat Burns and Doug Gilmour to pose with me for the back-cover photo of this book. We walked onto a grassy area in front of the hotel and Paul Hunter of the *Star,* who is covering this road trip, snapped a dozen or so pictures. Unfortunately, we took the photos beside the fully loaded team bus and the other players tried to razz us by banging on the inside of the bus windows. Boys will be boys.

On our way to The Pond, George Harrison's song *My Sweet Lord* was play-ing on the radio and it sparked a recollection of the infamous plot that Harold Ballard devised when The Beatles came to Toronto in August, 1965. Though the boys from Liverpool were scheduled for only one show at the Gardens, Ballard sold advance tickets for two concerts without informing Beatles manager Brian Epstein, who justifiably went ballistic when he found out. But, Ballard — at his con-artist best — warned him of potentially grave consequences from maniacal fans who, in his words, would "tear the building down with you guys in it" if Epstein cancelled the second show. As a result, The Beatles played two, and Harold milked a windfall in concession earnings by purposely delaying both concerts for over an hour, and turning on the Gardens' heating system during one of the hottest days of the year. He also ordered water fountains turned off in the building and he sold gallons of soft drinks to parched fans. Bob Stellick re-told the story on the bus ride today and got a chuckle from everyone seated near the front.

I walked into The Pond with Pat Burns and began gushing once again at how magnificent this facility is. The coach agreed, but voiced his overall preference for the United Center. We then talked briefly about the ice conditions around the NHL. Burns feels that Edmonton's Coliseum has the best ice in the league and the Montreal Forum has the worst. He also said Maple Leaf Gardens is close to the bottom and that New York's Madison Square Garden can be bad... "especially after the circus, with elephant-shit all over the place." Sounds inviting.

The Leafs skated for 45 minutes this morning before heading back to the hotel for a few extra minutes of rest and relaxation. Tonight's game with the Mighty Ducks will start at 8:05 p.m. — a half-hour later than usual — because the California Angels are also in town across the highway at Anaheim Stadium (playing Oakland), and the two games cannot start at the same time. As well, the *Prime Sports* cable-TV network has scheduled both the Los Angeles at Chicago and Toronto at Anaheim games tonight, and would like as small an overlap as possible (the Blackhawks and Kings get going two-and-a-half hours earlier). Of course, it'll be a late night for TV viewers back home, as *Hockey Night In Canada* won't go to air until 11 o'clock Eastern.

* * * * * *

Pat Burns has been head coach of the Toronto Maple Leafs for just under three years, having joined the club from Montreal in a surprise announcement on May 29, 1992. During his tenure behind the bench, the Leafs have played their best hockey since the Stanley Cup dynasty of the 1960s. Success came almost immediately to the hockey club, and the Maple Leafs of 1992-93 ventured to within four minutes of advancing to the finals against Montreal. Many observers, including myself, believe that if the team had gotten past Los Angeles in Game 7 of the Campbell Conference championship that spring, Toronto's quarter-century Stanley Cup drought would have ended.

As it were, Wayne Gretzky rallied the Kings to a late victory in that deciding encounter at the Gardens, but L.A. then succumbed to a Montreal club that triumphed in a remarkable ten consecutive overtimes — an astounding exploit that almost certainly will never be equalled. Exhaustion played an unequivocal role in the Los Angeles demise and the Maple Leafs — having endured 21 games in 41 nights themselves — would have been similarly fatigued. But the aura of a Stanley Cup tilt with their age-old rival, combined with the spectre of Burns defeating his former team, may have been enough to compensate.

Of course, we'll never know.

The season's momentum, however, spilled over to the start of the following campaign and the Burns-led Maple Leafs barged out of the gate with an NHL-record ten consecutive victories. The unparalleled streak came to an end in Montreal on a Saturday night (Oct. 30, 1993), and the Toronto club has never since been the same. Without warning or apparent reason, the novelty of winning dissipated; the raging competitive fires waned to a flicker. And no strategy in the interim has been able to fan the flames, not even a personnel about-face that over-hauled roughly one half of the club's roster. The current-day Leafs are a banal, middle-of-the-pack team — aging in key areas — with no distinct potential.

How does all of this sit with the coach?

Not too well. In fact, much worse than he's been willing to reveal publicly. While travelling with the Leafs during this lockout-shortened season, I've gotten to know Burns rather well. We've spent much of the past four months together in airplanes, busses, arenas and hotels. It's fairly simple to get a read on a person when you're in their company so frequently. Even a person as complex as Pat Burns.

When we arrived back at the hotel this morning, I asked the Maple Leaf coach for a few moments alone and we met in the lobby after lunch. He and I had a candid and wide-ranging chat for close to an hour in which we covered a bevy of topics.

"This season's been an obvious disappointment," he began. "Mainly because of the limited time we had to prepare after the lockout. And I knew it would be that way. In fact, I never thought the season would be saved. After Christmas, I figured it would be logically stupid to start back up again. And all the things I figured would happen did happen. A schedule was rushed. An almost-impossible travel schedule had to be put together. And there wasn't much preparation on the players' part. When people said the players were skating (during the lockout)... yeah, they were skating, but it was shinny hockey. And anyone who has played this game at the pro level knows that isn't good enough for conditioning.

"I'm happy to see that only three coaches have paid the price so far (George Burnett, Barry Melrose and Lorne Henning) because we really weren't in control of anything during the lockout. We were stuck in the middle between players and management and all we knew for sure is that a difficult situation would be dumped in our laps when it was over."

It may sound like wishful thinking today, but Burns insists he was excited about his hockey club during the pre-lockout training camp.

"I was really pumped up," he says. "We had a very tough camp and I felt the guys were ready to come out strong. Then, bang, the lights were turned out on the last day. And it hurt me, I was really stung by the whole situation... understanding, too, that labour relations often get messed up. Being a former union guy in the police department, I was able to comprehend what was happening, but it was a disappointment for me because I never actually *thought* it would happen."

As Burns mentioned, the lockout was a Catch-22 for coaches around the NHL. Technically, coaches are management. Realistically, they are mere extensions of the dressing room and their livelihoods are largely predicated on a reasonable rapport and kinship with the players. Burns felt it was impossible to strike that balance during the lockout.

"I just got out of town," he remembers. "I figured the best thing for me to do was shut up about the whole thing and go to my summer home (in Austin, Que.). I had feelings about the situation that I expressed privately with Cliff and I found my emotions swinging back and forth. One day, it was `What are the owners doing?!' and the next day, it was `What are the players doing?!' Balancing myself on that beam between players and management wasn't very easy."

And the end result of the lockout, for Burns, was a largely fresh group of players who are still — four months later — searching for an identity. One he isn't overly confident they'll discover this season.

"I think you would see a better Leaf team if we had a full 84-game schedule but, of course, we'll never know," he muses. "I hope we come together and mesh as a unit in the playoffs, but I'm not certain it'll happen this year. I was very serious when I made the statement at the start of the season that our goal was to make the playoffs. People were probably saying, `Oh, he's trying to hide behind that comment in case things go wrong,' but I wasn't. I knew it would be tough for this group of players to become a team so quickly."

The complexion and personality of the 1995 Maple Leafs underwent a drastic modification when Cliff Fletcher chose to deal Wendel Clark. While the former Leaf captain's game-by-game contribution was grossly exaggerated by those mourning the deal with Quebec, it's clear that he brought something to the table the Leafs have failed to replace. It's often been said about Clark that he has the "best first ten seconds" in hockey. Be it a fight, an important shift, or a burst of speed in the attacking zone, Wendel has always done things well *quickly.* He has an enviable capacity to shrug off undue pressure, which often enabled him to thrive in key situations for the Maple Leafs... like the playoffs.

"Replacing Wendel with another player on a forward line wasn't a problem," Burns explains. "But replacing the respect he brought to the team was another thing altogether. I know the day that trade happened, nobody in our organization was sure we were making the right move. But we knew that something had to be done, and if it meant taking one step backwards to make up two steps later on, then so be it. And let's not overlook the fact we got a pretty good player back in Mats Sundin.

"But I think what everybody seemed to overlook was the loss of two key defencemen in Sylvain Lefebvre and Bob Rouse. That has definitely hurt our team to a far greater extent than losing Wendel."

On many occasions this season — both privately and in scrums with the media — Burns and I have discussed the mysterious plight of Doug Gilmour. The Leaf captain's season-long travail has been repeatedly documented in this manuscript, with no plausible explanation. Theories have been plentiful; solutions have been scarce.

"It's been a horrible frustration for both of us," Burns admits. "I think it has a lot to do with the instant stardom that came with his success as a Maple Leaf. Many people in hockey were surprised that Doug became an overnight superstar in a tough hockey town like Toronto. He had always been a second and third-liner on other clubs, but he became the focal point of our team very quickly. Everything we did was built around Doug Gilmour and the remarkable way he responded surprised many people... perhaps *me* most of all.

"I had known him as a good checker; a guy who was a thorn in your side, and a great penalty killer. Suddenly, he used all of that energy to become a prolific point-getter and in the opinion of many, the best all-round forward in the National Hockey League for two straight years. I'm not sure that even Dougie believes he's really that good."

Like most of us, Burns feels the lockout messed up Gilmour. Taking the overachieving angle one step further, it's my opinion that Doug got himself into some kind of a "zone" when he arrived in Toronto — in particular, after Dave Andreychuk was acquired from Buffalo and placed on his wing. There was nothing fluky about the way he played; Gilmour earned every ounce of what he achieved through ceaseless determination. But it now appears that a delicate rythym was interrupted; a momentum that Gilmour himself may not have understood.

For two years, he had it all: endorsements... community charm... instant recognition... and most of all, phenomenal success on the ice. Though a deeply private individual, he seemed to bask in the adulation of being hockey's most talented pain in the ass.

Then came the lockout.

"I think Dougie's a guy who relies heavily on a gameplan," Burns explains. "He plays hard during the season and keeps himself fit in the summertime. After having both his feet operated on last summer, he was not able to maintain his normal off-season conditioning routine (which includes a lot of running) and that's probably where his trouble began. Had the season started as planned, I think he might have been able to play his way back into shape. He would have benefitted from the normal environment of the season. But then the players were locked out and it set him back even further.

"He went over and played in Switzerland, and I think something hit him there. I think he suddenly realized, `I can't stop... I have to be in the middle of the action.' And I believe he was thrown off by that."

Whatever the cause, Gilmour simply wasn't the same player when the lockout-shortened schedule began. Nor has he regained his dominance in the interim. He refuses to show any tangible frustration publicly, and even though I've privately seen the odd flood of emotion — like during our brief walk up the street from the Loews Santa Monica in March — I haven't noticed any drastic change in his off-ice demeanour. Then again, I'm not nearly as close to Gilmour as Burns is.

"Around the 30-game mark of the schedule, his frustrations boiled over and we had to sit down together and have it out," the Leaf coach remembers. "It was the first time in our association that we had any words between us and I think it was a bit of an awakening. Suddenly, Dougie realized, `Hey, I can't be doing this.'"

Asked to explain what "this" means, Burns repeated himself.

"Everything was built on frustration. He wasn't going into traffic with the puck, he was staying on the perimeter. Not that he was scared; it's just that his confidence was down. He started listening to all the suggestions from people... one day, that he should be playing on a line with (Dave) Andreychuk; another day, that he shouldn't be playing with Andreychuk, or he should be playing with two other guys. There were 20 different things. I think he listened to too many people and he stopped listening to the people who cared. And I'm one of those who does care about Doug Gilmour. A lot. Too much to go out and put pressure on him to carry this team the way he did for two seasons."

Burns and I then began to reflect on his tenure as coach of the Maple Leafs. Though the club has slipped back this year, it's fair to say Cliff Fletcher made a prudent decision in hiring Burns away from Montreal after the 1991-92 campaign. And the coach's agent, Don Meehan, also shines for aggressively steering Burns in the opposite direction of Los Angeles, where he almost signed as G.M. and coach of the Kings. The move to Toronto has been positive for everyone concerned.

"I have to be satisfied with what has been accomplished so far," Burns says. "My signing with the Maple Leafs happened very suddenly and I came into the situation blind. I remember going over the line-up that summer at my cottage and thinking, 'Geez, what in the world am I going to do with *this* team?' But Cliff turned things around pretty quickly — the acquisition of Dougie made us a good team much faster than anybody in the organization ever dreamed of."

Fletcher and Burns have a typical G.M.-coach relationship. They certainly don't agree on everything, and their personalities are an obvious mismatch. Fletcher is a conservative man who goes to great lengths to maintain his decorum. While other GMs will holler crassly at officials and players from their perch above the rink (John Ferguson's rages could be heard all over the Winnipeg Arena when he managed the Jets), Fletcher doesn't venture beyond slamming his fist on the table in frustration. At least, when others are present.

Burns, by comparison, is not *un*dignified, but he's obviously more comfortable at flaunting his emotions. And Fletcher doesn't hold back from privately reprimanding Burns whenever he deems it appropriate.

During the Winnipeg-Chicago road trip in mid-April, Burns came up to me in the lobby of the Drake Hotel. Mats Sundin was playing with a sore wrist and he couldn't shoot the puck worth a damn against the Jets the previous night. Burns asked me how I handled Sundin's injury on my post-game radio reports and I told him exactly what I've just told *you*. I wondered why he was interested, and he said Fletcher had just phoned him in a huff from Toronto, demanding to know why Burns was keeping Sundin's broken wrist a secret from him. Burns insisted Sundin's wrist was not broken and asked Fletcher where he came up with such a thing. The G.M. said that Darryl Sittler had "heard it on the radio" (it turns out, on CFRB) and had phoned him with the information.

This type of scrutiny — unfair at times — is not unusual with Fletcher, and it occasionally leads to a squabble among the two men.

"Cliff and I have disputes now and then, but they are usually based on how to use various players," Burns says. "And I don't think Cliff minds that. He's never left me with the impression that he wants a 'Yes' man behind the bench. He wants somebody who will stand up for his beliefs and I've been known to do that."

Conflicts between a G.M. and a coach are often fundamental: the G.M. drafts or trades for a player and he wants the coach to use that player. Otherwise, his decisions are open to question. And since the coach is employed by the G.M., an awkward circumstance can materialize. It happened on the Leafs with Drake Berehowsky, a player who Fletcher did not draft (he was still G.M. of Calgary when the defenceman was selected in 1990). Fletcher pushed for Burns to be patient with Berehowsky, who had been a first-round pick, but the coach concluded he could not play in the NHL and had little use for him. Burns ultimately won that debate as Berehowsky was dealt to Pittsburgh at the trade deadline last month. But he realizes for a coach, it's usually a two-way street... at best.

"That's something I learned in Montreal," Burns admits. "I have to take a back seat now and then and realize that a general manager cannot mortgage the future of a hockey team for a long period of time. A coach obviously lives for the moment and he welcomes anything that will make his team better immediately. We see the reasons why all the time, with coaches being fired left and right. But, a good general manager knows he has a long-term responsibility to the organization and he isn't as likely to agree to knee-jerk decisions.

"On the whole, though, Cliff has been very supportive during our three years together."

Born just over 43 years ago in St-Henri, Que., Burns never worked outside his native province till he left to join the Maple Leafs. His NHL career began with the Montreal Canadiens in 1988-89, but he doesn't subscribe to the theory that there's no place like home. In fact, he's far more enamoured with coaching in Toronto.

"There's no comparison at all," Burns claims. "The hockey climate and working conditions for a coach are so much better in Toronto. I've enjoyed this experience much more than I did my days in Montreal, where they take the game a bit too seriously. In Toronto, hockey's a pastime; in Montreal, it's a religion."

When reflecting on his youth, Burns admits he could never have imagined one day coaching his beloved Canadiens... and then, the Maple Leafs. As a youngster in the mid-60s, he would sneak into the Montreal Forum to watch practice, then wait outside for the players to emerge. Among his idols from that era was defenceman Jacques Laperriere, who'd later be his assistant with the Canadiens.

"Don't think *that* didn't blow my mind," Burns chuckles. "Here's a guy whose autograph I used to get and, suddenly, I'm his boss! When I first walked into the Montreal dressing room, I looked around and there was Larry Robinson... Bob Gainey was my captain... Mats Naslund was in another corner. And I thought to myself, 'Holy shit, is this for real?' I mean, I had purchased scalper tickets maybe three years earlier to go watch these same guys play. I would sit up in the white seats and cheer them on. Now, I was their coach. Try figuring that one out."

Of course, Burns didn't just show up one day at the Forum and get the job. After playing Junior hockey and bouncing around from one pro tryout to another, he finally abandoned his dream of being an NHL star and joined the police force in Gatineau, Que. However, he always stayed close to the game at the minor level and he eventually worked his way up (in 1983) to a head coaching position with Hull of the Quebec Junior League (a team co-owned by Wayne Gretzky). After four years there, he graduated to the pro ranks with Sherbrooke of the American League, and was hired by Serge Savard to replace Jean Perron in Montreal a season later (1988-89). He's been among the best at his trade ever since.

Burns could probably write a book himself just on the 16 years he spent as a policeman in Gatineau, which sits directly across the Ottawa River from our nation's capital. Like most border communities, Gatineau is a rough, crime-ridden area and Burns quite often had to use force as a deterrent. One particular moment of peril stands out.

"Every town has one bad family with six or seven brothers who are all tough," Burns explains. "And I think I fought the whole family at one time or another in Gatineau. One by one. Sometimes two at a time. And they even kicked the shit out of me a couple of times. They were a constant problem for the policemen of that city.

"On Christmas Eve one year, I think it was 1974, I was directing traffic in front of the liquor board commission, which is always jam-packed on that day for obvious reasons. It was around 4 o'clock in the afternoon and was starting to get dark out when I saw this car coming towards me kind of weaving from side to side. So, I pulled it over and, naturally, it was one of these brothers who was just piss-faced... pie-eyed to hell. I looked at him and said, 'Listen, you cannot drive right now in your condition. You only live three blocks away. Park your car here, walk home, and tell one of your brothers to come and pick it up.'

"Even though I had battles galore with this family, I didn't want to start fighting on Christmas Eve. Most people were in the spirit of the season and I felt that way as well. But the guy was obviously in no frame of mind to listen and he began cussing at me, yelling, 'Fuck you, who the hell do you think you are,' and stuff like that. Well, we wound up rolling in the snow and going at it. My back-up (officer) came over and we put the guy in the car and charged him with impaired driving. We didn't keep him, though. We just gave him a citation to appear in court on a certain date and he went home.

"Well, around an hour later, I went for my supper break. I picked up some Chinese food and brought it back to the station. I was sitting there, eating, when all of a sudden I heard this weird sound. It was like 'ping... ping... ping' and it seemed like something was bouncing off the outer wall of the station. I said to myself, 'What the hell is that?' and got up to have a look. Well I don't know if you've ever been fired on, but when someone shoots at you, it's not the same sound as if you're standing behind the gun: you can hardly hear the thing go off.

"So, I started walking around and we had an old fire truck in the station, because we were also the city's fire-fighters the first couple of years I was there. All of a sudden, the front tire of the truck blew out. Then as I was climbing the stairs, pieces of glass and cement were flying all over the place. I figured, 'What the fuck?' A small chunk of lead or cement then flew up and cut me just above the bridge of my nose — it was like something stung me. I put my finger there and felt the blood coming down. My other partner said, 'Somebody's shooting!' and we hustled the hell out of there.

"I went into the bathroom and looked in the mirror to see if there was a hole in my face. My partner said, 'You've been hit!' and I said, 'I can't be hit, it's on the forehead and I'd be on the ground if I got shot, you dope!' Then I saw the blood trickling down and began to panic a little. I remember thinking, 'Shit, am I alive?'

"Anyway, the upshot of the whole thing is that this bad-ass who I pulled over went home and got a rifle, then came back to the station and tried to kill me. We had a laugh about it later on, but that's the closest I came to getting knocked off during my 16 years as a cop."

The so-called "policeman" in Burns is frequently a conversation topic among his critics. How often during the past three years have we been witness to a TV clip that reveals the un-smiling Maple Leaf coach talking with a death-knell tone about life in the NHL? During his first year in Toronto, there were many times when I felt that Burns was the biggest prick I'd ever encountered. He seemed to get perverse enjoyment out of creating difficulty for members of the electronic media, and would go out of his way to make us feel inferior.

Having gotten to know Burns much better since that time, there is obviously another side to the man, but he doesn't quarrel with the fact he'll never be nicknamed "Chuckles."

"In 16 years as a cop, you learn to shut your mouth," Burns says. "That caused a problem with the media during my first year in Montreal because during press conferences, all I'd say was 'Yeah. No. Yeah. No.' That's what you're taught to do in the police force. Eventually, it was easier for me to open up, because I realized the media has a job to do that requires some rapport. But that's where my reputation got started and I'll probably never be able to live it down.

"Actually, I think the perception of me being grumpy is something that the press really enjoys. It gives them a subject to write and talk about when there's a slow day and it's a great way to start a story —'Old Forrest Grump was at it again' — that kind of stuff. But after a while, it actually gets you in a pissed-off mood when you hear it.

"I mean, there are some members of the media — like Barb Ondrusek (of CBLT, Channel 5) — who don't understand that you have to talk loud in practice. A bunch of big, heavy men are skating around and shooting pucks and you have to speak at a certain level to be understood. But she'll ask me afterwards, 'What are you angry about today?' You just shake your head and wonder where she's coming from."

At this point in the conversation, I felt it only fair to remind Burns that he isn't exactly the "Good Humour" man during his post-practice media scrums. These are the sessions where radio and TV reporters pin him up against a wall to the left of the dressing room and fire questions. His answers are more curt and less thoughtful than during his follow-up chat with the print media — or, during a one-on-one radio or TV interview.

"I don't like those scrum situations," he admits. "I much prefer sitting down like we are right now and discussing all kinds of things, not only hockey. Some of the questions in those media scrums — and you know, you've been there — just don't make sense. And you can see the resentment from the other reporters who have to wait for me to answer. I think to myself, 'These poor bastards want to get something done and you're asking me a dumb question like that!' It's part of the limelight I don't enjoy and I wish I didn't have to endure it on a daily basis."

Burns has varying relationships with members of the local media who regularly cover and travel with the team. After a slow start, I've been able to garner a decent rapport with the Maple Leaf coach: to the point where he'll confess things to me that are strictly off the record and not have to worry about them being repeated. That type of trust is the product of familiarity, and it takes time to develop. In the media scrums, however, I'm just another reporter and Burns will grumble at me as quickly as he will anyone else. I've learned to just play along.

Otherwise, I find myself treading lightly around Burns — simply because it would serve me no useful purpose to be antagonistic. I'm not hesitant to ask him a tough question, but I rely on his cooperation for the benefit of my radio listeners. Annoying him to the point of not wanting to speak with me would obviously be counter-productive.

The newspaper writers and columnists are normally less scrupulous. Burns can give them stout, one-word answers and they can build stories around them. I can't do that with sound.

The beat-reporters are Damien Cox and Paul Hunter of the Toronto *Star;* Dave Fuller and Lance Hornby of the Toronto *Sun*; David Shoalts of the *Globe & Mail*, and Larry Sicinski of the Hamilton *Spectator*. All but Shoalts travel with the team on a regular basis, as the *Globe* does not staff Maple Leaf road games until the playoffs. Burns gets along nicely with Cox, Hunter and Hornby, but he clashes with Fuller and Sicinski.

His running feud with Fuller is particularly intriguing, because the veteran *Sun* writer is less obtrusive than his counterparts. Dave is rarely inclined to flaunt the illusory machismo that others do while in the presence of Burns and you'd think that delivery would sit well with the Leaf coach. But Burns has never forgiven Fuller for using the Bill Berg "I wouldn't know him if I ran over him with a truck" comment... or for quoting him expressing frustration over Wendel Clark when the Maple Leaf captain was sidelined with an injury in January, 1993.

"If a reporter goes out of his way to disturb me, I think my best course is to just push the guy aside and not worry about him," says the coach. "Fuller has tried to provoke me a few times and has written some personal things I didn't like. So I'd rather not deal with the man.

"The thing people tend to misunderstand is that I don't have to like members of the media, and they don't have to like me. Nowhere is it written that we must live in harmony all the time. It's human nature to clash with people; it happens in the workplace every day. There were guys I dealt with on the police force who I couldn't stand and I'm sure others felt that way about me. I imagine it's the same with you... that not everybody at The *Fan* is in love with Howard Berger, and vise versa. So, personality clashes aren't that uncommon."

Which brings us to the rancour between Burns and Sicinski, the veteran *Spectator* columnist who makes the majority of Leaf road trips. Observing this act on a daily basis is tragically comical — a living sequel to Felix Unger and Oscar Madison. Burns is Tom, and Larry is Jerry. Nobody grates on the nerves of the Leaf coach quite as much as the Hamilton writer, and the results are poignant every time they meet. Actually, if you can overlook his penchant to argue, Sicinski isn't a bad guy. If you say black, he'll say white. If you ask him to stand up, he'll sit down. But, that's just Larry. Beneath all the blarney is a sensitive and loving family man who works extremely hard.

However, don't try explaining that to Burns. "Everyone knows Larry's a pain in the ass but I'm the only one who will tell him," the coach grunts. "He came up and asked me that stupid question in Edmonton earlier this season and I told him to fuck off. If you want to be part of a media scrum, that's fine... I usually give the writers a fair amount of my time. But, don't hang around afterwards and think that you'll get a personal audience just because you work for the Hamilton *Spectator.* That's Larry's approach and it stinks."

As Fuller mentioned after the "hate campaign" thing in Anaheim, he feels that Burns deliberately tries to bully the media the same way he bullies his players. But, the coach obviously disagrees.

"You're getting that opinion from a guy who has a problem with me," he says. "I don't bully anybody in the media, but if I don't like a Dave Fuller, I'll tell him. That's not bullying... it's fact. Now, if a Bob McKenzie, or a Jim Proudfoot came up and said that to me — or if *all* the media felt the same way — then I'd have to believe there's a problem. Otherwise, I consider the source and move on."

As for other members of the travelling media, the coach has mainly kind words. Lance Hornby is a sharp, effective reporter whose discreet, non-confrontational approach sits well with Burns. Ditto for Paul Hunter, although the Star reporter drew the coach's wrath several weeks ago for chronicling how Burns barred the media from a practice session. Hunter wrote that Burns contravened a League by-law and the coach saw red. The following day, Hunter was taking photographs at the visitor's bench in the Gardens and Burns had it out with him.

"You know Paul, you and me are very much alike... you're either a great guy or a fucking asshole!"

Burns and Cox seem to have a unique relationship as Damien makes a point of maintaining a closeness to the Maple Leaf coach. Some of his rivals accuse him of "brown-nosing", but Damien is entitled to utilize whatever method works best for him. He also tends to go lightly around the coach, yet he's the best analytical writer on the Maple Leaf beat.

"Damien's a guy whose sense of humour I enjoy, but he's not someone I hang out with," Burns says. "And in spite of accusations I hear from time to time, I *don't* give him exclusive material. That's bullshit."

While Burns disputes the notion that he's a control freak, there are some prime examples to the contrary. He is very much in charge of everything that transpires on a road trip: from the moment the players and coaches arrive at the airport, to the moment they get back. This is clearly personified by his "throne" at the front right-hand side of the bus, where other humans dare not tread. Pat can be the last person out of the arena or hotel, but that row will be open. Even Cliff Fletcher sits behind him when he comes on a trip.

"Well, it's the best seat on the bus," Burns says wryly. "I think you'll find that most coaches from Junior, to minor-pro, to the NHL sit where I do. I don't believe the players would appreciate it if I went back and sat with them. They have their own things to talk about.

"As far as being in charge, I think there *has* to be someone who plays that role. Maybe you haven't noticed, but both general managers I've worked for (Serge Savard and Fletcher) don't travel with the team very often because they understand that I'm in charge. Cliff knows that he can go do his own thing and if there's a problem, I'll handle it. He and I speak by phone on a regular basis and he never feels the need to travel on the same airplane or bus as the hockey club.

"It's not an ego thing for me, like some people believe."

Having been employed by both the Canadiens and Maple Leafs during his seven years in the NHL, I wondered if Burns would reveal the least-favourite player he's coached. It wasn't the fairest of requests and he danced around the question a tad. But the names Claude Lemieux and Russ Courtnall did pop up once or twice.

"I've known Claude Lemieux since Junior and I like him very much," Burns said. "But as a professional hockey player, he drove me nuts. He just didn't want to buy into the program. As far as Russ is concerned, we had our differences, but he gave me two very fine years. And really, I can't think of too many players who I didn't enjoy coaching."

On the flip side, the names roll off Burns' tongue.

"Chris Chelios. Patrick Roy. Doug Gilmour. Wendel Clark. These are people you're proud to be associated with. I think I said publicly that if I had another son, I'd want him to be like Wendel. And there are a lot of other players I've coached who are in that category."

As for a favourite moment in his NHL career, Burns is somewhat torn. Montreal made it to the Stanley Cup final in his rookie season of 1988-89, but he's not sure that accomplishment ranks ahead of the Maple Leafs' first-round playoff upset of Detroit two years ago.

"Just seeing the reaction of the team when Nicki's overtime goal went in is a memory I'll always take with me," he smiles. "It wasn't a situation where I wanted to cry and couldn't talk, but I just loved the ecstasy of the players at that moment. It was more of a pure excitement than going to the finals with Montreal, which was a big thing for *me* in my rookie season. But guys like Bob Gainey and Larry Robinson had been there many times before and they didn't get all giddy.

"Our dressing room after the Detroit win was completely different. It was absolute euphoria because it was so unexpected. I've never been a part of something quite that special."

The Leaf coach has a son and daughter from a previous marriage and currently lives with his girlfriend, Tina Sheldon, who is the marketing director for the *Nesbitt-Burns* Investment Group. The couple met in Montreal four years ago and Burns is 12 years her senior. Tina maintains a low profile, and is rarely seen in public with Burns.

"That's the way she wants it," he insists. "Tina likes her privacy and I respect that. She's definitely not a hockey wife. Her career is important and she works very hard. I think what really attracted me to her is the fact she won't sit around and do nothing. I've seen wives of players who make me just shake my head. I say to myself, 'What do you do all day?' Tina's not like that.

"She doesn't have to work — I make more than enough money to keep us going — but that's not how she wants it. She insists on sharing the expenses and doesn't expect a free ride. As far as getting married, we don't even discuss it. We've both gone that route before and there's no rush to do it again. I imagine we will one day, but I can't say when."

Burns also cherishes his privacy and hopes to ultimately get away from the big cities and bright lights of professional hockey.

"I love my off-season home," he says. "I've got a log cabin up in the Vermont area (in Austin, Que.) and I want to retire there one day. I can see myself getting up in the morning and going to the local town ten miles down the road for a newspaper and coffee. That may not sound like much of a life for a supposed hard-ass and egomaniac like me, but it's exactly what I want."

With that, the Maple Leaf coach excused himself and went back up to his room for a few hours of shut-eye before tonight's game.

*   *   *   *   *   *

Burns will not use Kenny Jonsson against the Mighty Ducks tonight and it's probably a wise decision. The rookie's performance flattened out after he recovered so nicely from that embarrassment in the second game of the season at San Jose. He's played a whole lot of hockey on a defence unit that has generally struggled and his development seems to have lagged. With Dmitri Mironov back in the line-up tonight, Burns now has six healthy veterans on the blueline, and he'll go with them.

Having no particular reason to rest, Jonsson walked across to the mall this afternoon with Kent Manderville and Matt Martin. I also took a stroll over there and ran into the Maple Leaf trio. We began chatting about today's somewhat predictable news out of Winnipeg, where the Jets have confirmed they'll be leaving for a destination in the U.S. — most likely Minneapolis. With the Quebec Nordiques reportedly on their way to Denver, the NHL will only have five Canadian teams next season.

The weather was just perfect late this afternoon and I had an hour to waste. So I went out to the pool and noticed Rich Sutter lounging by himself, reading the newspaper. The 13-year veteran hasn't been playing much lately and it's tormenting him. There are few elements in the game of hockey analogous to the Sutter brand of determination and while Rich hasn't distinguished himself recently, he yearns to be in the line-up.

"It's awfully tough not playing," he told me as we chatted in the hot afternoon sun. "I've never been one to argue with coaches because I know how difficult a job they have. And Pat Burns is someone who I've always respected. But I hope to get back in there for the playoffs. I'm pumped up about playing my former teammates and I obviously enjoy the challenge of playing against my brothers (Brent, and coach Darryl)."

Sutter hasn't seen much of his wife and three children since being traded by the Blackhawks in early March. "They're back home in Chicago and it's agonizing being apart," he moaned. "At least when I'm playing, it takes my mind off how much I miss them. When I'm not out there, I've got too much time to sit around and think."

The subtle difference between playing and not playing was evident when Bill Berg strolled out to the pool area fully dressed in the suit he'd be wearing on the team bus. Sutter laid bare-chested several feet away, in no obvious hurry to leave for the arena.

About 45 minutes later, the Leaf players gathered outside the main entrance of the Westin and loitered in the vicinity of the bus. It was absolutely delightful in the late-afternoon sun. I sat on a picnic-type chair with Joe Bowen and watched as a teenaged fan turned his videocam on the players: impervious to the admonishing of a hotel employee. Dave Ellett walked over and asked, "Howard, did you hire that guy as well?" in a wisenheimer reference to the photos Paul Hunter took of me, Burns and Gilmour earlier today. Typical Ellett.

Warren Rychel exited the hotel and looked at the video guy, now standing across the way. "Today's youth!" he marvelled, shaking his head. "When I was that age, we were lucky to have pocket-cameras. Now, they have video equipment." Dmitri Mironov looked around and noticed Bowen working over a big wad of bubble-gum. Their eyes met and "Tree" began to chew his cud in mimicking fashion. Joe grumbled an indignity in Russian and we got on board.

As the players poured out of the hotel, a man in his early 20s was practically begging for them to step across the driveway and autograph his binder of hockey cards. Most of the Leafs ignored his plea and went straight to the bus. "C'mon Chucky, go over there and sign," said Felix Potvin with a wry smile. Andreychuk, who doesn't enjoy the adulation of hockey stardom, rolled his eyes and replied, "I've seen that same guy in San Jose, L.A. and now here. He must have my autograph 20 times!" Mike Gartner took the time to go over and meet the fan. Then he boarded and the bus pulled away.

The season finale with the Mighty Ducks was rendered meaningless when the Blackhawks hammered Los Angeles at the United Center, securing home-ice advantage in the first round of the playoffs, and eliminating the Kings. But the Leafs should still be embarrassed by their revolting performance tonight. The game was an absolute travesty from the get-go, as the youthful Anaheim players — also, with nothing to gain — skated rings around their apathetic opponents in a 6-1 romp. Mind you, few of us expected the Maple Leafs to boldly shrug off the Chicago triumph and come out guns ablazing. Nothing about the club's deportment this season suggested the emergence of such character and neither did it materialize. Instead, the Leafs did precisely what Pat Burns figured they might when he confessed earlier today a desire to withhold the Chicago result from them. It was a sad, yet accurate commentary on his underachieving team.

While the Leafs lollygagged around the Pond ice surface, there was plenty of exasperation in the executive box. Bill Watters stormed out in the second intermission, took one look at me, and blathered that I'd be "devoting full time" to finishing this book by the end of next week.

In the dressing room afterwards, predictable excuses were rolling off the players' tongues. "The game meant nothing and it showed," said captain Doug Gilmour. "We played badly tonight but don't look too far into it. We're all pros and we'll be prepared for what's needed to win when the puck drops (in Chicago) on Sunday. It's a good lesson for us."

Added coach Burns: "I didn't think we'd be as flat as we were, but to err is human. It's a little worrisome going into Sunday. We have to stop talking big games or we'll be out of the playoffs pretty quick."

The coach's disdain for what he witnessed tonight was unmistakable as he sat motionless on the team bus moments later. In a move to break the stony silence, Watters leaned across the aisle and whispered, "One good thing... you won't have to worry about overconfidence after that display." Slumped in his chair, Burns then erupted loud enough for the dozen or so players already on board to hear: "Nope, there's no chance of any overconfidence from this talented group. Fuck the talent! It's meaningless if you haven't got any heart. You need balls to play in the playoffs. I'll take heart over talent any day."

As the bus pulled out of the Arrowhead Pond, Bob Cole of *Hockey Night In Canada* gave the Maple Leafs a thumbs-up salute. Coley will broadcast the Quebec-New York Rangers first-round series because HNIC producers believe it will attract the largest TV audience. However, the expression on Cole's face as we left the arena tonight seemed to be one of sadness. I got the impression he'll miss calling the Leaf games.

THURSDAY, MAY 4th
Toronto

As the Leaf players filed onto the team bus in front of the Westin South Coast Plaza at 6:15 this morning, *Another One Bites The Dust*, by the rock group Queen, was playing over the sound system... not exactly the words a team heading into the playoffs wants to hear. But after the club's sickly performance last night, it seems like an omen. The skies were overcast as we made the 45-minute trek up the San Diego Freeway to L-A-X and the team quickly boarded the Air Canada *Boeing-767*.

The trip home took just more than four hours. Ken Daniels and I spent much of it in the flight deck, gabbing with the captain and first officer. Many of the Leaf players slept through the flight. They should be well rested after last night's fiasco.

Standing around the luggage carousel at Pearson Airport, I talked with a relaxed Pat Burns. "That was sure frustrating last night, but I think my veteran players will come through in the playoffs," he opined. Then, he looked over and said, "I guess they'll be talking a lot about me at your radio station today."

"What do you mean?" I asked.

"Well, my agent (Don Meehan) was in Anaheim to see the game and Al Strachan has written that story in the *Sun*."

The coach had gotten wind of Strachan's column today... entitled: BURNS OUT? IT'S ELEMENTARY, with a sub-head CLUES SUGGEST MAPLE LEAFS AND THEIR COACH MAY PART WAYS AFTER PLAYOFFS. In a parody of a Sherlock Holmes episode, Strachan wrote:

"I'm afraid, my dear Watson, that we must conclude that the Toronto Maple Leafs will have a new coach when the next season opens.

"...Why, Holmes, have you reached this decision?"
"...Who knows, Watson. I'm not Nostradamus. But he does like boating, and Los Angeles is on the water. Furthermore, when Wayne Gretzky owned a Junior team, it was Burns who coached it. I'm afraid I'm not really sure yet where he is going, Watson. There are not enough clues available to reach a conclusion. All I can tell you is that there's sufficient evidence to assume he's going somewhere."

The not-so tongue-in-cheek column suggested that Burns has been at odds recently with a number of his players, including Dave Andreychuk, Doug Gilmour, Jamie Macoun and Mike Gartner. It also hinted that Cliff Fletcher has grown weary of his coach's preponderance towards defensive hockey. Strachan credited speculation within his hockey pipeline as the source for the column.

When I asked Burns about the prosect of him leaving, his response was ominous:

"In this game, Howie, you can't tell anyone to fuck off."

PLAYOFFS
SATURDAY, MAY 6th
Chicago

The Maple Leafs and Chicago Blackhawks are meeting for the second consecutive year in the playoffs and it's rather intriguing to reflect on the last time Chicago defeated Toronto in the spring.

The Blackhawks prevailed in a best-of-five Stanley Cup final back in 1937-38 — winning the series three games to one. A few notes about that particular NHL season should provide an historical perspective of just how long ago it really was:

* There were a total of eight teams in the NHL. The Maple Leafs, New York Americans, Montreal Canadiens and Montreal Maroons comprised the Canadian Division, while Boston, Chicago, Detroit and the New York Rangers were in the American Division.
* Maple Leafs Gordie Drillon (52 points) and Syl Apps (50 points) finished one-two in the scoring race. No Toronto player has since won the points championship for the Art Ross Trophy.
* Harold (Mush) March, the man who scored the first-ever goal at Maple Leaf Gardens in November, 1931, was still playing for Chicago.
* The legendary Eddie Shore was on defence for the Bruins.
* Walter (Turk) Broda played all 48 regular-season games in goal for the Maple Leafs, recording a 2.64 average and six shutouts.
* Frank Calder was president of the NHL.
* Future NHL president Clarence Campbell was still a referee.
* The coaches were: King Clancy (Maroons), Red Dutton (Americans), Cecil Hart (Canadiens), Dick Irvin (Toronto), Art Ross (Boston), Lester Patrick (Rangers), Bill Stewart (Chicago) and Jack Adams (Detroit). NHL trophies are currently awarded in the name of four of the eight coaches that season: The Hart, Art Ross, King Clancy, and Jack Adams.
* Cliff Fletcher and Bob Pulford were two years old.

The Blackhawks won the Stanley Cup that year despite having by far the worst regular-season record of the six teams that qualified for the playoffs. The 'Hawks had 37 points, and they knocked off the Canadians and Americans (both of whom had 49 points), and the Leafs (who had 57). They won the Stanley Cup on April 12th of that year, downing Toronto 4-1 at Chicago Stadium.

Charles L. Coleman, who authored the venerable three-volume series THE TRAIL OF THE STANLEY CUP, wrote about that series finale:

> *Toronto had high hopes of winning the second game at Chicago and forcing a return to Toronto for the final. However, Chicago, supported by another great turnout of fans, had other plans.*
>
> *Cully Dahlstrom opened the scoring but Gordon Drillon equalized on a nice play with Apps. Carol Voss stole the puck from (George) Parsons in front of the Toronto net and whipped it behind Broda. A minute later, Jack Shill scored from the blueline. Harold March added another to make it safe for Chicago.*
>
> *Although there was plenty of heavy checking, only five penalties were called. Red Horner was forced out during the second period by pulled ligaments in his knee.*
>
> *Manager Bill Stewart, with no previous experience as a hockey coach, had done the impossible and brought the Stanley Cup to Chicago. Owner Fred McLaughlin was highly elated.*

Of the five goalscorers that night, only Dahlstrom and March are still alive. Since then, the Maple Leafs have prevailed against Chicago in five playoff meetings, including the 1962 Cup final, and a memorable Cup semifinal in 1967 — the last year the Leafs were champions.

This spring's Western Conference quarterfinal begins tomorrow night at the United Center, where the Maple Leafs were 1-1-1 in three regular-season meetings. The Blackhawks will not have their captain and leader Jeremy Roenick in the line-up, which should give the Leafs a bit of an edge. However, virtually nothing about Toronto's regular-season performance bodes well for prosperity in the playoffs.

My flight to Chicago left sunny and warm Toronto at 9:45 this morning and after landing at O'Hare Airport, it seemed that my luggage had gone someplace else. Chris Cuthbert and Mark Askin of *Hockey Night In Canada* waited patiently with their bags to share a cab ride with me, but the damned conveyor belt kept going round and round with the same two pieces of luggage — neither of them mine. I finally went upstairs to the Air Canada ticket counter and appraised the agent of my plight. Just as she took my baggage claim-check, Chris ran up the escalator and told me it finally had arrived. What a relief *that* was!

The hotel situation in Chicago this weekend is a terrible mess. A food and grocer's convention has attracted more than 140,000 people to this city and hotels are booked solid as far north as Milwaukee. To the chagrin of the Toronto media, the Maple Leafs' publicity department was able to find rooms only at the Chicago Hilton and Towers, and only on the elite upper floors. As a result, our radio, TV and newspaper bosses are on the hook for $205 per night (U.S.), not including tax. The poo-bahs at The *Fan* almost had coronaries when I informed them, but there literally is no other choice at the moment.

Before leaving home, I phoned a service that had the availability of all Chicago hotels and was told there was one room at a *Comfort Inn* near Wrigley Field... "but, the toilet isn't working." Wonderful. It's like a car rental company saying, "Sir, we've got a lovely mid-size for you, but it has no steering-wheel." My bowels and I politely declined.

The cab ride to our hotel today was as hair-raising as any of the bumpy flights I've been on this season. Destiny decreed that I had the front seat, right next to the wild-man in the turban, who zigged and zagged, and lurched, and screeched until the three of us were ready to puke. How we avoided a collision is still a mystery. I spent much of the ride on my knees facing Chris and Mark in the back seat, and the concept of vomiting brought to mind another broadcasting fable.

My two *Molstar* pals howled as I recounted the night former Maple Leaf broadcaster Ron Hewat barfed on the air, right in the middle of a game. The Leafs were getting hammered by the New York Islanders at the Gardens late in the 1977-78 season and Hewat shared the microphone with partner John McGillvary. My father and I were at the game and it was so one-sided, we left midway through the third period. While driving home, we listened to the action on CKFH-1430, and right in the middle of an Islander rush, Hewat suddenly stopped calling the play. All me and Dad could hear were crowd noises in the background. We looked at each other with confused expressions when poor McGillvary came on in a panic.

"Uh, number five in the blue shoots it into the white zone... the goalie of the white team fires it back off the boards...", that kind of thing. Now, colour commentators aren't expected to be quite as familiar with uniform numbers, so McGillvary was in a predicament. I would have died if Joe Bowen or Ken Daniels had walked out on me during those pair of broadcasts in the regular season.

Still, it didn't explain to us what had become of Hewat. That is, until McGillvary finally decided to appraise the audience.

He began by saying, "Ladies and gentlemen, you probably realize that Ron Hewat is no longer doing the broadcast. He's not"... and just as McGillvary said "feeling well", someone could be heard retching his guts out in the background. McGillvary cupped his hand over the mike as poor Hewat heaved up in a garbage-pail behind him. It mustn't have been all that funny for the broadcasters, but Dad and I almost drove off the road in hysterics. Radio can sure be a humbling business.

Relating old yarns helped to divert our attention from the crazed taxi driver and Cuthbert, who will call the Toronto-Chicago series with Harry Neale, had a few of his own.

"Being nauseous sure isn't fun for a broadcaster," he said. "I got sick one night in the middle of a game in Vancouver. My normal pre-game fare is a clubhouse sandwich and that day I decided to go on a health kick and order coleslaw instead of fries. I swallowed one mouth-full of the stuff and realized it was spoiled. It had just a horrible smell and I decided to leave it there and concentrate on the sandwich.

"Well, one fork-full was enough. As soon as we went on the air, I broke out in a cold sweat and by the end of the period, I couldn't open my mouth. I remember every time I tried to say `Petri Skriko', I felt my insides coming up. I told the producer (Larry Issac) I was going to be sick and might have to bail out, but he didn't hear me. My partner that night, Jim Peplinski, took over and threw to a commercial in the final minute, and Issac wound up giving him shit.

"Thank goodness Vancouver had a private bathroom right behind our broadcast location. I spent a good 15 minutes in there and have no idea what I'd have done if we were in the old Chicago Stadium."

Cuthbert also remembers losing his voice in Calgary on the morning of Game 6 of the 1991 playoff series between the Flames and Edmonton.

"I went to the Oilers' doctor and he phoned a colleague in Calgary and got me a cortisone prescription," Chris recalled. "The pharmacist gave me the bag and asked, `Do you know what you've got here?' He said it was a powerful drug and told me to keep drinking throughout the day. I downed about eight cans of ice-tea that afternoon and just before the game, my voice miraculously returned. I literally could not squeak out a syllable at noon-time, but the drug must have worked.

"I usually take a bathroom break in the first intermission, but Grapes was already on with *Coach's Corner* so I decided not to. Well, about four minutes into the second period, I thought I was going to burst. All of that ice-tea was ready to come out and I simply couldn't go anywhere. One of our workers pulled a wastebasket between my legs but Peplinski was with me again, and I knew if I went ahead and peed, he'd broadcast it to the entire country. Somehow, I made it through."

291

Chris believes a bigger nightmare than an upset stomach or a full bladder would be a sudden bout of the hiccups. "It's against the rules to even mention that to a broadcaster before a game," he warned.

My $205 room in the Hilton is quite wonderful, with an overlooking panorama of Lake Michigan out the two windows. It's a long suite, with a full bathroom and shower at each end. In order to take full advantage of the exaggeratted room rate, I've decided to pee in one and crap in the other.

A suppertime television report on the Maple Leafs and Blackhawks was so typical of the way Chicago treats hockey. It showed a video clip of yesterday's Leaf practice at the Gardens and the announcer doing the voice-over said, "...Leaf captain Doug Gilmour thinks it'll be a long, tough series." A close-up facial shot of a musing Dave Andreychuk was then flashed on the screen with Gilmour's name beneath it. Unreal.

Tonight, we all gathered at *Gameskeepers* Sports Bar in the north end of Chicago to watch the Stanley Cup playoff openers on giant-screen TVs. We downed chicken wings and nachos as Washington beat Pittsburgh and Quebec came back from a 4-1 deficit to edge the Rangers 5-4 in the final minute of regulation time. Harry Neale couldn't help but comment on our pricey hotel.

"That's alright, I'll be walking out of there with soap, towels, sheets, robes... you name it," he cracked.

SUNDAY, MAY 7th
Chicago

There isn't much left of old Chicago Stadium anymore.

The Maple Leaf bus drove past it on its way into the United Center for the morning skate. All that remains standing is the eastern tier of the arena — about one-quarter of the original structure. It looks like someone took a giant cleaver and chopped away all but the area between the east goalline and blueline. That red and yellow stairwell that led fans to the upper northeast corner of the Stadium is miraculously still intact, as it was on our last trip here in mid-April.

The Maple Leafs-Blackhawks series is pretty much a rumour here in Chicago, as the sports denizens are all tantalized by the Bulls-Orlando Eastern Conference NBA series, which begins today in Florida. The radio talk-shows are entirely monopolized by basketball chatter and the hosts make no effort at all to change the subject. The newspapers are just as biased. A one-story preview of the hockey series appears on Page 22 of today's Chicago *Sun-Times* sports pullout section. The first ten pages are devoted to the Bulls, followed by reports from yesterday's Kentucky Derby; the baseball recaps, and college football news.

Sun-Times hockey writer Brian Hanley believes the Blackhawks will win the series, though he provides much evidence to the contrary:

> *Potvin has struggled this year and Doug Gilmour even more so. Still, Leafs have had Hawks' number almost every season. Hawks are 11-19-1 vs. Toronto in post-season meetings dating to 1931. BRIAN HANLEY'S PICK: Blackhawks in six.*

Our hotel is in the theatre district of the Chicago Loop, about a 20-minute walk south on Michigan Ave. from the so-called "Magnificent Mile". The Leafs are up there in their normal haunt, The Drake Hotel. It's a much more lively and happening area, and I'm going to try and move closer to that part of downtown after the weekend.

After arriving at the United Center and having dinner in the media lounge, I ventured outside and bought a copy of The *Blue Line*. I can't help but crack up when I read some of the material in that off-the-wall publication. In tonight's issue, there's a full-page photo of Chicago's owner Bill Wirtz and general manager Bob Pulford being accosted by some factitious space creature under a headline WIRTZ, PULFORD SEEK PLAYOFF ADVICE FROM INTELLIGENT LIFE FORM. Part of the accompanying story reads:

> *Bill Wirtz denied ever meeting the Alien, insisting the Hawks were never seriously looking to sign an extraterrestrial to beef up the team's flagging powerplay. Said Wirtz: "The last thing we need is another overpaid foreigner who won't take the body."*

The publication's unequivocal disdain for Wirtz is apparent on the cover. There's a cartoon of the Blackhawk owner sitting across the desk from a silly looking doctor. He's pulling bank notes out of his wallet and saying, "Doctor, it hurts when I go like this."

Blue Line has the following assessment of the Maple Leafs heading into the series against Chicago:

> *It is in the playoffs when Wendel Clark will be most sorely missed by the Leafs. Clark was traded in the off-season for*

Mats Sundin. Sundin can and probably will score a goal a game, but he still won't have the impact Clark had on these games. Clark was mean, and always made big, disruptive hits. When he was on the ice, everyone kept one eye on the puck and one eye on him.

Toronto's defence is also a question mark. The Leafs shut out the Hawks 1-0 three times in last year's first round. Their defence, however, is nowhere near as formidable this season. Their goals-against average rose from 2.85 to 2.98. Sylvain Lefebvre and Bob Rouse stifled the Hawks in last season's first round, but neither is a Leaf today.

Felix Potvin has looked ordinary this season. He is not the same goaltender he was when he stoned the Hawks in the first round last season. Pretty much unflappable in his first two seasons in the NHL, Potvin has for the first time in his career started letting in bad goals.

My prediction on this series is recorded thusly in my notebook: "I choose Chicago in 6... May 7, 1995 - 6:32 p.m. CST."

Incredibly, the Maple Leafs had one of their easiest games of the entire season during tonight's playoff opener at the United Center. A 5-3 victory was very flattering to the Blackhawks, who received brutal goaltending from Ed Belfour and fell to pieces in the third period. The Leafs have now earned five out of six points in their last three games here in Chicago and have gotten off to a roaring start in this series.

There were several turning points in tonight's game. The first one occurred at 8:52 of the second period and was a phenomenal screw-up by referee Paul Devorski. Leafs were leading 1-0 on Mats Sundin's goal when Devorski called a delayed penalty against Chicago. Randy Wood took off down the left-wing boards and fired a slapshot at Belfour. The puck squirted past the goalie and into the crease behind him. Attempting to knock it away with his stick, Belfour instead poked it into the net and the Leafs seemingly had a 2-0 lead. As Harvey Whittenburg announced the goal to the United Center audience, a conversation ensued over near the timekeeper's bench and Devorski suddenly waved it off.

Somehow, the referee figured Belfour had smothered Wood's shot and had blown his whistle to stop play before the goalie turned and knocked it into his net. Devorski was in the Leaf zone when Wood sped away with the puck, and was forced to slow down when Garth Butcher and Joe Murphy began fencing.

He had barely gotten to center-ice when the puck entered the net, and his angle was such that Wood screened his view of Belfour. Still, it was a dreadful mistake at a critical juncture of the game.

Over in the supervisor's booth, NHL director of officiating Bryan Lewis had a technically correct, yet lame explanation. "Devorski phoned up here for some help and I told him it was his call," Lewis said. "He then confirmed he had blown his whistle before the puck entered the net and he disallowed the goal." Asked why the scoring play was announced over the P.A. system, Lewis replied, "I don't know the answer to that." As per usual, Lewis would not confess that Devorski had made a mistake, though he did admit he'd be "pissed off" if it happened a second time.

Down on the ice, the Leafs put up only a mild argument, realizing they could do nothing about Devorski's ruling. "You can't choke back a quick whistle," said captain Doug Gilmour after the game.

It hasn't taken a lot to dislodge the Maple Leafs from a gameplan this season, and all of us were expecting some kind of emotional cave-in after the bad break. Lo and behold, the Buds started running around in their own end and Chicago — rejuvenated by the quick whistle — got excited for the first time. Patrick Poulin and Tony Amonte scored goals in a 1:28 span and the Leafs were suddenly behind by one.

The game's primary turning point occurred in the final minute of the period, and was very much courtesy of Belfour. Paul DiPietro, who will never be confused for Mats Sundin, carried the puck around in back of the Chicago net and stuffed it in on his forehand with 33.7 seconds remaining. Sundin's opening goal had also been on a wrap-around at the other end, and the Chicago fans booed Belfour rather heartily.

"Paul's goal was the most important moment of the game for us, no question," Pat Burns said afterwards.

During the second intermission, Leaf assistant coach Rick Wamsley angrily confronted Lewis about the disallowed goal in the press area and created a bit of a scene. But Lewis held his composure and calmly explained the ruling once again. "That's brutal, Bryan," Wamsley barked as he walked away shaking his head.

After witnessing the exchange, I walked over to a draped-off area at the opposite end of the press box which is set aside for members of the Chicago Blackhawk alumni. A big, husky man who seemed to be in his 60s was chatting with an usher at the entrance to the room. He stood with sort of a hunched back, as if suffering from an arthritic ailment. His face was vaguely familiar, but I couldn't quite make the connection until the usher said, "Nice seeing you, Moose." Then I realized who it was: Elmer Vasko — the large, stocky defenceman who wore No. 4 for the Blackhawks when I was a kid. "Moose" played on Chicago's 1961 Stanley Cup team and was an original member of the Minnesota North Stars after the 1967 expansion. In fact, that's how I remember Vasko — wearing the green and white of Minnesota on those CBS Sunday afternoon telecasts in the late-60s. He always reminded me, facially, of actor George Kennedy.

I introduced myself, and we chatted idly for a few moments. When he shuffled away in apparent discomfort, I asked the usher if Vasko was ill, and found out he does indeed suffer from arthritis. Still, he's an avid supporter of the Blackhawks, and it was nice re-visiting a face I hadn't seen since my youth.

Another former 'Hawk whose face was more familiar sat at a table in the Alumni room. Reggie Fleming played on the '61 Stanley Cup team and was among the most willing scrappers in the NHL of that era. When he stood up to get a drink tonight, however, he looked like a gigantic egg. Now almost 60, Ol' Reg ain't missing any meals. He must weigh a good 300 pounds.

Having gained a surge of momentum with DiPetro's late wrap-around, the Maple Leafs came out strongly and completely owned the third period of tonight's game. Mike Gartner put the Leafs in front to stay when he banged in Dave Andreychuk's feed at the lip of the goalcrease just 1:25 into the period. Toronto played strong defensive hockey and nursed its one-goal lead past the 10-minute mark. Then the Leafs received a break from Devorski every bit as large as the misfortune of Wood's disallowed goal in the first period. And it put the game away.

Murray Craven of the Blackhawks carried the puck into the Maple Leaf zone and circled rather carelessly near the blueline. Mats Sundin poked it away into the neutral zone and began racing after it. Behind the play, Craven — trying to catch Sundin — was blatantly hooked to the ice by Todd Gill, and the big Swede swept in on a clear breakaway. He deked to his forehand and easily beat Belfour to give Toronto a 4-2 lead, as Craven threw a mild tantrum out near center ice.

"Devorski owed us one and I guess he missed Todd's hook," Burns noted afterwards. "Paul's like that."

Before the Blackhawks could recover, Andreychuk beat Belfour to a loose puck and scored to make it 5-2. With great effort, Andreychuk sprawled flat on his belly and poked it past the Chicago netminder, who had come out to meet him. The goals were scored 14 seconds apart and the United Center emptied in a rush.

Hawks' coach Darryl Sutter replaced Belfour with Jeff Hackett at that point, but it was way too late. Hackett's first shot was an easy glove save off Bill Berg, and those remaining in the audience let loose with a good old Bronx cheer. Jeff Shantz scored a meaningless goal for the Blackhawks and the Maple Leafs skated off with a 5-3 victory.

Today was the 50th anniversary of the end of World War II — when the Germans unconditionally surrendered to the Allies in Europe — and *Sun* hockey writer Lance Hornby used the analogy in his game story:

> *It was V-E Day for the Maple Leafs: a victory over Eddie The Eagle.*

Indeed, the Maple Leafs had exposed the Blackhawks' achilles heal. Ed Belfour has generally not been a clutch playoff performer; in fact, he's choked in the majority of his post-season appearances, and tonight can be included among them. However, Chris Chelios didn't quite see it that way and he came to the defence of his goaltender.

"He shouldn't take the blame, because it's our fault," Chelios said. "We could have been down by three or four goals after the first period. `Eagle' made some big saves to keep us in it. It was a total team loss and Eddie is not included in that."

Chelios then went on to verbally berate everyone else in the 'Hawk dressing room. "We fell apart," he groused. "Call it pressure. Panic. I don't know what to call it. We choked. Everyone played terrible, like a bunch of rookies, including myself."

Meanwhile, the Maple Leafs were celebrating a lop-sided victory in the opener, and praising Mats Sundin for showing the way offensively.

"After what he's been through before, I think it was important for Mats to have a big game like this," said Burns in reference to Sundin's struggle in the playoffs with Quebec two years ago. "He's never gotten by the first round in his career. He's never realized what it takes to succeed in the playoffs, but he saw it tonight, watching Dougie, Felix and Andreychuk take their games up a notch.

"And he took his game up, too. If we get nights like this from him, whew, it'll be great. But, he's still learning."

Burns re-united Gilmour and Andreychuk for the first time since early in the season and placed them on a line with Mike Gartner. They looked very comfortable and the Leafs generated an unusual amount of offence. "We just wanted to throw a little kink at them," explained the Leaf coach. "We weren't exactly burning up the league with our attack, so I wasn't scared to make a few changes."

There were several-thousand empty seats for the first-ever playoff game in the United Center. The announced attendance of 19,042 had to be deceiving as the vast majority of seats at both ends of the arena were not occupied; no more than 17,000 fans were actually in the building. The hockey game partially overlapped with the Bulls at Orlando opener. In fact, transistor radios and even a few miniature TVs were evident in the press box so the hockey reporters could keep their ears and eyes on the basketball proceedings.

In the end, it was a fairly rotten day to be a Chicago sports fan. The Blackhawks, Bulls, White Sox and Cubs all went down to defeat.

The Maple Leaf team bus was quite raucous after the game. It was also filled to capacity with members of the travelling road show. Each year in the playoffs, the club brings along its entire front office and medical staff. With us for the first time this season were team doctors Leith Douglas, Michael Clarfield, Darryl Ogilvie-Harris, and long-time club dentist Ernie Lewis. Darryl Sittler was also on the bus along with former Leaf players and scouts George Armstrong and Dick Duff (Army is still with the team). As well, the entire media relations staff of Bob Stellick, Pat Park and Casey VandenHeuvel was on board.

The bus was parked inside the United Center, at the bottom of the loading ramp. At one point, loud rumbling noises could be heard at the back, followed by an outbreak of sickly groans.

"Driver, please, we need some air... they're farting up the whole bus," Burns appealed from his front-row seat.

"Someone's passing away," added Bill Watters.

The players blamed third-string goalie Pat Jablonski.

Our compassionate driver pulled the vehicle outside, enabling him to leave the engine and air conditioning system on.

I sat next to Darryl Sittler on the way back to the hotel and was reminded of a repugnant, yet hilarious tale from his rookie season with the Maple Leafs. Back in the early-70s, the Leafs had a wet sauna next to their dressing room at the Gardens. The players would pile in there to unwind after practice and occasionally, the sauna would be filled to capacity. Such was the case one afternoon when George Armstrong, in his final professional season, tried to join his teammates. He stood with the sauna door open and looked around for a place to sit, which brought a deluge of gripes from the relaxed players, who angrily informed him there was simply no room for anyone else.

Armstrong responded by urinating on the coals, and slamming the door shut. A cascading mist of body fluids filled the sauna, and almost asphyxiated the players, sending them in a mad dash for fresh air.

"There was plenty of fucking room in the sauna after that," Armstrong laughed, remembering the incident.

"It stunk like hell," recalled Sittler, who was among the victims. "Our eyes were burning out."

The former captains looked at each other and shook their heads.

MONDAY, MAY 8th
Chicago

It was dark and gloomy outside this morning, as a steady rain pelted Chicago. My conscience arose, and I made a number of phonecalls, trying to find some cheaper accommodations. The old Seneca Hotel up on East Chestnut Street had a room tonight for $125, and the Westin Hotel was available for $105 tomorrow. Both are located in the "Magnificent Mile" area and are much closer to where the Maple Leafs are staying, so I packed up and moved — saving the radio station a combined $180 U.S.

The Seneca is a residence-hotel, and the rooms look very much like those which Norman Bates rented in the movie *Psycho*. I was half scared to death when I showered this morning before leaving for practice.

The Leafs skated at the United Center for about an hour today. Pat Burns spent part of the practice inspecting the metal glass supports in the end zone to the left of the team benches. They protrude an inch or so and are a threat to cause an untrue bounce when the puck is shot in. Midway through the workout, Mike Ridley lost his balance on a line rush and slammed back-first into the corner boards — sending an eerie echo through the empty arena. Athletic therapist Chris Broadhurst scampered onto the ice and Leaf doctors Douglas and Clarfield rushed down to the bench area. Ridley got up, caught his breath, and was slowly assisted towards the medical staff. Everyone breathed a sigh of relief when he was able to shake off the heavy spill and continue practising.

The ever-frolicking Tie Domi engaged in a couple of mock tussles with teammate Todd Gill during the session this morning. Afterwards, in the dressing room, Domi pulled me aside. "Go over to Giller, shove the microphone in his face, and ask him what it's like to get the shit beat out of him by me," Domi requested. I did so, hesitantly, and Gill just smiled and shook his head. "It never happened, and will never happen," he insisted, as Domi cackled away in delight.

About 30 minutes later, as the bus turned right out of the United Center, we could see the wrecking ball hammering away at what's left of Chicago Stadium. "Ooooh, I've got to get some of that dust for my den," chided Warren Rychel, seated near the back. Just about everything that is retrievable from within the

Stadium demolition site is being either sold or kept as a souvenir. Rychel, of course, is a comedian.

The Maple Leafs' regular driver here in Chicago is Eric Hickman, who works for *Keeshin* Bus Lines. Young and personable, Hickman is well-liked by the players and coaching staff. Yesterday, however, the Leafs were chauffeured by Eric's older and crustier colleague, Harold Rucker, who apparently went from the hotel to the United Center by way of Kansas City. When Pat Burns politely inquired as to what part of the country the Leafs were in, Rucker snapped at him.

"Oh, that's just Harold," Hickman laughed today. "He was driving the New York Knicks to Chicago Stadium a few years ago and the players were being obnoxious. All of a sudden, he pulled the bus over to the side of the road, got out, and said he wouldn't continue on until they calmed down. He doesn't roll with the punches very well and the Knicks won't have him as their driver anymore."

The Maple Leaf publicity department took the Toronto media out for dinner tonight to a popular Italian restaurant called *Bice* (pronounced Bee-chee). Thankfully for the other patrons, we were segregated in a private room upstairs, as a dozen or so bottles of wine created quite a din. It was Jim Proudfoot's 62nd birthday today, but the Toronto *Star* columnist had a rough time at dinner. All three of his courses arrived late for some reason.

He ordered a delicious-looking tuna appetizer, as did somebody at the table behind us. The waiter placed the dish in front of Proudfoot, but then suddenly removed it. "I was just about to stab it with my fork when it disappeared," lamented the veteran sportswriter. A few minutes later, poor Jim leaned on his elbow, shaking his head as the rest of us devoured our main courses. The waiter kept coming by and apologizing — promising to "rush" his veal dish. Some birthday.

TUESDAY, MAY 9th
Chicago

As the Maple Leaf bus approached the United Center along Madison Ave. this morning, a young black man waved a couple of Chicago Stadium bricks in the air the way a scalper waves tickets. People have taken to sneaking into the Stadium construction site and lifting pieces of the old building. Their freelance operation works in direct contrast to the in-house enterprise across the road, where Bill Wirtz is hawking mounted and labelled Stadium bricks for $25 at souvenir kiosks.

I decided to skip the formal stuff and do business the underground way. During the Maple Leaf skate, I ventured outside and approached the brick scalper. It was a glorious sunny day, and he seemed happy to have a customer. I offered $4 for the two chunks of concrete in his hand but he wanted $10. We held intense negotiations for about 15 seconds and he wound up accepting $5. "Enjoy your piece of the Stadium," the man said.

After the morning workout, the Leaf players mingled in the loading area outside the team bus. "Playoff weather, huh?" mused Dave Ellett in the 75-degree sunshine. Doug Gilmour sat in the driver's seat, playing with the bus radio. "Hey, Howie, what if I drove away with this thing?" he asked. "Think I'd be thrown in jail?"

I just rolled my eyes and sat down.

The temperature cooled late in the afternoon and a monstrous fog rolled in off Lake Michigan, blanketing the downtown area. I was on the 21st floor of the Westin Hotel and couldn't even see across the street. If you're a fan of the NFL, you might recall a comparable circumstance during a Bears-Philadelphia playoff game in December, 1988. A dense fog descended on Soldier Field at halftime and the balance of the game was imperceptible on TV. How the players were able to see the football that day was beyond comprehension.

The Maple Leaf bus departed the Drake Hotel for the United Center at 5:15 this afternoon and gradually drove into sunshine as it motored away from the lake. The scene from the west end of the city was eerie. A thick, white cloud — about two miles long — formed a giant blanket over the downtown core, obstructing Chicago's huge office towers. Even the 96-story Hancock Building at the north end of Michigan Ave. was invisible. There was blue sky above the cloud, and on either side of the downtown strip. It was an extraordinary sight.

During the 20-minute ride, I sat next to the sauna-destroyer. I've come to realize over the years that George Armstrong is one of hockey's all-time great practical jokers. It's funny, but as a youngster growing up in the '60s, I had this squeaky clean image of my Maple Leaf heroes. Of course, media was altogether different in those days. There were no scandal newspapers and tabloid TV shows, and it seemed like a universal degree of respect prevailed; more-so than today. If someone had told me 20 years ago that the captain of the Maple Leafs had pissed in a sauna, I wouldn't have believed it. But, the players of that 1960s Stanley Cup dynasty played hard and lived even harder.

Johnny Bower — whom I spoke to recently — was among the few conservative members of that group, and the great former goalie was often the victim of Armstrong's pranks. The two players were inseparable friends, and remain so today. "Oh, the Chief was always doing something to get a laugh at my expense," Bower remembered. "I guess I was a willing target."

301

The Maple Leafs of that era still fall over laughing when reminded of the day Armstrong switched Bower's false teeth in the dressing room. "Boy, I'll never forget that one," Bower said. "Like always, I put my teeth in a little cup above my locker and went out for practice. We had lost the night before and I was hoping the players would stay out a bit longer and take shots. But as soon as (Punch) Imlach ended the workout, everyone except (Larry) Hillman bolted off the ice, which I found to be quite strange. Larry took a few shots, then we both went to the room.

"When I got to my locker, I instinctively reached for my teeth and put them into my mouth. But the upper ones suddenly felt too tight, and the lower ones were way too loose — they were floating around in there like water. I couldn't figure it out until I looked up and saw that all the guys had their faces buried in towels. That's when I knew someone had pulled a joke on me and I immediately blamed (Eddie) Shack. He was always pulling stunts and I said to him, 'Shackie, I'll get even with you, so help me God, if it takes the rest of my life.' He looked up and said, 'Nine times out of ten, it *would* be me, but not this time, John.'

"Then I looked over at the Chief and even *he* had his head down. That was the tip-off for me. George could always look you right in the eye and keep a straight face when he was pulling a practical joke. But this time, he was all red from laughing. He shook one of his gloves and out fell my teeth. The rest of the guys completely lost it and were all rolling on the floor in hysterics. I spit out the teeth that were in my mouth and said, 'Where the hell did you get *these*?'

"Army told me he had a friend who owned a funeral parlour. I said, 'Jesus Christ, you got them from a corpse?' I thought the other guys would need oxygen, they were laughing so hard. It was just the type of thing we needed after losing the night before and even Punch broke into a grin when we told him what the Chief had done."

The most infamous of all Maple Leaf stories from that era involves the late Tim Horton. The club was in Quebec City for an exhibition game and a number of the players went to a bar afterwards. Horton was known to have the odd nip and was feeling no pain when he left the place with Bower, Armstrong and defence partner Allan Stanley.

"We had a curfew, and me and Chief were making sure that Tim got back to the hotel okay," Bower recalls. "We walked past a construction site that was cordoned off by cement drums. Well, Tim went over and started moving them out of the way. He just picked up two or three of them and carried 'em off to one side. We tried telling him to put them back, because if somebody drove through the passage Tim had created, they'd fall right over a cliff. But, he wasn't listening to us and when we heard a police car coming, me and Chief ran like hell.

"Someone had apparently called the cops to report that a group of hockey players were making noise and the police hauled Tim off to jail. They called Punch at about 3 a.m. and said they had one of his players. When he asked, 'Which one?', they told him it was Timmy and Punch said, 'Leave him there till morning.' We bailed him out around 8 o'clock and, boy, was Imlach angry. He fined Tim $25 and we had a double-practice when we got back to Toronto later that day."

Armstrong laughed when we talked about that story on the bus ride tonight. "We used to do some crazy things but, in those days, you could get away with it," he explained. "There were a couple of sportswriters on every road trip and they'd usually come to a bar or restaurant *with* us. We knew that if something happened, they would never write it. But today, you've got newspaper columnists, and TV and radio people looking for stories all the time. The players have to be much more careful."

We passed by the ruins of Chicago Stadium a few minutes later and Armstrong peered wistfully out the window.

"Boy, there's sure some great memories," he mused. "I must have played over 200 games in that building."

"We won our first Stanley Cup there (in 1962)," added Dick Duff, sitting across the aisle. "I think the fans were ready to tear it down when I scored the winning goal that night."

"Yeah, you almost gave it away, too," chided Armstrong.

The Maple Leafs had a 3-2 series lead over the Blackhawks and Game 6 of that final was scoreless heading into the third period. In a most uncharacteristic move, Duff coughed up the puck behind his own net to Bobby Hull, who beat Don Simmons to give Chicago a 1-0 advantage at the 8:58 mark. However, Bob Nevin tied it up for Toronto moments later, and Duff scored the winner with 5:46 remaining on a nifty pass from Horton.

"Actually, I never bring up that giveaway," Armstrong whispered to me, a bit embarrassed that he'd done so seconds earlier. "Duffy still gets mad when he thinks about it, even though we ended up winning the Stanley Cup on *his* goal. He was a tough S.O.B. and was one of the best playoff performers I ever saw. He could really turn it up a notch."

The *Blue Line* was at it again tonight, venting its humorous spleen on 'Hawk G.M. Bob Pulford, who was also a member of the Toronto Stanley Cup dynasty in the '60s. On the cover — under a headline THE BEST MOVE BOB PUL-

FORD COULD MAKE — is a cartoon of the G.M. reading through an assortment of pamphlets from places like the "Happy Acres Retirement Village" and "End 'O The Line Home For The Aged". Real nice.

On the inside, is a list of BOB PULFORD'S TOP 10 MOVES. Among them are:

*   Turning the pillow over to the cool side.
*   Hitting the snooze button.
*   Stealing the covers from his wife.
*   Ignoring the waiver wire.

On another page, is a feature called TIM WEIGEL'S PROBING WEINER. It has a photograph of a smiling, gap-toothed Weigel saying, "My four previous wives want to know why I never gave *them* the probing weiner." It then says:

> *Tim asked members of the Toronto Maple Leafs this probing question: "What do you think about the Illinois House voting to lower the blood-alcohol level for drunk driving to .08 from .1?"*

The mock article "quotes" Doug Gilmour, Pat Burns, Tie Domi and Dave Andreychuk talking about the issue.

Burns says: "In order to absorb the excess alcohol in my system, I'll just need to consume larger quantities of tacos, donuts, twinkees, hohos, steaks, fries, butter, bacon, eggrolls and, of course, that delicious Connie's Pizza."

Andreychuk says: "As a Canadian citizen, I am exempt from all such laws. In fact, back in Ontario, you're *required* to have at least .05 in your system at all times. Besides, how will Bill Wirtz get to work each day if they approve this?"

The Maple Leafs were the ones in good humour again tonight, but they'd have been awfully grumpy if not for Felix Potvin. Hockey writer David Shoalts of the *Globe & Mail* summed up the evening in his story:

> *CHICAGO - There was a heist here last night.*
> *That wasn't surprising, given this city's history of gangsters, but this job was pulled off in front of 19,017 witnesses, and there was a clean getaway.*
> *The perp was one Felix Potvin, a shifty goaltender, and the rest of his Toronto Maple Leaf teammates. The victims: the*

Chicago Blackhawks, 3-0 losers here, and now facing a short road to elimination from the Stanley Cup playoffs.

They say all good teams have goalies who steal a game now and then, and Potvin did just that for the Leafs. Chicago ran up a lop-sided 42-17 edge in shots, but wound up on the losing end. Somehow, after such a mediocre regular season, the Maple Leafs have come to the United Center and captured the first two games of this series.

"We're just going to take this win and run out of town," said Dave Andreychuk. "We stole it."

Potvin was obviously marvellous in recording his fourth playoff white-washing of the Blackhawks the past two years, but there was some deception in the final statistics. The Maple Leaf defence did a superb job of keeping the Chicago skaters clear of the slot area, and many of the shots were from the perimeter. It was more a case of quantity than quality for the Blackhawks and rebounds were also at a premium. Potvin was sharp, indeed, but he didn't have to stand on his head. He was far more spectacular, for example, in the 2-1 win he stole at Dallas early in the season. That night, he was defenceless; tonight, he was not.

Still, the accolades poured out of the Leaf dressing room. "They were better than us tonight, we have to accept that," said Pat Burns. "We just had one guy who was better than both teams on the ice and he wore No. 29 with the big mask. That was one of the best games Felix has played for me since we've been together in Toronto."

Chicago came out flying and swarmed the Leafs in the first period, building a 12-5 advantage in shots. Potvin made great saves on Bernie Nicholls and Jeff Shantz but, typical of this game, Toronto actually had the best scoring opportunity, as Randy Wood was thwarted by Belfour on a shorthanded breakaway at the 11-minute mark. Chicago's shot lead went to 20-5, and the Leafs did not record a second-period shot until there was 6:17 left on the clock. But they wound up scoring the first goal of the game, and their timing couldn't have been better.

Mike Ridley broke his stick and skated towards the bench to grab a replacement. His abrupt reappearance in the Chicago zone caught Jeff Shantz by surprise and Ridley stole the puck from the 'Hawk forward. He then sent a rising slapshot past an equally astonished Belfour with 6.8 seconds left on the clock.

"I don't remember too much about the play because it happened so fast," said Ridley. "I just skated back into the Chicago zone and swept the puck away from one of their players. I knew there wasn't much time left and I had to get a shot away quickly. Thankfully, it went in, and really gave us a big lift coming into the dressing room."

Said Shantz: "I never really saw Ridley. He came out of nowhere and surprised me. I was just trying to get the puck out of our zone."

In the third period, referee Paul Stewart provided the Blackhawks with every conceivable opportunity to stay in the game. Andreychuk went off with a double-minor for high-sticking at the five-minute mark, but Potvin kept Chicago at bay. The Leafs scored to make it 2-0 just before the midway point when Mats Sundin — cruising in the slot — converted Andreychuk's pass from behind the net.

Doug Gilmour received an assist for his 65th career playoff point as a Maple Leaf: tying him with Dave Keon for second place on the all-time club list, two points in back of Darryl Sittler.

Stewart then assessed the Leafs a couple of marginal penalties you rarely see in a playoff game. He sent Ridley off for holding, and Randy Wood for tripping, but the 'Hawks failed to do any business with their feeble powerplay. Patrick Poulin of Chicago was awarded a penalty shot by Stewart with 1:49 left on the clock, after Bill Berg was deemed to have intentionally dislodged the Maple Leaf net from its supports. But Potvin coolly blocked the attempt with his pads, showing the confidence of a seasoned playoff warrior.

Chicago coach Darryl Sutter pulled Belfour with 1:30 remaining but Mike Gartner slid a shot into the vacated Blackhawk goal in the dying seconds, and the Maple Leafs were sittin' pretty.

"Stewie gave them every chance to get back into the game," Burns sighed afterwards. "But our penalty killing was pretty good tonight. It will have to be good during this series if we're to beat Chicago."

The media tried to get Potvin to compare tonight's performance with the generally average regular season he had, but the Leaf goalie wouldn't bite. "I played some good games and some bad games this year," he said. "I really don't want to talk about it."

Meanwhile, in the Chicago dressing room, the players were making all the standard comments of a team in their position. "Toronto hasn't won this series yet," noted Chris Chelios. "We've had our ups and downs this season, so we should realize as much as anyone that the ball can get rolling just as easily the other way."

Added Murray Craven: "We're not devastated by any stretch of the imagination. Game 1 was much more frustrating for us. We played a lot harder tonight and perhaps got shortchanged when we didn't get the win. We had every kind of shot, and Potvin stopped them all. Now, it's time to forget this and start preparing for Game 3."

Once again, the United Center attendance figure was deceiving. The same number of empty seats was evident as in Game 1, and the Bulls were not playing Orlando tonight. The end zone seats — miles away from the action — are probably a little too pricey for the playoffs.

*   *   *   *   *   *

The Blackhawk players weren't barking up a tree when they claimed not to be out of the series after Game 2. Indeed, they went to Toronto and pulled the exact same trick on the moribund Maple Leafs — winning Games 3 and 4 at the Gardens.

The Leafs couldn't contain Chicago's two wheelhorse defencemen during the 3-2 loss in Game 3. Gary Suter blew a pair of slapshots past Felix Potvin and Chris Chelios scored a shorthanded goal on a solo rush. Ed Belfour was the star of Game 4, as he made 30 saves in a 3-1 Chicago victory that tied the series. He was particularly impressive in the first ten minutes, when the Maple Leafs came out full of energy and had a half-dozen excellent scoring chances. The Blackhawks led 2-0 when Jamie Macoun's long screen shot eluded Belfour at 1:57 of the third period. But Belfour was solid the rest of the way and Jeff Shantz clinched the victory with an empty net goal.

It's conceivable now that the Maple Leafs will blow a third consecutive playoff series in which they've won the first two games on the road. It happened in 1977 against Philadelphia and 1987 against Detroit. They'll have to win at least one more game at the United Center to avoid it happening again.

Apparently, several Leafs had near-death experiences on the flight home from Chicago after Game 2. "You think that flight to Dallas last month was bad?" Mats Sundin said to me the other day. "That was nothing compared to this. I've never seen the guys so scared." Once again, the Leaf plane took off into storm clouds... it appears to be a recurring theme of this entire season.

A minor controversy ensued after Chicago G.M. Bob Pulford was caught smoking in the Gardens' press box during Game 3 by Hockey Night In Canada cameras. Lighting up in a public venue is a violation of the City of Toronto by-laws and the City's Environmental Health Services department told Pulford — through the Maple Leafs — to butt out. He obliged and began chewing on copious amounts of gum.

When Pulford arrived at his press box location for the start of Game 4, two cigarettes and a book of matches were laid out in front of him — courtesy of St. Louis Blues' pro scout and prankster Bob Plager.

SUNDAY, MAY 14th
Chicago

After the experience of flying through a thunderstorm in St. Louis last month, I couldn't help but keep an eye on the skies above Toronto this afternoon. Susan and I hosted a Mother's Day brunch at our home in Thornhill, Ont. and the humidity produced ominous-looking clouds. There was a heavy thunderstorm watch in the Toronto area, and I figured to be in for some more hair-raising moments aboard an aircraft.

Like a blessing, however, the overcast parted on my way to Pearson Airport late in the day, and by the time I boarded the Air Canada DC-9, the skies were clear and the sun was shining. Thank goodness for little miracles. The flight departed uneventfully around 5:30 p.m., and I used an upgrade coupon. The 90-minute trip was nice and smooth, and the only downside was an annoying fly that refused to leave my area of the plane and bother someone else; the damned thing stayed in *Executive Class* for the entire flight. I guess it wanted a meal as well.

I couldn't help but chuckle when our captain came over the speaker and introduced himself. His name was George Herman, and I wondered if his wife's name was Ruth. Baseball fans know what I'm talking about.

There was a spectacular view of Chicago as we descended off Lake Michigan at the supper-hour. All of the giant skyscrapers that had been shrouded by that massive fog last week were glistening in the late-afternoon sun. Wrigley Field sat empty in the north end below us, and the unmistakable white exterior of the enormous United Center could be seen in the distance. We touched down at O'Hare around 6:05 p.m.

Toronto *Sun* photographers Michael Peeke and Greg Reekie were also on the flight and were renting a car here in Chicago. They offered me a ride downtown and while they arranged for the car, a lady standing in line asked me if I worked for The *Fan-590* (I was wearing a jersey with the call-letters). I answered affirmatively and she introduced herself. It was Dawn Coe-Jones — Canada's top female golfer — who was on her way to Dayton, Ohio for a speaking engagement. Stating correctly that she's been a guest on our radio station several times, we chatted idly for a few moments and when I left with the *Sun* guys, Reekie wondered if I'd asked her about the "Ben Wright thing" — referring to the CBS golf analyst's alleged claim a few days ago that, "Women don't play as well as men because their boobs hamper their backswing."

Having just met Coe-Jones for the first time, I informed Reekie that the subject of her boobs had not arisen during our brief chat.

Leaving the airport, the subject of airline security came to mind. An over-pass of the Kennedy Expressway just outside the O'Hare terminal is actually a taxi-way for planes. As we were heading towards downtown, a giant British Airways *Boeing*-747 inched along the over-pass in full view and range of auto-mobiles driving in either direction. Doesn't seem like the safest place in the world for a jetliner full of people.

The Toronto media contingent here in Chicago gathered for dinner tonight at *Gibson's* Steakhouse on Rush St. About ten of us descended on the place and we sat a few tables away from a group of Oakland baseball players, including Mark McGwire and Terry Steinbach. The A's flew here today from Minneapolis to begin a series with the White Sox tomorrow.

The denizens of Rush St. were in a euphoric mood afterwards, as their beloved Chicago Bulls had defeated Orlando this afternoon at the United Center to square that NBA series at two games apiece. It will be interesting to see which of Chicago's two playoff competitors lasts the longest. At the moment, it seems like the Bulls are in tougher.

MONDAY, MAY 15th
Chicago

After playing so well in the first two games of this series, Leaf captain Doug Gilmour was less conspicuous in the pair of weekend losses and was the subject of media attention today.

A headline in large block letters on the front of the Toronto *Sun* said: WILL THE REAL DOUG GILMOUR PLEASE STAND UP? There was a photo of Gilmour and a quote from Leaf president Cliff Fletcher saying, "I can't recall any player carrying a team on his back the way Doug has for the past two seasons. We knew it couldn't go on forever."

An eloquent column by Steve Simmons explored the issue in depth. This is part of what he wrote:

> *It is difficult to think about Doug Gilmour today and not remember all the yesterdays. It is difficult to comprehend his internal pain and not consider the gifts he has relayed along the way.*
>
> *No one has to tell Doug Gilmour anything right now. He knows it better than anyone, what's happening, and worse,*

what isn't. You can see it in his play and in his eyes: no one completely understands his demise, least of all him. This is supposed to be his time of year, the time that made him a legend, and it isn't happening.

(Now), the opinion is, something is wrong. Gilmour looks injured. It might be the feet. It might be the back. It might be both. And worse, it might be neither.

That is the greatest of the Maple Leafs' fears. What if this isn't a blip? What if all that ice time and all that production cannot be found again? Joe Frazier was never effective after his three classic fights with Muhammad Ali.

Is there still a championship fight left in Doug Gilmour?

A slightly different perspective of the Gilmour quandary appeared in Garth Woolsey's Toronto *Star* sports column today:

No doubt, (Gilmour) has yet to rise above the crowd in this playoff series against Chicago. That's hard to do, some would say, when you're being clutched and grabbed, and you're carrying a 6-foot-5 monkey named Steve Smith on your back.

But, Gilmour inherited the leader's cape when (Wendel) Clark was traded to Quebec and with it, the expectations. Although he was not the one responsible for turning over one-third of the roster, the Leafs are supposed to be Gilmour's team and, as such, he's supposed to overcome such merely human obstacles.

It might well be that the Leafs will go as far as conductor Doug, captain Gilmour takes them; could be a short trip, or long. One way hero, the other bum.

But a leader can't make the journey alone.

During the Maple Leafs' skate this morning at the United Center, Pat Burns had a long one-on-one session with Gilmour in the center-ice area. He also took Randy Wood and Paul DiPietro aside. There seemed to be an air of tension on the ice, but the dressing room afterwards was quite relaxed. The players felt comfortable to be back on the road — in the brand new arena where they have fared so nicely.

On the bus ride back to the hotel, there was a large plastic bag of chocolate chunks that a local store had brought to the Maple Leafs. It was open in the seat next to Darryl Sittler, who invited everyone to help themselves. After consuming handfulls of the delectable treats, a dreadful thought came upon Leith Douglas, the team doctor.

"What if all of this is *X-Lax*?" he wondered.

Several players froze in the middle of a chew, as onerous visions flashed through their minds. Then Douglas laughed out loud.

"Wouldn't that be the ultimate sabotage!" he roared.

"At least no one would beat the shit out of us," came a reply from the back... followed by more laughter.

A rather large mistake had been made after today's workout and there was hell to pay for Bob Stellick on the ride back to the United Center late this afternoon.

"Did you tell the bus to leave the arena this morning?" wondered Burns.

"Yeah, I did. Why do you ask?" Stellick responded.

"Because I was still in the fucking place doing an interview for television... that's why."

"Oh, sorry, I thought you took a cab."

"I did take a cab — thanks to you!"

"Did you get a receipt?"

"Nope... it was on the house, a ten-dollar cab ride. And if I were you, Bob, I'd never be late for a bus again."

"Here, take this," Stellick said, leaning forward with a $10 bill.

"Thanks... but still, don't ever be late!" the coach warned.

The tongue-in-cheek exchange made me wonder if this was, indeed, the final bus ride I would take with the Maple Leafs this season. Would we be back here for Game 7 on Friday? Or will the Blackhawks win again tonight, and eliminate the Leafs in Toronto on Wednesday?

Part 1 of that equation materialized, as the Maple Leaf playoff tumble continued with a 4-2 loss in Game 5. Chicago had the pivotal match under control pretty well from beginning to end, though it took a pair of third-period goals to produce the final outcome.

Damien Cox penned an appropriate lead in his Toronto *Star* story:

It would be wrong to suggest this is an aberration, a season suddenly gone wrong.

In fact, the Maple Leaf playoff collapse that continued with a 4-2 pratfall for the benefit of the surging Chicago Blackhawks, is in fact a continuation of a campaign that started poorly and is on the brink of ending in truly ignominious style.

"We're not going to give up," insisted Todd Gill afterwards. "We will fight them tooth-and-nail until the final nail is in the coffin."

Poor Gill had a rough night; one of those games where he's giving maximum effort (like always), but is zigging when he should zag. Trying to poke the puck away from Denis Savard behind the Maple Leaf net in the first period, Gill instead handed it right to the Chicago veteran, who fed a wide-open Murray Craven in front. Craven had time to make a sandwich and phone home before picking the left-hand corner on Felix Potvin, giving the Blackhawks the all-important 1-0 lead.

The Maple Leaf powerplay, which has been an embarrassment during the second half of the season, was completely hopeless in the first two periods tonight. Otherwise, the outcome may have been different. With Sergei Krivokrasov in the penalty box for pulling down Warren Rychel in the first period, Burns put Mats Sundin on the point with Dave Ellett. But the Leafs were able to get the puck over the Chicago blueline only once — on a dump-in from the neutral zone. Early in the second period, the Maple Leafs were two men *short* when Jamie Macoun registered a shot on goal — that's the kind of night it was for the boys in blue.

Another powerplay opportunity went amiss midway through the period and the Blackhawks capitalized. Brent Sutter was just emerging from the penalty box when Chris Chelios sent Tony Amonte in on a clear breakaway from center ice. Amonte beat Potvin on the stick side for a 2-0 Chicago lead. The 'Hawks scored again 19 seconds later when Craven tapped in a Jeff Shantz set-up, but Chicago captain Dirk Graham was penalized for holding the stick and the goal was disallowed.

The Maple Leafs had trouble advancing the puck beyond center-ice on the powerplay, and another man-advantage went to waste.

It took a completely makeshift forward line of Paul DiPietro, Bill Berg and Mats Sundin to finally get the Leafs going. The trio buzzed around the Blackhawk goal in the final minute and Sundin scored on a high backhand shot from the right side of the cage. The Leafs have now tallied in the final minute of the second period in all three games of this series at the United Center. Momentum being a foreign word to the Leafs, they allowed Tony Amonte to streak in alone on Potvin seconds after Sundin's goal. But the Chicago winger shot high and The 'Hawks took a 2-1 lead to the dressing room.

Something bizarre happened early in the third period: the Leafs scored a powerplay goal. Dave Andreychuk banged in Gilmour's pass and the game was deadlocked, 2-2. But the night's turning point occurred less than three minutes later, and once again, Todd Gill was front and center. Bernie Nicholls appeared to out-muscle Gill as he cut to the Leaf net from the left side. While shielding Gill with his right arm, Nicholls shovelled a pass to Joe Murphy, who poked it behind Potvin for the eventual winning goal. Only afterwards, did we find out what really happened on the play.

"Nicholls had a hold of my stick and (referee Rob) Shick didn't see it," Gill explained. "If I had fallen to the ice, Nicholls would have fallen with me and I would've gotten a holding penalty. It was a classic no-win situation."

Over in the Chicago room, Nicholls made no attempt to shroud the truth. "Yes, I definitely had a good grip on Gill's stick," he casually admitted. "But, it's not a penalty unless they catch you doing it. And, in the playoffs, you've got to try every trick in the book."

Murray Craven — the best player on the ice tonight for either team — clinched the victory for Chicago with a breakaway goal late in the final period.

For the first time in this difficult season, Doug Gilmour showed his frustration after the game by bolting past a group of reporters wanting to speak with him. Typically, he wasn't the least bit rude or abrupt with anyone — softly explaining that he had nothing to say.

Everywhere else in the Leaf room, there was obstinacy in the face of reality. Anyone who has watched the Maple Leafs closely this season realizes, as Damien Cox wrote, that nothing at all strange is unfolding in this series. In fact, the Toronto club is following its season-long script to a 'T': grab an opponent by the throat, and let go. There has been a singular lack of killer instinct from the very outset, and this playoff series is merely the exclamation point.

"It's very disappointing," said Mats Sundin. "Tonight, I thought dominated the second half of the game, but we can't become frustrated. We're at least as good as Chicago."

The same form of denial was evident in Jim Proudfoot's Toronto *Star* column, entitled LEAF COACH MAINTAINS SERIES STILL UP FOR GRABS.

Pat Burns isn't about to vary the message he's been trying to sell the Maple Leafs ever since they began losing control of their opening Stanley Cup playoff series against the Chicago Blackhawks.

> *But, the coachly pitch is going to be a lot less believable now because the Toronto team has fallen an important victory behind in a competition it once led 2-0.*
>
> *And the Blackhawks...are in position to earn advancement to the next playoff stage either (Wednesday) evening in Toronto, or back here 48 hours later.*
>
> *The Leafs' only chance, meanwhile, is to sweep both matches.*
>
> *Burns keeps assuring them they can.*
>
> *"This is an even series," he maintained, "and we can win it if we make up our minds to. Chicago's defence is better than ours. Our forwards are better than theirs. The goalkeeping, I think, is a wash. So, there's no reason we can't win. This was a toss-up and still is."*

Like everyone in the Toronto media covering this series, Proudfoot also felt compelled to address Gilmour's dilemma:

> *Gilmour, a dominant force for the Leafs in playoff triumphs of 1993 and '94, has had a dreadful series at the end of a mostly dismal campaign. In fact, of Toronto's customary offensive nucleus, only Sundin has been adequately productive.*
>
> *"I met with Gilmour for half an hour Sunday," Burns said. "I pointed out that only two people will take the heat if we lose this thing — him and me. We're in it together. He agreed he has to be a lot better."*

So must the entire Leaf team or it's lights out on Wednesday.

*   *   *   *   *   *

The Maple Leafs' two best players throughout this season combined to keep the team alive in Game 6 at the Gardens.

Randy Wood finished off a classic Mats Sundin rush by shovelling a rebound past Ed Belfour at 10:00 of the first overtime period, giving the Leafs a 5-4 victory, and squaring the series at three games apiece.

But this was a game the home side desperately tried to squander. The Leafs took what seemed like an insurmountable 4-1 lead at 55 seconds of the third period, only to have Chicago rebound with three unanswered goals in the next 14 1/2 minutes. Brent Sutter converted a Denis Savard rebound at the 15:23 mark to cap the comeback, and send the Gardens' audience into a collective state of shock.

Like last spring in the Conference semifinals against San Jose, the Leafs came within a hair of being eliminated at home in Game 6. A year ago, it was Johan Garpenlov ringing a slapshot off the crossbar behind Felix Potvin in overtime, only to have Mike Gartner save the day a few minutes later. In this series, it was veteran Murray Craven sliding a weak backhand off the right goalpost early in the extra session.

But the Leafs have lived to fight another day.

THURSDAY, MAY 18th
Chicago

I flew back to Chicago at mid-afternoon today and if it's the last plane ride of this Maple Leaf season, it was one hell of a send-off!

The captain meandered in and around about a dozen storm-fronts and the trip — which normally takes about 75 minutes — lasted almost two full hours. The usual straight-in approach to O'Hare westward over Lake Michigan also went astray, as Air Traffic Control sent the plane north, halfway to Milwaukee, before allowing it to turn around. I could have used a good, stiff drink when we finally landed.

During the warm-up of last night's game at the Gardens, I had a chance for the very first time to chat with the legendary Soviet goalie Vladislav Tretiak. Now the Blackhawks' goaltending coach, Tretiak was sitting by himself in the press box and I wandered over to him — not knowing how well he spoke or understood English. I pointed to the north goal below us and said, "Remember Peter Mahovlich?"

Tretiak broke into a wide grin and shook his head.

"You expect me to forget *that*?" he replied.

Of course, I was referring to Game 2 of the famous Canada-U.S.S.R. hockey summit of 1972, when the young Mahovlich scored one of the most memorable goals ever on Canadian soil — a full breakaway deke in which he landed splat on top of Tretiak. It helped the Canadians to a victory that avenged a shocking wipeout in Montreal two nights earlier. And, of course, it ultimately led to Paul Henderson's dramatic series-winning goal in Moscow 24 days later.

"Even though we lost, that series was the highlight of my life," said Tretiak in quite acceptable English. "Until then, I was only known in Soviet Union and Europe. After that, I was known internationally. It was the best hockey I ever played in."

Tretiak remembered playing in the Gardens for the first time in 1969, three years before the famed summit. "It was against the Canadian national team and Ken Dryden was in goal," he said. "I also played here in 1974 against the WHA team and in the Canada Cup in 1976 and '81. So, I have lots of good memories from this arena."

The backdrop to this entire series from a Chicago standpoint has been the controversy swirling around Jeremy Roenick. The Blackhawks' leader and best player has been out of action since injuring his leg in a collision with Darian Hatcher of Dallas, April 2. Initially feared to be career-threatening ligament damage, the ailment was re-diagnosed as a deep bone bruise after the swelling subsided, but it was a virtual certainty that Roenick would not be able to suit up against the Leafs.

The Chicago centerman began skating on his own early last week. He travelled with the team to Toronto for Games 3 and 4 of this series and was motoring around Maple Leaf Gardens with a small parachute attached to his waste after the Blackhawk practices. With a new contract to be negotiated in the summer, Roenick and his agent, Neil Abbott, have been accused of erring on the side of caution and using Roenick's absence as a negotiating ploy. Chicago's team doctor, Louis Kolb, hinted last week that Roenick's knee was strong enough for game action, but a visit to the famed orthopaedic surgeon, Dr. James Andrews, in Birmingham Tuesday revealed a less-promising report (his leg-strength still required improvement).

"I'm listening to both doctors, but I'm following the advice of Dr. Andrews a little more seriously because he doesn't have any ties to the Blackhawks," Roenick said the other day.

More controversy ensued after Game 5 at the United Center Monday, when Bernie Nicholls criticized Abbott's motives during a post-game radio interview. "He's getting bad advice from bad people," Nicholls said about Roenick. "Agents think of themselves, don't kid yourself."

After the Blackhawks' pre-game skate in Toronto yesterday, the two players spent 15 minutes discussing the situation outside the dressing room. "He was wondering what the other guys were thinking," Nicholls explained. "We never questioned J.R.; obviously, he will know when it's time to come back. We were only questioning his agent. Playoffs are a time to play. If J.R.'s agent wants to talk about a contract, it should be left behind closed doors."

Roenick had this to say: "Bernie thinks Neil is telling me not to play and that simply isn't true. Neil just wants to make sure the injury is completely right. And when I come back and play, he wants me to be an asset, not an ordinary Joe

Shmoe. I don't want any of my teammates to think I'm not playing because of my contract. When I'm ready, I'll tell you guys. It will be no one else's decision, period, end of story.

"And I'm not ready yet."

The Maple Leafs obviously have renewed optimism about this series after the overtime victory the other night. The Blackhawks may have the home-ice, but all Game 7 situations are a crap-shoot. And this playoff, in particular, has been terribly unpredictable. "Everyone believes we can do it," said Dave Andreychuk after arriving back in Chicago. "There is no doubt in this room that we can win."

There are several factors that would improve the Leafs' chances of surviving tomorrow's winner-take-all showdown. Among them, would be the long-overdue emergence of winger Benoit Hogue, who has been practically invisible since joining the club from the Islanders on Apr. 7. In the *Star* today, Paul Hunter wrote a rather cheeky lead under a headline: LEAFS STILL WAITING FOR HOGUE TO ARRIVE.

*Six weeks ago, the Maple Leafs acquired Benoit Hogue
from the New York Islanders.
Any day now, he's expected to show up.*

Something has happened to the 28-year-old veteran this season. He scored 36 goals for a mediocre Islander team last year, and Maple Leaf G.M. Cliff Fletcher gave up a sure-fire goaltending prospect in Eric Fichaud with the expectation that Hogue would reacquire his offensive spark in a Toronto uniform. However, the struggling forward managed only three goals down the stretch in the regular season, and he hasn't been anywhere near the net so far in the playoffs.

Perhaps his was the case of a player thriving in a non-pressure situation. While it's reasonable to suggest there's always *some* onus to perform at the NHL level, regardless of the circumstance, Hogue tallied 99 goals over three seasons for an Islander team that everyone knew was going nowhere. Observing him in a Leaf sweater, I've noticed a player who is terribly hesitant to involve himself physically in any aspect of the game. Hogue must have scored a lot of garbage goals on the Island, because he's not the least bit interested in battling for real estate near the net. He's been strictly a perimeter skater thus far, and I've seen him repeatedly put on the brakes to avoid collisions. You're not going to score many playoff goals tip-toeing around like that.

"I still believe I'm a good hockey player," he told Paul Hunter. "I can help hockey teams, but it's just not happening right now. It's tough on me and it's hard sometimes to face my teammates because I've played against these guys for eight years and they know how I can play. Right now, I'm not showing any offensive skills.

"I have to shoot more often. Instead of looking around for open guys, I have to be more confident in myself to take the shot. I'm not quitting. I'll come around."

I went for dinner tonight with Jim Proudfoot to *Harry Caray's* restaurant and enjoyed a surprisingly excellent meal. Normally, these haunts under the name of famous sports personalities aren't fussy about their food, but Harry's was exceptional.

It was a doubly fine evening for Proudfoot, who enjoyed his veal-parmigiana dish, and fell head-over-heals in love with our waitress.

There was much depression in the city later tonight, as the Bulls were eliminated from the NBA playoffs by Orlando at the United Center. All of Chicago's TV stations had satellite-remote set-ups outside the arena and the tears were flowing freely. Of all the grieving fans who were interviewed, only one — a young female — made any reference to that other pro team, when she said, "Now, it's 'Let's go Blackhawks!'"

FRIDAY, MAY 19th
Chicago

Chicago Stadium is no more.

The last vestiges of the old cavern have been destroyed since we were here earlier in the week, and for the first time since the late-1920s, there is no building at 1800 W. Madison Street. — just a pile of rubble and twisted metal. Soon, the northeast corner of Madison and Wood will serve as a parking lot for the United Center. Hopefully, the City of Chicago will see fit to erect some form of monument in memory of the loudest and most unique arena in NHL history.

For reasons that need not be explained, there was a quiet tension around the Maple Leafs today as they prepared for the one-game showdown with the Blackhawks. Virtual silence prevailed on the bus rides to and from the United Center this morning; it was strictly business.

The hockey club has an airplane all fuelled up and ready to head in one of three directions. By winning tonight, the Leafs will begin their next playoff round Sunday in either Calgary, St. Louis or Toronto (against Vancouver). Of course, they could return to Toronto and *watch* the next round, as well. The same tentative plans pertain to the media, and we have therefore packed our bags for the possibility of a one-week journey on the road. It's just that time of year.

Like all of us, Pat Burns hasn't a clue what to expect. Game 6 the other night proved once again that this Maple Leaf team plays it minute by minute, with no reliance on, or aversion to momentum. The coach has been left to watch and wonder, himself.

"I can't figure it out anymore and I've given up trying," he said. "We have no consistency. There seems to be commitment for one period, and no commitment for the next. Why? — I have no idea. This is by far the most perplexing team that I've coached in the NHL."

'Hawk coach Darryl Sutter was at his crabby best after the morning skate. What *is* it with this guy? His brother, Rich, who I've gotten to know quite well with the Leafs, says Darryl is a fabulous man, but all I've been privy to this season is a brooding argumentative grouch. One aspect of this playoff series that seems bizarre is that in most games, the team that comes out the strongest ultimately winds up losing. The 'Hawks were strong at all times in Game 2 and lost. The Leafs were all over Ed Belfour in the first 10 minutes of Game 3 and lost. And Chicago had a terrific first period in the Game 6 overtime defeat on Wednesday.

When I mentioned that anomaly to Sutter this morning, he glared at me with contempt and said, "I don't know what you're talking about." I then made the audacious error of replying, "Well, it has been that way throughout the whole series," enabling him to angrily shoot back, "The WHOLE series?"

"Well, you know what I mean."

"No, you said the WHOLE series!"

At which point I silently told him to go find his mother's teeth, and walked away. Boy, can some people be jerks.

After eating dinner tonight in the United Center media lounge, I walked across the street and stared into the gravel pit that used to be Chicago Stadium. Some guy was walking around the construction site with a videocam and he came over to the fence where I was standing. "How 'ya doing?" he asked. "Can I get you a brick or something?"

Turns out this guy was a friend of one of the construction workers who'd been allowed to roam around and take pictures. "I'll try and find you a common brick from the exterior of the building and a red one from the inside," he mentioned. Of course, I'd never met this fellow before and I found it rather odd that he was anxious to go through all that trouble for a complete stranger. Not one to look a gift-horse in the mouth, however, I waited patiently at the fence, and the man came back five minutes later with the two Stadium chunks he'd promised. They were beauties — and both fully intact. I asked him if there was a catch to his generosity and he replied, "Nope. Glad to do it. Have a nice day." I suppose there are people in this world who merely enjoy being helpful and friendly. This gentleman was certainly among them.

Tonight's edition of The *Blue Line* has a cartoon of Jeremy Roenick sitting with crutches across from the team doctor, who's holding a page of test results. The caption says, "I have good news and bad news, Mr. Roenick. The tests show your knee is fine, but the pain in your ass is Bernie Nicholls."

There's a Top Ten list of REAL REASONS WHY THE UNITED CENTER ISN'T SELLING OUT. Among them are:

* Fans are saving their money for next year's inevitable ticket price increase.
* Hawk fans under mistaken impression that hockey in Chicago ends by May 1st.
* Over 3,000 fans have been dismissed by Judge Ito for illegal conjugal visits.
* One key reason: Ebola virus-flavoured nachos.

I'm going to miss that silly publication.

* * * * * *

The Maple Leafs are kaput!

Chicago put the Buds on ice tonight with a lop-sided 5-2 victory at the sold-out United Center, ending one of the most frustrating and erratic hockey seasons in recent Maple Leaf annals.

The turning point in the game was a floating shot from the left point by Chicago defenceman Eric Weinrich late in the second period that eluded Felix Potvin through a screen. It broke a 1-1 tie and the Leafs did not seriously threaten to get back on even terms the rest of the way. Denis Savard and Dave Andreychuk had traded goals in the first period, but the Blackhawks — driven by the largest and loudest crowd of the series — controlled the vast majority of the play.

Chicago's 2-1 lead in the first half of the third period might as well have been 6-1 the way its defence stymied Maple Leaf advances. A turnover in the neutral zone by Todd Gill led to the ultimate winning goal. Gill's attempt to pass the puck about 15 feet to Dave Ellett was intercepted by Blackhawk winger Joe Murphy, who went in on a breakaway and beat Potvin with a high backhand —

making it 3-1 Chicago. However, there was no indication before then that the Maple Leafs were going to mount any kind of offensive, so it wouldn't be fair to pin this one on Gill. Everyone in the building could sense some Blackhawk insurance.

Patrick Poulin's wrist shot 26 seconds later removed any element of doubt, even though Dmitri Mironov was finally able to count another Leaf tally with 3:13 left on the clock. I couldn't help but think back to Mironov also scoring the Maple Leafs' *first* goal this season — in Los Angeles — four months ago tomorrow night. Murphy clinched the Chicago victory with an empty net goal and the United Center erupted in ecstasy when the final buzzer sounded.

Though tonight's defeat seemed imminent from the opening faceoff, a post-game sense of shock permeated the Maple Leaf dressing room. Doug Gilmour showered quickly — as always — and sat barefoot in shirt and tie at his locker for the longest of time. Two seats to his left, Rich Sutter sobbed uncontrollably. He perked up for a moment and then broke down again when brother Darryl came into the room to console him. Rich had been a Blackhawk, of course, for the first half of the season, and now his former teammates were taking another step towards the Stanley Cup without him. Who could blame the guy for hurting?

"This was a season I just want to forget — a very average one for me," confessed Gilmour, who repeatedly denied that any specific ailment had slowed his production. "Losing in the first round of the playoffs is something this team isn't used to. It's very disappointing. I just want to get away from things and come back strong next year."

Pat Burns seemed more resigned to the defeat.

"This whole season never felt right, from the moment the players shook hands in the exhibition games," he said. "We didn't have enough time to put things in place (after the lockout) and we never figured out what style we wanted to play. I told the guys to keep their heads up. It was a disappointing loss, but we earned the right to be here."

SATURDAY, MAY 20th
Toronto

Exactly four months after their season to nowhere began at the Great Western Forum, the Maple Leaf players filed into the Gardens for the unpleasant ritual of cleaning out their lockers. The uncomfortable and strange-looking play-off beards had been shaven and the floor of the arena was no longer covered with ice. A sure sign the season has ended.

There were some very strong analyses in the paper today, beginning with Damien Cox on the front page of the Toronto *Star* sports section:

>*It was supposed to be the year for the big step forward; a year to finally answer the echoes of 1967. Instead, the Maple Leafs have taken major strides backwards for the second consecutive year.*
>
>*(The) apologists will say that pushing the (Chicago) series to seven games was a substantial achievement, and will have the usual thick volume of rationalizations to explain away this year's failures.*
>
>*The realists won't buy any of them and will instead identify the Leafs as what they are — not-good-enough occupants of the mushy middle that typifies the parity stricken NHL.*
>
>*They are roughly equal to the likes of Buffalo, Dallas, Washington and Boston, but not close to the calibre of Detroit, Quebec or the New York Rangers.*
>
>*This wouldn't be so striking — or, depending on where you sit, alarming — if only two springs ago, the Leafs hadn't come within a Game 7 triumph of qualifying for the Stanley Cup final.*
>
>*It's clear now that the moves executed by general manager Cliff Fletcher to make the Leafs a Stanley Cup contender not only didn't achieve that goal, but instead produced a less-capable — and far less promising — club.*
>
>*The season was filled with so many excuses that if they were layers of the ozone, we'd all have fewer sunburn worries this summer.*
>
>*(In) retrospect, a 6-1 season-ending loss in Anaheim that the Leafs tried to shrug off as meaningless was, in fact, meaningful. The pride that once would never have permitted such a result, simply wasn't there.*
>
>*(Harsh) reality hurts, but it has arrived in the Leaf camp in a big way. Next season will depend on the ability of the Leaf braintrust to read this one for what it was. Which was not much.*

Jim Proudfoot's *Star* column appeared under a headline LEAFS IN NEED OF BIG OVERHAUL AFTER PLAYOFF FALL. He wrote:

The Maple Leafs, pretty well everybody involved, must be awarded failing grades for their 1994-95 efforts, which ended in ignominious collapse against the Chicago Blackhawks last night.

Start with general manager Cliff Fletcher when passing out demerits.

He was right to revamp a Toronto team in decline, beginning almost a year ago, but few of his trades had the desired effect — so much so, that it's difficult to envision a bright future without a further extensive overhaul.

Coach Pat Burns never did find a way of dealing with the telescoped regular schedule, shortened to 48 games because of labour discord. Others in his line of work around the NHL managed to overcome the disadvantages the Leafs found insurmountable.

And almost without exception, the players making up Toronto's hitherto reliable nucleus failed to approach the excellence of the previous two campaigns — the first of the Fletcher-Burns regime. They weren't even close, actually — guys like Doug Gilmour, Dave Ellett, Jamie Macoun, and even Felix Potvin.

Head trainer Chris Broadhurst, however, was outstanding.

(If) this was a rebuilding year, progress was indeed a subtle thing, hard to detect.

Dressed casually, Pat Burns and Cliff Fletcher appeared in the media lounge at the Gardens this afternoon to answer a few of the many questions surrounding this team. Wanting to speak with Burns for a one-on-one interview, the Leaf coach lit up a cigarette and led me into the vacated *Hockey Night In Canada* studio next door. The following question and answer session ensued.

BERGER: Pat, what you said after the loss to Chicago about the season never feeling right from the beginning, certainly wasn't a revelation to anybody who spent time with the team this year. It wasn't a feeling that snuck up on anyone and yet it was something you obviously couldn't say until you did.

BURNS: *It was a funny season but I still believe in this team, I told the guys that today. At times, it looked like we would jell as a team, but it never quite happened. Some guys had frustrating years and it wore off on the others. I think leadership has to come from guys who are playing well, and that's why Doug Gilmour had such a tough year. I felt for him all year long. He wanted to give me that leadership but, hey, when you're not playing well, it's tough to stand up in the room and say we have to do this, or we have to do that. I walked in the room last night in Chicago and I didn't know what to say. Guys were crying and brooding. But today, I told them to keep their heads up. I believe in the guys in that room and if there's to be changes, well, that's part of the game. We're all trying to figure out what really went wrong this season, and if I do come up with a solid answer, I'll definitely let everybody know, but I think it's going to be a tough one.*

BERGER: I'm wondering if the players you have in the dressing room right now can play the gritty type of hockey that your teams last year and the year before played. It doesn't seem fit for this group.

BURNS: *I don't believe that. I think if there's a commitment, they can. We just didn't have time to work on much this year. We were a suitcase team that was on the road for extended periods and I felt like many of our practices were rushed. The practice-to-game ratio was very low and that hurt us.*

BERGER: But that gritty, grinding style of hockey — isn't that more of a mind-set than something physical?

BURNS: *Yeah it is, and everyone has to be willing to pay the price. One thing we did learn this year was the value of conditioning. The guys are getting their off-season training programs this morning and this club has to come into camp in top shape on Sept. 9. That cannot be an out again. We're going to really monitor it this year and if anybody comes into camp out of shape, they're going to be in deep trouble. We're going to have to come back ready to go through another grinding travel schedule with one thing in mind — our bodies must be able to take it. I think our bodies couldn't take a lot this year.*

BERGER: I'm not going to ask you less than 24 hours after being eliminated from the playoffs to start coming down on individuals, but it's obvious your defencemen have to be re-evaluated rather extensively over the summer.

BURNS: *I agree. But the way we played as a team didn't help our defence. Our forwards were often caught in no-man's land and weren't willing to come back and help out. And that was never a problem the two previous years. There could be one or two changes on defence, but we're not going to overhaul the entire team like we did last summer.*

BERGER: You've said you want to come back as coach; Cliff has said he wants you back, so it seems pretty cut-and-dried. But, obviously, that doesn't preclude another team from asking Cliff permission to speak with you in the summer about a coaching vacancy or a dual role as G.M. and coach. Where does that enter the equation?

BURNS: *Well, that's a different issue altogether. That situation hasn't come up yet. No one has ever spoken to Cliff, or to me, about a job somewhere else. If it arises, and Cliff tells me about it, then we'll have to sit down but right now, I want to remain a Toronto Maple Leaf. I know that the fans want a winner and sooner or later, they're not going to pick on the players; they're going to look down behind that bench and say, "Maybe he's the problem." And I understand that. That's part of hockey and I'm ready to live with it. Criticism is part of coaching and I'll take that criticism, as long as it's fair. But the option of leaving for another team has not come up.*

BERGER: You talked about Doug Gilmour before. Do you just wait for training camp in September and keep your fingers crossed?

BURNS: *I have a lot of respect for that man and I'm definitely not throwing the towel in on Doug Gilmour. I believe he has a lot of hockey left in him and I can see where the events of this season screwed him up. I mean, at Christmas time, which would have been nearing the halfway point of a normal season, he still didn't know if he'd be playing hockey in the NHL, or in Switzerland, or at all. I've told Doug to come back to camp in physical condition and be ready to put this season aside — to just forget about it. That won't be easy for him because he's a guy that has a lot of pride and worries about things like this. But I really believe he can be our leader once again.*

* * * * * *

Gilmour had quite a media audience surrounding him in the dressing room today and I waited for the mob to disperse before talking with the Maple Leaf captain in an adjoining room.

BERGER: Doug, what was the toughest part of this season — not playing like you have in the past, or spending so much of it trying to explain why?

GILMOUR: *Well, the whole thing was a learning experience, that's for sure. I usually like to do my talking on the ice and not so much with the media, but this season was different. I look back and say to myself, "This is what happened this year... what can I do next year to change it?" There's no use in being negative about it, but I don't want it to happen again either. When I reflect on the lockout, and going to Switzerland, and some of the other aspects of this season, I realize I would have done things differently. But I'm not going to make excuses. We're all professionals in this room and it's my job to come back next season and produce. I'll keep this experience in my back-pocket.*

BERGER: You came to Toronto from Calgary and took this city by storm, and you then carried this team on your back for two consecutive years. Did that make it more difficult to live through a tough season?

GILMOUR: *Well, after the two seasons you just mentioned, I think I definitely had an established set of goals. And, in that regard, this was a horribly disappointing year. But, Howie, I'm too positive to look at what happened and surrender myself to it. There's not a lot of quit in me and that's why I've been successful; it's just a matter of hard work and a good attitude. Now, I can't tell you that I'm going to come back next year and pick up where I left off before this season. But I will say that all of us in this dressing room will come to camp much more prepared and in better physical condition. After that, I can't make any predictions.*

BERGER: You have a very positive veneer about you, but I saw it crack a bit for the first time the past few weeks.

GILMOUR: *Well, I didn't speak to the media towards the end of the Chicago series but people have to understand my situation. I knew I was having a tough time and so did everyone else in this dressing room. It was enough of a distraction during the regular season and it obviously wasn't talked about while we were winning the first two games of the series. But after that, it became a big issue once again and I decided I didn't want my teammates coming by and saying, "Did you see today's article,*

Doug?" The playoffs is a time to stay focused individually. I didn't want anyone feeling sorry for me when we were in a tough situation together. We usually don't give a crap what the media says, but it's not fair for the focus to be on one person. By keeping quiet the past week, I tried to deflect some of that focus.

BERGER: In my experience, you have never been one to gloat over the good times or come up with alibis for the bad times. You said after the loss to Chicago you didn't want to use injuries as an excuse, but I believe you can give *us* the information and let *us* decide if it's an excuse or not. Can you reveal anything now that you obviously couldn't have while the team was still playing?

GILMOUR: *Well, you should know... you tripped me going off the bus and I hurt my ankle. (He laughs). No, I'm not going to use any physical ailment as an excuse. I'm not going to say I was 100 percent either. I had the operation on my feet last off season and wasn't able to stay in proper condition. That's why I went to Switzerland, trying to get into the physical shape I wanted to. But, it just never felt comfortable. During the season, I had ample opportunities to produce and I was stopped — it just didn't happen for me. I hope it will next year.*

And with that, Doug Gilmour and the Toronto Maple Leafs left the Gardens for the final time in this dismaying season.

The question is, how many of them will return?

POSTSCRIPT
SATURDAY, JULY 8th
Edmonton

Toronto's version of the little team that couldn't underwent more surgery at the 1995 National Hockey League entry draft. President and general manager Cliff Fletcher made three deals in what he promised to be a further re-tooling of his disappointing hockey club.

For the second consecutive year, I had a wildly busy afternoon on the floor of the league's annual welcoming party and swap meet. Unlike a year ago in Hartford — when Fletcher practically warned everyone of a pending move — there were few indications the Leafs would acquire a front-line player, in spite of the necessity.

The lack of quality and depth along the blueline was painfully evident to all Leaf observers throughout the abbreviated '95 schedule. With a graphic inability to move the puck from their own territory, the Leafs had no transition game, no powerplay, and an agonizingly limited attack. Reinforcements were clearly on the agenda.

The day began with a blockbuster announcement that overshadowed the balance of the proceedings. Even before the draft started, Buffalo was said to have traded scoring star Alexander Mogilny to Vancouver. It was confirmed within moments, and the selection of hot-shot defenceman Brian Berard by Ottawa as the No. 1 pick in the draft wasn't quite so dramatic or newsworthy. The Mogilny deal had every bit as much impact on the NHL event as the Wendel Clark-Mats Sundin swap last summer.

As the draft began, those of us covering the Maple Leafs wondered if Fletcher would be able to make a significant move. In the lobby of the Westin Hotel last night, Fletcher paused on his way to agent Don Meehan's annual draft party and confirmed that he was working on three deals, but didn't know if he'd be able to swing any of them. The Silver Fox revels in the horse-trading aspect of his profession and mentioned that after briefly showing his face at Meehan's bash, he'd head back up to his suite and remain awake by the telephone most of the night.

"I love this stuff," he said, rubbing his hands together, as he walked into the Westin ballroom.

Of course, during his four years with the Maple Leafs, Fletcher has pulled off three of the most stunning trades in the history of the club and the league. On

Sept. 19, 1991, he began a rapid housecleaning by executing a seven-player transaction with Edmonton. Fletcher traded Vincent Damphousse, Luke Richardson, Scott Thornton and Peter Ing to the Oilers for Grant Fuhr, Glenn Anderson and Craig Berube. However, when the Leafs wobbled through the first half of the 1991-92 schedule — winning only 10 of their first 41 games — it was obvious something even more dramatic was required.

The final straw was a 12-1 thrashing at Pittsburgh on Boxing Day, 1991, and Fletcher acted quickly.

A day after the New Year, came word of an extraordinary deal with Calgary that, numerically, was the biggest in NHL history. The Leafs sent four regulars and their back-up goalie to the Flames. Gary Leeman, Michel Petit, Soviet-born defenceman Alexander Godynyuk, Berube (part of the Edmonton trade) and Jeff Reese went to Calgary for Doug Gilmour, Jamie Macoun, Rick Wamsley, Kent Manderville and Rick Nattress. Never before had 10 players switched uniforms in one trade. Gilmour had been an effective centerman for the Flames, contributing largely to the 1989 Stanley Cup championship. But he had fallen into disfavour with G.M. Doug Risebrough over a contract snit and was happily cast aside. Rarely in the annals of hockey has such a grievous error been made.

Had Gilmour been acquired *alone* for the five players, the Leafs would've come out ahead as the energetic Kingston, Ont. native became the most effective Toronto forward ever. Not since the prime years of Darryl Sittler's magnificent career had the Maple Leafs employed such an impact player. Gilmour erupted for 238 scoring points in his first two regular seasons with the blue and white, and contributed 63 more in playoff competition — leading the way in consecutive advancements to the Stanley Cup semifinals. While Fletcher had always been respected for his managerial acumen, the pilfering of Gilmour placed him in the elitist of company. It was the shining moment of his career.

But the Leaf G.M. didn't stop there. He parleyed another segment of the Edmonton trade to acquire a big gunner for Gilmour. When rookie Felix Potvin flashed the skills to play regularly in the NHL, Fletcher sent Grant Fuhr to Buffalo for left-winger Dave Andreychuk. Known as a streaky but productive goalscorer during a decade in a Sabres uniform, Andreychuk came to the Leafs with 29 tallies in the first two-thirds of the '92-93 campaign. He added another 25 in just 31 games alongside Gilmour and became only the third player to reach the 50-goal plateau while wearing a Maple Leaf jersey (the others being Rick Vaive and Gary Leeman). Again, the Fletcher touch turned to gold.

Nobody expected anything from Fletcher's Maple Leaf regime until at least the five-year mark; such were the straits of the organization. Overcoming the mayhem from two decades of meddlesome mismanagement by the late Harold

Ballard would be no simple chore. Continued patience was requested as Fletcher set about his duties.

The acquisition of Gilmour, however, expedited the plan beyond anyone's hopes and by the middle of Fletcher's second year, the Maple Leafs were among the better teams in the NHL. When they danced through an ethereal march to the '93 semifinals, and came within four minutes of playing legendary rival Montreal for the Stanley Cup, expectations began to soar unmanageably. Hindsight clearly proves it was a case of too much, too soon, for when the Leafs again advanced to the final four a season later — and were demolished by the Vancouver Canucks — moans of unfulfillment permeated the hallowed walls of Maple Leaf Gardens.

Suddenly, the so-called five-year plan was completely forgotten and Fletcher's Leafs were branded underachievers. Pressure mounted for a further restructuring and it seemed that only a trip to the Stanley Cup title round would cast the Toronto skaters in a favourable light. With that in mind, Fletcher again struck explicitly. Aiming to improve a lagging offence and inject some youth into an timeworn roster, the G.M. nabbed Swedish phenom Mats Sundin from the Quebec Nordiques in a six-player deal that sent shockwaves through the Hartford Civic Center, 35 minutes before the start of the 1994 entry draft. He later acquired 70-point-a-year centerman Mike Ridley from the Washington Capitals.

Fletcher reluctantly departed with revered captain Wendel Clark and steady defenceman Sylvain Lefebvre, but felt the long-term gain was worth the short-term concession. When Lefebvre's solid blueline partner Bob Rouse transferred his services to Detroit via free agency, however, Fletcher's Leafs were in a quandary — from which they failed to emerge throughout the season past.

Which brings us to earlier today here in Edmonton.

Amid last night's trade conjecture, Fletcher offered a delectable tidbit midway through the first round of the entry draft. He told on-sight reporter Rod Smith of The *Sports Network* (TSN) that he had acquired "a front-line defenceman" whose identity would be forthcoming (presumably after the player in question could be informed). TV sets were sprinkled throughout the media interview area beneath the Coliseum stands and Smith's chat with Fletcher was clearly audible.

Upon hearing Fletcher's claim, I immediately checked with a source who was seated in a corner chair of the arena. His information had the Maple Leafs dealing winger Benoit Hogue to the Pittsburgh Penguins for veteran defenceman Larry Murphy. Two other media contacts on the floor of the Coliseum had similar details. These situations are the kind that fuel my competitive fires. To me, there is no greater challenge for a reporter than pursuing information during a live event. Especially in the presence of a "rival" national network — in this case, TSN. The newspapers can (and do) present finer details, but during an afternoon event like today's, time is not of the essence.

In *my* circumstance, I understood that TSN had the knowledge and manpower to be on top of any story, as it happened. Anchor Paul Romanuk and hockey analyst Bob McKenzie (of the Toronto *Star*) were perched on a platform above the proceedings, while reporters Smith and Gary Green were free to meander among club tables on the draft floor — an area restricted to the general media throng. As the only other electronic entity reporting live to the Toronto market — and with the competitive nature of our business — I felt driven to be first on the air with the Maple Leaf trade.

Back at The *Fan* studios in Toronto, anchors Stormin' Norman Rumack and Roger Lajoie were in the midst of a two-hour draft broadcast. While I believed I had correct information on the Leaf-Pittsburgh swap, I did not want to go on air without some form of contact with the Maple Leaf table. Thankfully, coach Pat Burns caught my eye, and I summoned him to the iron fence that separates the media from NHL personnel.

I flat out asked Burns if the club had acquired Murphy for Hogue. Having learned early on during my travels this season that Burns is not a comfortable liar, it came as no surprise when he nodded affirmatively — while correcting my information on the Leaf end of the deal.

"Yeah, we got Murphy but I think we traded (Dmitri) Mironov... I'm not sure," said the coach.

"But, you *do* have Murphy, right?" I asked.

"Yup."

That's all the confirmation I needed, and I rushed to the phone. When the producer answered and said he had not yet heard the trade (he had TSN on in the control room), it came as an overwhelming relief.

I relate this escapade not to sound pompous. The fact is, nobody has ever broken a story without taking a chance, and regular listeners to our radio station may recall that I jumped to incorrect conclusions twice during the lockout: errors that were duly noted by broadcast columnists at the Toronto *Star* and *Sun*. This can be a humbling profession at times. It's sure no fun being reminded in print of a blunder, but I like to think my employers can live with the occasional screwup — so long as it's borne out of pugnacity, not indifference.

I tell this story only to relate the whirlwind aspects of covering a live occasion like the NHL draft. And the surge of energy it provides me. In the case of earlier today, my anxieties were strangely fuelled by Leaf assistant general manager Bill Watters, with whom I had worked so closely at the radio station for three years prior to his departure. I am entirely unaware of any media personnel to which Watters reveals "off the record" information, and can only emphasize that he has never volunteered any secrets in my direction. I believe he is extra mindful not to be seen as collaborating with a former work-mate, and as such, I've generally abstained from approaching him for information.

What I *can't* quite understand is why he went out of his way to try and make me look bad today. Moments after discussing the trade on the air, I was minding my business when I heard Bill call my name. I turned around and found him leaning against the boards in the media section, surrounded by a trio of Toronto newspaper writers.

"Howie, I hear you've traded Mironov for us," Watters said with a sarcastic, almost venomous air.

Had I not received proof of the deal from Burns, his tone may have intimidated me. But I felt confident in my information, and I knew Bill well enough to realize he would take extreme measures not to betray the sanctity of his boss, Cliff Fletcher. By putting on this side-show for the writers, he was absolving himself of any wrongdoing — even in the absence of such. I just accepted it as Bill being Bill and walked away. To be sure, however, I re-checked with my sources, and they reconfirmed the Murphy for Mironov swap.

Unlike Burns, Watters can be rather skilful at deception. When he wants to "tell it like it is," nobody is more direct or forthright, but his current job often precludes such behaviour. Moments after his chin-wag with the newspaper types, he was back on the NHL side and I called him over to the fence. In this one-on-one setting, I was hoping to find out why he was upset, having not been provoked by me in any way. But, he remained defiant as ever. And when columnist Al Strachan of the *Sun* walked over, Bill raised his voice and barked several times, "You just don't get it, do you Howie?" He was damned right. I had no idea at all what he was attempting to suggest. After years of co-existing amicably, Bill Watters had a bone to pick with me. But, why?

If his aim was to plant reasonable doubt in my mind, it worked. I went back to the phone and called the station. As the line was ringing, Burns rushed over to the fence and waved at me with a wide-eyed look. Then he began gesticulating like a baseball umpire on a "safe" call at the plate. However, I took it to mean exactly the opposite. He seemed to be warning me that something had gone awry. I went back on the air and suggested there may be a snag in Toronto-Pittsburgh trade and that I'd return shortly with further information.

After more checking, I was told there'd been some consternation at the Maple Leaf table. Fletcher was apparently annoyed that news of the deal had leaked before he had a chance to inform Murphy by telephone. A reasonable concern. But, the trade had definitely not been rescinded. I also heard that Fletcher had possibly admonished Burns for being the informant, which he most certainly was not. The coach merely confirmed details I'd received elsewhere, and simply refused to lie when I gave him the opportunity to do so.

Back to the phone I went, and told our listeners about the mix-up, adding that the deal would be officially announced within minutes. And it was — NHL senior vice-president Brian Burke doing the honours from the podium at the front of the draft floor.

About 20 minutes later, I was standing near the fence when Burns wandered over and confirmed there had been some "excitement" at the Maple Leaf table when the deal was made public.

"Did he give you shit?" I asked, in reference to Fletcher.

Burns just smiled and shrugged.

After initially reporting the transaction, I approached the fence and summoned Penguins' general manager Craig Patrick, who was seated nearby. When I asked him to comment on trading Murphy for Mironov, he seemed flustered and went to great lengths to convince me no such deal had even been discussed. But, moments after it was announced, Patrick was nice enough to walk over to me and confess that he simply could not comment at the time. He then spoke in detail about the trade.

Later in the afternoon, when TSN's draft coverage was over and we were in the midst of a Blue Jays broadcast from Oakland, Fletcher approached us at the fence and again announced the completion of a deal — his third of the day (he had earlier acquired journeyman defenceman Rob Zettler from Philadelphia). Fletcher said he'd be back with the details once the players could be informed. Sound familiar? With our coverage having ended, there was no purpose in frantically trying to uncover the news and I patiently waited for the Leaf G.M. to return, which he did as promised.

"We've traded Mike Ridley to Vancouver for Sergio Momesso," he told the gathered media clan from Toronto.

In the span of five hours, Fletcher had done yet another partial re-make of his hockey club. And had completed the three trades he spoke about last night. Unquestionably, the deal for Murphy should be a boost for the Leafs, who desperately require some direction on the powerplay. In shipping Mironov to Pittsburgh, the Leafs have yielded almost five years in age, but have undeniably acquired the better player. Even at 34, Murphy was a second team all-star last season and unless he loses it in the coming year, he'll be the quarterback the Leafs have needed while skating with the man advantage.

As well, the deal rids the Leafs of the player who most dismayed Burns. With the exception of a short span towards the end of the 1993-94 season, Mironov either refused or was unable to flash the skills that were so prominent during the 1992 Winter Olympics in Albertville, France. His confidence with the puck played a large role in helping the Russian unified squad to a gold medal victory. But the same conviction hardly ever surfaced in crucial situations while wearing the Maple Leaf uniform, and it drove Burns to distraction.

Zettler is a sixth or seventh defenceman, who will replace Grant Jennings on the roster and likely dress sparingly. After only a month and change with the Leafs, Jennings was not offered another contract, and later signed with Buffalo.

The Ridley for Momesso switch comes as a puzzlement to just about everyone. Fletcher's theory for making the trade is plausible, but he may not have acquired enough in return for a 70-point-a-year centerman. This deal has been made solely for the emotional and physical benefit of Doug Gilmour. By trading Ridley, the Maple Leafs are telling their captain, "We believe in you, and are confident you can bounce back with a much improved season." Neither Fletcher nor Burns were particularly fond of the arrangement that forced Mats Sundin to play wing this past season. It was necessitated by the club's alarming lack of offensive spark — much of it due to the unforseen decline of Gilmour.

The club wants Sundin back at his natural center-ice position on a full-time basis and if Gilmour does recover, Ridley is simply too good to be used effectively as a third-line player. So the philosophy is sound. But reality may be a problem. If Gilmour's prolific days are indeed behind him, the Leafs will be right back in the quandary they found themselves a year ago, when they brought in Sundin and Ridley to solidify a dreadful shallowness at center.

Gilmour will also be asked to compensate for the disparity in the offensive aptitude of Ridley and Momesso. Ridley has produced 25 to 30 more points per season than Momesso, whose size on the wing should come in handy. Added production from Benoit Hogue, Mike Gartner and Mike Craig will also help re-coup the traded numbers... again, in theory. Momesso will be looked upon to provide the playoff spark he's shown in recent years —particularly against the Leafs in the '94 semifinals.

Just another routine NHL draft for Cliff Fletcher.

PHOTOS AND A BRIEF BIO
FOR EACH OF
THE TEAM MEMBERS
I TRAVELED WITH.

THE CAST

CLIFF FLETCHER General Manager

Tied with Harry Sinden of Boston for consecutive years of service among active general managers, Cliff has quickly accomplished the goal with which he was entrusted when the late Don Giffen brought him to Toronto. On that spring day in 1991, the Maple Leafs regained credibility and respect. And two years later, they came within four minutes and one bad bounce of making it to the Stanley Cup final for the first time in 26 years. Fletcher became a G.M. in the NHL in the 1972-73 season, with the expansion Atlanta Flames. He moved with the team to Calgary in 1980 and the Flames won the Stanley Cup in 1988-89. He quickly righted the Maple Leafs with acquisitions like Doug Gilmour, Dave Andreychuk, Glenn Anderson, Jamie Macoun and Bill Berg. Respected widely for his low-key, business-like approach, Cliff played a significant role in maintaining cool heads during the lockout. Despite his overt stance in opposition of the work stoppage, he proved he was a team player when he spoke on behalf of the league at the infamous Board of Governors meeting in New York, Sept. 30, 1994, when the season was officially postponed. Cliff faces another tough challenge in the foreseeable future — guiding the Maple Leafs back into contention for the Stanley Cup before a critical and anxious public.

BILL WATTERS Assistant General Manager

One of hockey's high-profile player agents in the 1970s and '80s, Bill joined the Maple Leafs shortly after Cliff Fletcher came on board. He spent five seasons alongside Joe Bowen in the broadcast booth as colour commentator on Leaf radio and was co-host of the supper-hour magazine show *Prime Time Sports* from its inception in late-1989 until he joined the Leafs in October '91. Few people in the game have a sharper tongue

than Mr. Watters and he's put it to valuable use over the years. As an agent, his clients included former Leaf captain Rick Vaive and current Chicago coach Craig Hartsburg (who played with Minnesota). Bill assumes much of the media responsibilities of the Maple Leaf front office — an arrangement that suits both he and Fletcher. He also handles contract negotiations and aspires, one day, to be in the big chair himself. He makes the vast majority of road trips and is known for keeping things generally loose around the hockey club.

PAT BURNS Head Coach

One of hockey's most respected coaches, Burns' availability came as a surprise to Cliff Fletcher and he was hired quickly away from Montreal in May, 1992. Almost joined the Los Angeles Kings before agreeing to coach the Leafs, then guided Toronto to the Stanley Cup semifinals in his first two years behind the bench. A former cop, Burns can have a growly demeanour and his critics say he takes himself and the game too seriously. From a media point of view, I enjoy his candid, forthright approach and was able to discover a different side of the man during my travels with the Leafs this past season. Away from the spotlight, he is far less aggressive and has an engaging (zany?) sense of humour. Drives his players hard during practices and games and the jury remains out on whether his approach can be effective in long-term situations.

MIKE KITCHEN Assistant Coach

Had he been five inches taller and 30 pounds heavier, "Kitch" may have developed into one of hockey's better defencemen in the late-70s. Even today, at 39, he is likely the fastest skater in the Leaf organization — as evidenced by his tireless work during practice each day. A member of the last Toronto Marlie Memorial Cup squad in 1975, Kitchen played for Don Cherry at Colorado in 1979-80 and survived the experience. He is frequently the target of wisecracks from Pat Burns, but the head honcho leans heavily on him in practice and behind the bench during games. Sits behind Burns on the team bus and is generally quiet and reserved.

RICK WAMSLEY Assistant Coach

Not so quiet and reserved, "Wammer" inherited his current position from Mike Murphy, when the latter joined New York Rangers after the 1993-94 season. His role differs from Murphy, who worked closely with the Maple Leaf forwards. An ex-goalie in the NHL (Montreal, St. Louis and Calgary from 1981-93), Wamsley spends much of his time in the presence of Felix Potvin, Damian Rhodes and Pat Joblonski. On game nights, he charts the action and throws conniptions in the press box, while in radio contact with fellow assistant Kitchen. Rick devotes many hours to charitable work and is another valuable person to have around the team when the tension mounts.

No. 1 DAMIAN RHODES Goaltender

When history recounts this lockout-shortened campaign, not many Maple Leaf players will be remembered for having career years. "Dusty" will be an exception. Damian subbed almost spectacularly for Potvin on 13 occasions and his 2.68 average was .23 better. He displayed all the qualities of a bonafide first-string netminder — something he knows he'll never be in Toronto while Potvin is still alive. While it may have come as a slight disappointment to Damian, his value to the club was proven when the Leafs failed to deal him at the trade deadline. A diligent worker off the ice who impressed Pat Burns with his sheer dedication, Rhodes is a luxury the Maple Leafs may not be able to afford in the long run. After trading prospect Eric Fichaud, however, Cliff Fletcher will wait till he receives maximum value for such a likeable and talented athlete. Damian Rhodes deserves good things.

No. 29 FELIX POTVIN Goaltender

While he was far from the Maple Leafs' biggest problem, the "Cat" had his least-spectacular season in a Toronto uniform. He was still solid, with a 2.91 average, but he allowed more weak goals by the opposition than in his entire career beforehand. At times, he appeared even bored. Perhaps we've come to expect too much from this young phenom.

Or maybe he was a victim of an overall regression in the Maple Leafs' defensive posture. Whatever the case, Potvin was not quite as sharp as he'd been earlier in his career. Terribly soft-spoken, but with an obvious inner confidence, Felix is a player I haven't come to know. He shuns the spotlight and rarely initiates by-play with the media. For the first time in his young career, he had to endure some criticism this season and his ability to allow for such observation was impressive.

No. 2 GARTH BUTCHER Defenceman

One of the most hated opponents of the Maple Leafs during his years in St. Louis (1991-94), "Butchey" could not deliver the same abrasiveness in his first season with Toronto. Part of the Wendel Clark-Mats Sundin trade, Garth was steady on the Leaf blueline, but was not the physical, nasty player he used to be. An absolute delight to deal with off the ice, Butcher is quick with a smile and I don't think he boarded the bus without saying "Hi boys" even once this past season. A true pro, he handled criticism well, and never lost his cool in the dressing room — even after the game at St. Louis, Apr. 21, when a questionable penalty call against him by referee Don Koharski sent Pat Burns over the edge.

No. 3 GRANT JENNINGS Defenceman

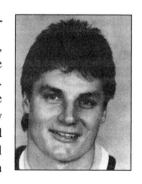

With two Stanley Cup rings from his years in Pittsburgh, Grant provided the Maple Leafs with size and experience late in the season, but could not overcome his slow-moving feet. Acquired from the Penguins for Drake Berehowsky at the trade deadline, Jennings alternated with rookie Kenny Jonsson in the final three weeks of the regular season, and during the playoffs. Quiet, with a dry sense of humour, I still laugh when I recall how he gave that poor cab driver in Edmonton a hard time on the final road trip of the regular season. A short-term project whose presence didn't hurt the Maple Leafs, neither did Jennings help a whole lot and he wasn't offered a contract for 1995-96. He signed as a free agent with Buffalo in late August.

No. 4 DAVE ELLETT Defenceman

Acquired from Winnipeg in November, 1990, Dave has been the best Maple Leaf defenceman in the first half of the '90s, but has never graduated to "front line" status, despite an abundance of natural ability. Lacks patience with the puck and it shrouds an excellent all-around package of size, skating and shooting skills. Leafs would like him to play a more physical game, but Ellett hasn't been quite so willing to mix it up along the boards since suffering a shoulder separation in Washington near the end of the 1992-93 regular season. Nicknamed "Roy" for his resemblance to the Robert Redford character in *The Natural*, Ellett is among the most intelligent and analytical quotes in the Leaf dressing room, but he doesn't go out of his way to pal around with the media.

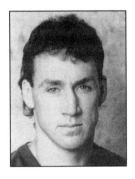

No. 7 MIKE RIDLEY Centerman

If consistency is the staple of professional athletics, then "Rids" is the model athlete. He played in all 48 regular-season games this past season — one of only three Maple Leafs to do so — and has missed only 26 games since breaking into the NHL with New York Rangers in 1985-86. During that time, Mike has quietly averaged almost 70 points per season — even during his years with offensively challenged Washington. Why then did the Leafs trade this man to Vancouver after just one season? It's a question that does not offer an immediate answer. Ridley had a dour temperament and seemed uncomfortable in frivolous situations. He never said a whole lot and his unfluctuating demeanour was interpreted, at times, by Pat Burns to be of a less-than competitive value to the team. He liked to spend time by himself on the road. I recall my wife Susan and I approaching him as he stood alone in the St. Louis Union Station late one night. We attempted to strike up a conversation, but he seemed not at all interested in company, so we walked away. He sure knew how to play, though.

No. 9 MIKE CRAIG Right Wing

The Leafs acquired "Craiger" from the Minnesota/Dallas Stars because of his tenacious efforts in games *against* Toronto early in his career. The free agent signing cost Leafs center Peter Zezel and defence prospect Grant Marshall and was not at all worth the outlay during the lockout-shortened season. Craig was a non-factor on a Maple Leaf team begging for the offensive skills he flashed sporadically while with the Stars. He was a much "softer" player than he had shown, but his youthfulness and quick release are qualities the Leafs probably should not give up on — at least until they are wasted for another full season. Off the ice, Craig is quiet but friendly. He likes reading the gossip tabloids.

No. 10 BILL BERG Left Wing

An early season knee injury prevented "Bergy" from being quite the pest he normally is on the ice. One of my favourite people on the Leaf team, Bill is a walking paradox. Off the ice, he's practically invisible and does absolutely nothing to rock the boat. He treats everyone equally — his teammates and the media — and is always available for a chat, in good times or bad. During games, however, he's reputed to be among the most hated players in the NHL. He apparently has an agitating tongue on the ice, but don't try and get him to admit it. Nobody in hockey can shrug quite so inno-cently. A tenacious checker and penalty killer, he missed his long-time linemates Peter Zezel and Mark Osborne this past season. But he's still a valuable member of the team, and a guy Pat Burns would never bowl over in a car.

No. 11 MIKE GARTNER Right Wing

While his prolific scoring days appear to be behind him, "Garts" will be the first member of the current Maple Leaf team to qualify for the Hockey Hall of Fame. He scored 12 goals in 38 games this past season and now has 629 goals in his 16-year career. Only Wayne Gretzky, Gordie Howe, Marcel Dionne and Phil Esposito have more among players in NHL history. Mike suffered a horrific injury early in the season when a monstrous bodycheck by Edmonton's Bryan Marchment sent him to hospital with a partially collapsed lung. He stayed pretty much to the perimeter the rest of the season, though he is a player who can mix it up when he wants to. President of the NHL Players' Association, Gartner is a smart, well-spoken man who remains refreshingly unaffected by his success. A season devoid of labour strife could rekindle his scoring touch.

No. 13 MATS SUNDIN Centerman

Considering Doug Gilmour's season-long problems, the Maple Leafs likely wouldn't have made the playoffs if not for the "Big Weed." Sundin came over from Quebec with the unenviable chore of "replacing" Wendel Clark and he shone brightly in the task. The club's best player night in and night out averaged a point a game while alternating between center and wing. Leaf management believes he'll be even more effective if he stays at his natural pivot spot in 1995-96 — thus its rationale for trading Mike Ridley to Vancouver. The challenge now is to provide Sundin with wingers who can score. Always easy with a smile, Mats was a delight to deal with and we struck up a sound relationship from the very start. He learned my name late in the season, and would bellow out "Howeeeee" in the dressing room after games or practices. At 24 years of age, Sundin should be the cornerstone of the Toronto franchise for the next decade.

No. 14 DAVE ANDREYCHUK Left Wing

After a slow start to the season, "Chucky" got it in gear and wound up with 22 goals: second on the Leafs to Mats Sundin's 23. He thus would have attained his career average of between 35 and 40 goals had the schedule not been reduced by the labour dispute. His totals were more impressive in the light of Doug Gilmour's struggle — the duo had a spectacular chemistry in the two seasons prior to last. Andreychuk is a streaky goalscorer and a streaky sort of character off the ice. He moves about with an ever-smouldering intensity that remains in check (except on bus rides from the airport when he feels his teammates owe him money... remember Vancouver?). In no way is he unfriendly, but he seems generally detached, and very much in his own little world. Dave will be even more effective in 1995-96 if he plants his immense carcass in front of the opposition net more often. And, of course, if Gilmour is able to bounce back.

No. 15 DMITRI MIRONOV Defenceman

Having seemed like a sure-fire star in the making a season earlier, "Tree" couldn't get it done this year and was traded to Pittsburgh at the NHL draft for Larry Murphy. During the '94 playoffs, the Soviet-born defenceman showed abundant confidence carrying the puck, and a hard, accurate one-time shot from the point that came in awfully handy on the powerplay. But that confidence practically disappeared this past season — perhaps because of the serious shoulder injury he suffered in late-March against Edmonton. It kept him out of 14 games and Dmitri was terribly hesitant to engage himself physically upon his return. That did not sit well with Pat Burns, who disdained Mironov's passive play. Slowly overcoming a language barrier, Mironov could prosper with the change of scenery provided by his transfer to Pittsburgh.

No. 16 DARBY HENDRICKSON Center/Left Wing

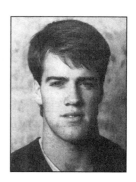

The Maple Leafs' fourth-round selection in the 1990 draft appeared in only eight games this past season, mainly as an injury replacement. He is basically an unknown, having played his first two NHL games with the Leafs against Chicago in the 1994 playoffs. With the shallowness of the Maple Leaf forward ranks, Darby will have an opportunity in 1995-96 to establish himself as a regular NHLer.

No. 18 KENT MANDERVILLE Left Wing

The 1995-96 season will be "Mandy's" fourth in the NHL and it's clear that he has only one more chance to make a favourable impression with Pat Burns. Acquired from Calgary in the Doug Gilmour deal, the former Canadian Olympian is still with the Leafs thanks to the patience (and authority) of general manager Cliff Fletcher, who traded for him. He floundered through a dreadful lockout-interrupted season, recording a mere assist in 36 games. At 6-foot-3, 207 pounds — and with good skating ability for a big man — Manderville's lack of production is a source of aggravation for Burns, who would rather see him moved elsewhere. Every so often, when motivation behooves him, Kent is an effective penalty killer and makes decent use of his size. But he absolutely must do so more often, or his NHL career will fizzle... at least, in Toronto.

No. 19 KENNY JONSSON Defenceman

The Maple Leaf hierarchy, led by Cliff Fletcher, did the "Little Weed" no favours by practically branding him the second coming of Bobby Orr. The club's first-round draft choice in 1993 does have undeniable skills that should blossom in the coming years. But he seemed burdened by all the advance hype in his first season with the Maple Leafs and it likely affected his performance. Having studied English at high-school in his native Sweden, Jonsson communicated well with his teammates, though he was painfully shy early in the season. He emerged from that shell as the year progresssed and reacted well to forking over $5,000 for a team dinner at Vancouver... his rookie initiation. However, as he came of age socially, his play deteriorated, and the Leafs may have to bring him along more delicately in his sophomore season. His ability to sluff off the criticism from his glaring mistakes in the season-opening road trip to Los Angeles and San Jose was impressive.

No. 20 RICH SUTTER Right Wing

This classy NHL veteran never seemed to overcome the disappointment of being traded by the Chicago Blackhawks early in the season... away from his two brothers: forward Brent and head coach Darryl. The 'Hawks dealt him to Tampa Bay, where he never caught on, and the Lighting sent him to the Leafs in mid-March. Initially, he seemed destined for a checking role alongside Mike Eastwood and Bill Berg, however the line failed to click in the long run. A decent, soft-spoken individual, Richie poured his heart out to me by the hotel pool in Anaheim during the season-ending road trip, saying how much he missed being away from his wife and two daughters, who were back in Chicago. When the Maple Leafs were eliminated by the Blackhawks in the first round of the playoffs, his emotions boiled over and he cried his eyes out in the Toronto dressing room. It was heart-wrenching to see the respectable NHL career of such a fine person ending so sadly. The Leafs did not offer him a contract for 1995-96 and he may have trouble catching on elsewhere.

No. 21 WARREN RYCHEL Left Wing

Having lost the abrasiveness of Ken Baumgartner for the season, Cliff Fletcher acquired Rychel from Los Angeles in early February. Nicknamed "Bundy" for his facial resemblance to the precocious son of Al and Peg in the TV sitcom *Married ... With Children*, Warren stepped forward when the situation called for brawn, but he was otherwise inconspicuous. He does possess some fine character and he became immediately popular with his new Maple Leaf teammates. A frequent practical joker, Warren's impact on the Leafs might be enhanced in conjunction with Baumgartner and Tie Domi for a full NHL season.

No. 22 KEN BAUMGARTNER Left Wing

If rotten luck was money, the "Bomber" would be filthy rich. Having spent countless hours in negotiations to end the NHL labour dispute, Baumgartner — vice-president of the Players Association — got into a grand total of two games before undergoing a season-ending shoulder operation. He suffered the initial injury during a scrap with Dennis Vial of Ottawa, Feb. 28, 1994, and — in hindsight — should not have been in the line-up to start the campaign. As the disappointing year progressed for the Maple Leafs, Baumgartner's absence was progressively bemoaned by the coaching staff and management, even though he had never played a significant role on the hockey club. Popular with his teammates and the media, everyone is rooting for Ken to bounce back and prove just *how* badly he was missed.

No. 23 TODD GILL Defenceman

A living, breathing testament to perseverance, "Giller" completed his 11th season in a Maple Leaf uniform, and is by far the longest-serving member of the hockey club. A holdover from the gory years of Harold Ballard's regime, Todd has played the best hockey of his career under Pat Burns, though he regressed considerably in the lockout-shortened schedule. But, there are few more willing "gamers" on the Maple Leaf roster and his spot on the club remains secure. Todd is an athlete I've been proud to know over the years. Every season — like clockwork — he'll commit a ghastly error that'll cost the Leafs two or three games singlehandedly, but never does he dwell on misfortune, and he's always available to the media after such an embarrassment. That kind of character is difficult to find, and it provides a clear explanation as to how Todd's been able to withstand his extreme highs and lows. Fans are quick to get on his case, but the treatment is frequently unfair.

No. 24 RANDY WOOD Left Wing

When Cliff Fletcher reflects on the dissatisfaction of the 1995 season, he'll be able to find some solace in one of his shrewdest acquisitions. The Buffalo Sabres — hardly a team with Stanley Cup promise — somehow left Wood unprotected in the September, 1994 waiver draft, and Fletcher claimed him for a song. The Princeton, N.J. native went on to score 13 goals for the Leafs and was arguably the club's most reliable skater on a nightly basis. Gritty determination and a kamikaze-like willingness to crash the net made "Woody" an immediate fan favourite at the Gardens and popular among his teammates. Educated and well-spoken, he's an excellent guy to chat with on any number of topics and he should be an integral piece of the Maple Leaf puzzle for several years to come.

No. 25 PAUL DIPIETRO Center

Acquired the day before the trade deadline from Montreal, where he used to play for Pat Burns, DiPietro was not much of a factor. When Fletcher traded Mike Eastwood to Winnipeg the following day, DiPietro became the club's checking centerman, but he wasn't nearly as proficient as either Eastwood, or Peter Zezel. Perhaps he shouldn't be judged on his short tenure with the club to date, but he'll have to show a lot more in the coming season to justify the abandonment of Eastwood, who was rounding into a solid NHLer at the time of his trade.

No. 28 TIE DOMI Right Wing

One of hockey's premier shit-disturbers is back where he began his NHL career (in 1988). Acquired from Winnipeg for Mike Eastwood at the trade deadline, Domi was brought on board to lend muscle to the Maple Leaf playoff effort. Only problem is, nobody fights in the playoffs anymore. While away from Toronto, the charismatic Domi gained fame and notoriety for his willingness to scrap, and is best remembered for his battles with Detroit behemoth Bob Probert. In partic-

ular, a lengthy punch-up at Madison Square Garden when he played for the Rangers. Domi fared well and skated to the penalty box motioning at his waste

347

as if to be donning the NHL heavyweight championship belt. The Gotham fans ate it up. A decent skater, Domi has the ability to play some hockey as well, and he feels at home in Toronto, where he's a fan favourite.

No. 32 BENOIT HOGUE Center/Left Wing

Among the biggest disappointments of the Maple Leaf season was this player's inability to find the net. Or even be near the net. Looking to upgrade the team's attack late in the season, Fletcher acquired Hogue from the New York Islanders in a deal of sheer extortion. Leafs were forced to part with can't-miss goaltending prospect Eric Fichaud, who might've never played in Toronto because of his age proximity to Felix Potvin. But, Fichaud may have fetched a lot more on the open market in years to come, than a player whose scoring skills have vanished. A 36-goal shooter on Long Island in 1994-95, Hogue was either a casualty of the lockout-shortened season, or a flash in the pan. Few players in a Maple Leaf uniform have more onus to perform this coming season that Hogue. Otherwise, it may turn out to be Fletcher's worst deal.

No. 33 MATT MARTIN Defenceman

The Maple Leafs' fourth-round selection in the 1989 draft has both the size and the brains to be a solid NHL defenceman. Whether his skills are up to par will be determined only when he gets a shot at full-time employment. That could very well come this year. In his second season of part-time duty with the Leafs, Martin played in 15 games and looked very comfortable at times in his own zone. A likeable and coachable kid who is only 24, Matt has many supporters in the Leaf dressing room and seems to require only confidence. Time will tell.

No. 34 JAMIE MACOUN Defenceman

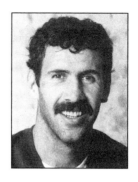

A grizzled veteran of 12 NHL seasons, "Cooner" remains among the most reliable of Maple Leaf blueliners, though his play — like others —took a step backwards this past season. The second-best player acquired from Calgary in the Doug Gilmour deal, Macoun seems to be nearing the end of the line. However, a reliable offensive-type partner (like Larry Murphy) could revitalize him. The Macoun-Butcher defence pairing simply didn't work, even though Pat Burns kept going with it all season long. With a lack of direction on the powerplay, Macoun was horribly mis-cast as a point man; his best season was 11 goals, a decade ago. Nobody on the Leafs is more adept at bitching and moaning, but Jamie usually does it tongue-in-cheek and he's thorough and cooperative with the media.

No. 93 DOUG GILMOUR Centerman

After all he has done for the Maple Leaf organization since coming here from Calgary, "Killer" was entitled to an off year. While there is no question he was a shadow of his former self this past season, Gilmour — in my opinion — earned an exemption from criticism. For one year, anyway. We'll soon find out if a spinal-disc injury and sore feet were the main factors behind his overall decline, or if he's simply tuckered out from playing an incredible amount of hockey the past three years at such high intensity. Gilmour hasn't the size to plough around the ice like fellow centermen such as Joel Otto or Mark Messier. Yet, he likes to play "big" all the time. Maybe he's simply exhausted his fuel. One thing is for certain: if you spend any time around the Maple Leafs — or if you are merely a fan of the club — it's impossible not to root for this guy to bounce back. No Leaf player in my lifetime has been so singlehandedly responsible for reversing the fortunes of the team. Few have been as valuable and responsible to the community. If any player deserves a vote of patience from the fans, it's Gilmour. And nobody should be surprised if he rebounds with gusto.